O Maidens in your Savage Season

8

Story by **Mari Okada**
Art by **Nao Emoto**

Relationships and story so far in this savage season:

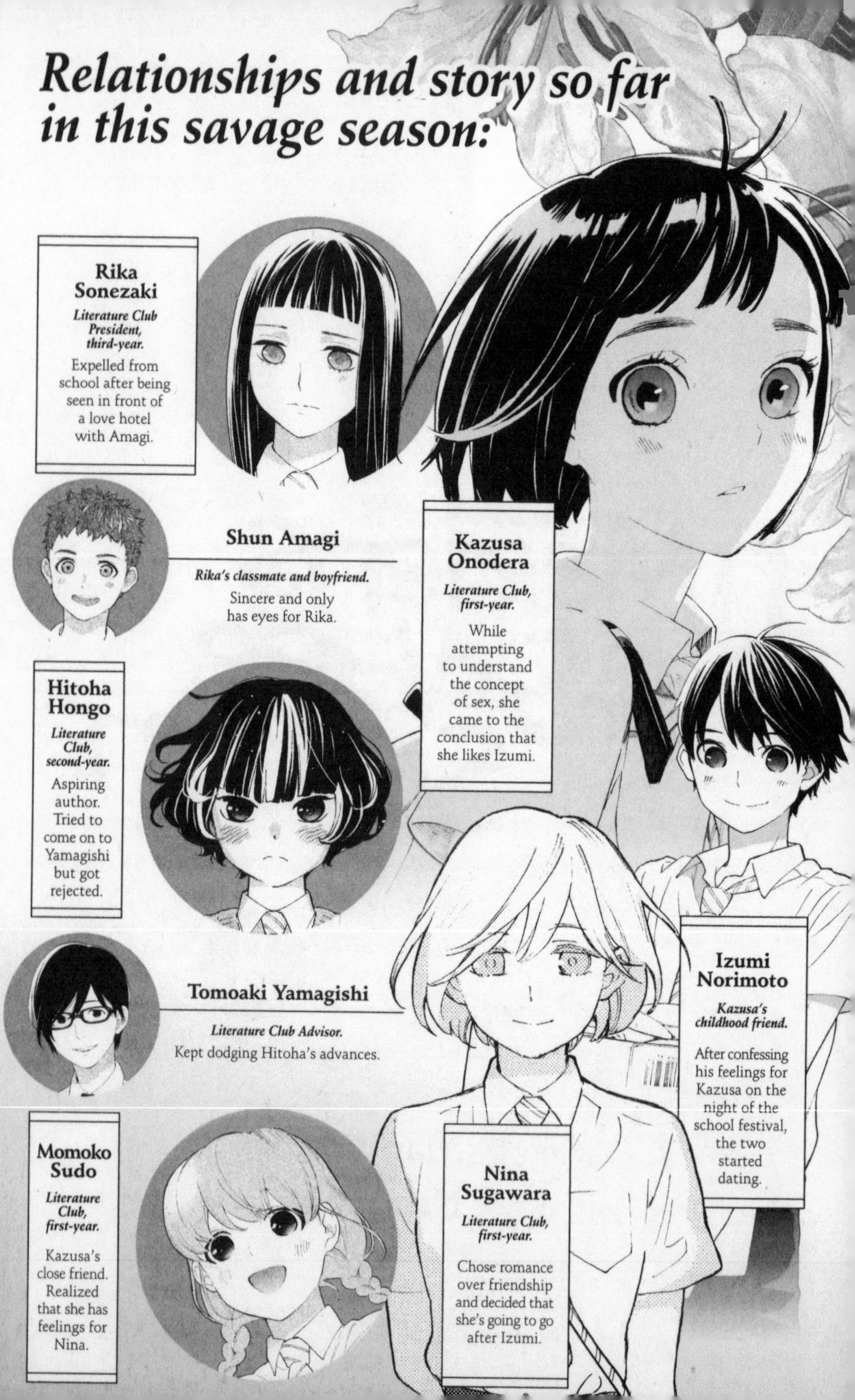
Rika Sonezaki
Literature Club President, third-year.
Expelled from school after being seen in front of a love hotel with Amagi.
Shun Amagi
Rika's classmate and boyfriend.
Sincere and only has eyes for Rika.
Kazusa Onodera
Literature Club, first-year.
While attempting to understand the concept of sex, she came to the conclusion that she likes Izumi.
Hitoha Hongo
Literature Club, second-year.
Aspiring author. Tried to come on to Yamagishi but got rejected.
Tomoaki Yamagishi
Literature Club Advisor.
Kept dodging Hitoha's advances.
Izumi Norimoto
Kazusa's childhood friend.
After confessing his feelings for Kazusa on the night of the school festival, the two started dating.
Momoko Sudo
Literature Club, first-year.
Kazusa's close friend. Realized that she has feelings for Nina.
Nina Sugawara
Literature Club, first-year.
Chose romance over friendship and decided that she's going to go after Izumi.

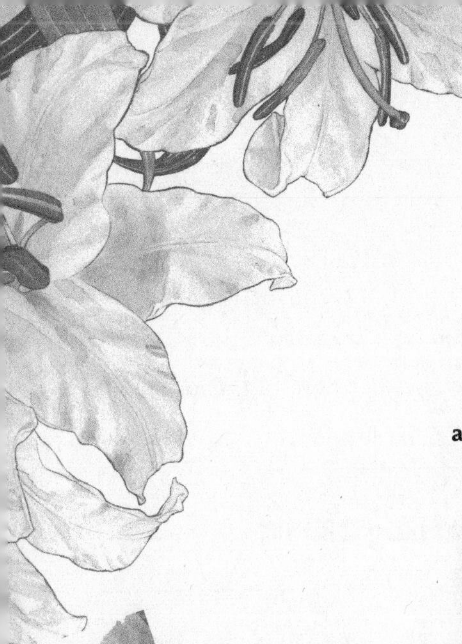

In this season, time's too precious to just sit around and wait.

As the girls' struggles with "sex" and "romance" get all tangled up, the school makes matters worse by announcing a Zero Dating policy. Kazusa and the others barricade themselves in the school to protest the administration's decision to expel Sonezaki. There's no question. It had to be done.

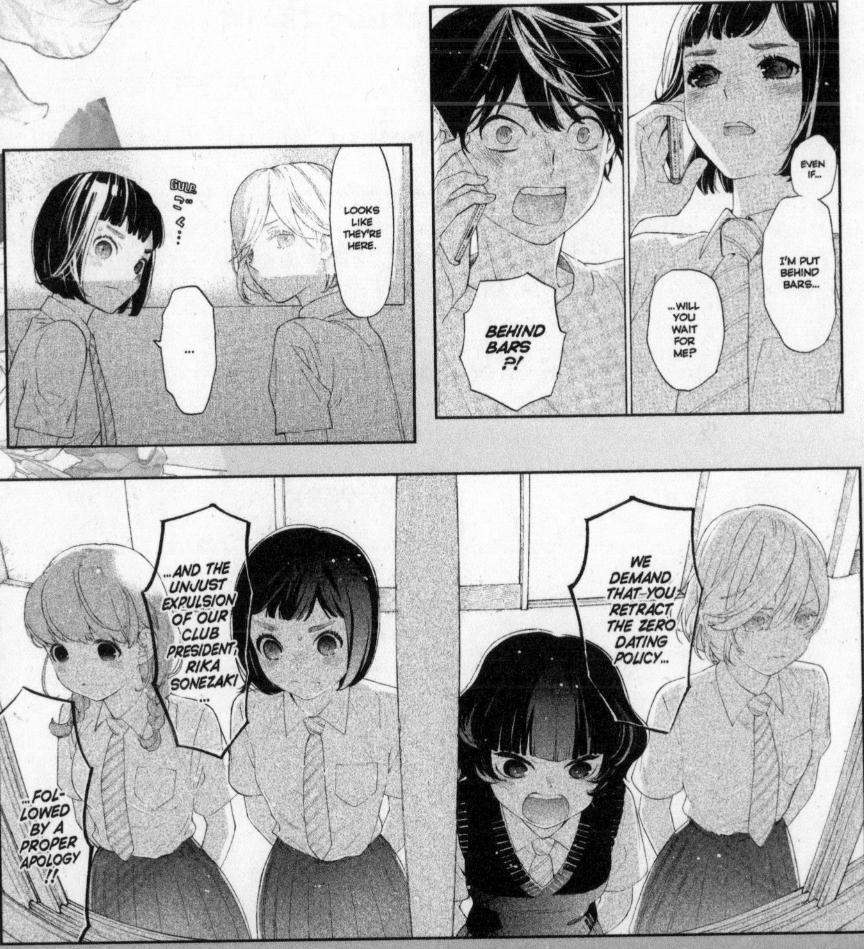
EVEN IF...
I'M PUT BEHIND BARS...
...WILL YOU WAIT FOR ME?
BEHIND BARS ?!
LOOKS LIKE THEY'RE HERE.
GULP
...
WE DEMAND THAT YOU RETRACT THE ZERO DATING POLICY...
...AND THE UNJUST EXPULSION OF OUR CLUB PRESIDENT, RIKA SONEZAKI...
...FOL-LOWED BY A PROPER APOLOGY!!

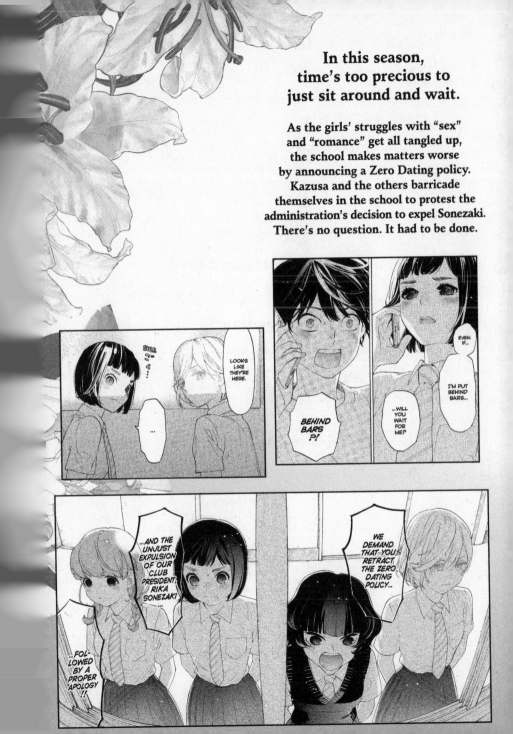

【 *Contents* 】

Meeting 28

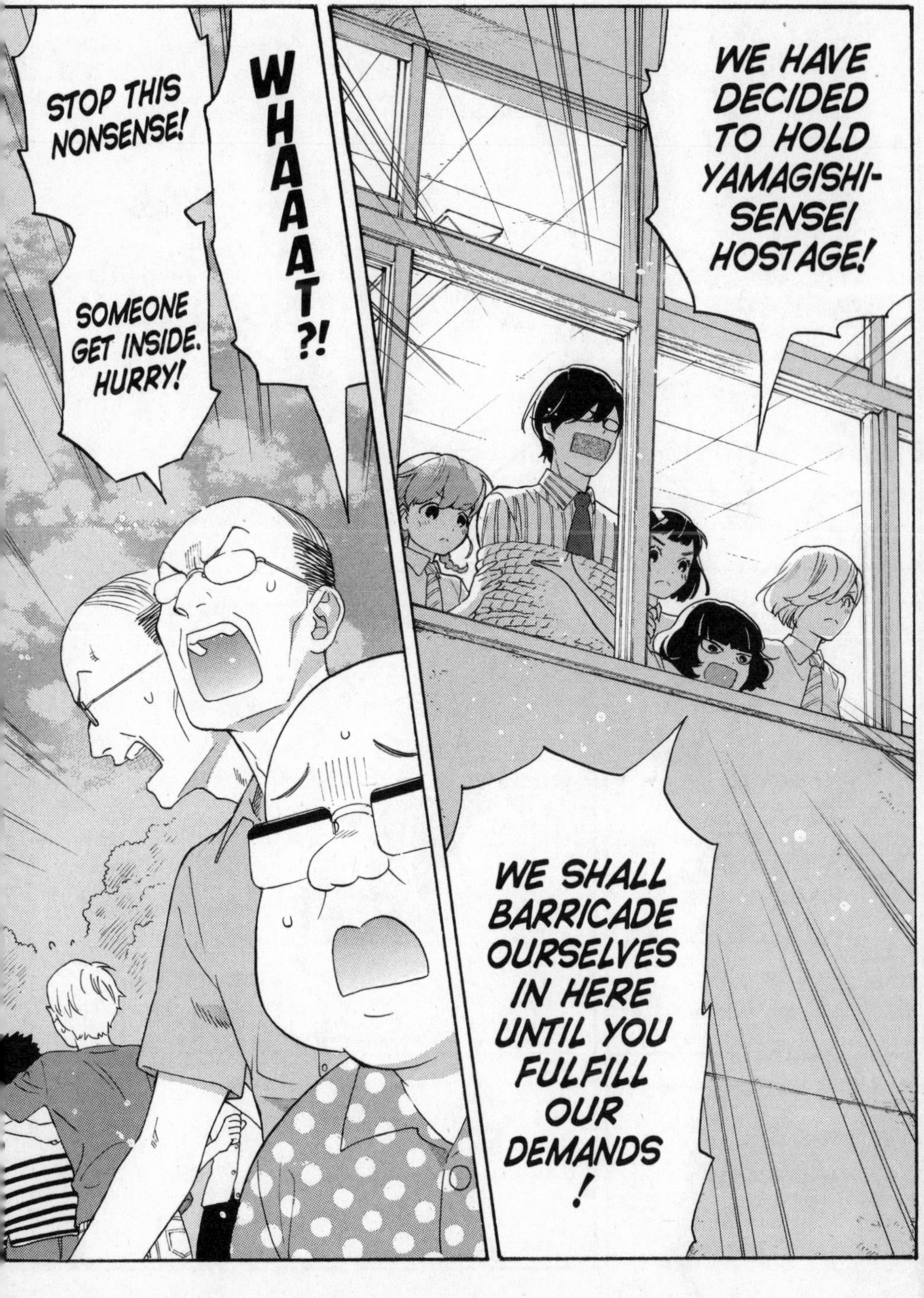
WE HAVE DECIDED TO HOLD YAMAGISHI-SENSEI HOSTAGE!
WE SHALL BARRICADE OURSELVES IN HERE UNTIL YOU FULFILL OUR DEMANDS!
WHAAAT?!
STOP THIS NONSENSE!
SOMEONE GET INSIDE. HURRY!

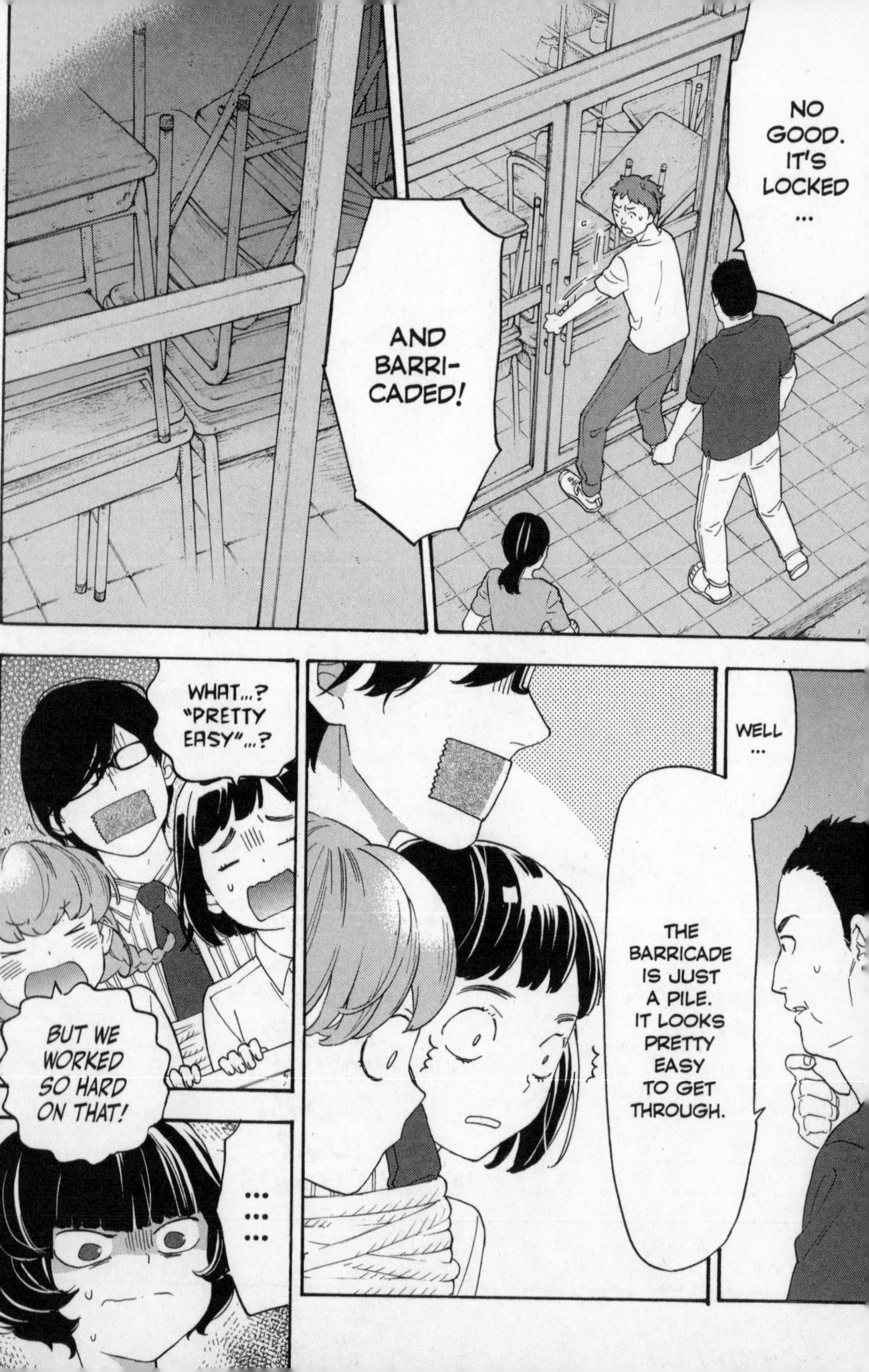
NO GOOD. IT'S LOCKED ...
AND BARRI-CADED!
WELL ...
THE BARRICADE IS JUST A PILE. IT LOOKS PRETTY EASY TO GET THROUGH.
WHAT...? "PRETTY EASY"...?
BUT WE WORKED SO HARD ON THAT!
... ...

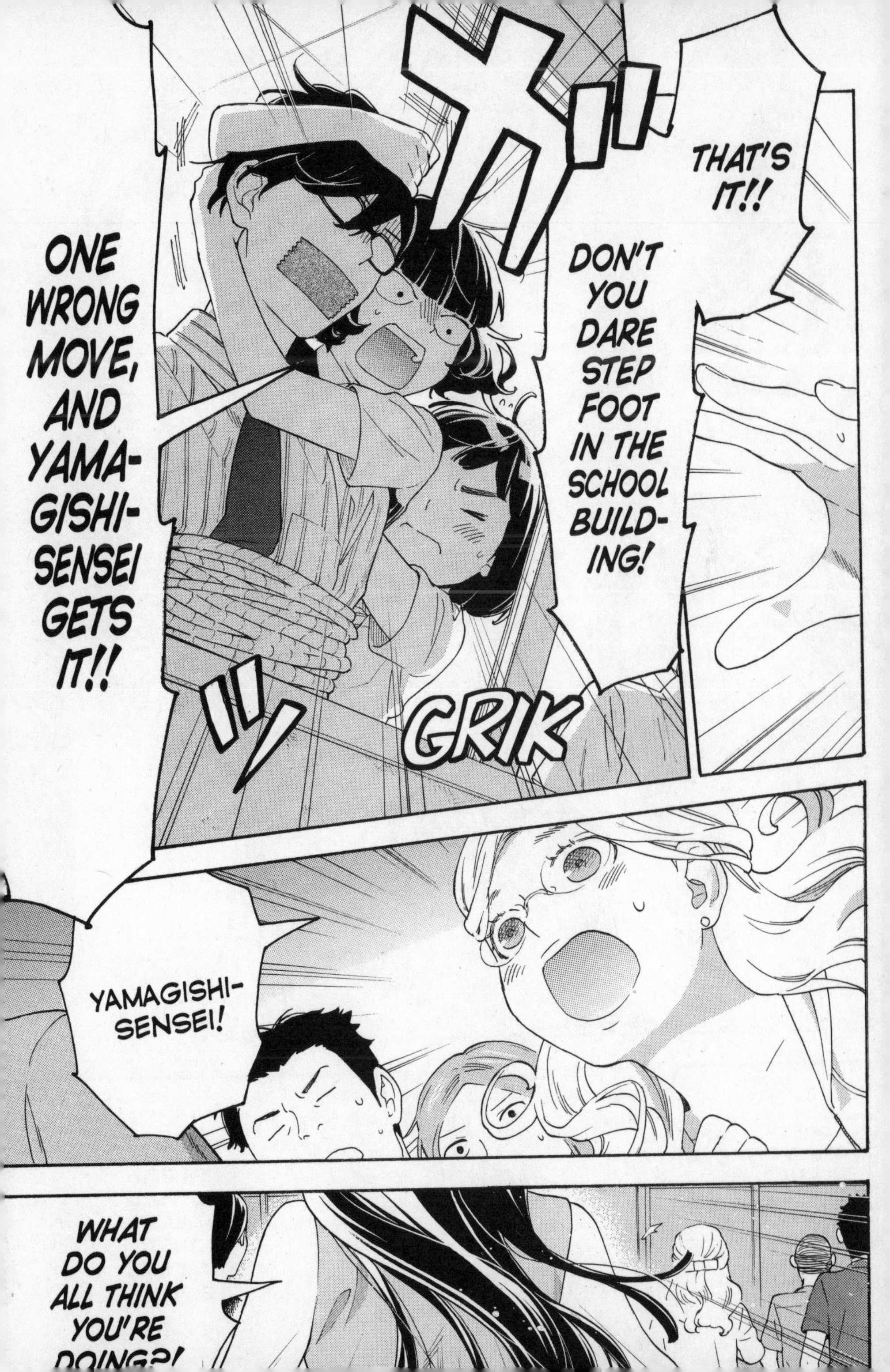
THAT'S IT!!
DON'T YOU DARE STEP FOOT IN THE SCHOOL BUILD-ING!
ONE WRONG MOVE, AND YAMA-GISHI-SENSEI GETS IT!!
GRIK
YAMAGISHI-SENSEI!
WHAT DO YOU ALL THINK YOU'RE DOING?!

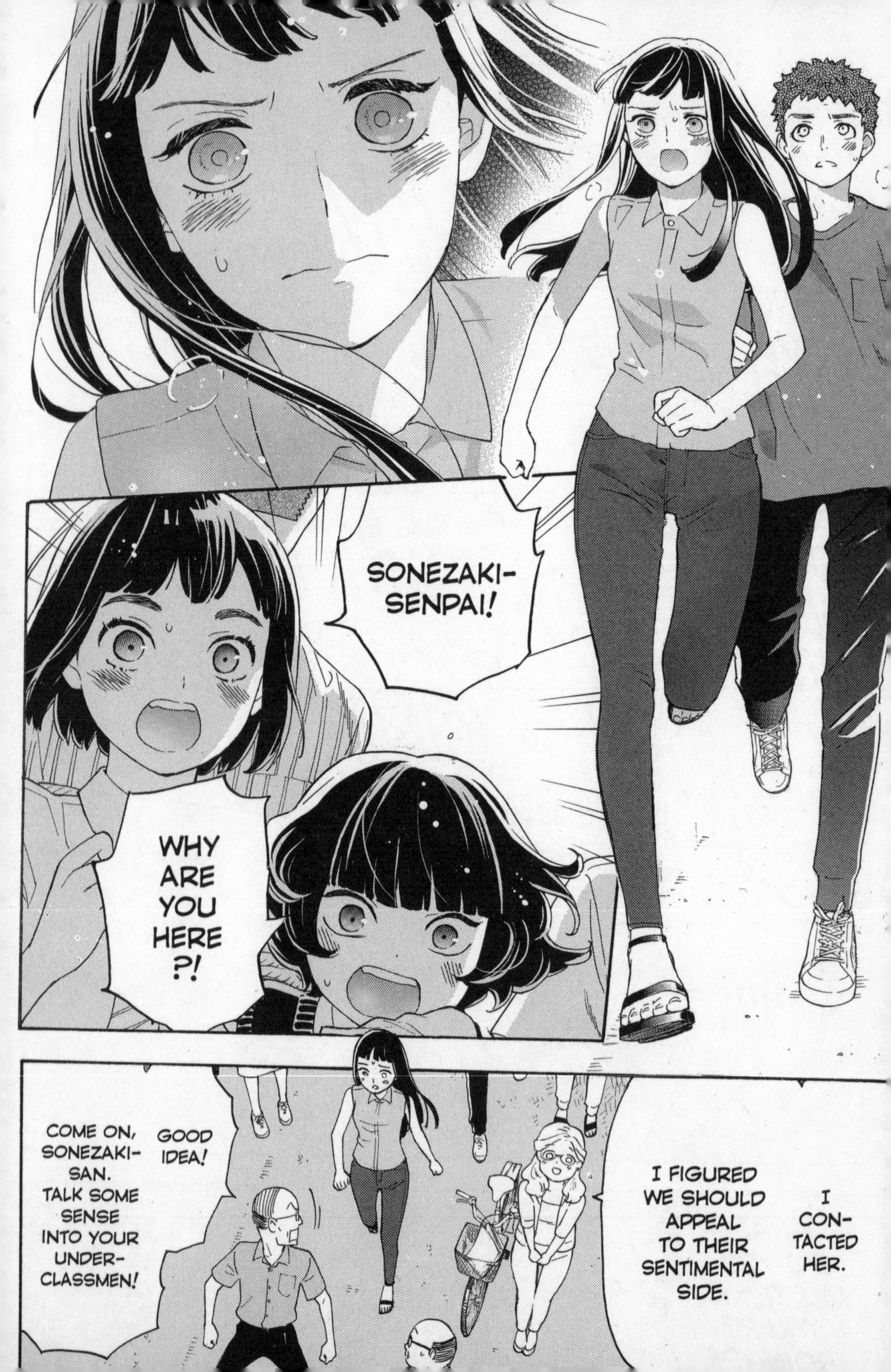
SONEZAKI-SENPAI!
WHY ARE YOU HERE?!
I CONTACTED HER.
I FIGURED WE SHOULD APPEAL TO THEIR SENTIMENTAL SIDE.
GOOD IDEA!
COME ON, SONEZAKI-SAN. TALK SOME SENSE INTO YOUR UNDERCLASSMEN!

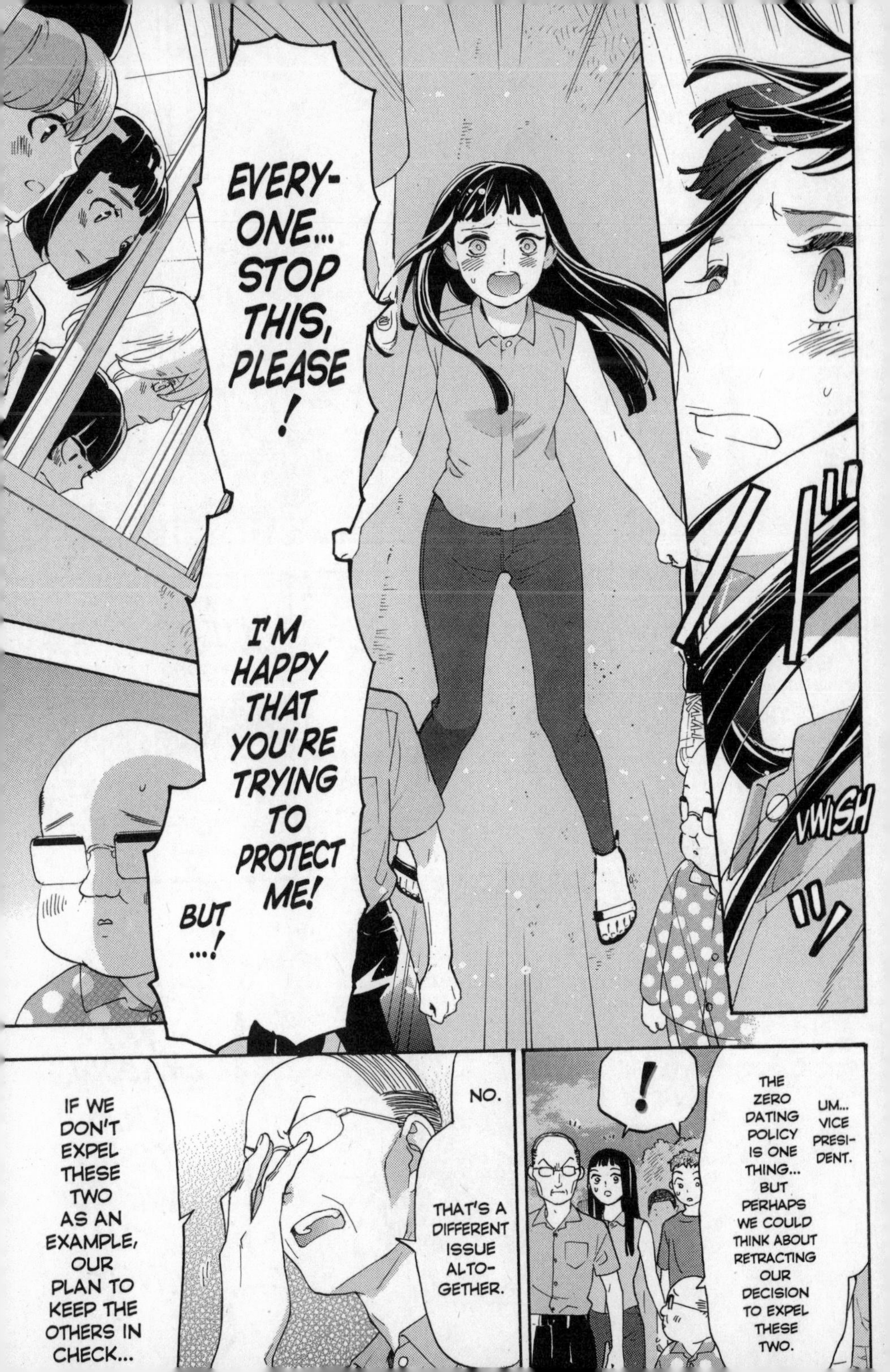
VWISH
EVERY-ONE... STOP THIS, PLEASE!
I'M HAPPY THAT YOU'RE TRYING TO PROTECT ME!
BUT...!
UM... VICE PRESI-DENT.
THE ZERO DATING POLICY IS ONE THING... BUT PERHAPS WE COULD THINK ABOUT RETRACTING OUR DECISION TO EXPEL THESE TWO.
!
NO.
THAT'S A DIFFERENT ISSUE ALTO-GETHER.
IF WE DON'T EXPEL THESE TWO AS AN EXAMPLE, OUR PLAN TO KEEP THE OTHERS IN CHECK...

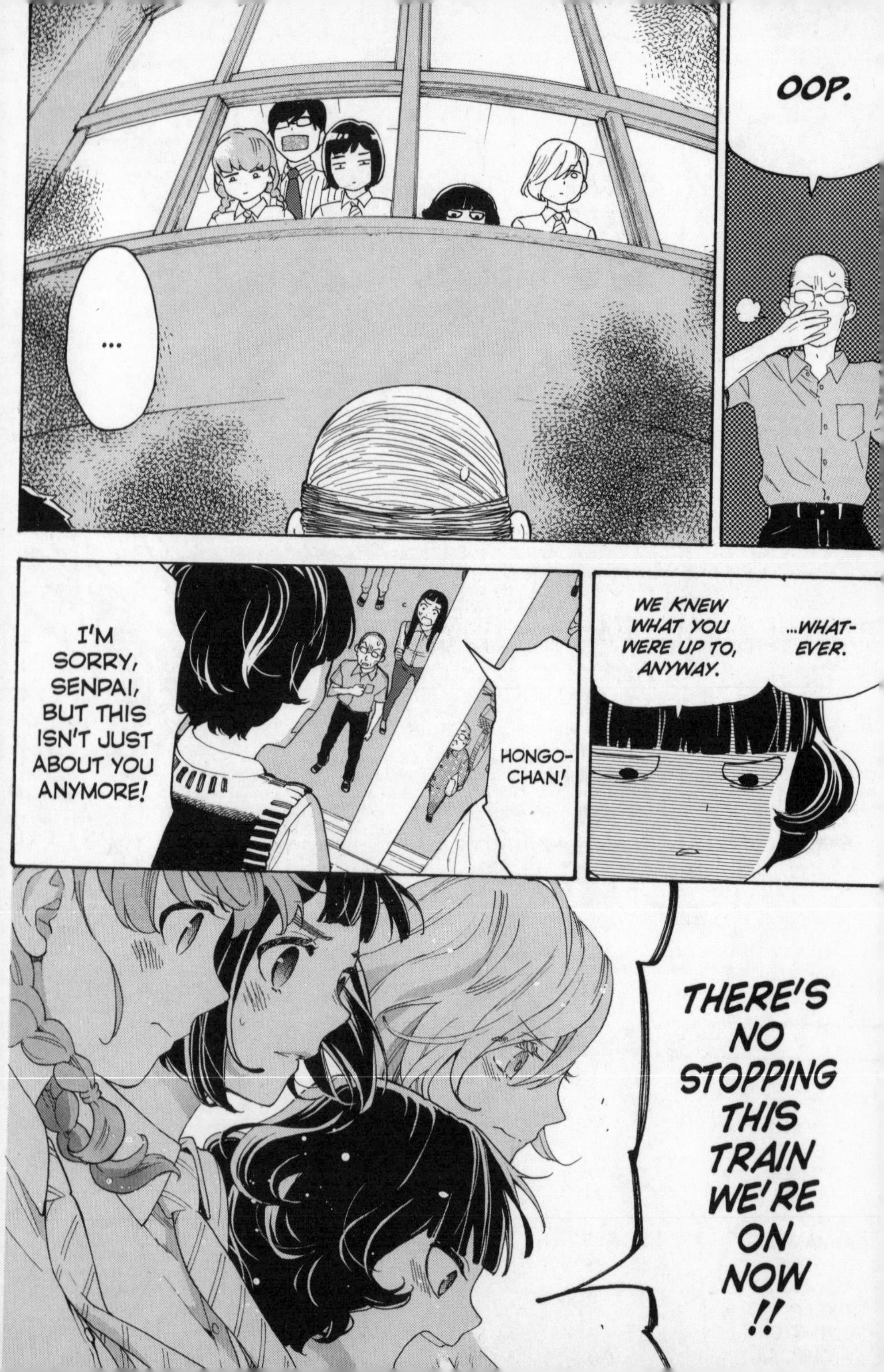
OOP.
...
...WHAT-EVER.
WE KNEW WHAT YOU WERE UP TO, ANYWAY.
HONGO-CHAN!
I'M SORRY, SENPAI, BUT THIS ISN'T JUST ABOUT YOU ANYMORE!
THERE'S NO STOPPING THIS TRAIN WE'RE ON NOW!!

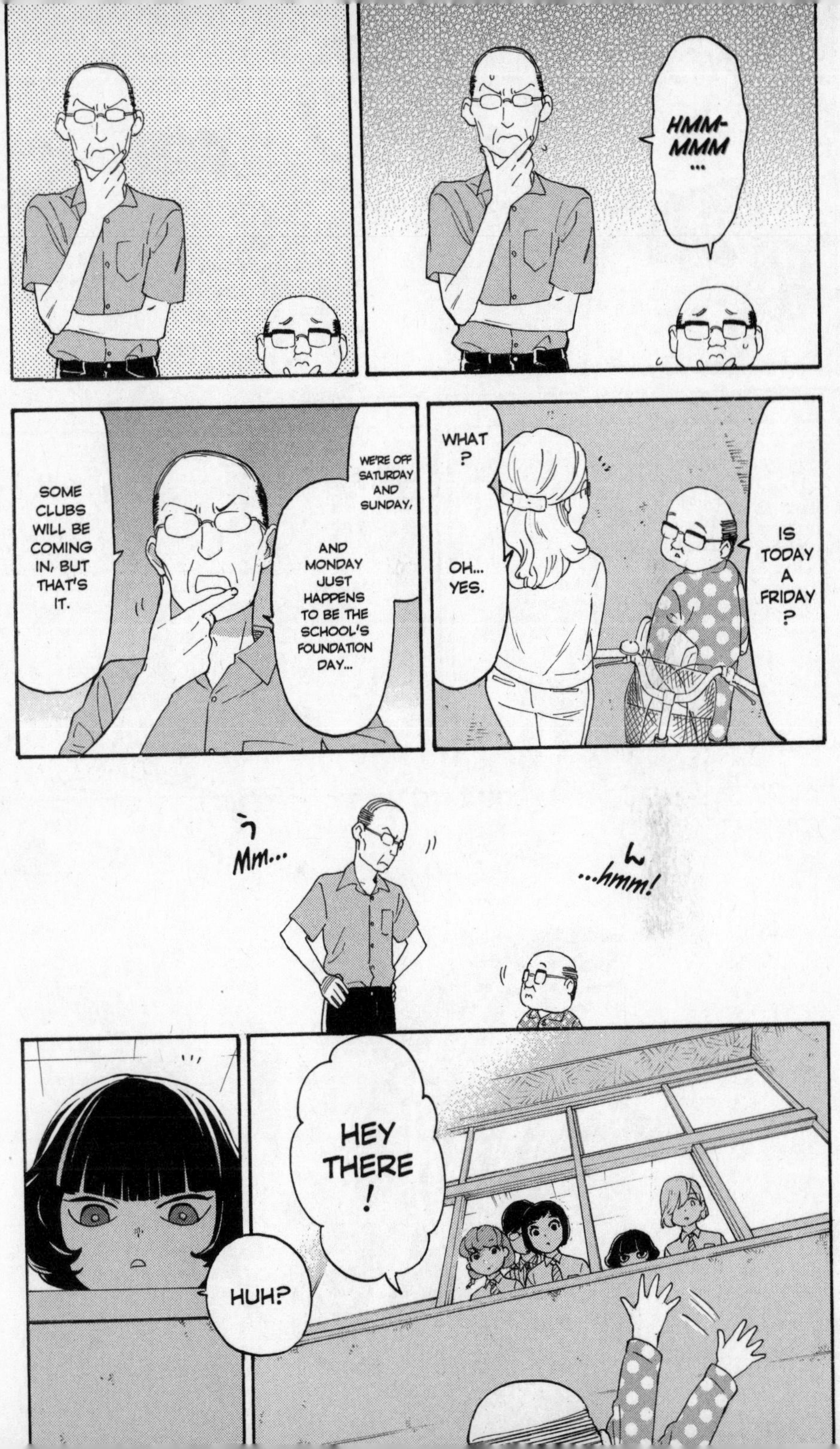
HMM-MMM ...
IS TODAY A FRIDAY?
WHAT?
OH... YES.
WE'RE OFF SATURDAY AND SUNDAY,
AND MONDAY JUST HAPPENS TO BE THE SCHOOL'S FOUNDATION DAY...
SOME CLUBS WILL BE COMING IN, BUT THAT'S IT.
Mm...
...hmm!
HEY THERE!
HUH?

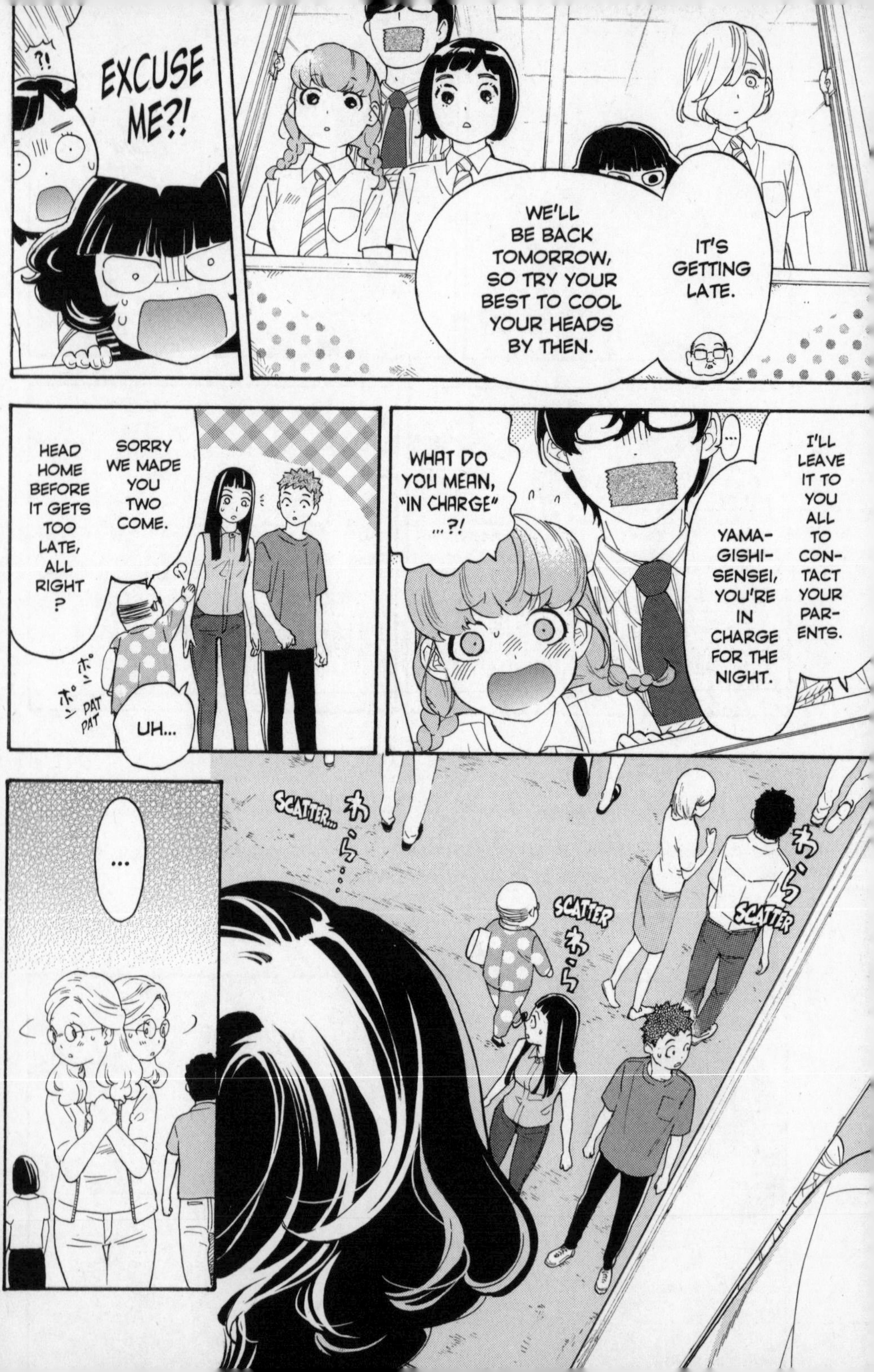
IT'S GETTING LATE.
WE'LL BE BACK TOMORROW, SO TRY YOUR BEST TO COOL YOUR HEADS BY THEN.
?!
EXCUSE ME?!
I'LL LEAVE IT TO YOU ALL TO CONTACT YOUR PARENTS.
YAMAGISHI-SENSEI, YOU'RE IN CHARGE FOR THE NIGHT.
...
WHAT DO YOU MEAN, "IN CHARGE"...?!
SORRY WE MADE YOU TWO COME.
HEAD HOME BEFORE IT GETS TOO LATE, ALL RIGHT?
PAT PAT
UH...
SCATTER
SCATTER
SCATTER...
...

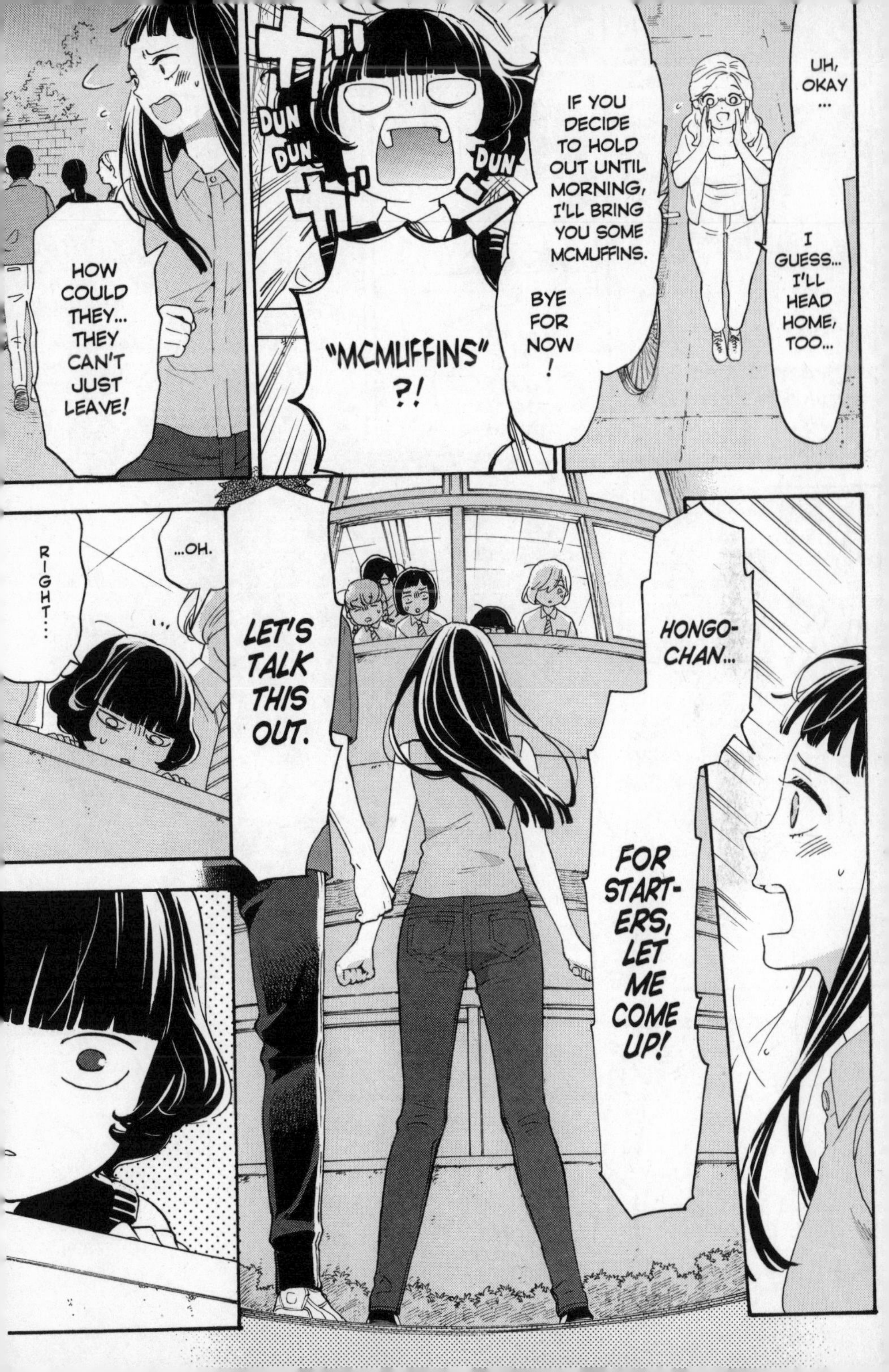
IF YOU DECIDE TO HOLD OUT UNTIL MORNING, I'LL BRING YOU SOME MCMUFFINS.
BYE FOR NOW!
UH, OKAY...
I GUESS... I'LL HEAD HOME, TOO...
DUN DUN DUN
"MCMUFFINS" ?!
HOW COULD THEY... THEY CAN'T JUST LEAVE!
HONGO-CHAN...
FOR STARTERS, LET ME COME UP!
LET'S TALK THIS OUT.
...OH.
RIGHT...

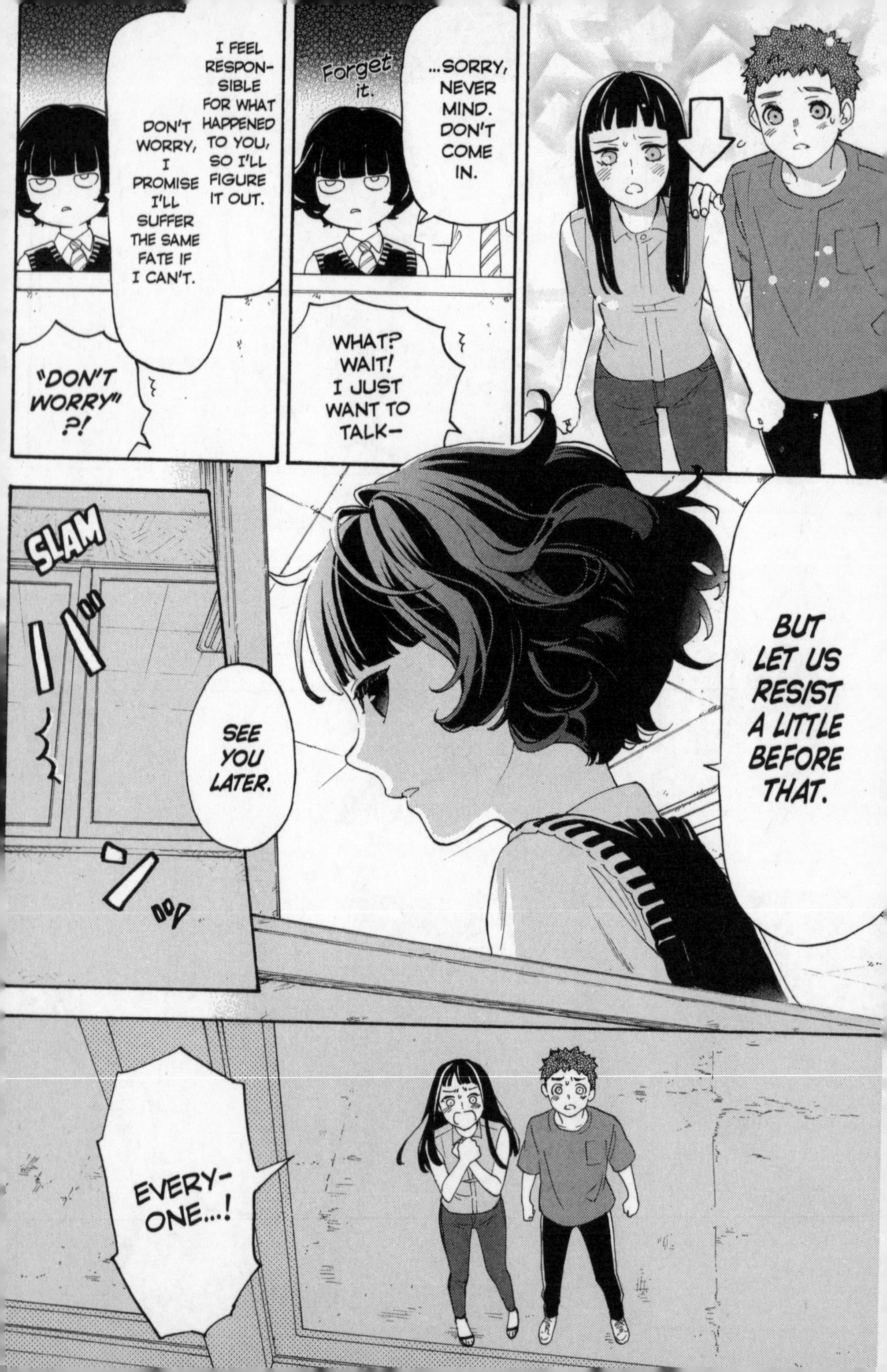
Forget it.
...SORRY, NEVER MIND. DON'T COME IN.
WHAT? WAIT! I JUST WANT TO TALK—
I FEEL RESPONSIBLE FOR WHAT HAPPENED TO YOU, SO I'LL FIGURE IT OUT.
DON'T WORRY, I PROMISE I'LL SUFFER THE SAME FATE IF I CAN'T.
"DON'T WORRY" ?!
BUT LET US RESIST A LITTLE BEFORE THAT.
SEE YOU LATER.
SLAM
EVERYONE...!

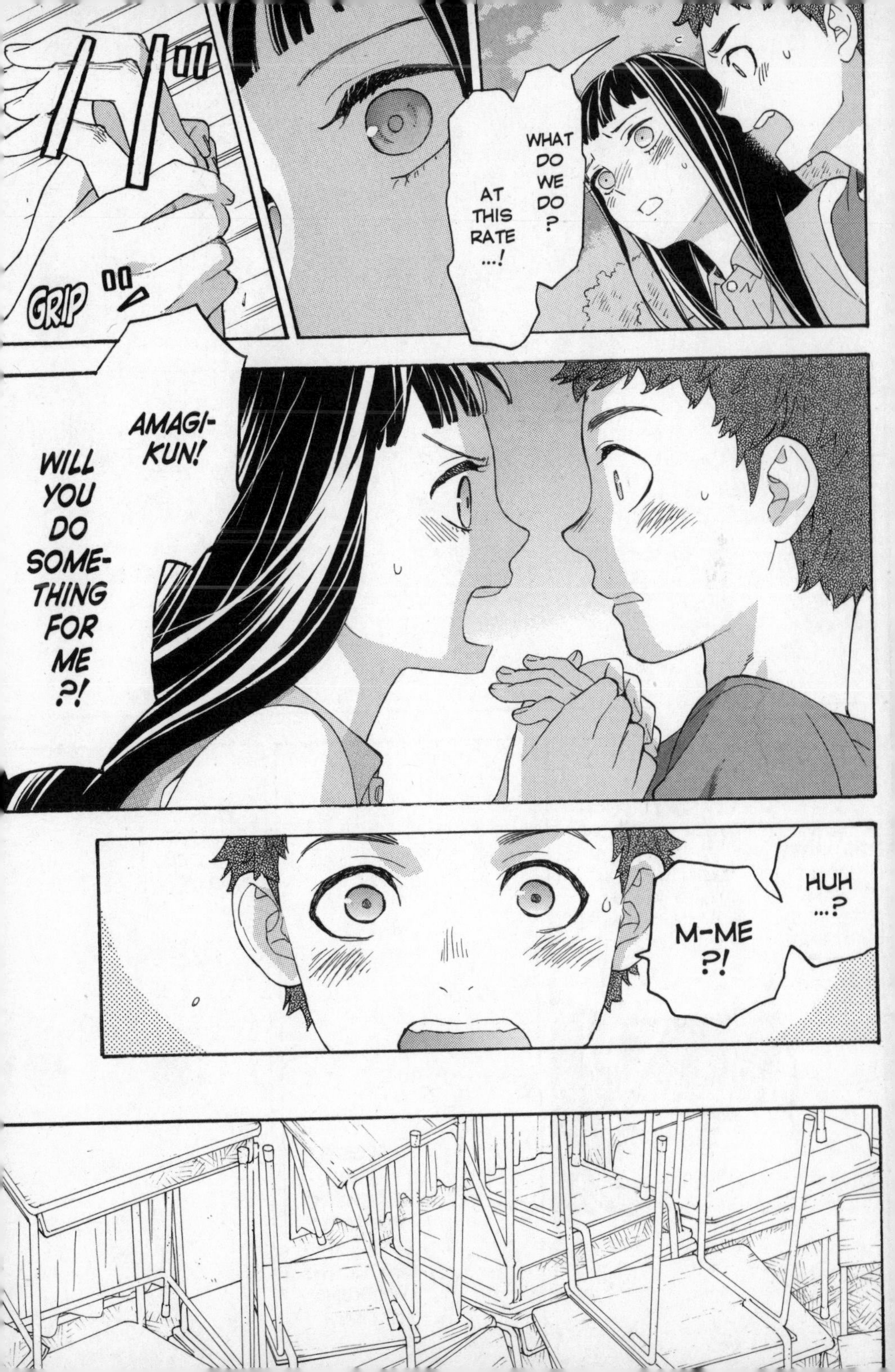
WHAT DO WE DO?
AT THIS RATE...!
GRIP
AMAGI-KUN!
WILL YOU DO SOMETHING FOR ME?!
HUH...?
M-ME?!

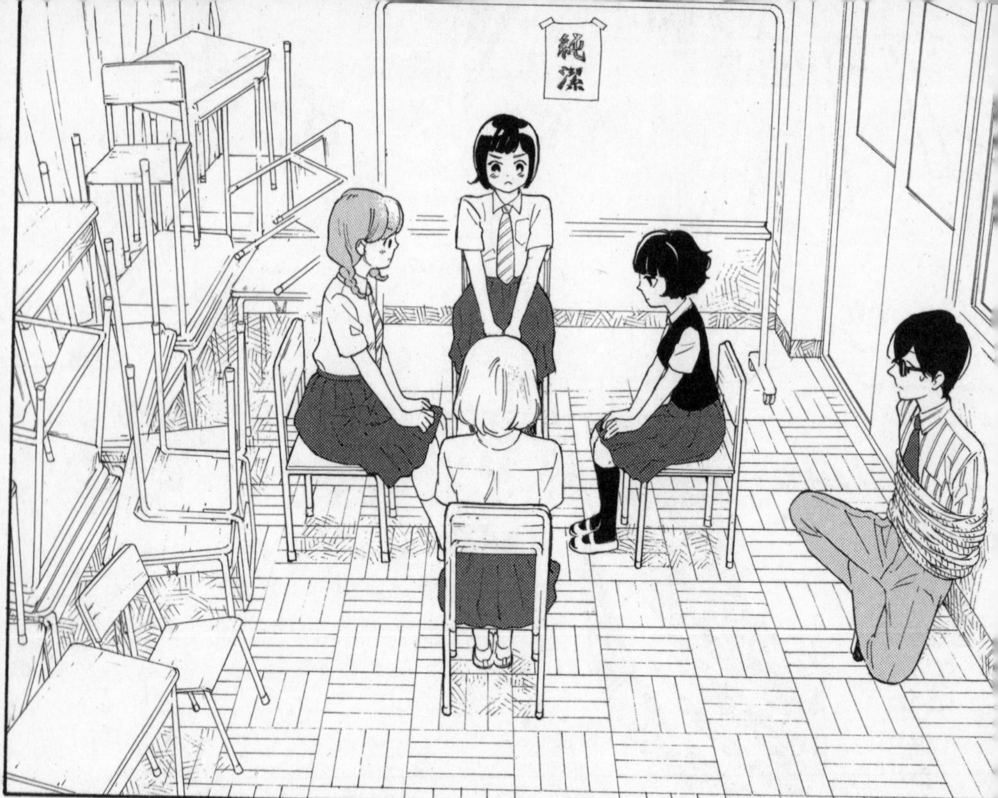
純潔
SIGN: Chastity

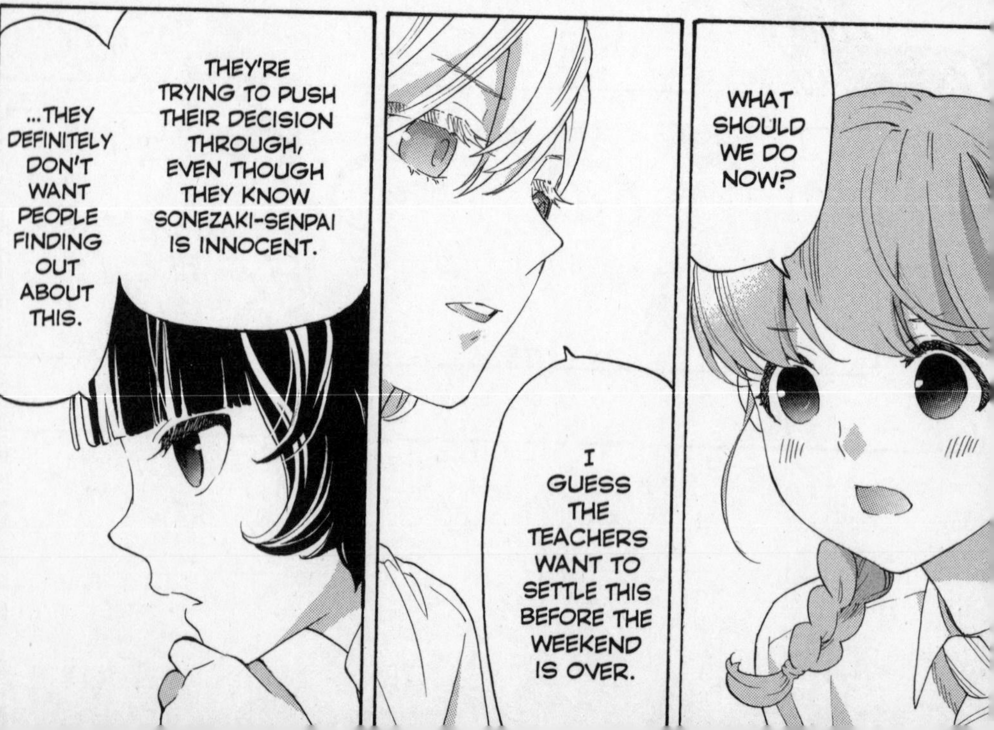
WHAT SHOULD WE DO NOW?
I GUESS THE TEACHERS WANT TO SETTLE THIS BEFORE THE WEEKEND IS OVER.
THEY'RE TRYING TO PUSH THEIR DECISION THROUGH, EVEN THOUGH THEY KNOW SONEZAKI-SENPAI IS INNOCENT.
...THEY DEFINITELY DON'T WANT PEOPLE FINDING OUT ABOUT THIS.

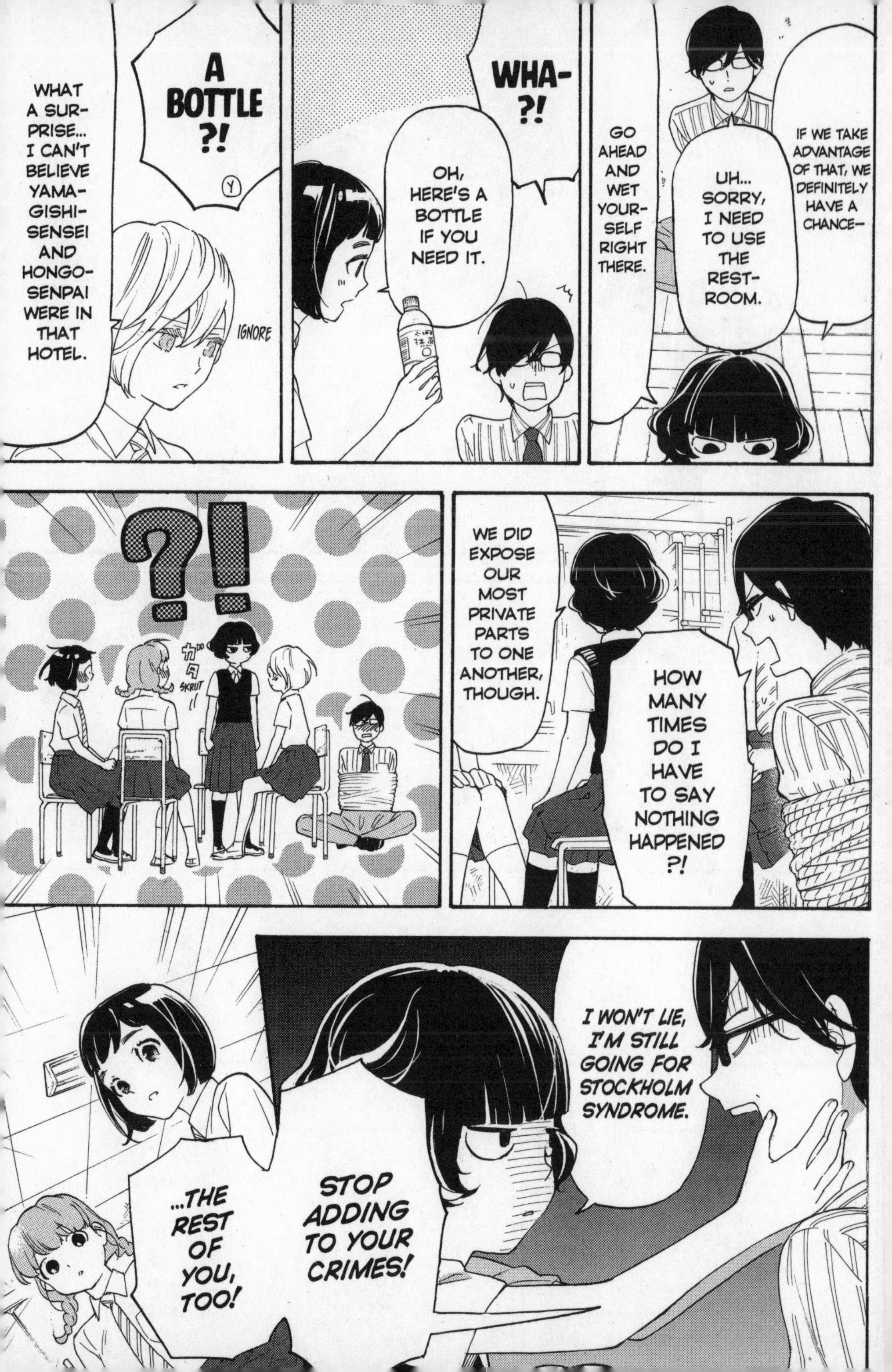
IF WE TAKE ADVANTAGE OF THAT, WE DEFINITELY HAVE A CHANCE-
UH... SORRY, I NEED TO USE THE REST-ROOM.
GO AHEAD AND WET YOURSELF RIGHT THERE.
WHA-?!
OH, HERE'S A BOTTLE IF YOU NEED IT.
A BOTTLE?!
IGNORE
WHAT A SUR-PRISE... I CAN'T BELIEVE YAMA-GISHI-SENSEI AND HONGO-SENPAI WERE IN THAT HOTEL.
HOW MANY TIMES DO I HAVE TO SAY NOTHING HAPPENED?!
WE DID EXPOSE OUR MOST PRIVATE PARTS TO ONE ANOTHER, THOUGH.
?!!
SKRUT
I WON'T LIE, I'M STILL GOING FOR STOCKHOLM SYNDROME.
STOP ADDING TO YOUR CRIMES!
...THE REST OF YOU, TOO!

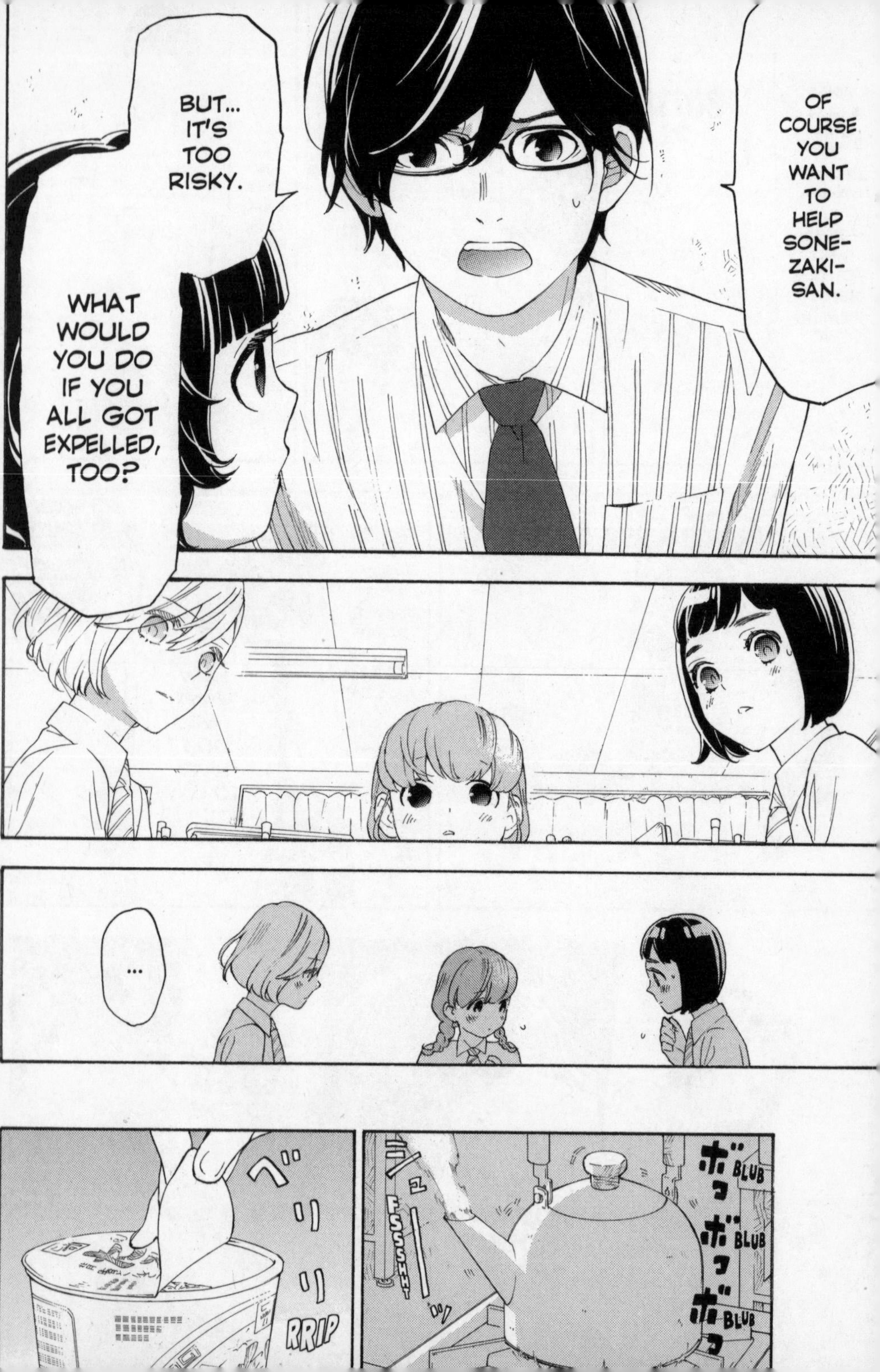
OF COURSE YOU WANT TO HELP SONE-ZAKI-SAN.
BUT... IT'S TOO RISKY.
WHAT WOULD YOU DO IF YOU ALL GOT EXPELLED, TOO?
...
BLUB
BLUB
BLUB
FSSSHHT
べりり
RRIP

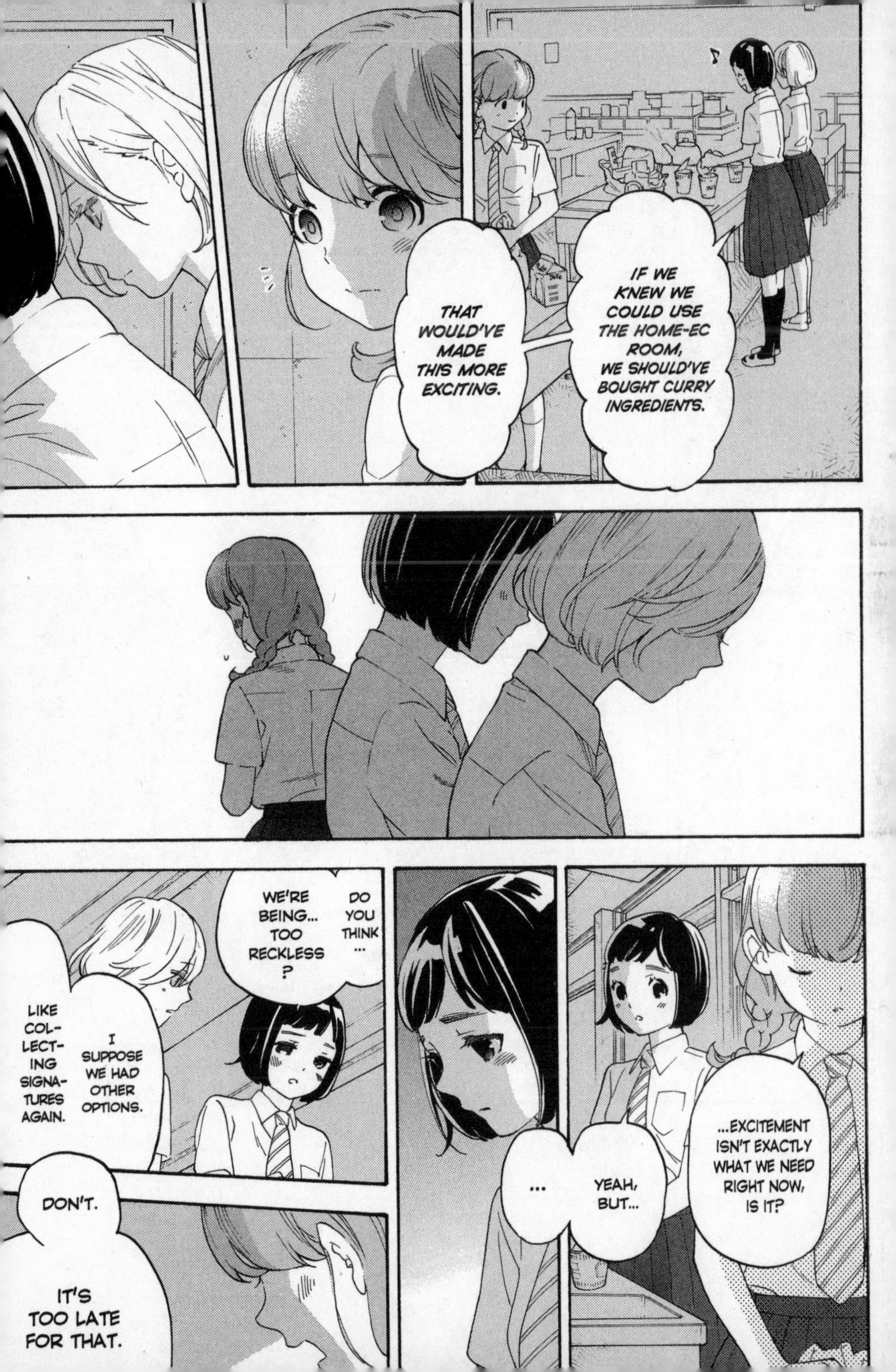
IF WE KNEW WE COULD USE THE HOME-EC ROOM, WE SHOULD'VE BOUGHT CURRY INGREDIENTS.
THAT WOULD'VE MADE THIS MORE EXCITING.
...EXCITEMENT ISN'T EXACTLY WHAT WE NEED RIGHT NOW, IS IT?
YEAH, BUT...
...
DO YOU THINK...
WE'RE BEING... TOO RECKLESS?
I SUPPOSE WE HAD OTHER OPTIONS.
LIKE COL-LECT-ING SIGNA-TURES AGAIN.
DON'T.
IT'S TOO LATE FOR THAT.

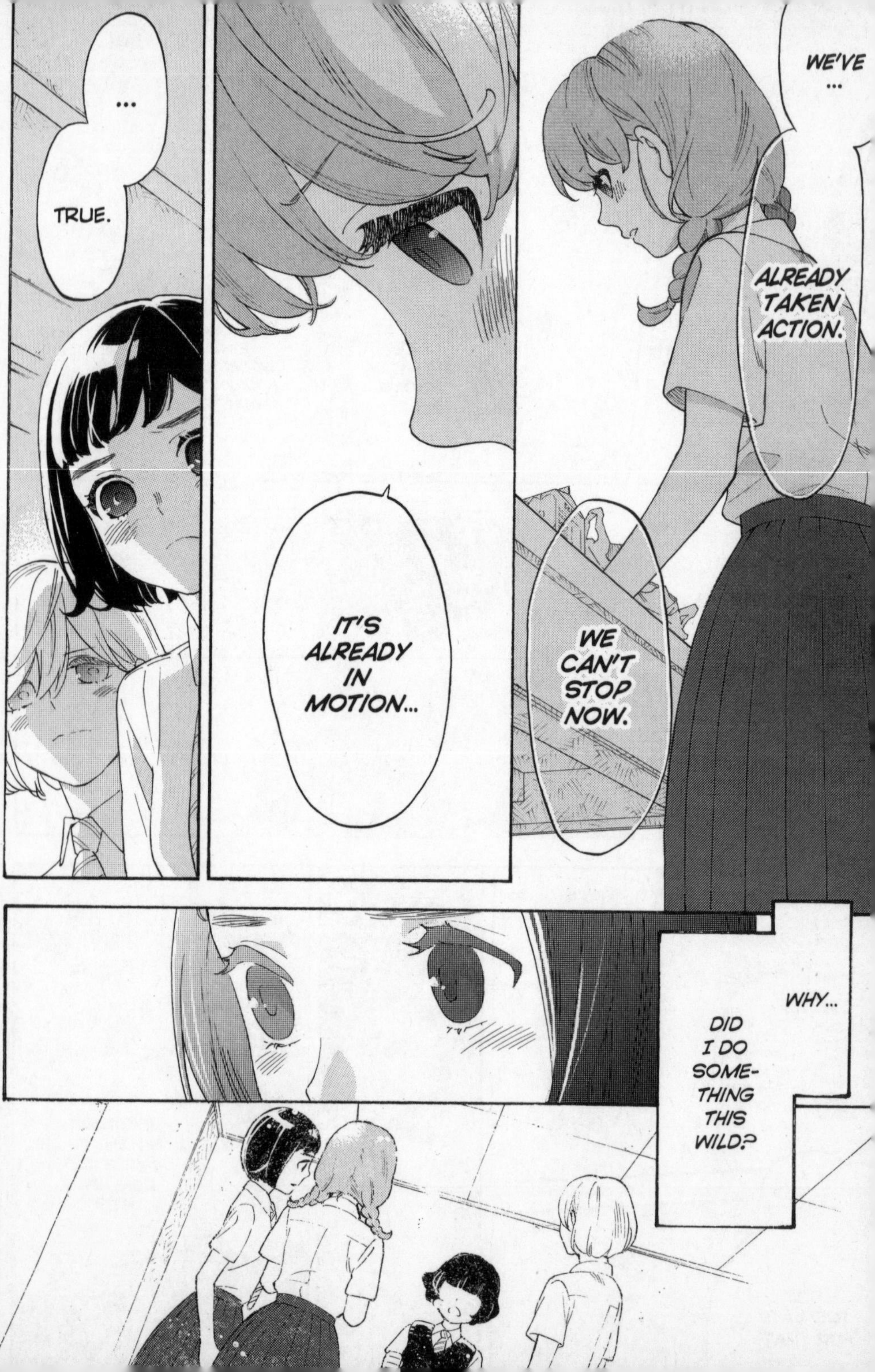
WE'VE ... ALREADY TAKEN ACTION.
WE CAN'T STOP NOW.
IT'S ALREADY IN MOTION...
... TRUE.
WHY...
DID I DO SOME-THING THIS WILD?

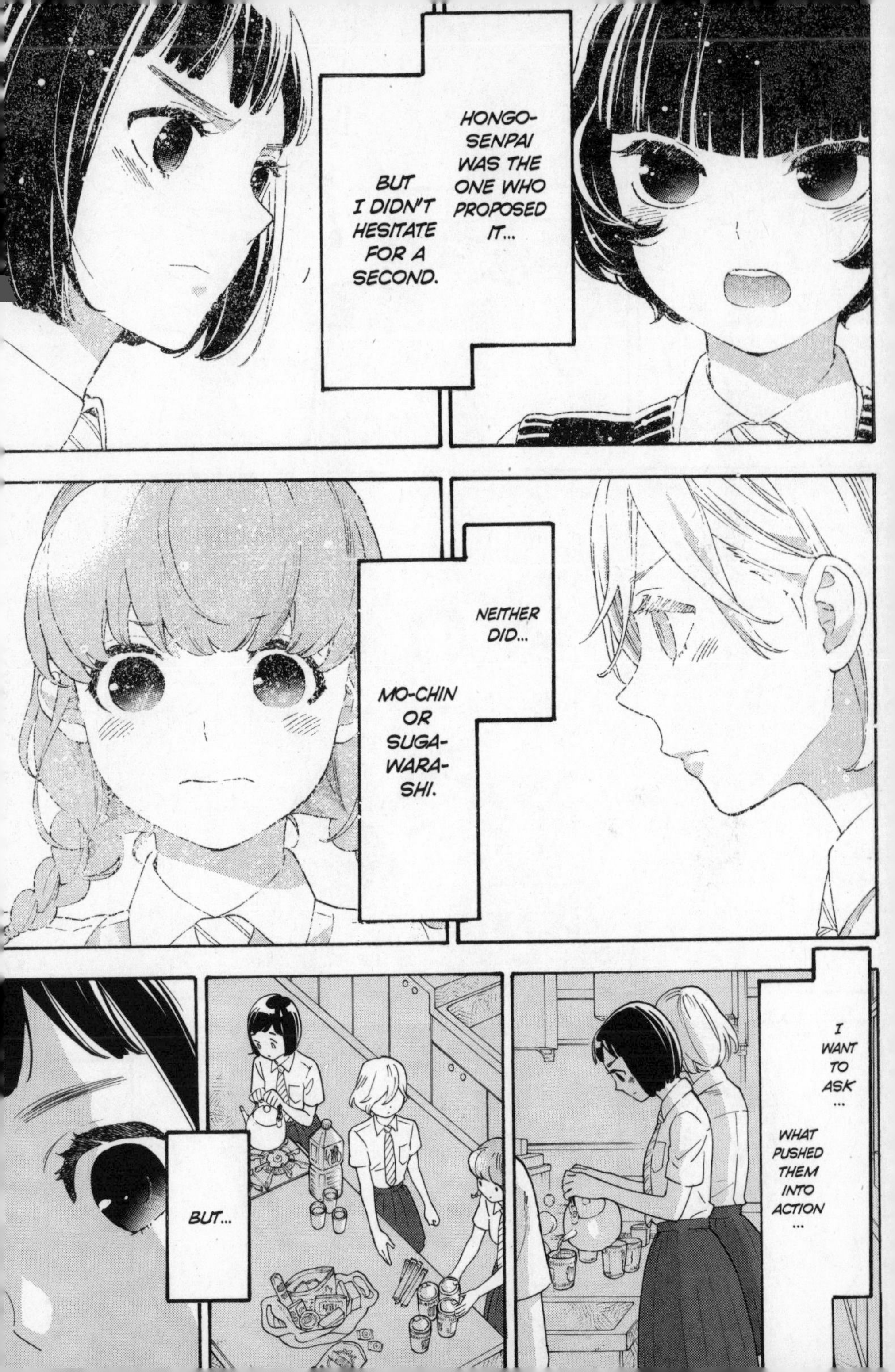
HONGO-SENPAI WAS THE ONE WHO PROPOSED IT...
BUT I DIDN'T HESITATE FOR A SECOND.
NEITHER DID...
MO-CHIN OR SUGA-WARA-SHI.
I WANT TO ASK...
WHAT PUSHED THEM INTO ACTION...
BUT...

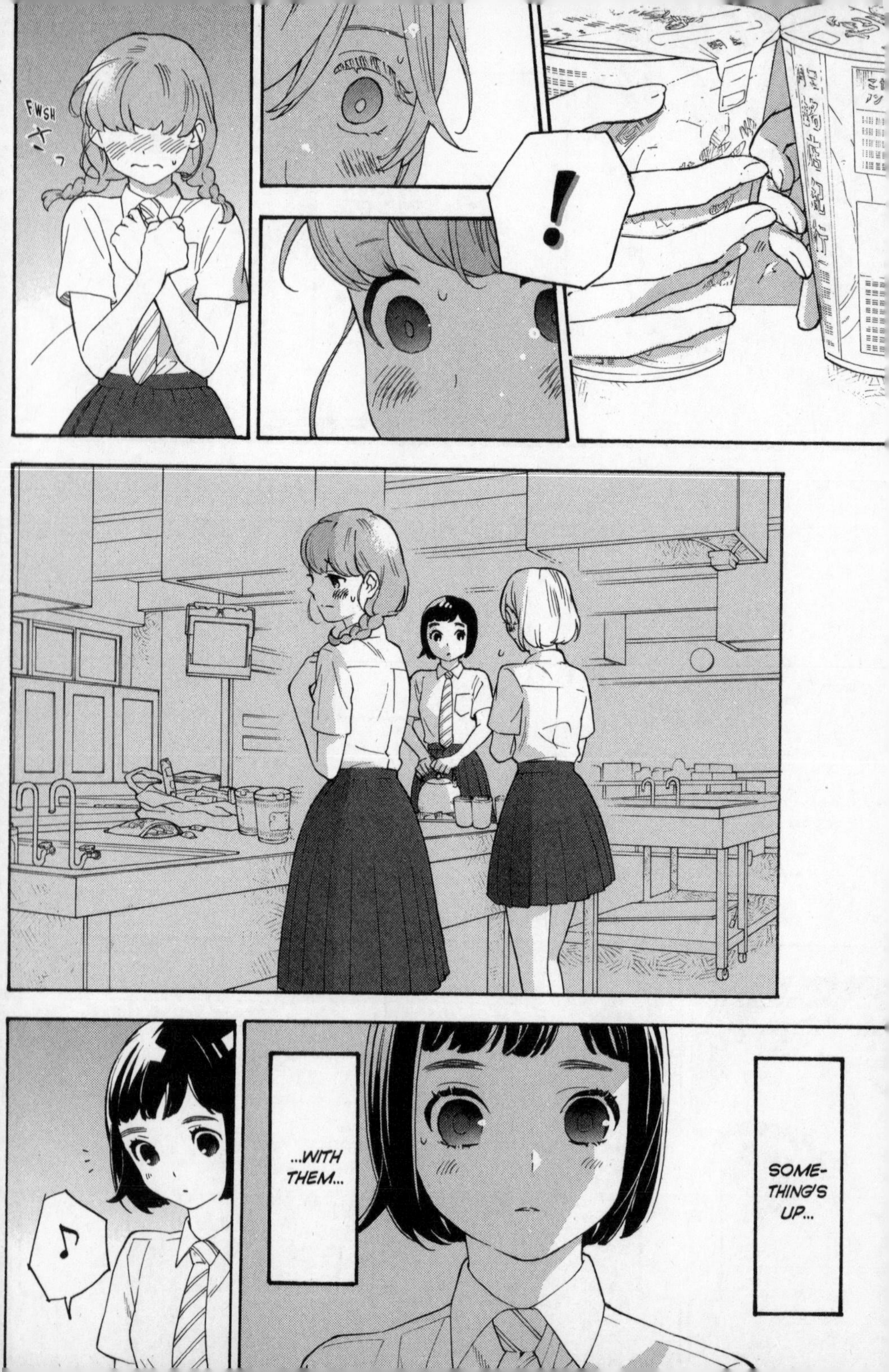
!
FWSH
SOME-THING'S UP...
...WITH THEM...
♪

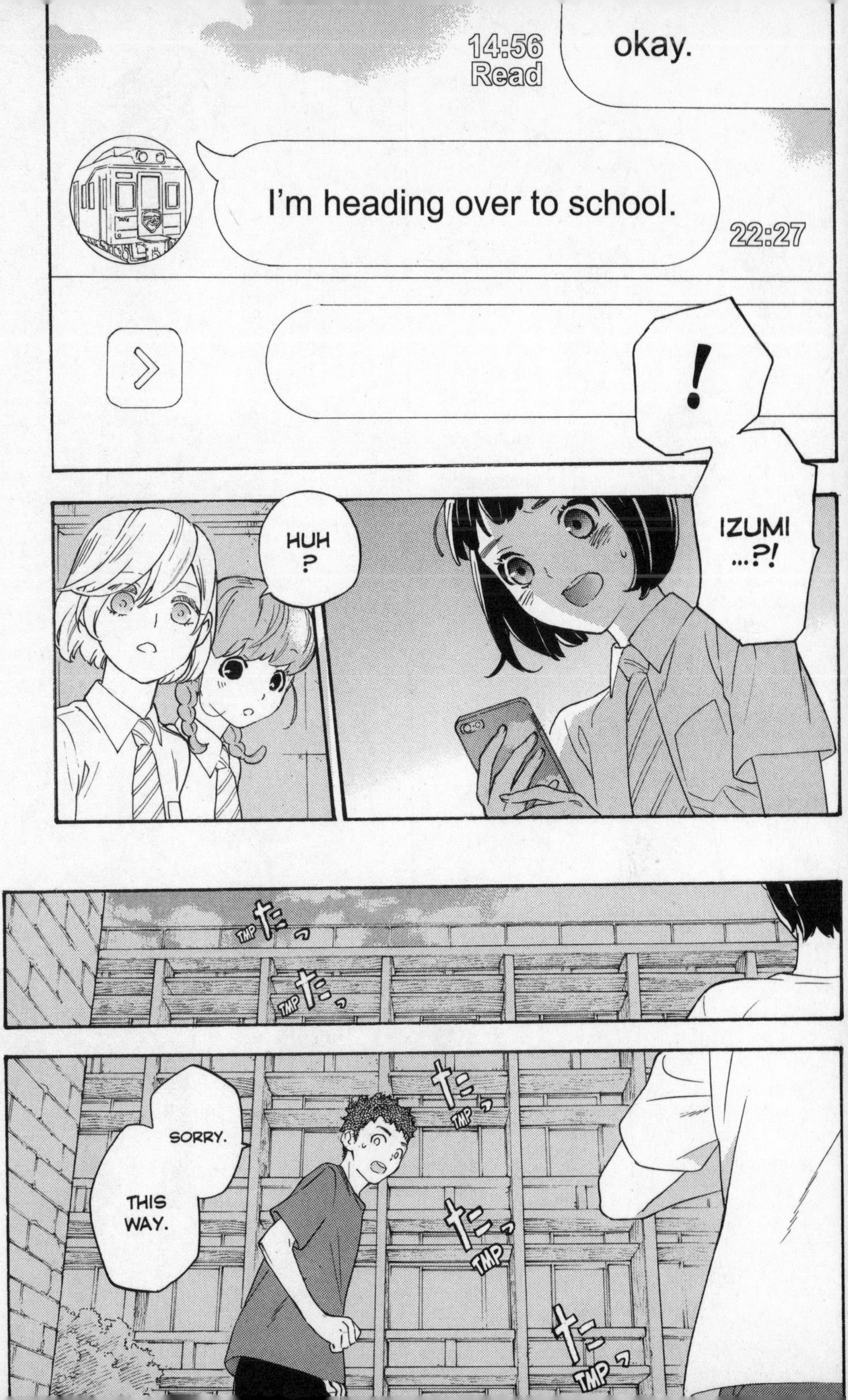
okay.
14:56 Read
I'm heading over to school.
22:27
!
IZUMI ...?!
HUH ?
TMP
TMP
TMP
TMP
TMP
SORRY.
THIS WAY.

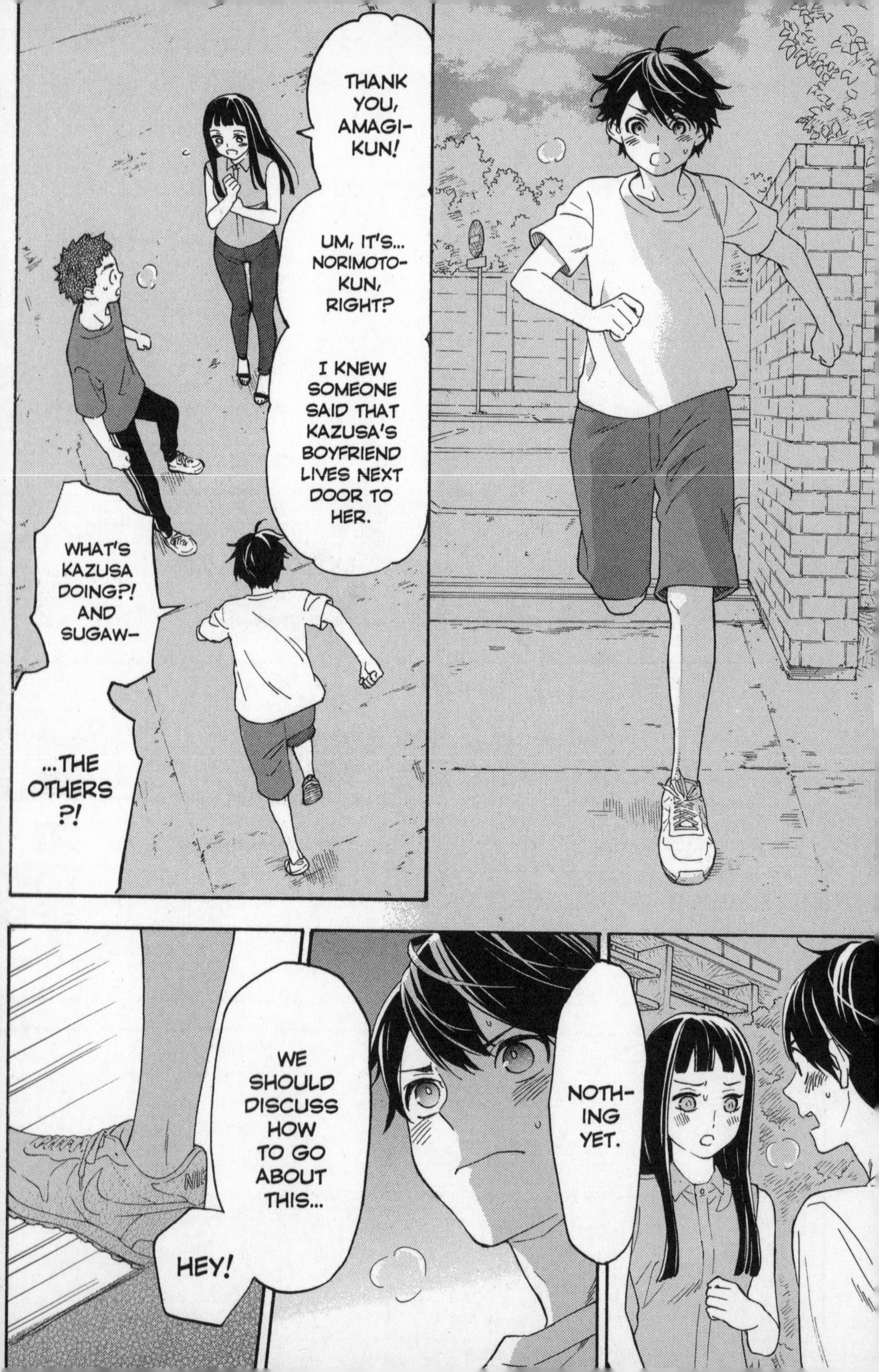
THANK YOU, AMAGI-KUN!
UM, IT'S... NORIMOTO-KUN, RIGHT?
I KNEW SOMEONE SAID THAT KAZUSA'S BOYFRIEND LIVES NEXT DOOR TO HER.
WHAT'S KAZUSA DOING?! AND SUGAW-
...THE OTHERS?!
NOTH-ING YET.
WE SHOULD DISCUSS HOW TO GO ABOUT THIS...
HEY!

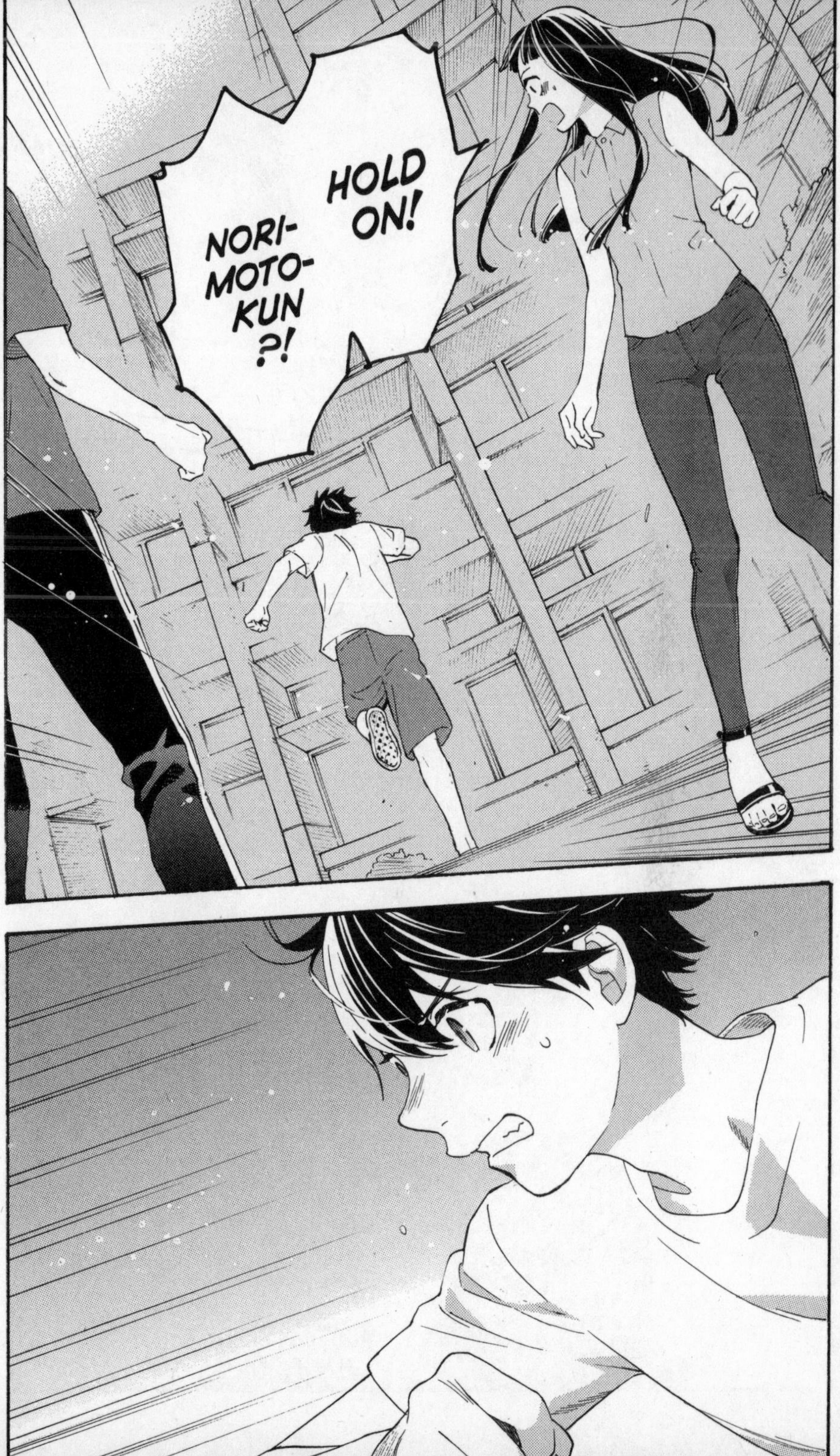
HOLD ON!
NORI-MOTO-KUN?!

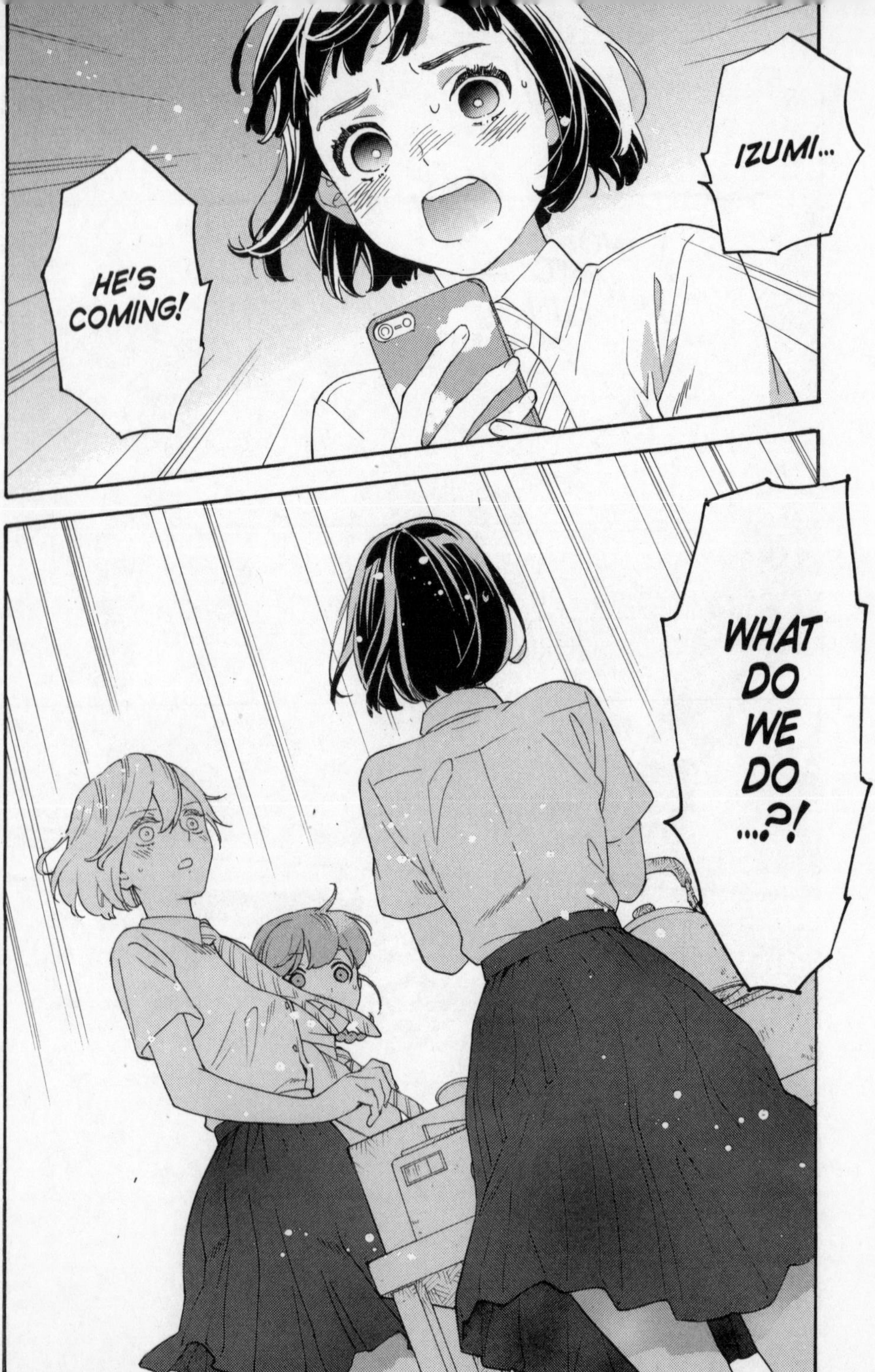
IZUMI...
HE'S COMING!
WHAT DO WE DO ...?!

O Maidens
in your Savage
Season

荒ぶる季節の乙女どもよ。

【あらぶるきせつの
おとめどもよ】

Meeting 29

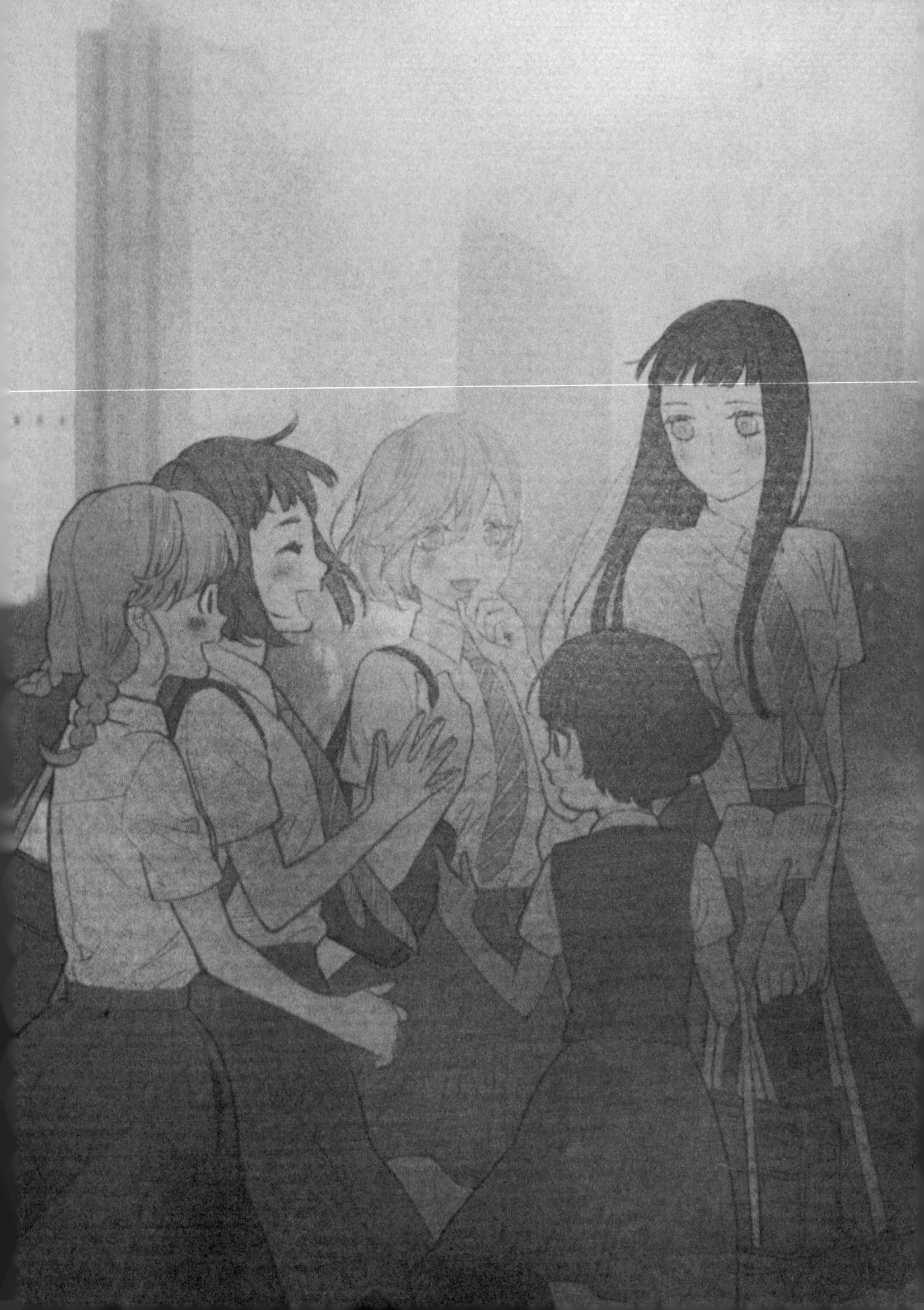

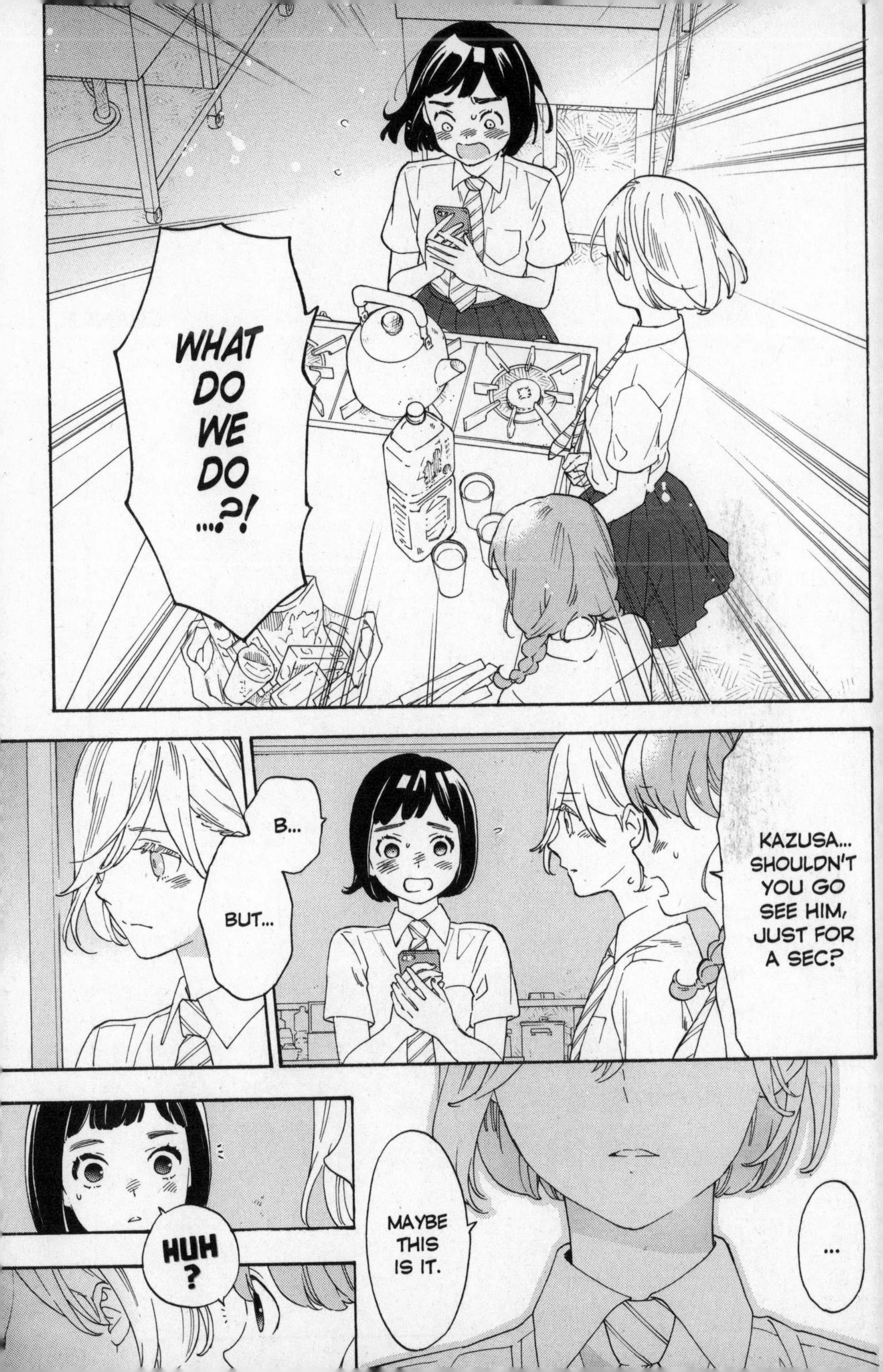
WHAT DO WE DO ...?!
KAZUSA... SHOULDN'T YOU GO SEE HIM, JUST FOR A SEC?
B...
BUT...
...
MAYBE THIS IS IT.
HUH?

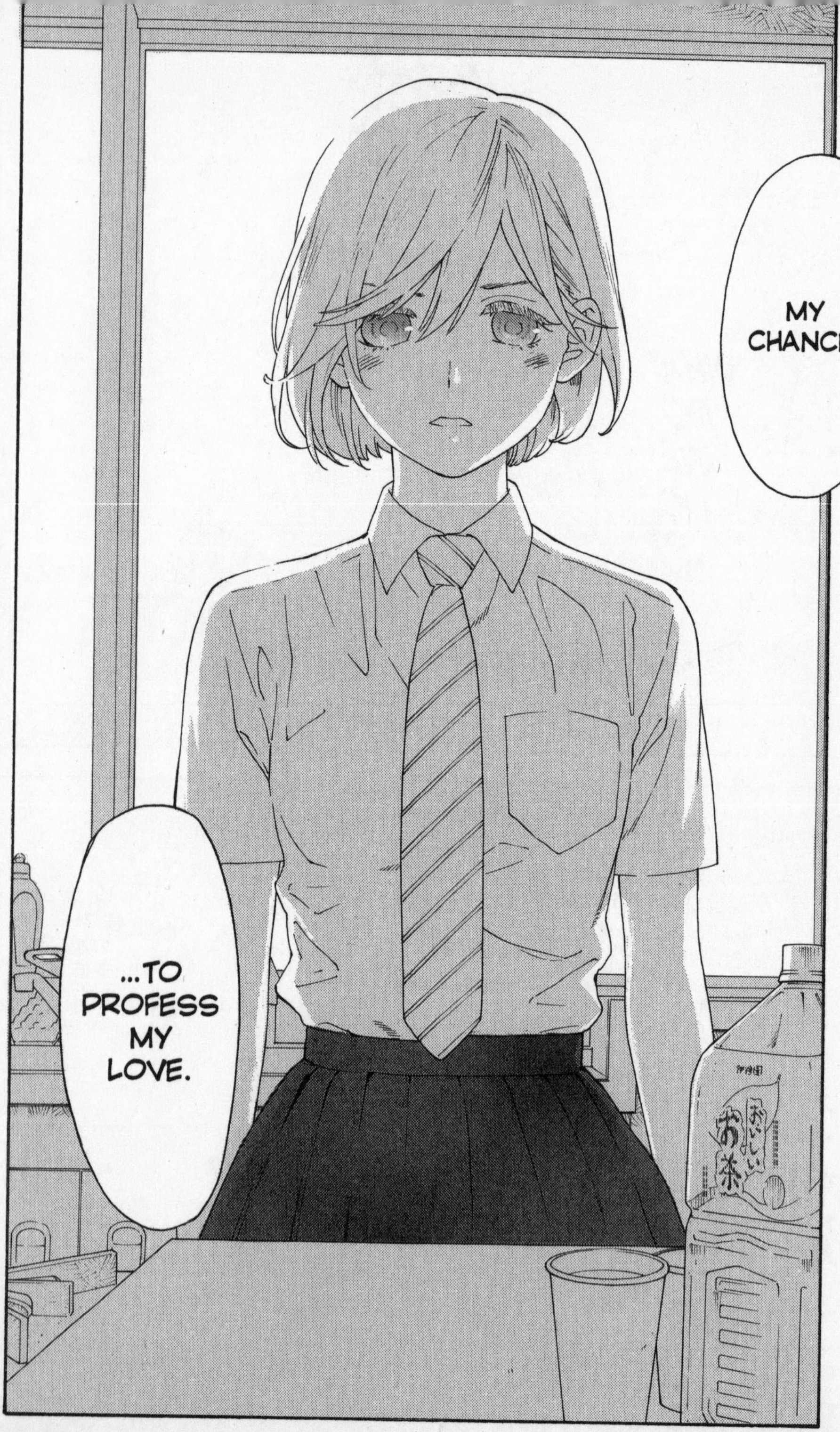
MY CHANCE...
...TO PROFESS MY LOVE.
おいしいお茶

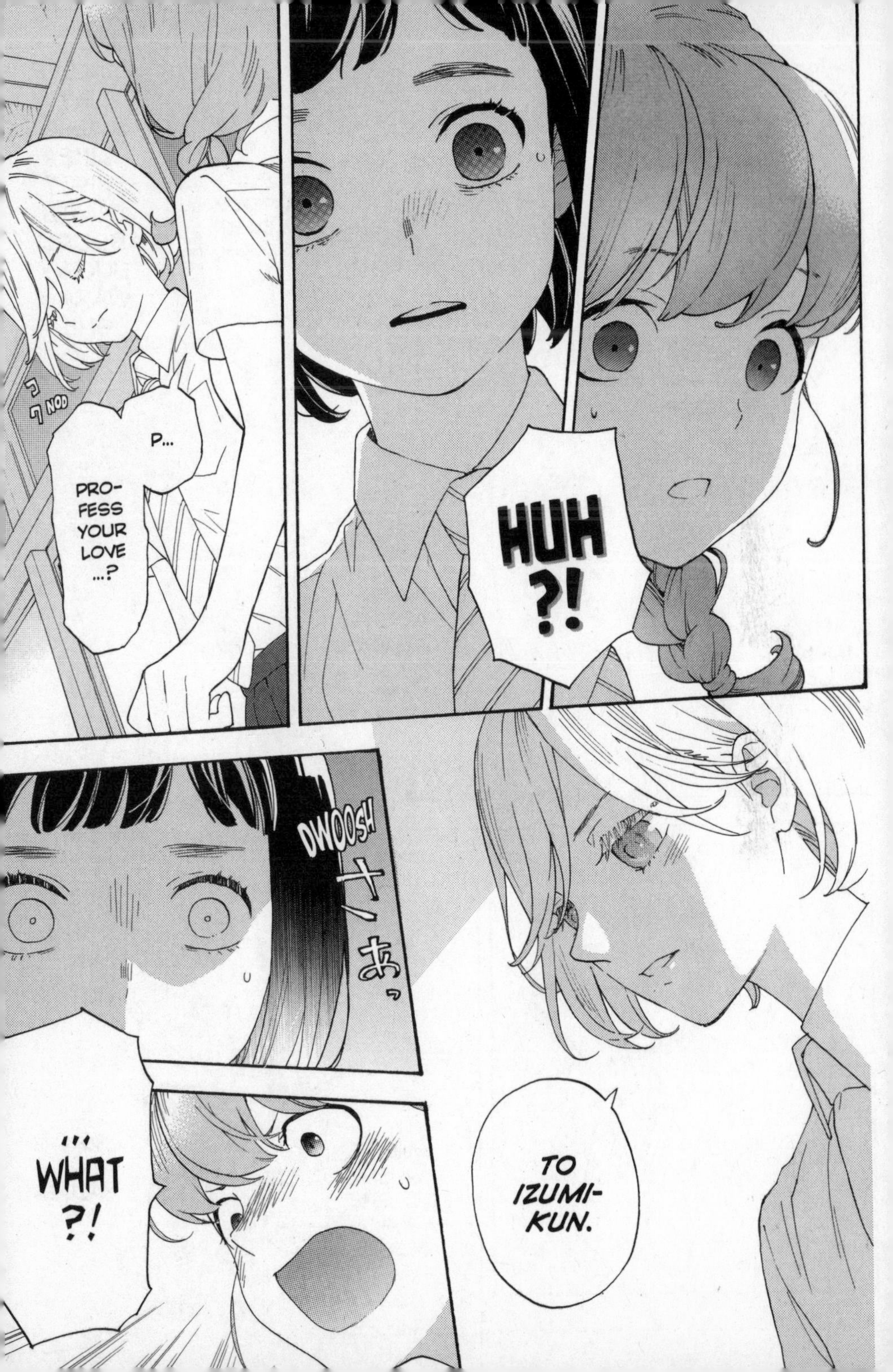
HUH ?!
NOD
P...
PRO-FESS YOUR LOVE ...?
TO IZUMI-KUN.
DWOOSH
... WHAT ?!

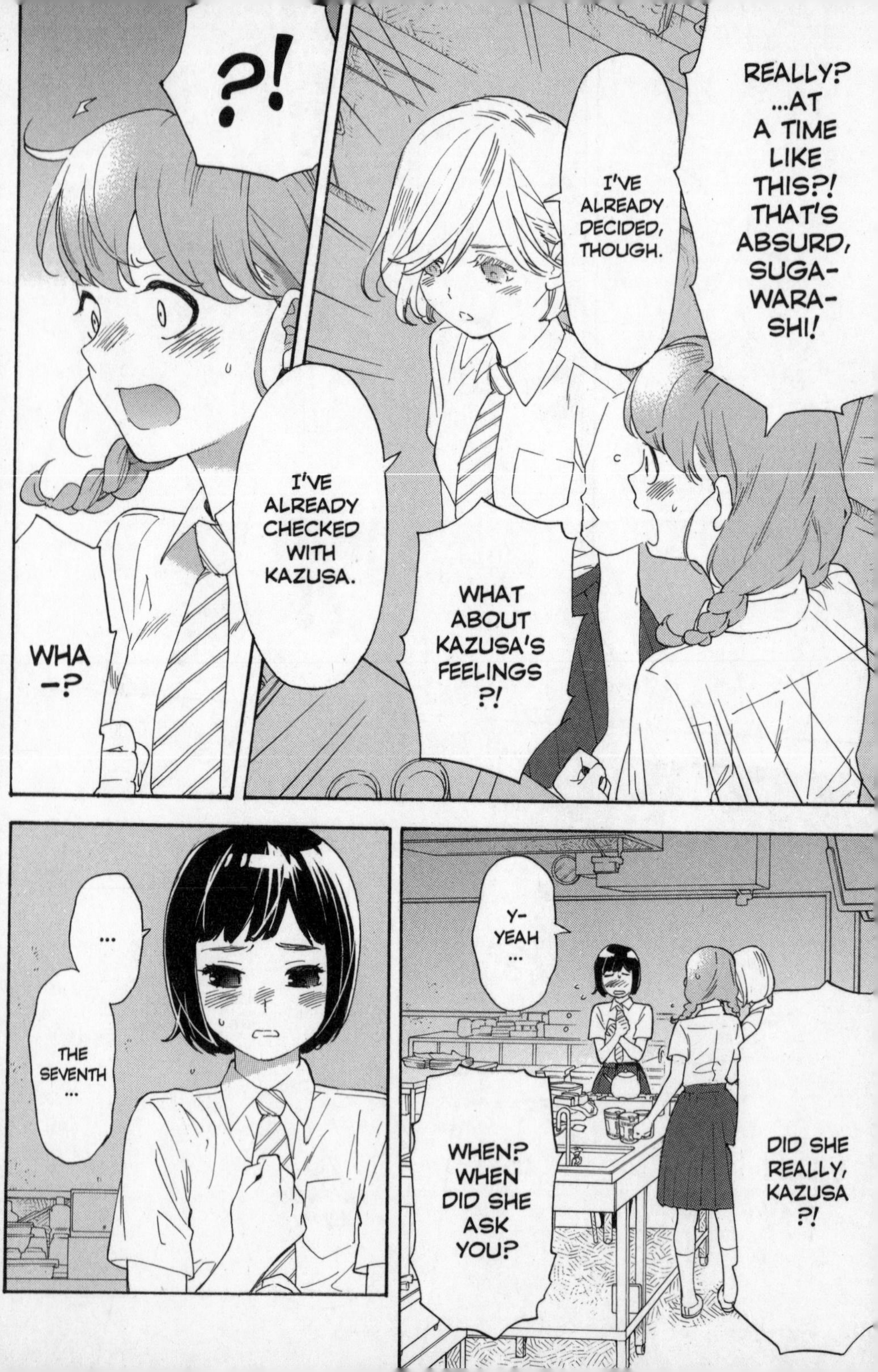
REALLY? ...AT A TIME LIKE THIS?! THAT'S ABSURD, SUGA-WARA-SHI!
I'VE ALREADY DECIDED, THOUGH.
WHAT ABOUT KAZUSA'S FEELINGS ?!
I'VE ALREADY CHECKED WITH KAZUSA.
?!
WHA -?
DID SHE REALLY, KAZUSA ?!
WHEN? WHEN DID SHE ASK YOU?
Y-YEAH ...
...
THE SEVENTH ...

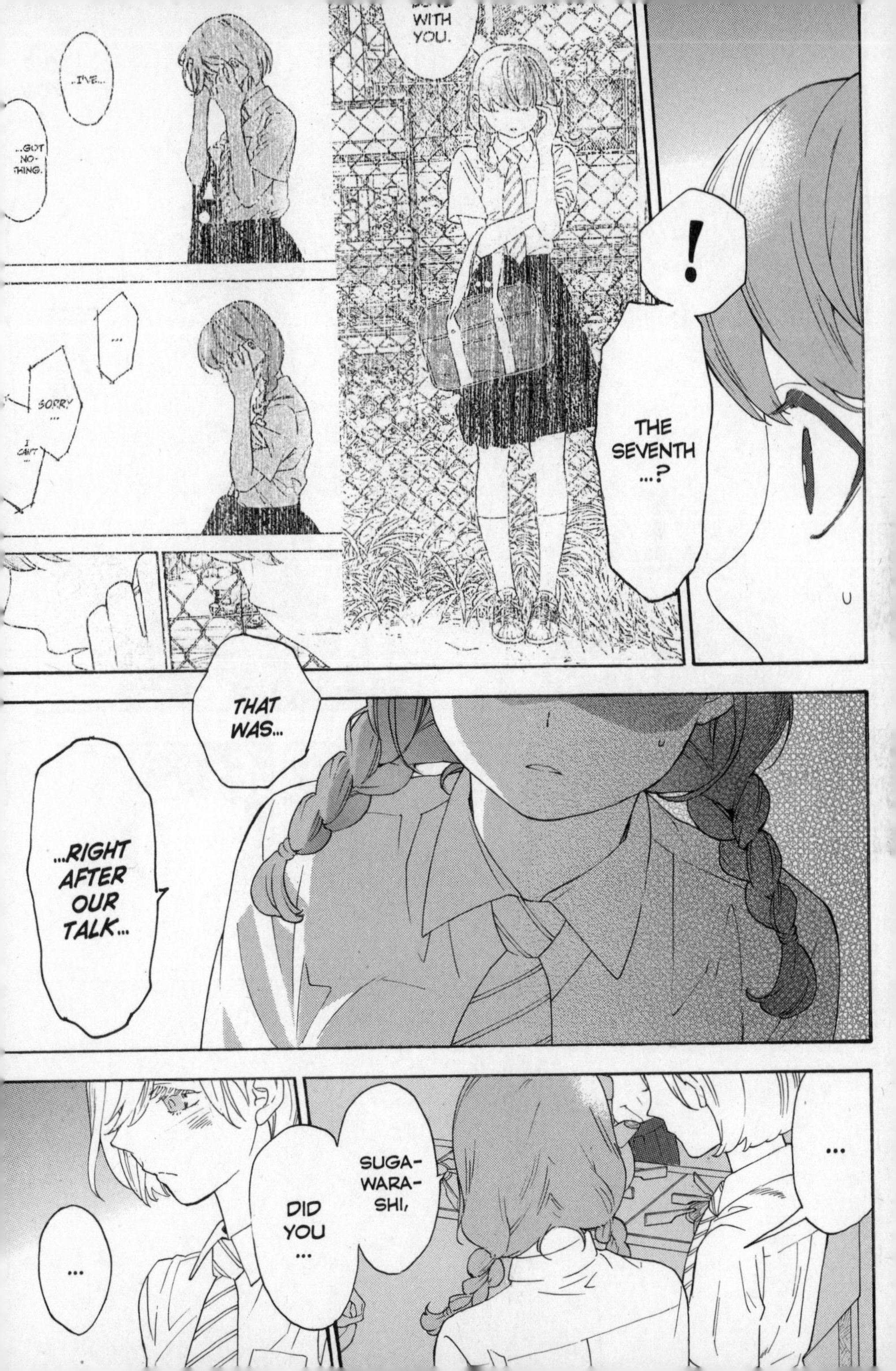
!
THE SEVENTH ...?
WITH YOU.
...I'VE...
...GOT NO-THING.
...
SORRY ...
I CAN'T ...
THAT WAS...
...RIGHT AFTER OUR TALK...
...
SUGA-WARA-SHI,
DID YOU ...
...

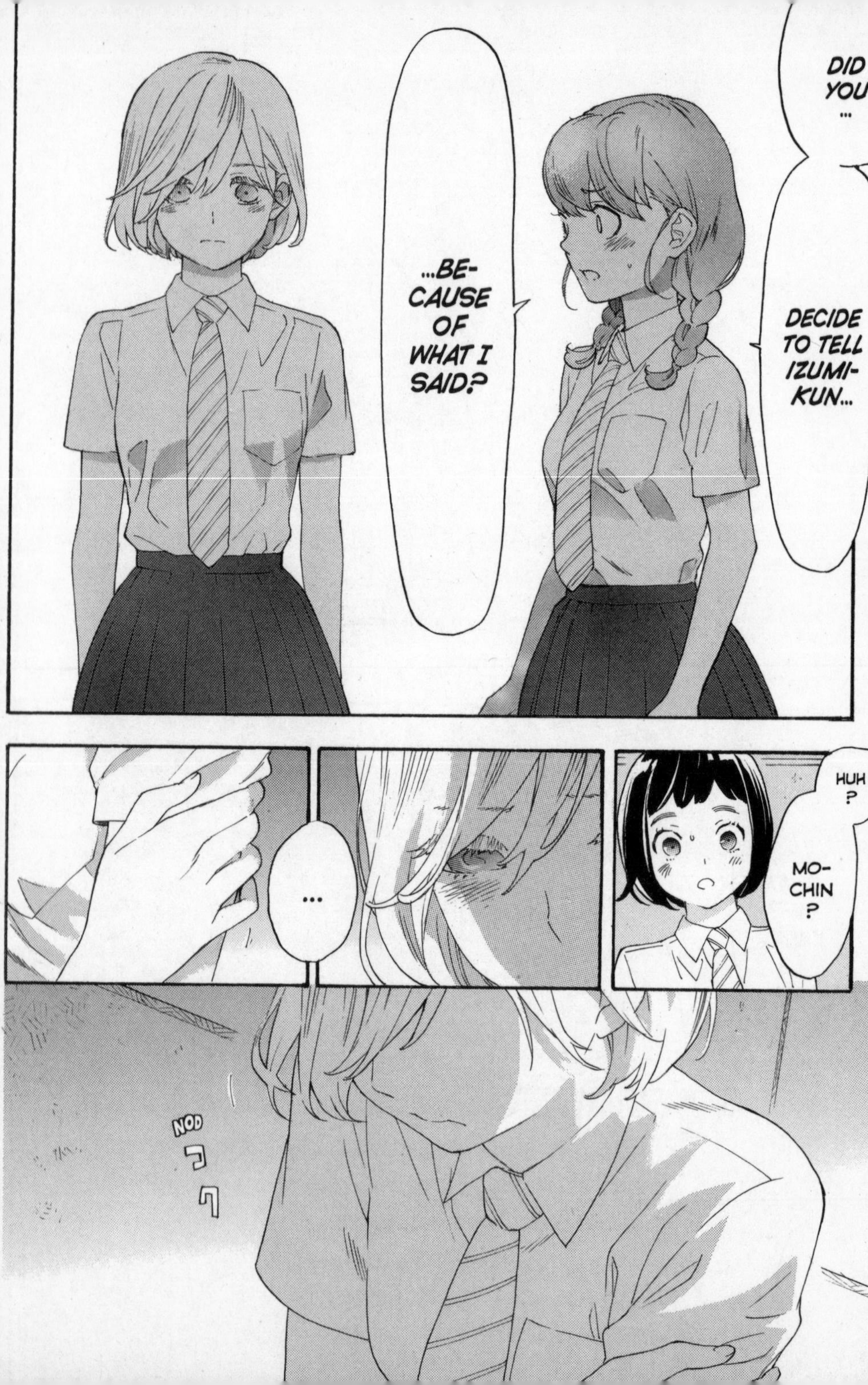
DID YOU ... DECIDE TO TELL IZUMI-KUN...
...BE-CAUSE OF WHAT I SAID?
HUH? MO-CHIN?
...
NOD
コク

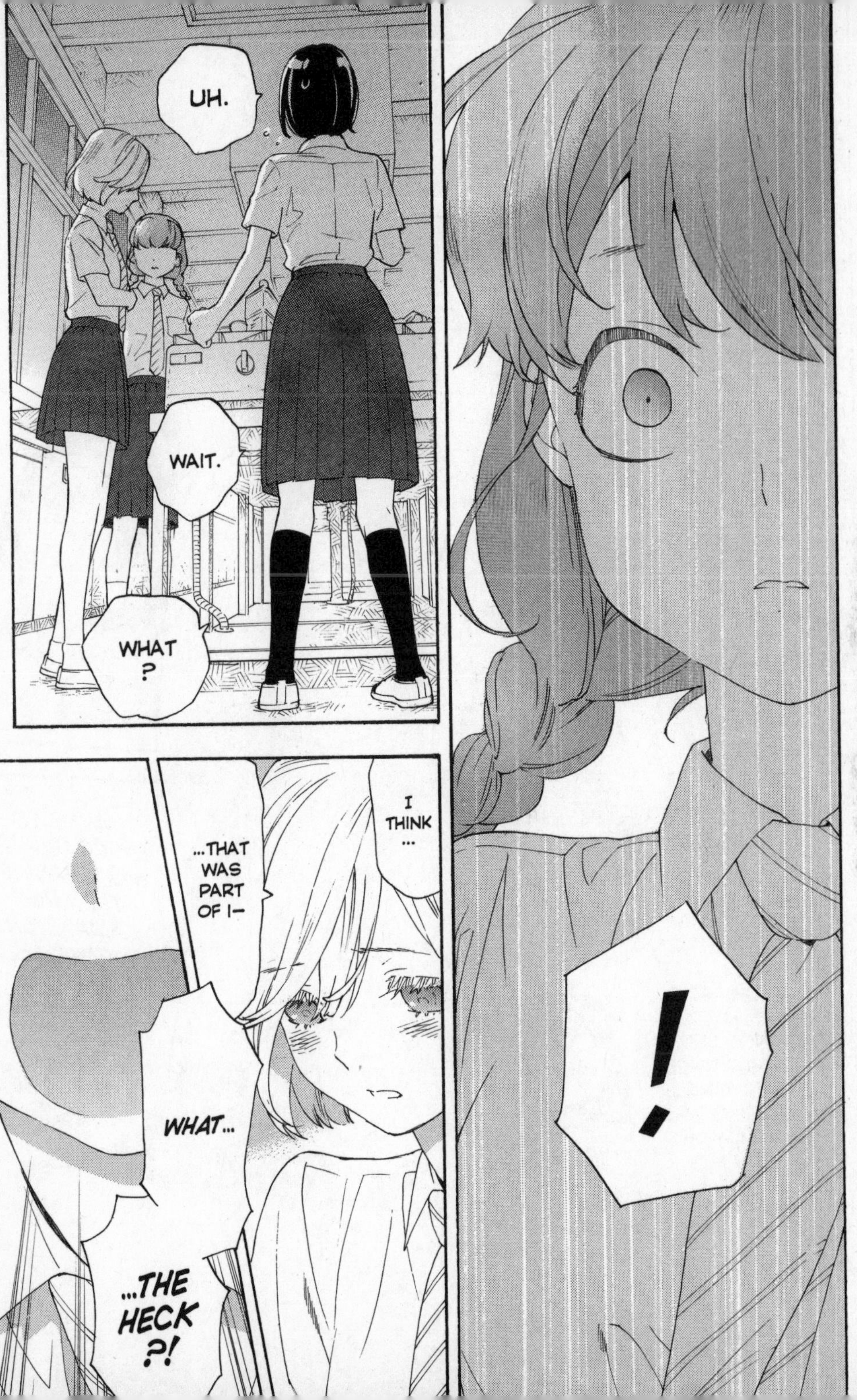
!
UH.
WAIT.
WHAT ?
I THINK ...
...THAT WAS PART OF I—
WHAT...
...THE HECK ?!

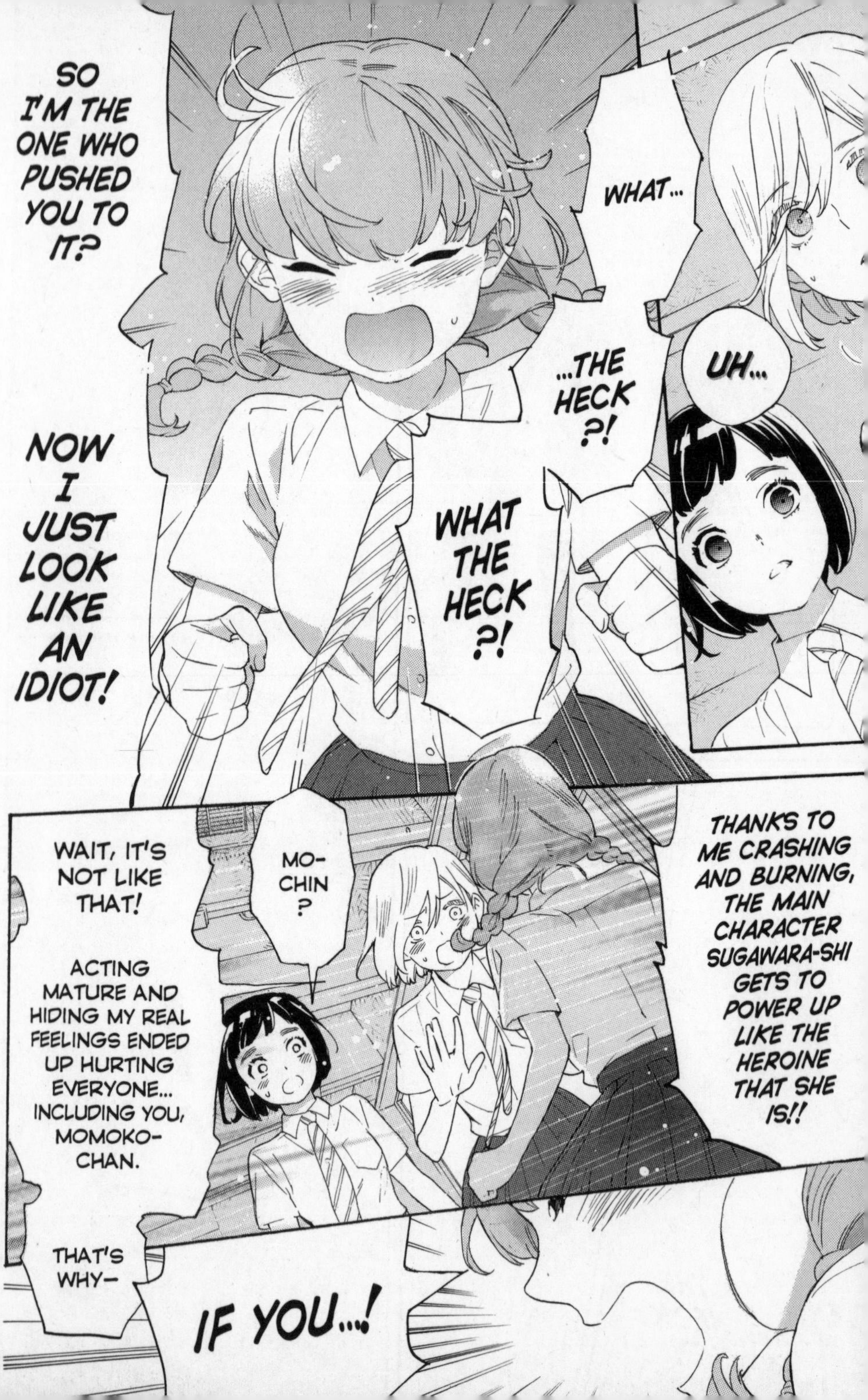
WHAT...
...THE HECK?!
UH...
WHAT THE HECK?!
SO I'M THE ONE WHO PUSHED YOU TO IT?
NOW I JUST LOOK LIKE AN IDIOT!
THANKS TO ME CRASHING AND BURNING, THE MAIN CHARACTER SUGAWARA-SHI GETS TO POWER UP LIKE THE HEROINE THAT SHE IS!!
MO-CHIN?
WAIT, IT'S NOT LIKE THAT!
ACTING MATURE AND HIDING MY REAL FEELINGS ENDED UP HURTING EVERYONE... INCLUDING YOU, MOMOKO-CHAN.
THAT'S WHY—
IF YOU...!

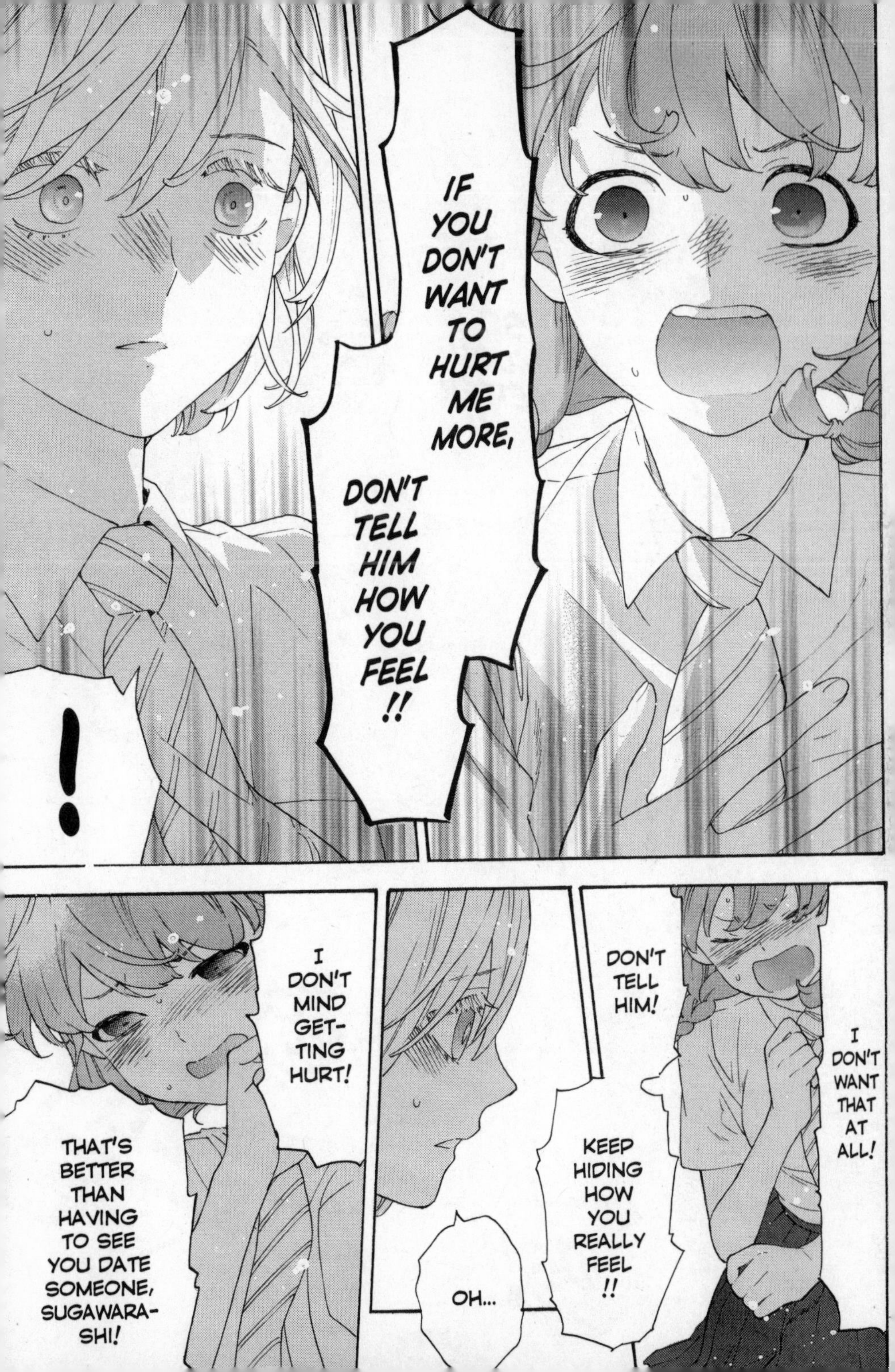
IF YOU DON'T WANT TO HURT ME MORE,
DON'T TELL HIM HOW YOU FEEL!!
!
DON'T TELL HIM!
I DON'T WANT THAT AT ALL!
KEEP HIDING HOW YOU REALLY FEEL!!
OH...
I DON'T MIND GET-TING HURT!
THAT'S BETTER THAN HAVING TO SEE YOU DATE SOMEONE, SUGAWARA-SHI!

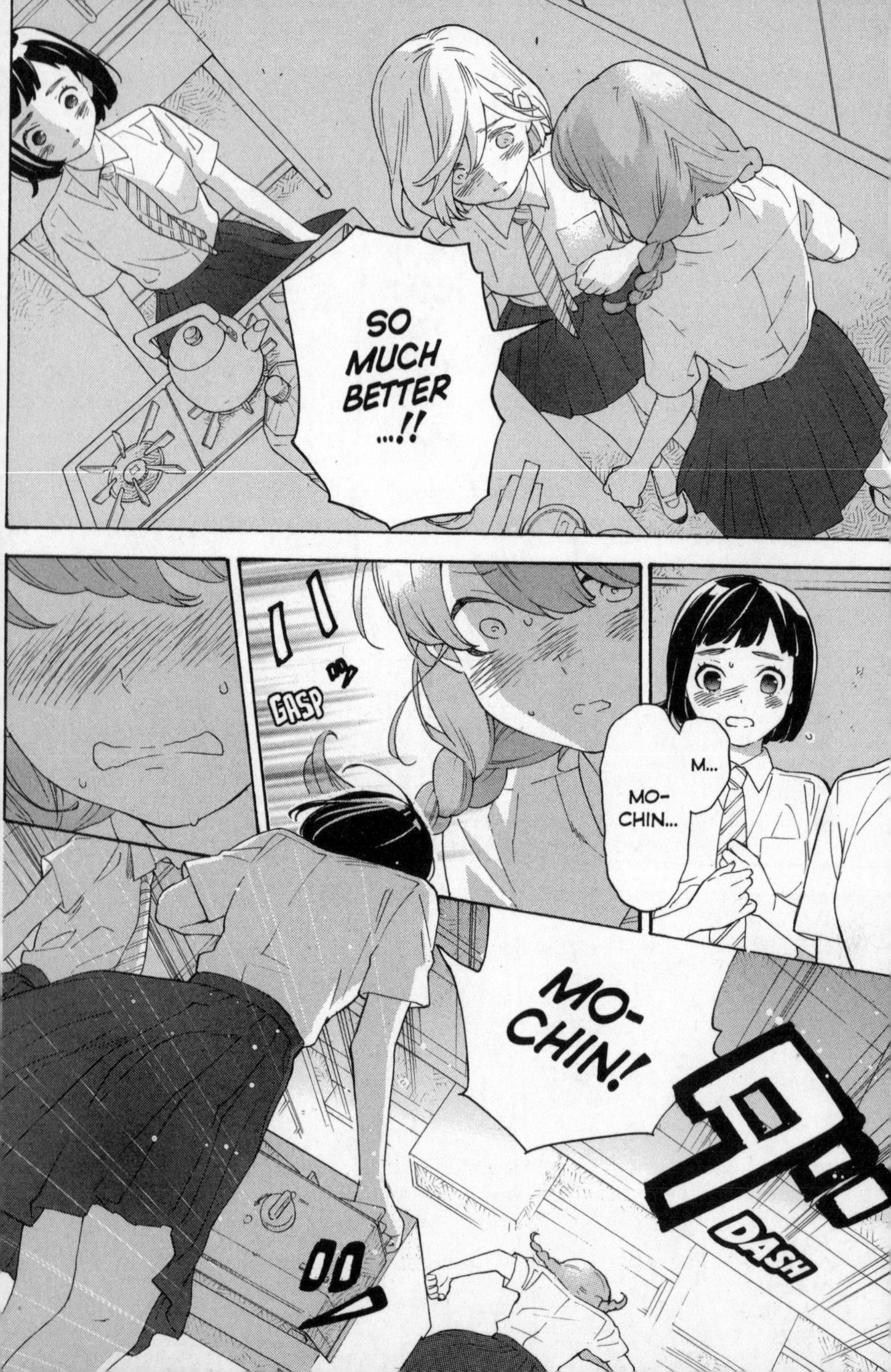
SO MUCH BETTER ...!!
M... MO-CHIN...
GASP
MO-CHIN!
DASH

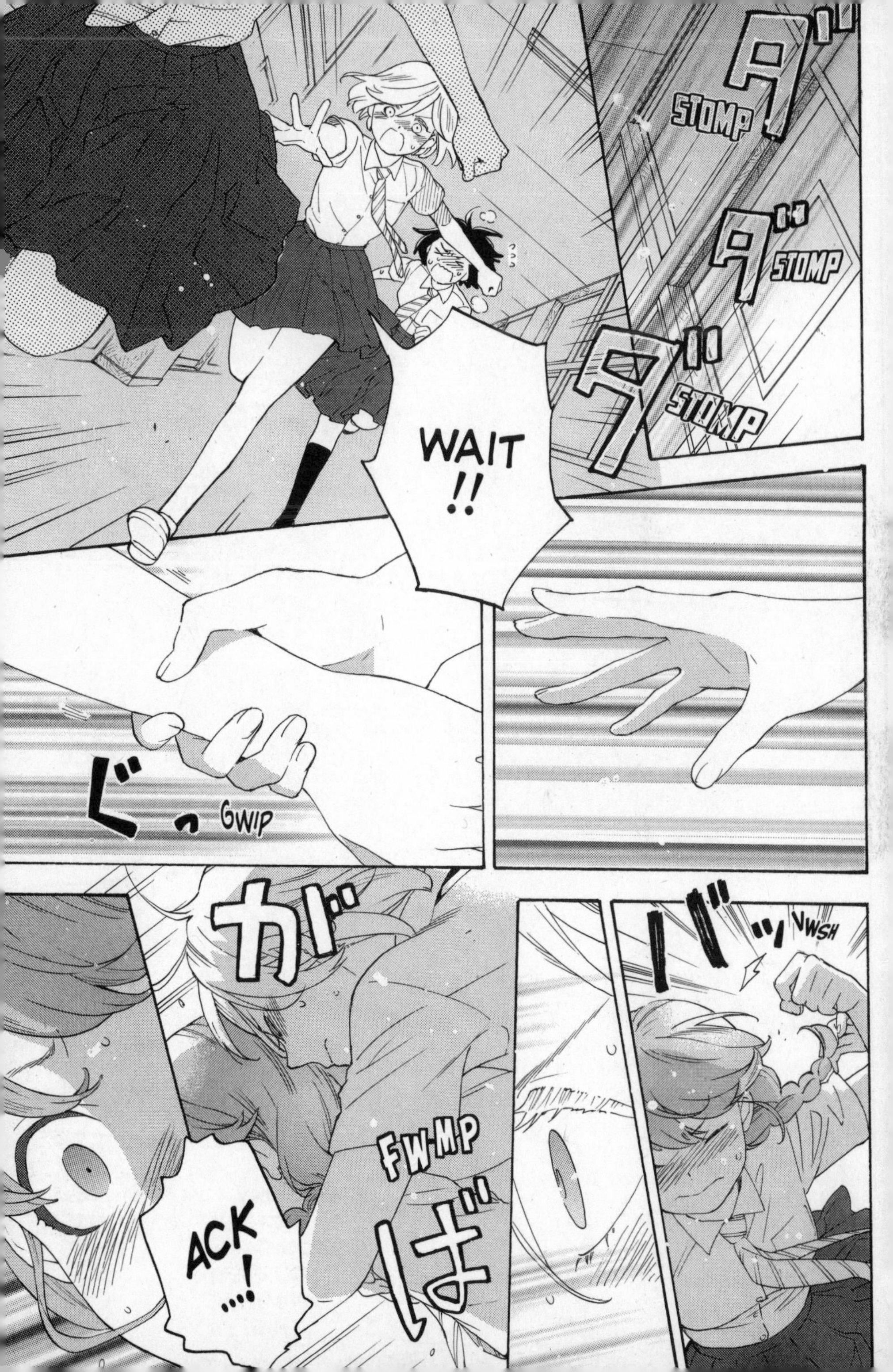
ダ
STOMP
ダ
STOMP
ダ
STOMP
WAIT !!
ぐっ
GWIP
バッ
VWSH
ガッ
FWMP
ばっ
ACK ...!

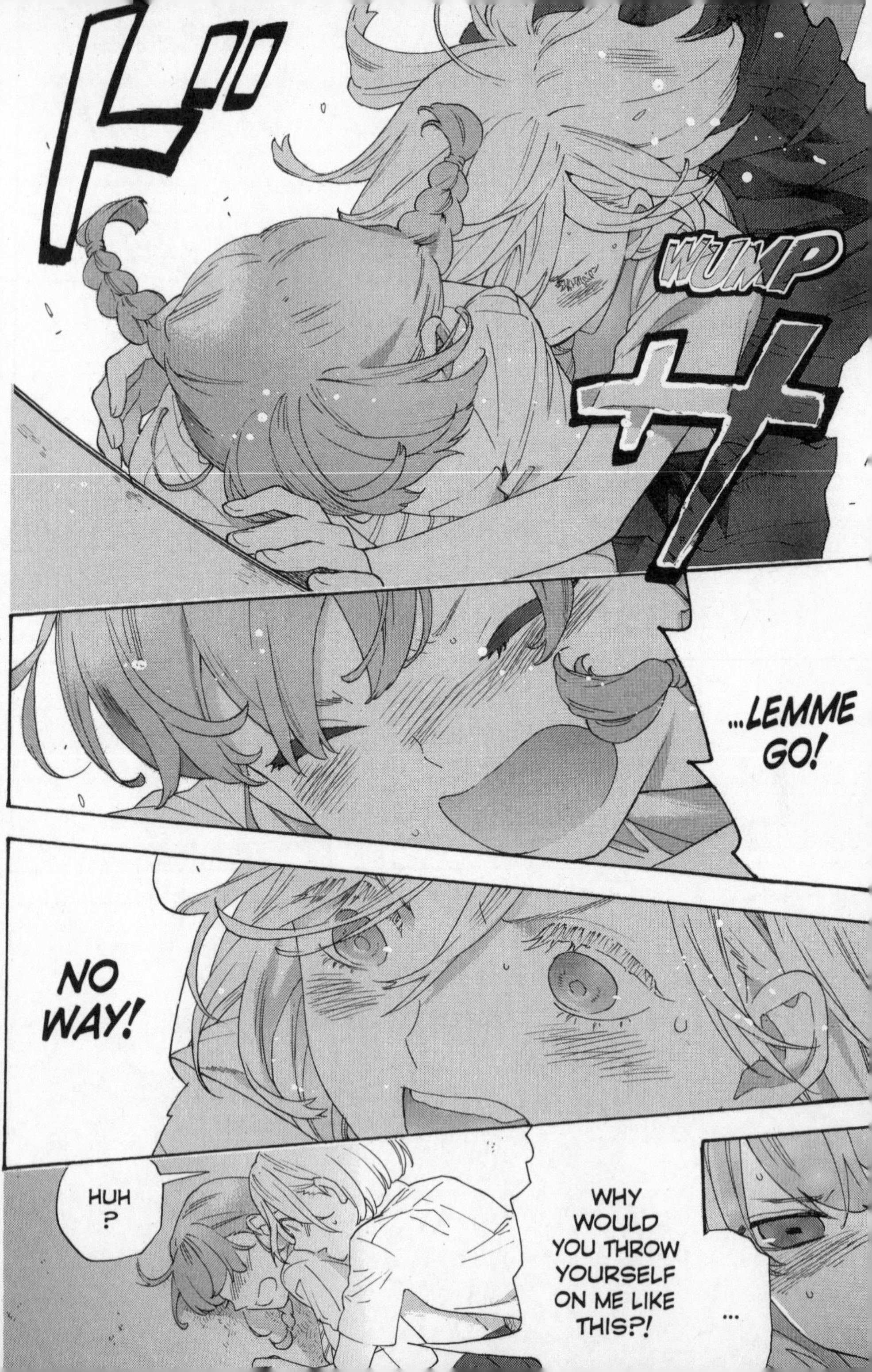
WUMP
...LEMME GO!
NO WAY!
...
WHY WOULD YOU THROW YOURSELF ON ME LIKE THIS?!
HUH?

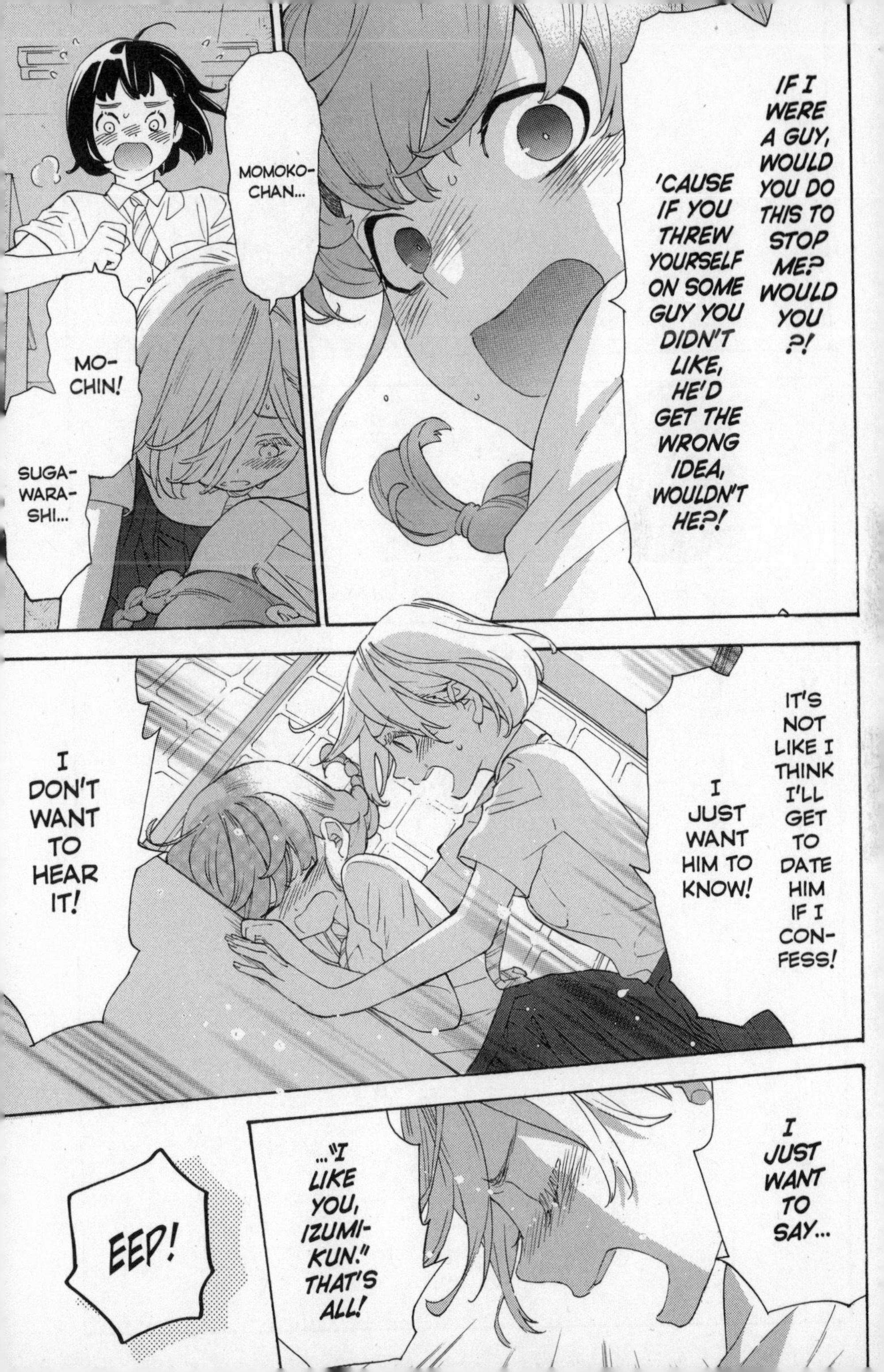
IF I WERE A GUY, WOULD YOU DO THIS TO STOP ME? WOULD YOU ?!
'CAUSE IF YOU THREW YOURSELF ON SOME GUY YOU DIDN'T LIKE, HE'D GET THE WRONG IDEA, WOULDN'T HE?!
MOMOKO-CHAN...
MO-CHIN!
SUGA-WARA-SHI...
IT'S NOT LIKE I THINK I'LL GET TO DATE HIM IF I CON-FESS!
I JUST WANT HIM TO KNOW!
I DON'T WANT TO HEAR IT!
I JUST WANT TO SAY...
..."I LIKE YOU, IZUMI-KUN." THAT'S ALL!
EEP!

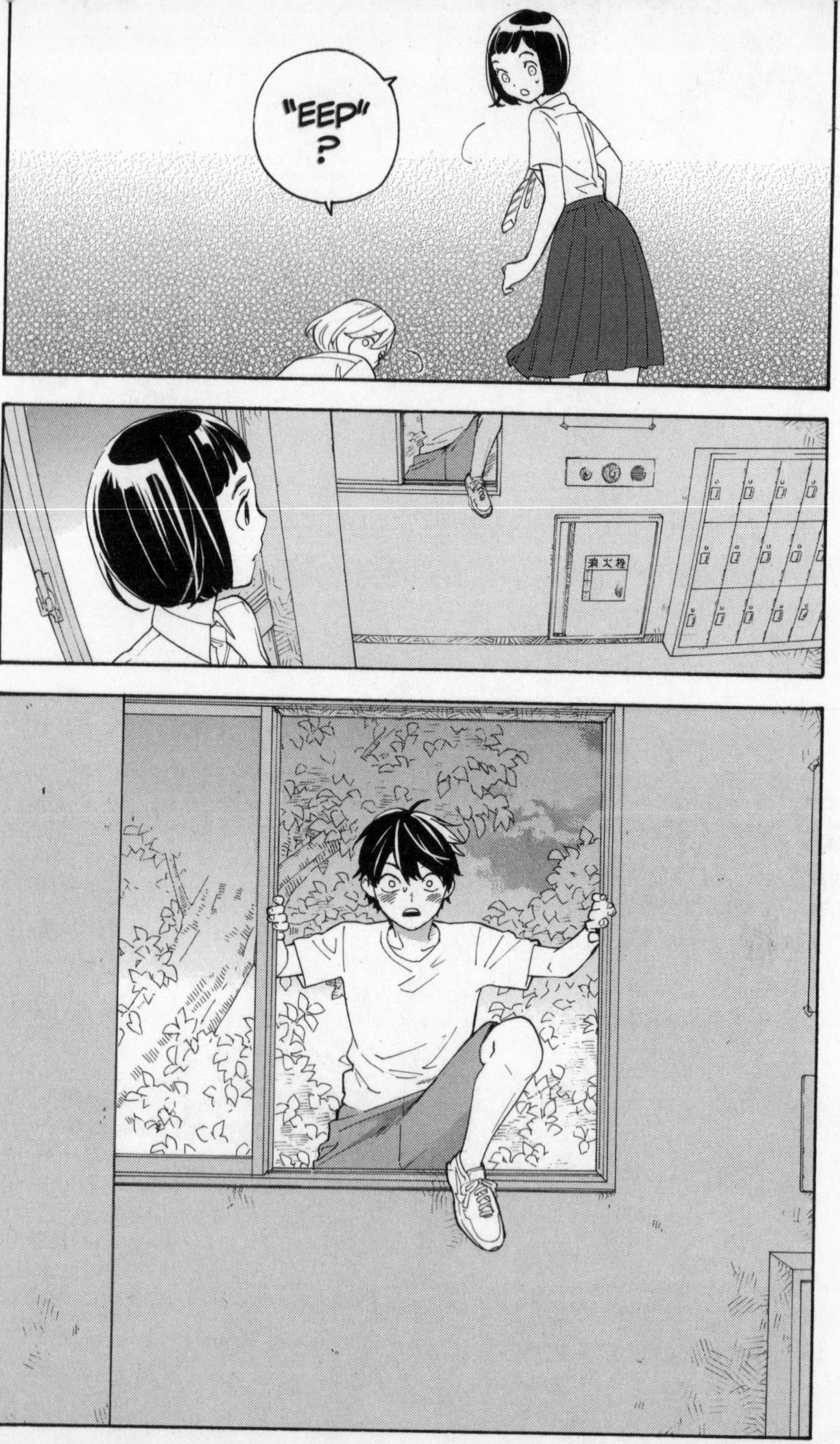
"EEP"?
消火栓

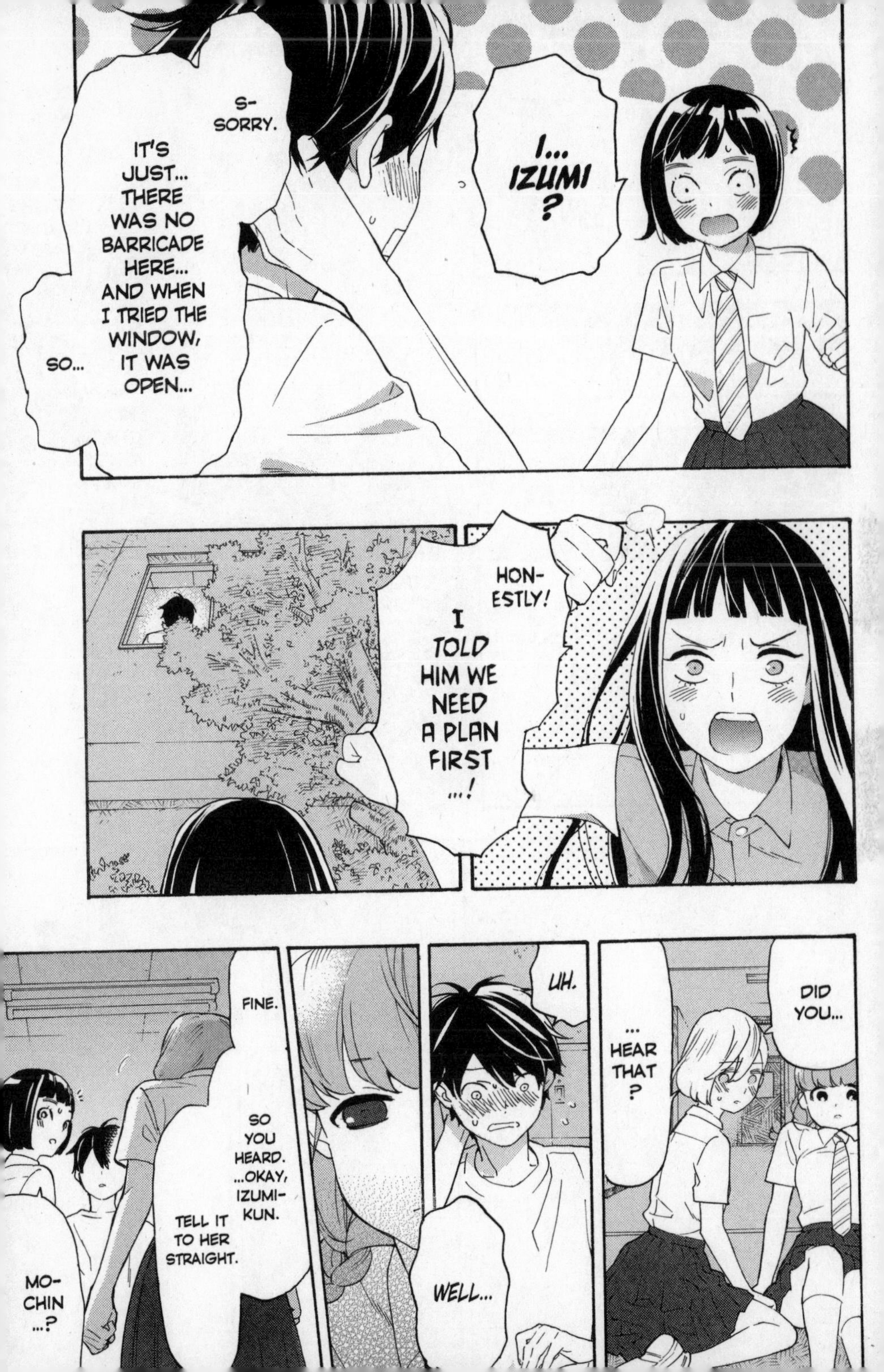
I... IZUMI?
S- SORRY.
IT'S JUST... THERE WAS NO BARRICADE HERE... AND WHEN I TRIED THE WINDOW, IT WAS OPEN...
SO...
HON-ESTLY!
I *TOLD* HIM WE NEED A PLAN FIRST...!
DID YOU...
...HEAR THAT?
UH.
WELL...
FINE.
SO YOU HEARD. ...OKAY, IZUMI-KUN.
TELL IT TO HER STRAIGHT.
MO-CHIN...?

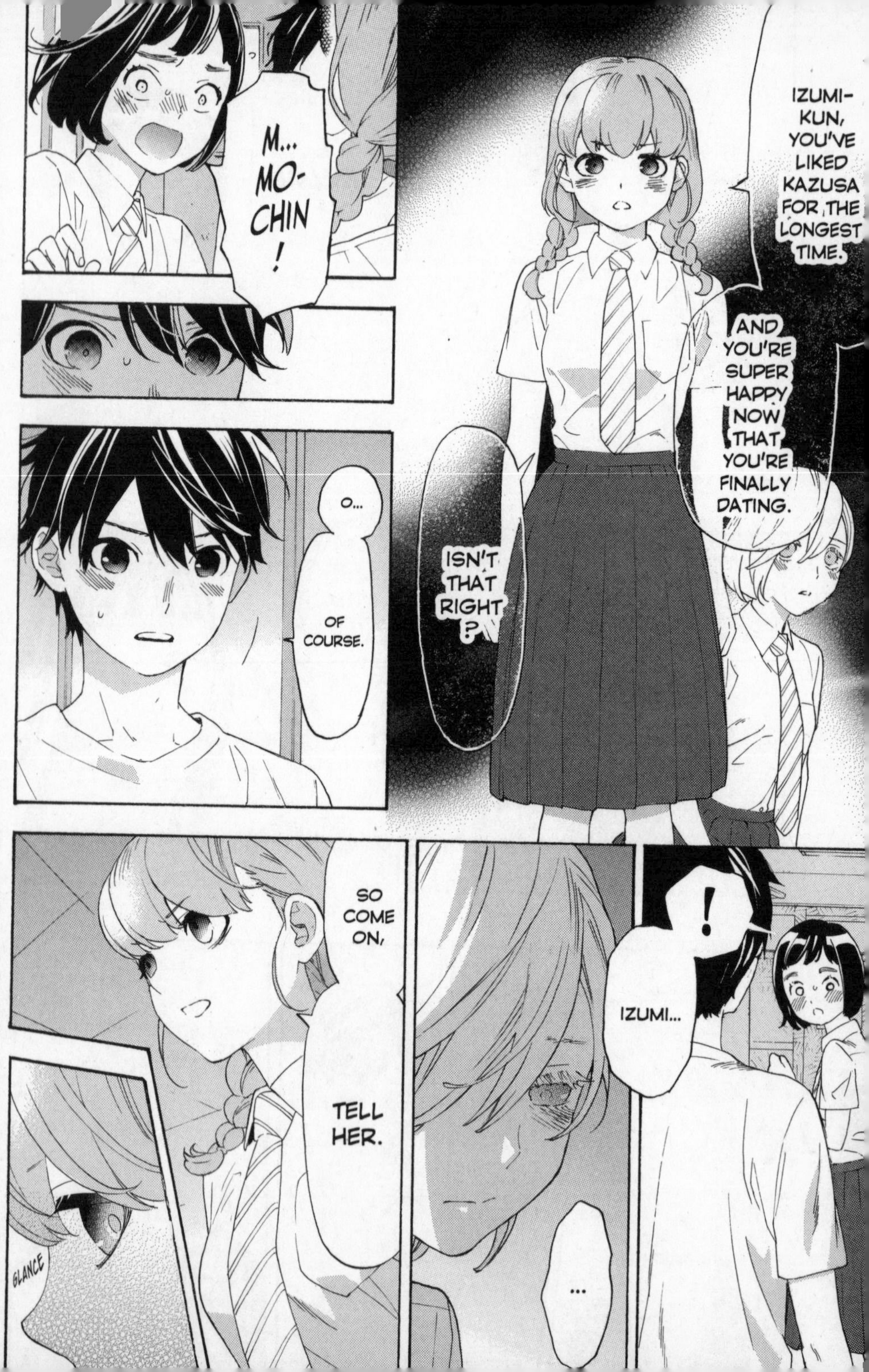
IZUMI-KUN, YOU'VE LIKED KAZUSA FOR THE LONGEST TIME.
AND YOU'RE SUPER HAPPY NOW THAT YOU'RE FINALLY DATING.
ISN'T THAT RIGHT?
M... MO-CHIN!
O...
OF COURSE.
!
IZUMI...
...
SO COME ON,
TELL HER.
GLANCE

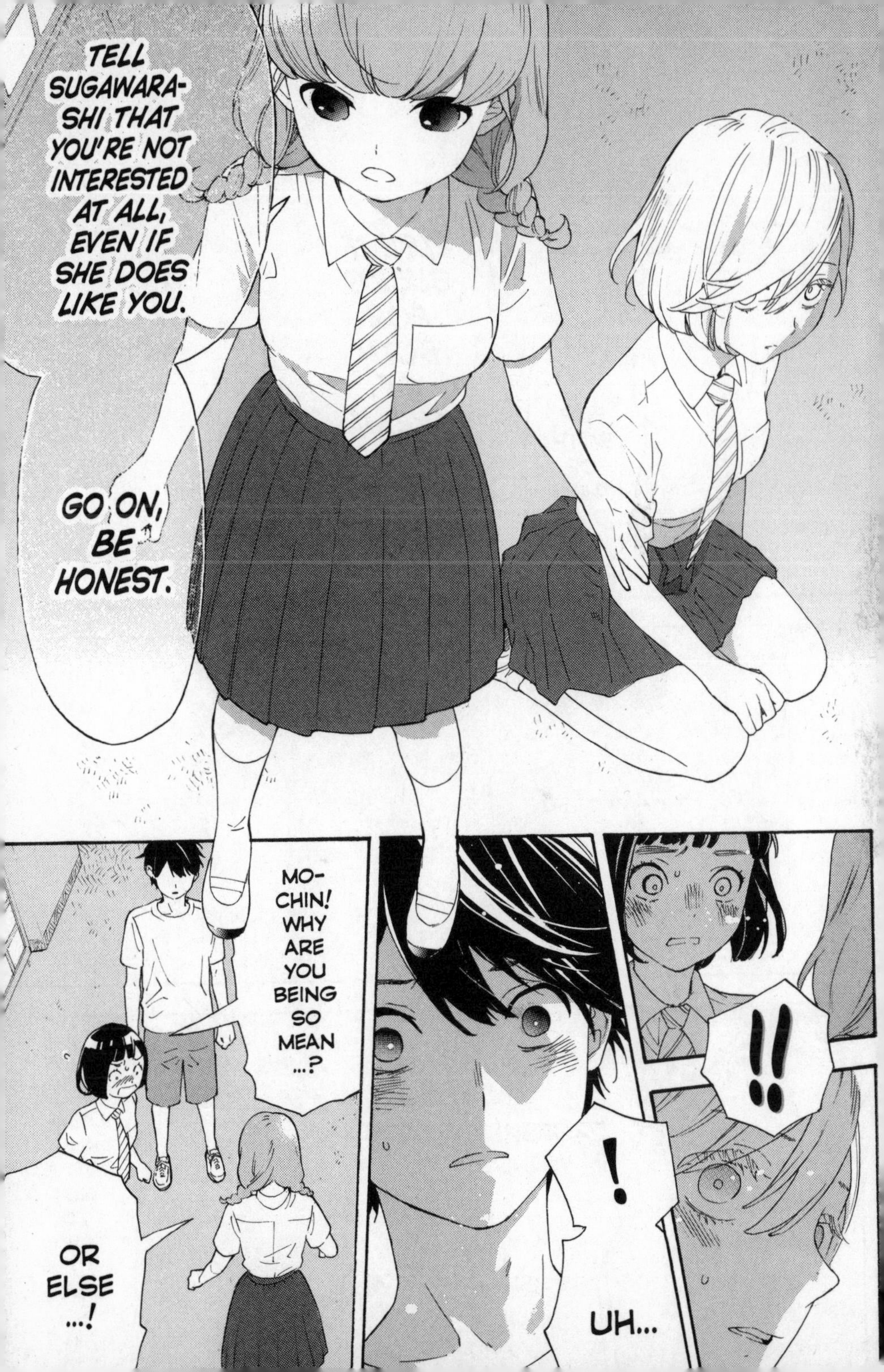
TELL SUGAWARA-SHI THAT YOU'RE NOT INTERESTED AT ALL, EVEN IF SHE DOES LIKE YOU.
GO ON, BE HONEST.
!!
!
UH...
MO-CHIN! WHY ARE YOU BEING SO MEAN ...?
OR ELSE ...!

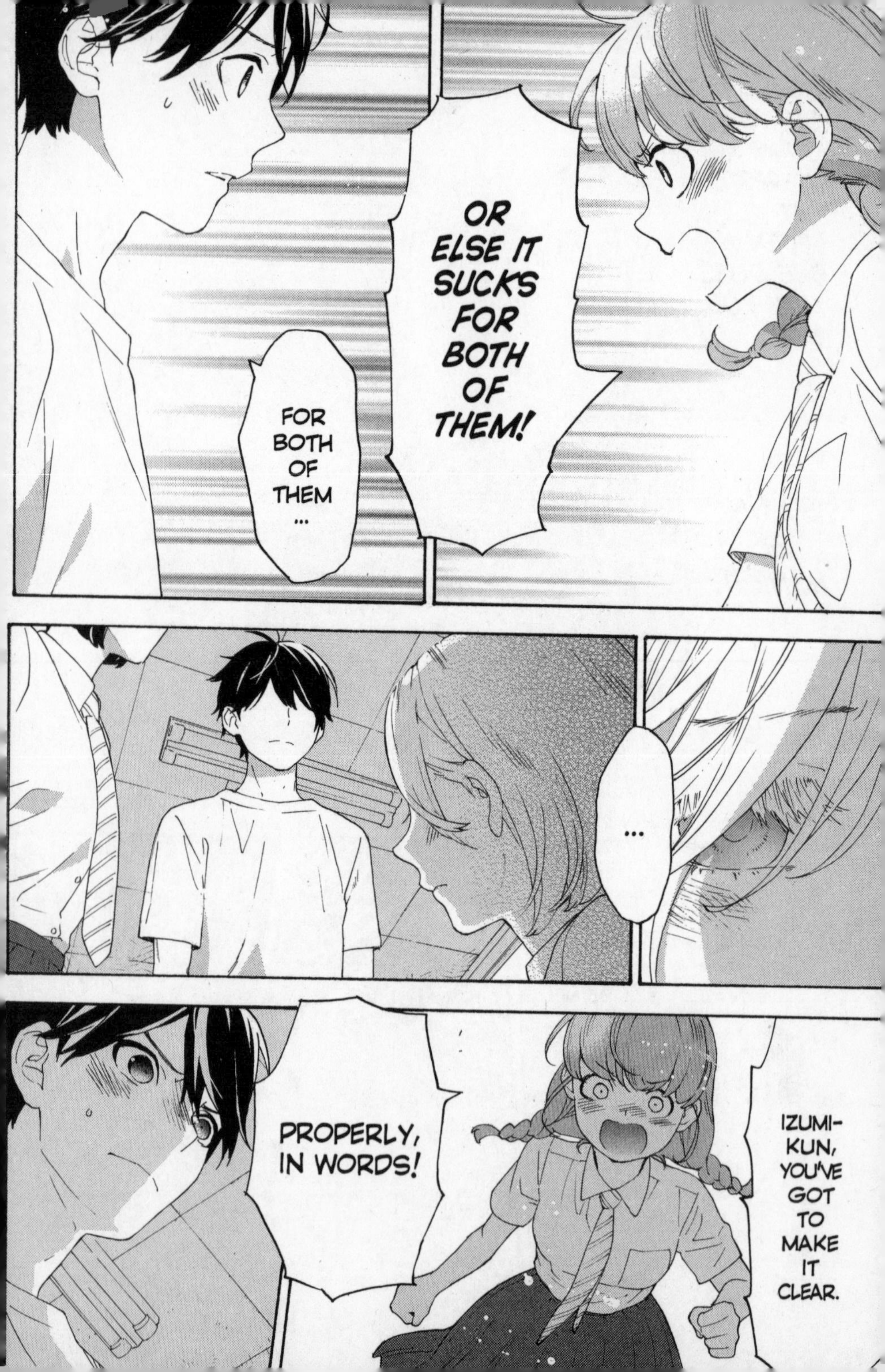
OR ELSE IT SUCKS FOR BOTH OF THEM!
FOR BOTH OF THEM ...
...
IZUMI-KUN, YOU'VE GOT TO MAKE IT CLEAR.
PROPERLY, IN WORDS!

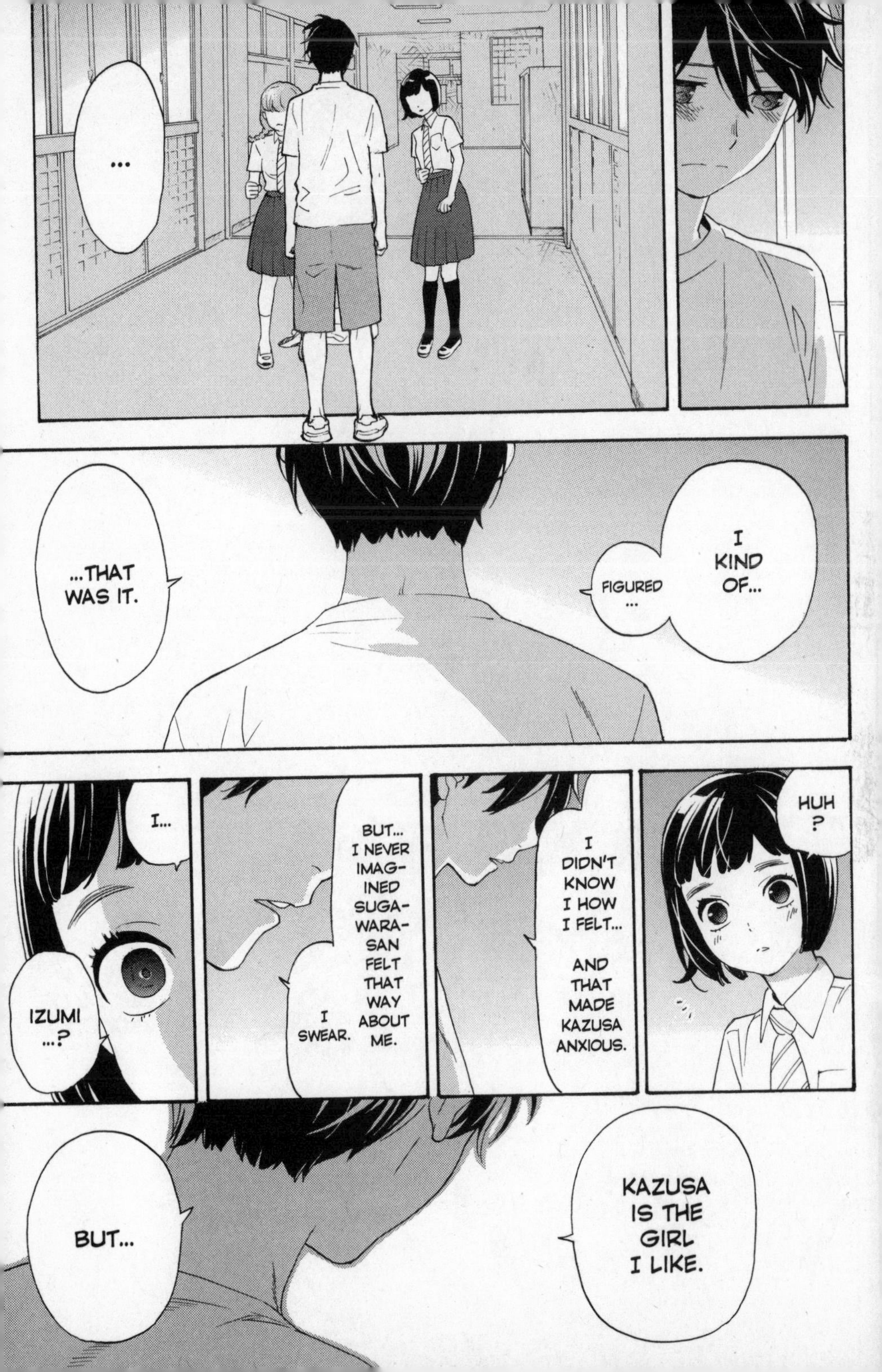
...
I KIND OF... FIGURED ...
...THAT WAS IT.
HUH?
I DIDN'T KNOW I HOW I FELT...
AND THAT MADE KAZUSA ANXIOUS.
BUT... I NEVER IMAG-INED SUGA-WARA-SAN FELT THAT WAY ABOUT ME.
I SWEAR.
I...
IZUMI ...?
KAZUSA IS THE GIRL I LIKE.
BUT...

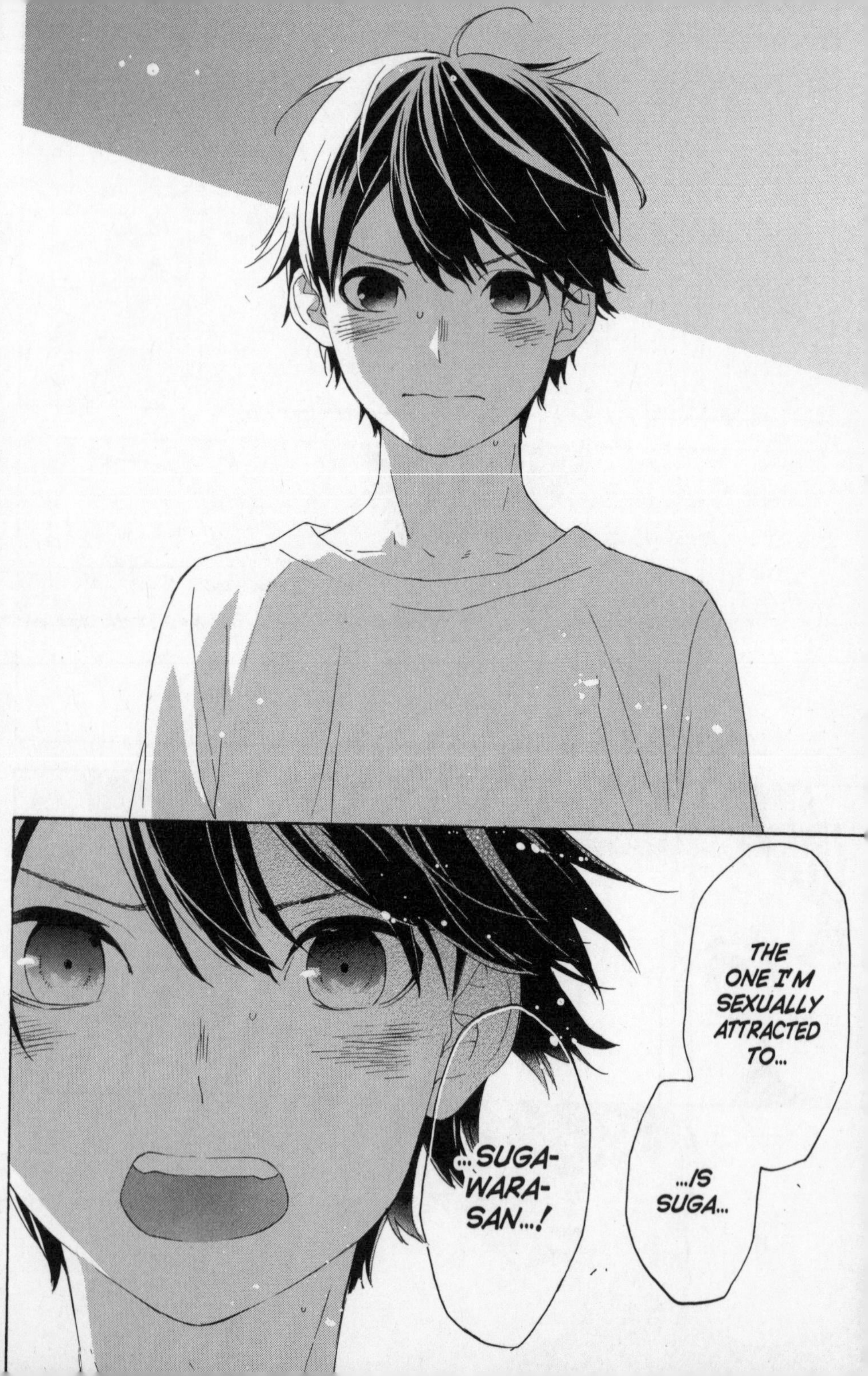
THE ONE I'M SEXUALLY ATTRACTED TO...
...IS SUGA...
...SUGA-WARA-SAN...!

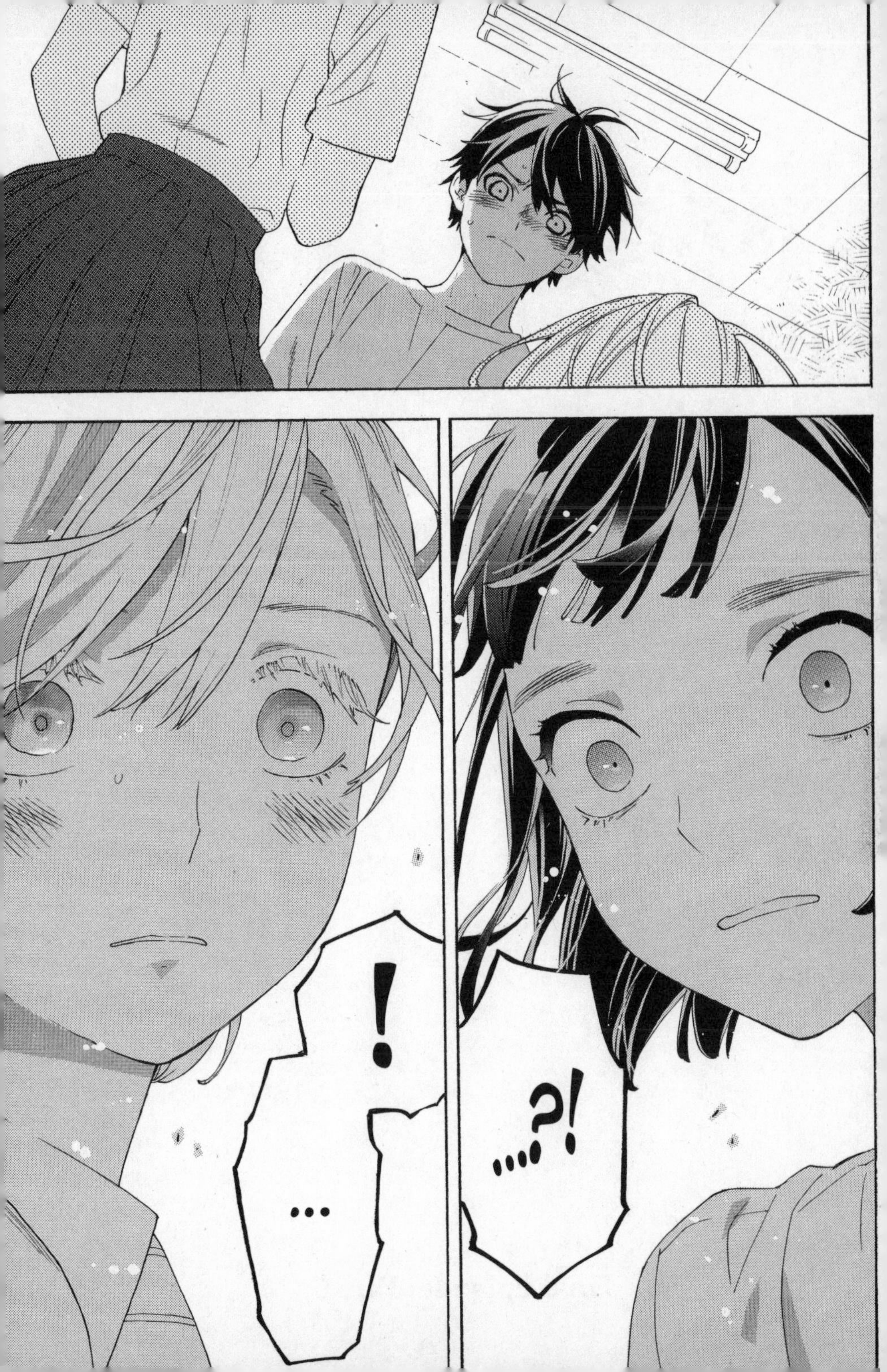
...?!
!
...

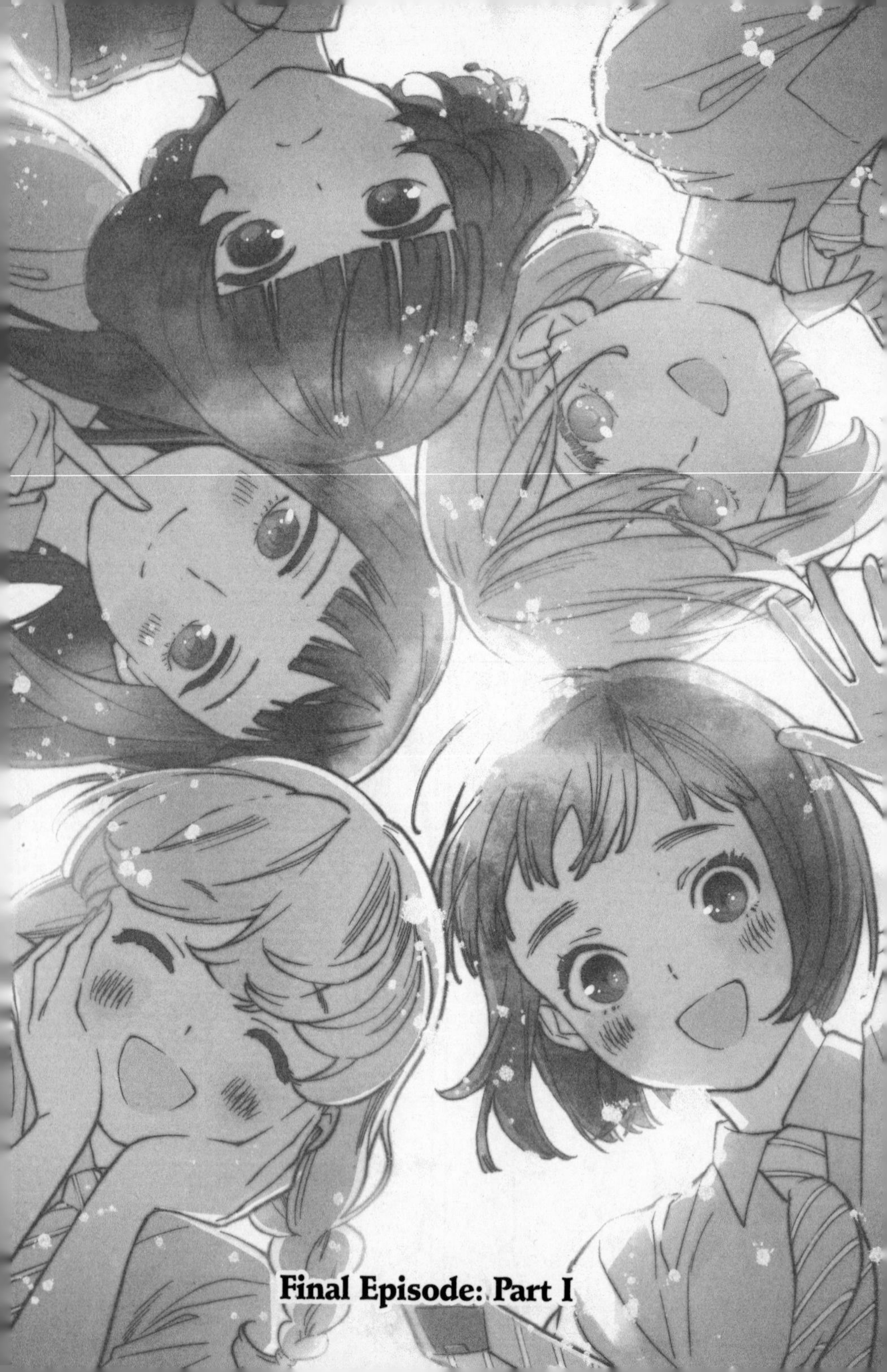
Final Episode: Part I

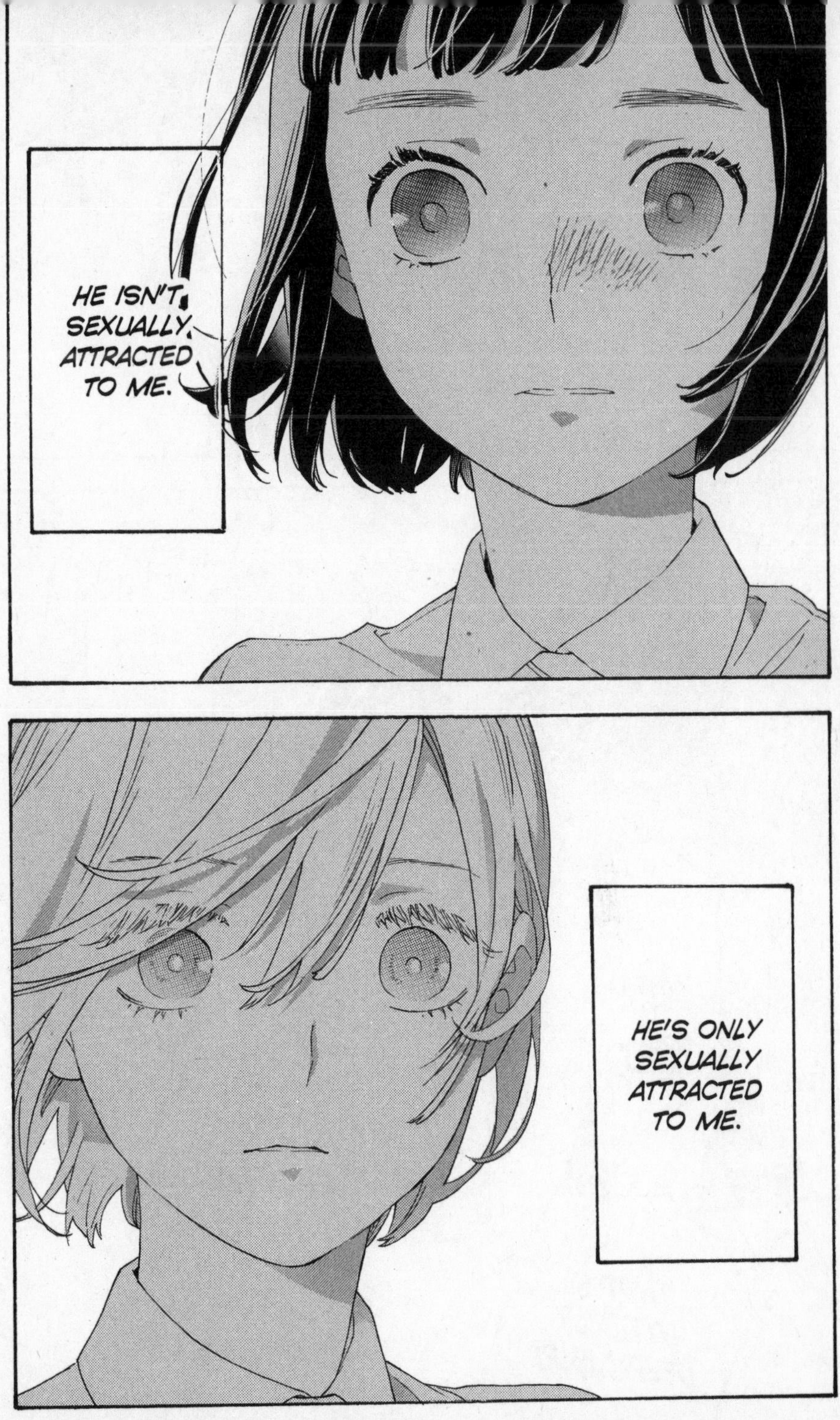
HE ISN'T SEXUALLY ATTRACTED TO ME.
HE'S ONLY SEXUALLY ATTRACTED TO ME.

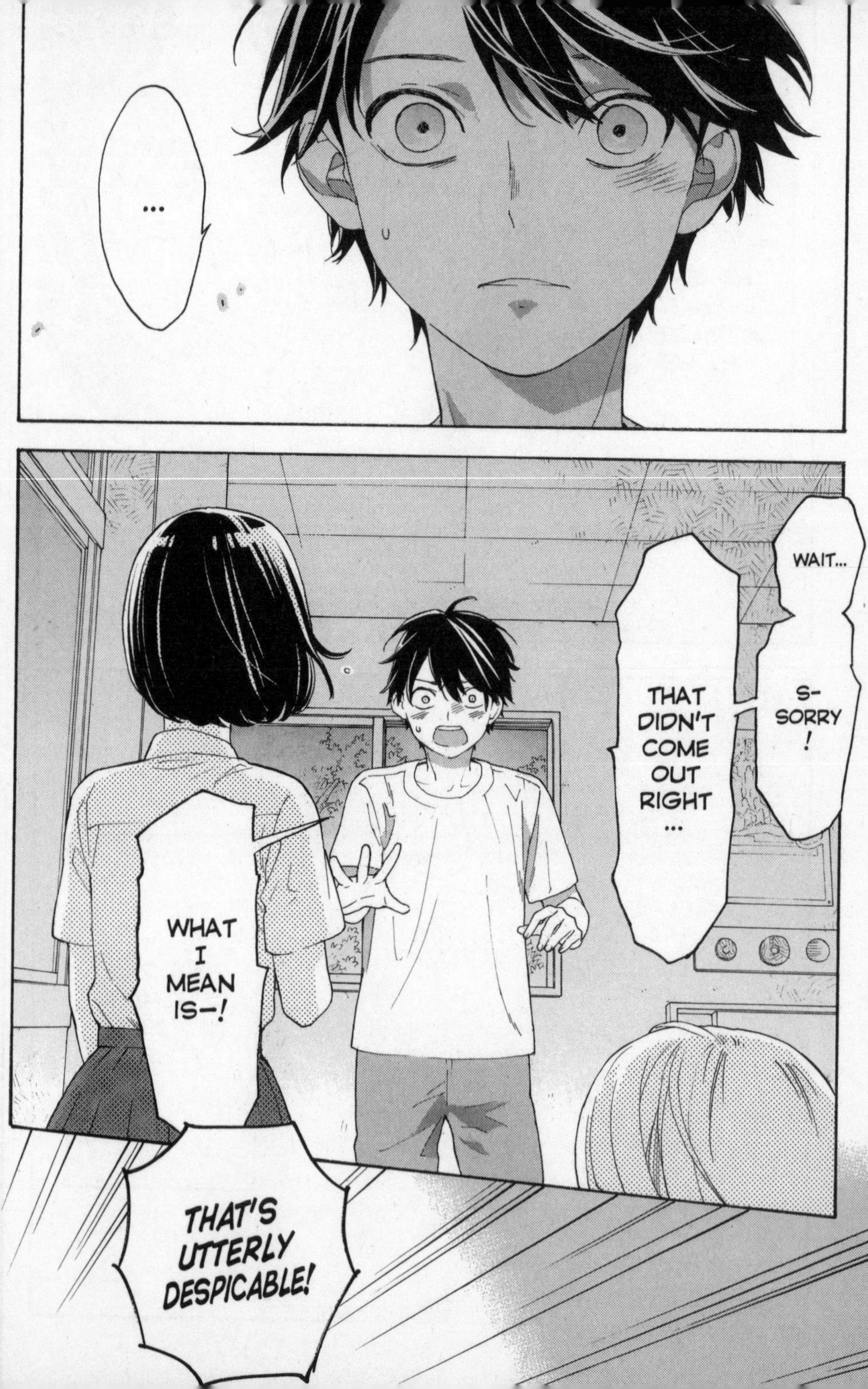
...
WAIT...
S-SORRY!
THAT DIDN'T COME OUT RIGHT...
WHAT I MEAN IS—!
THAT'S UTTERLY DESPICABLE!

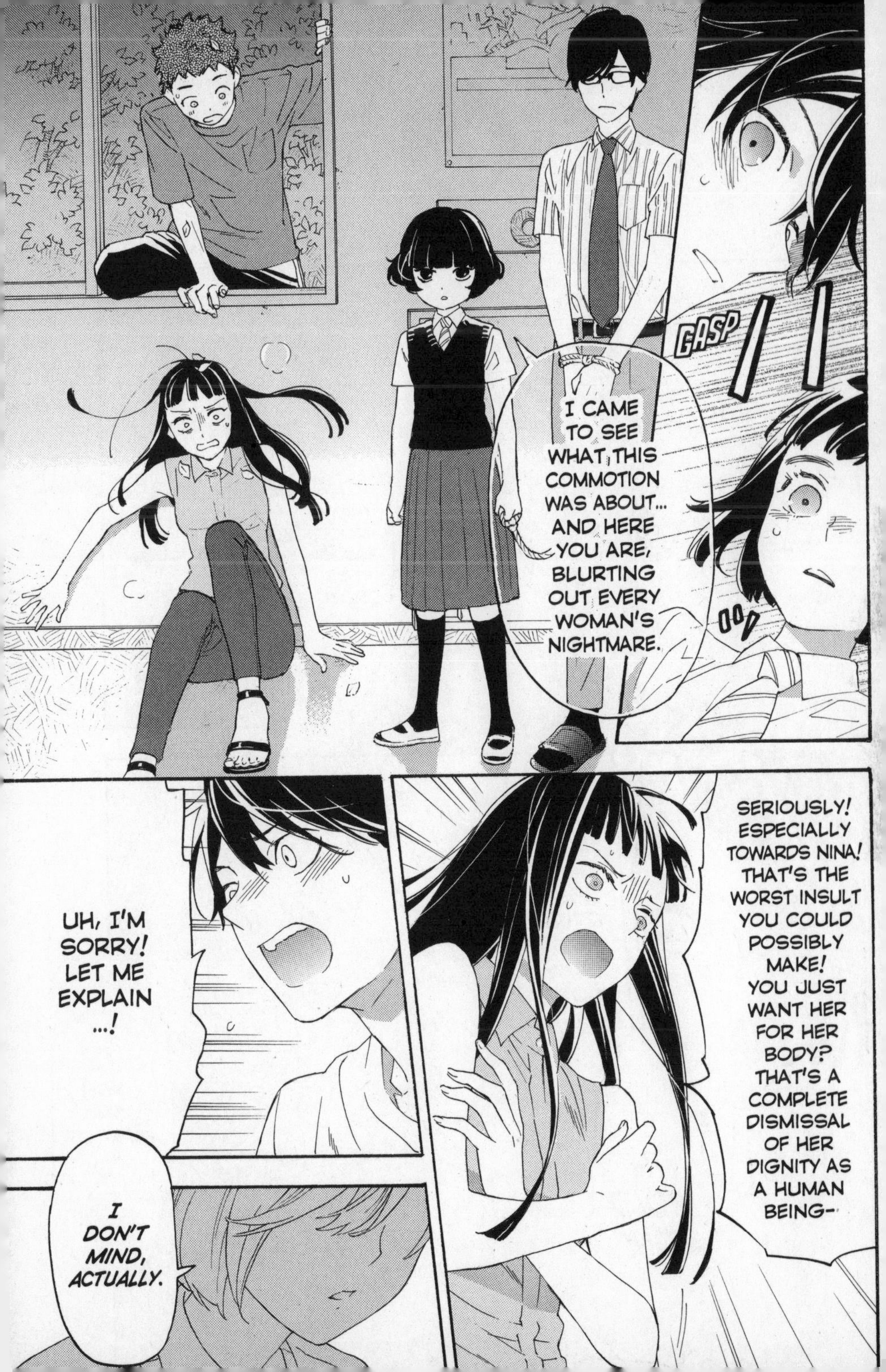
GASP
I CAME TO SEE WHAT THIS COMMOTION WAS ABOUT... AND HERE YOU ARE, BLURTING OUT EVERY WOMAN'S NIGHTMARE.
SERIOUSLY! ESPECIALLY TOWARDS NINA! THAT'S THE WORST INSULT YOU COULD POSSIBLY MAKE! YOU JUST WANT HER FOR HER BODY? THAT'S A COMPLETE DISMISSAL OF HER DIGNITY AS A HUMAN BEING-
UH, I'M SORRY! LET ME EXPLAIN ...!
I DON'T MIND, ACTUALLY.

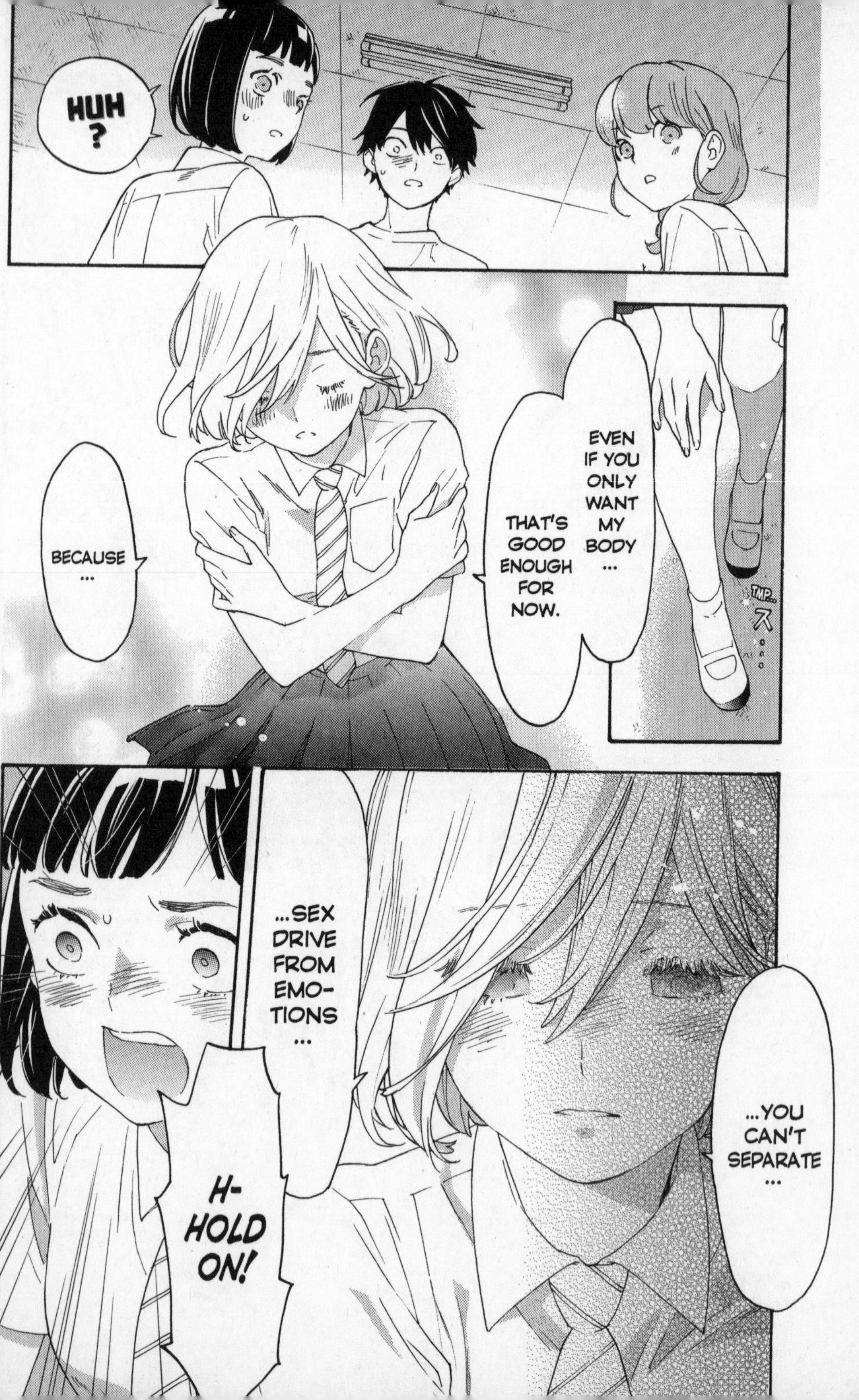
HUH?
EVEN IF YOU ONLY WANT MY BODY... THAT'S GOOD ENOUGH FOR NOW.
TMP... ス
BECAUSE...
...YOU CAN'T SEPARATE...
...SEX DRIVE FROM EMO-TIONS...
H-HOLD ON!

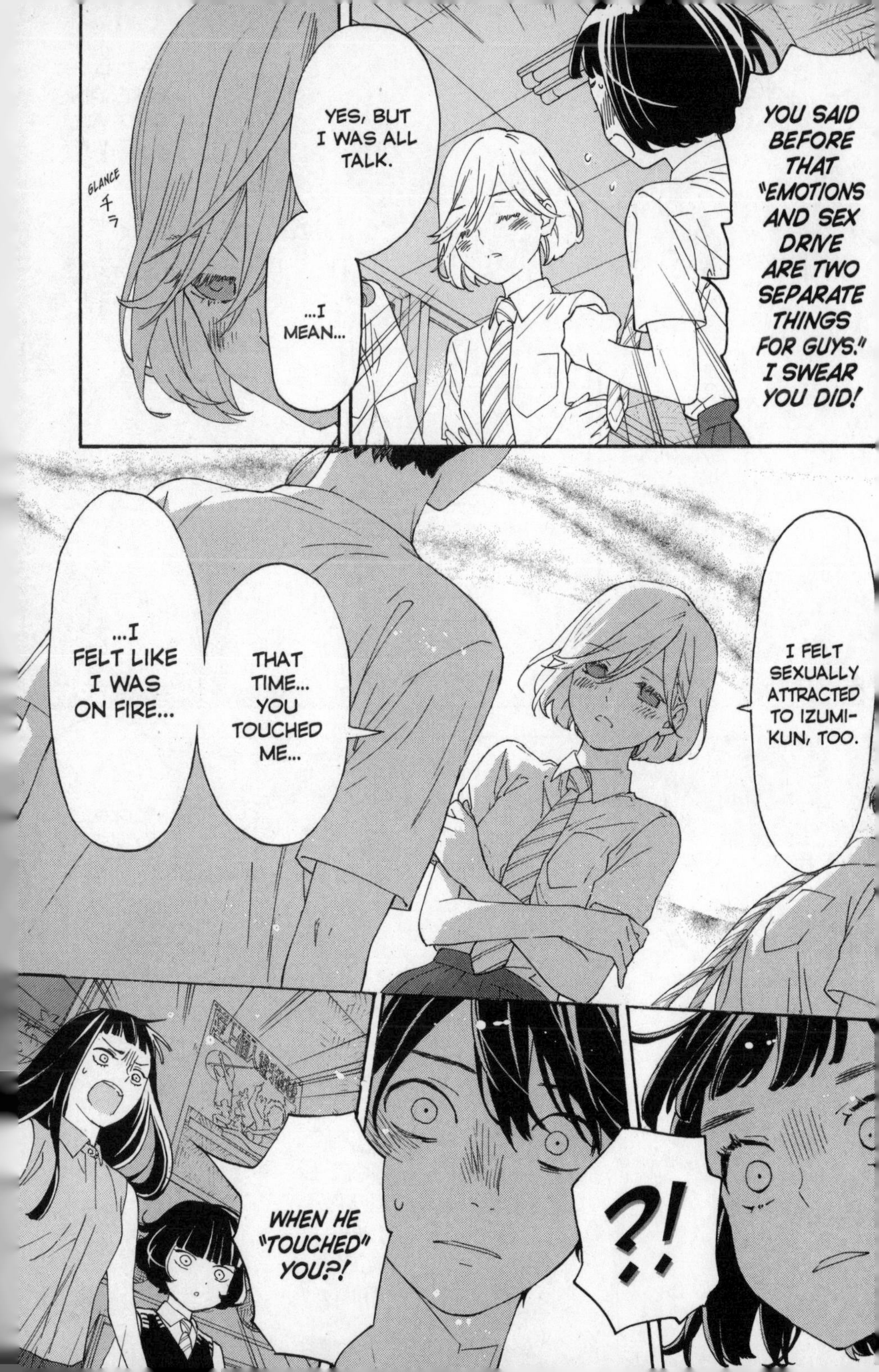
YOU SAID BEFORE THAT "EMOTIONS AND SEX DRIVE ARE TWO SEPARATE THINGS FOR GUYS." I SWEAR YOU DID!
YES, BUT I WAS ALL TALK.
...I MEAN...
GLANCE
チラ
I FELT SEXUALLY ATTRACTED TO IZUMI-KUN, TOO.
THAT TIME... YOU TOUCHED ME...
...I FELT LIKE I WAS ON FIRE...
?!
WHEN HE "TOUCHED" YOU?!

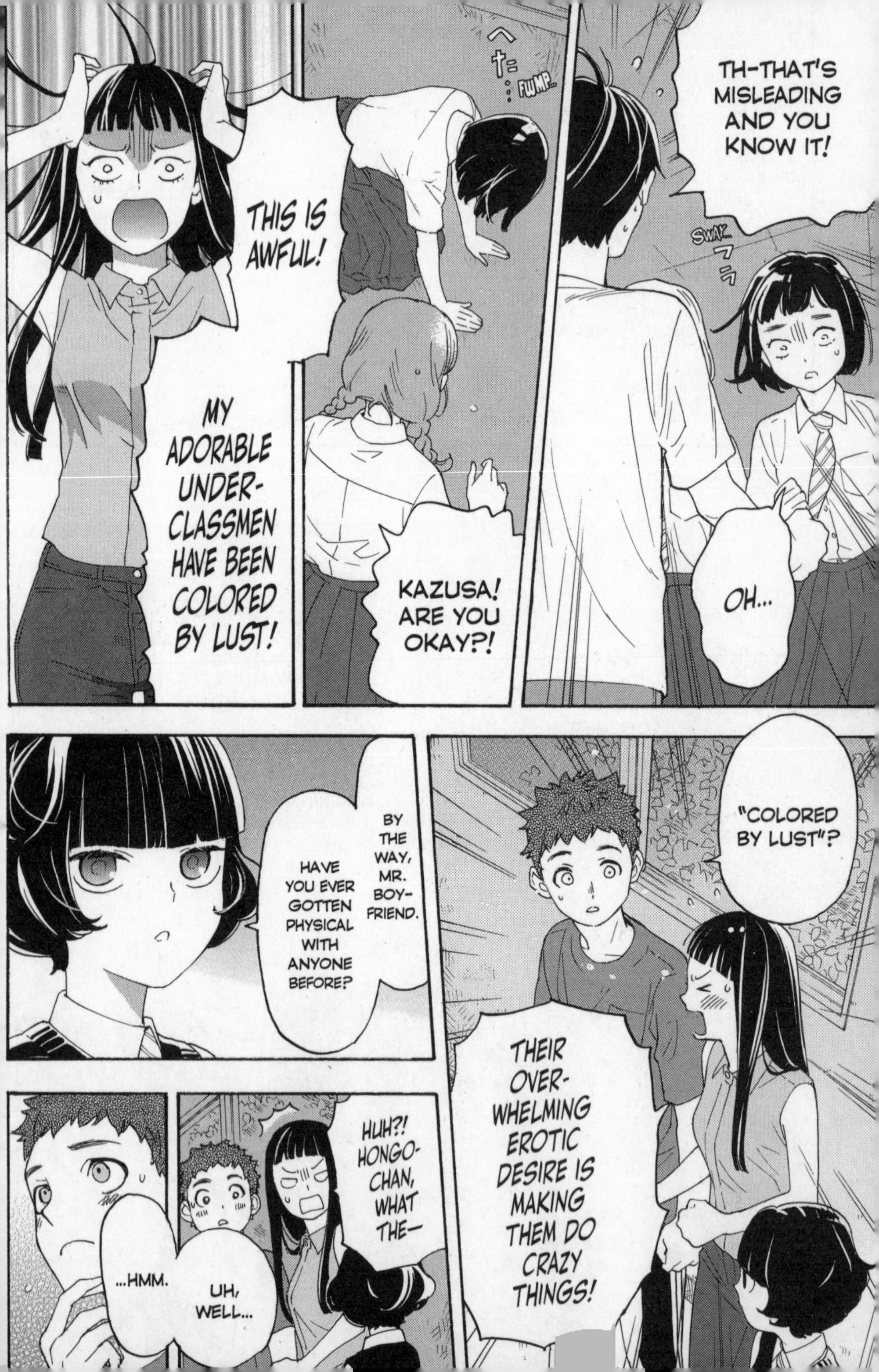
TH-THAT'S MISLEADING AND YOU KNOW IT!
SWAY...
OH...
FWUMP...
KAZUSA! ARE YOU OKAY?!
THIS IS AWFUL!
MY ADORABLE UNDER-CLASSMEN HAVE BEEN COLORED BY LUST!
"COLORED BY LUST"?
THEIR OVER-WHELMING EROTIC DESIRE IS MAKING THEM DO CRAZY THINGS!
BY THE WAY, MR. BOY-FRIEND.
HAVE YOU EVER GOTTEN PHYSICAL WITH ANYONE BEFORE?
HUH?! HONGO-CHAN, WHAT THE-
UH, WELL...
...HMM.

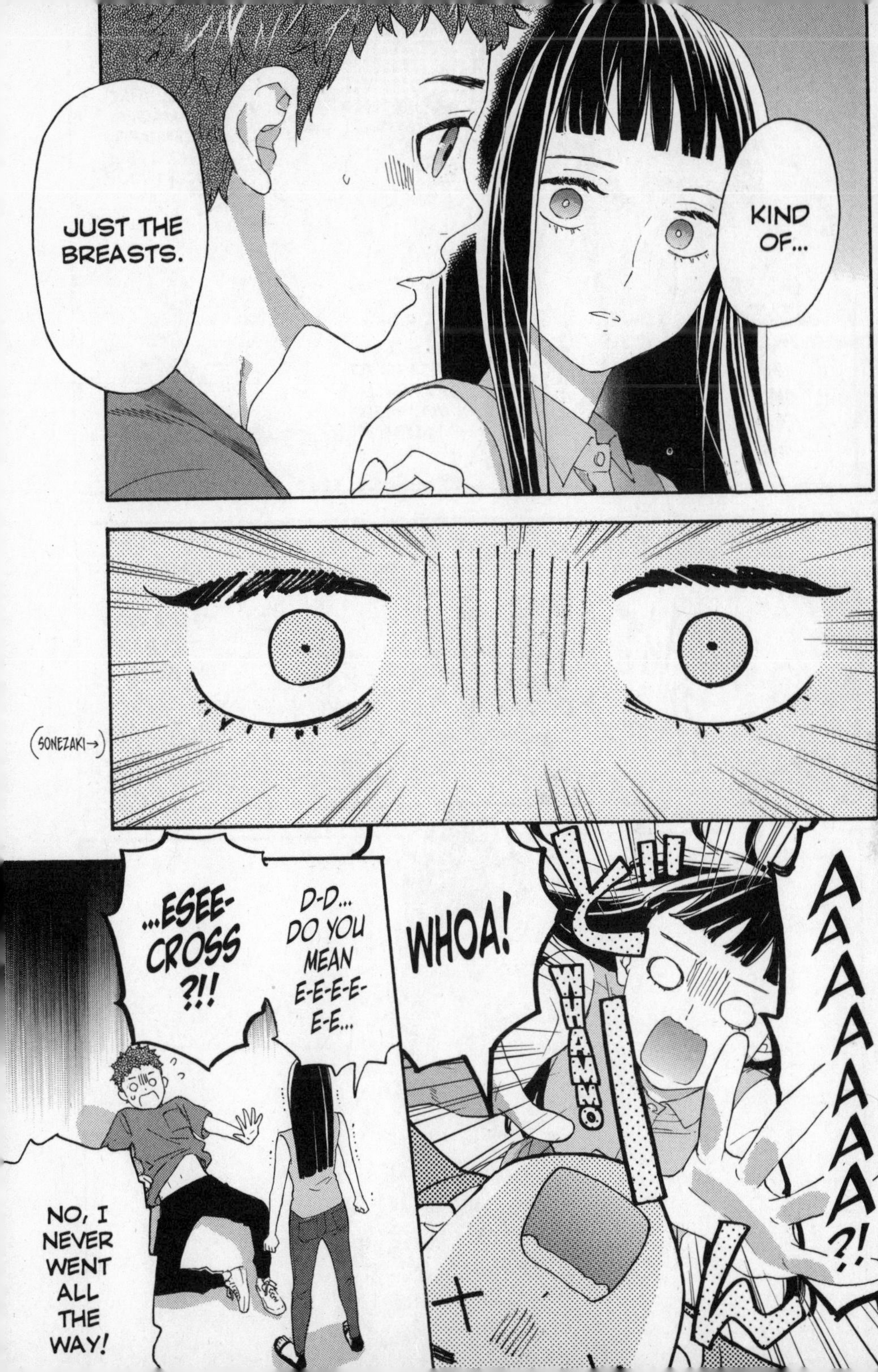
KIND OF...
JUST THE BREASTS.
(SONEZAKI→)
AAAAAAA?!
WHAMMO
WHOA!
D-D... DO YOU MEAN E-E-E-E-E-E...
...ESEE-CROSS?!!
NO, I NEVER WENT ALL THE WAY!

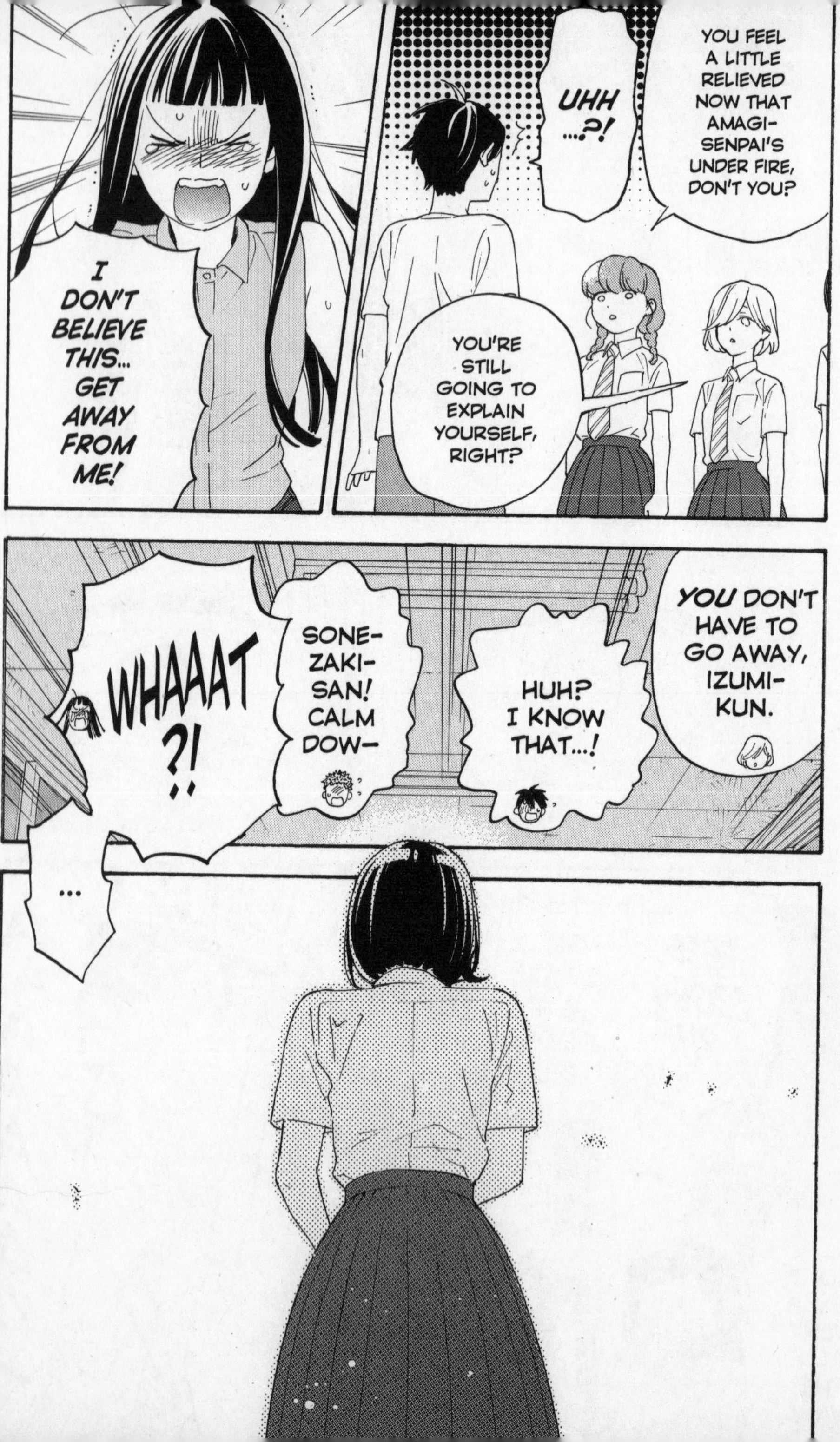
YOU FEEL A LITTLE RELIEVED NOW THAT AMAGI-SENPAI'S UNDER FIRE, DON'T YOU?
UHH ...?!
YOU'RE STILL GOING TO EXPLAIN YOURSELF, RIGHT?
I DON'T BELIEVE THIS... GET AWAY FROM ME!
YOU DON'T HAVE TO GO AWAY, IZUMI-KUN.
HUH? I KNOW THAT...!
SONE-ZAKI-SAN! CALM DOW-
WHAAAT ?!
...

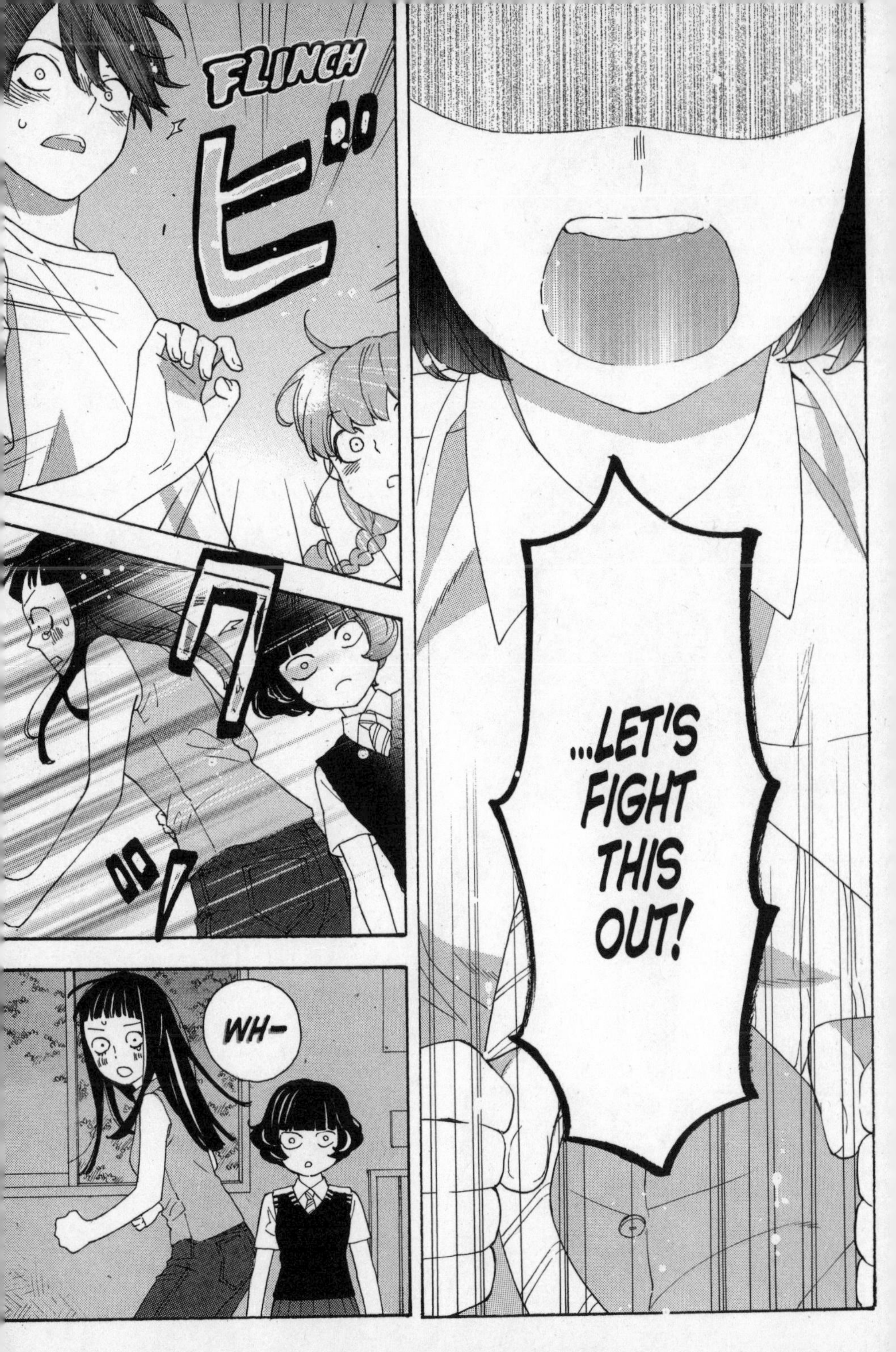
...LET'S FIGHT THIS OUT!
FLINCH
WH-

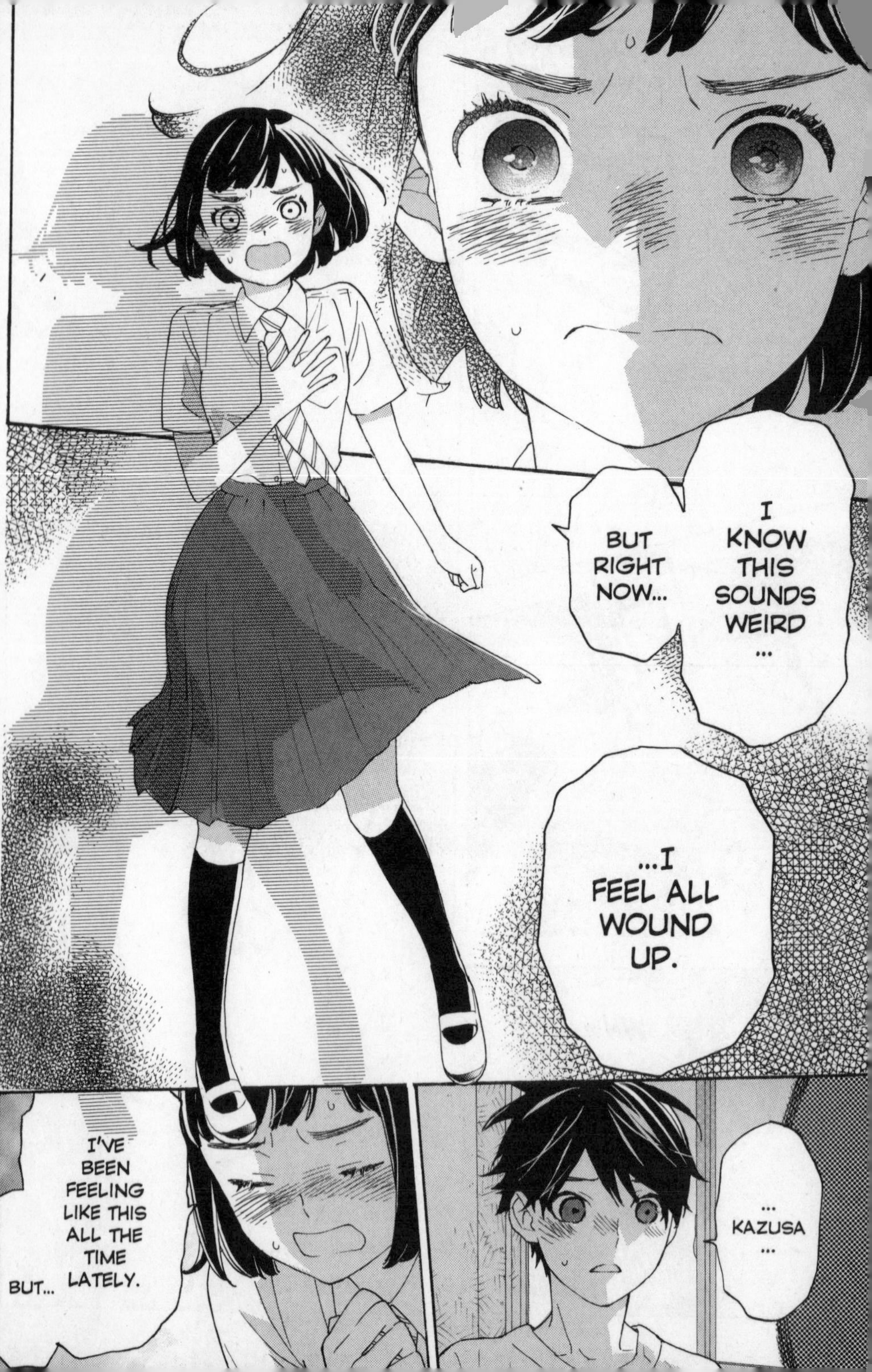
I KNOW THIS SOUNDS WEIRD ...
BUT RIGHT NOW...
...I FEEL ALL WOUND UP.
... KAZUSA ...
I'VE BEEN FEELING LIKE THIS ALL THE TIME LATELY.
BUT...

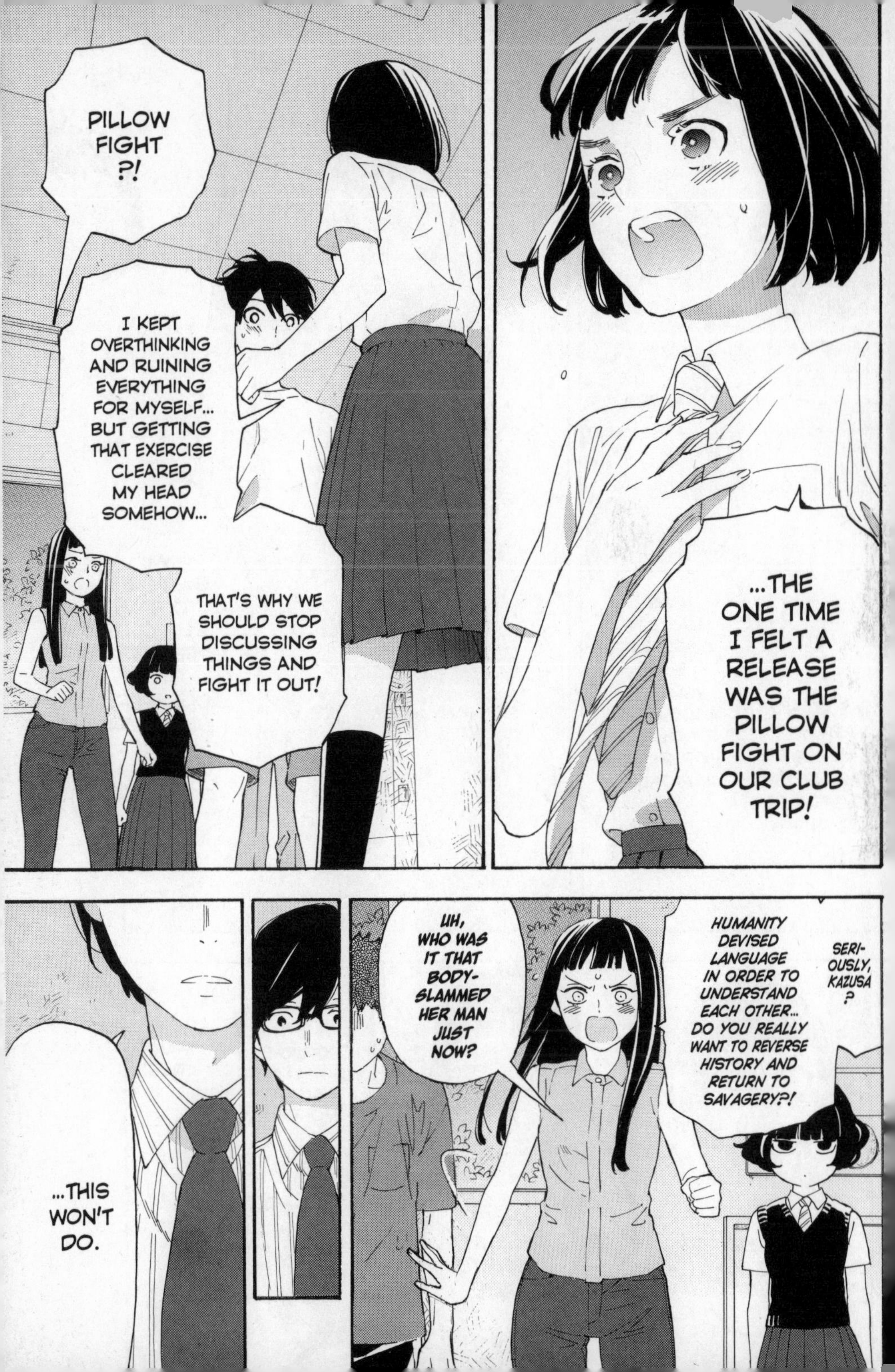
...THE ONE TIME I FELT A RELEASE WAS THE PILLOW FIGHT ON OUR CLUB TRIP!
PILLOW FIGHT ?!
I KEPT OVERTHINKING AND RUINING EVERYTHING FOR MYSELF... BUT GETTING THAT EXERCISE CLEARED MY HEAD SOMEHOW...
THAT'S WHY WE SHOULD STOP DISCUSSING THINGS AND FIGHT IT OUT!
SERI-OUSLY, KAZUSA ?
HUMANITY DEVISED LANGUAGE IN ORDER TO UNDERSTAND EACH OTHER... DO YOU REALLY WANT TO REVERSE HISTORY AND RETURN TO SAVAGERY?!
UH, WHO WAS IT THAT BODY-SLAMMED HER MAN JUST NOW?
...THIS WON'T DO.

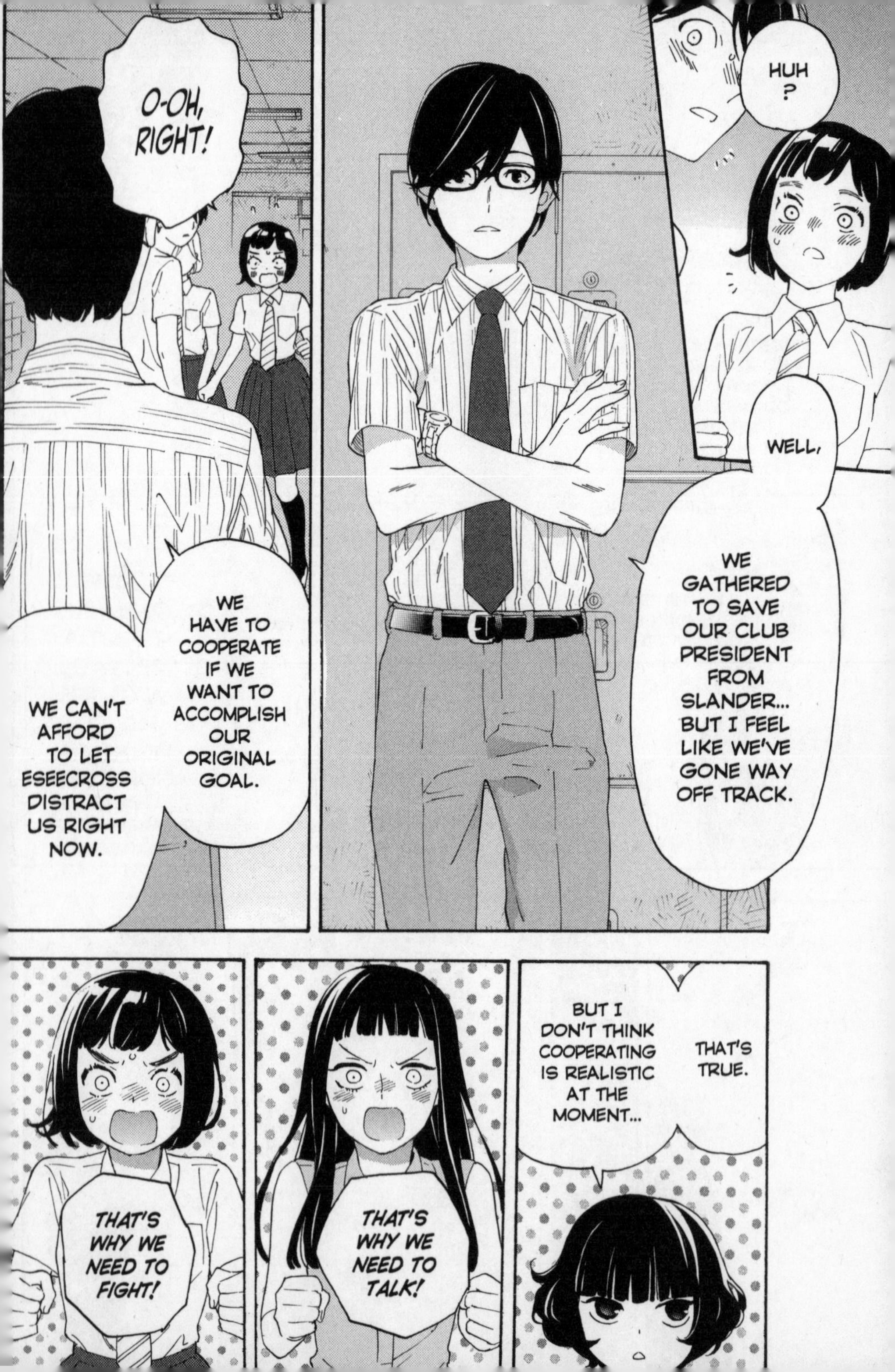
HUH ?
WELL,
WE GATHERED TO SAVE OUR CLUB PRESIDENT FROM SLANDER... BUT I FEEL LIKE WE'VE GONE WAY OFF TRACK.
O-OH, RIGHT!
WE HAVE TO COOPERATE IF WE WANT TO ACCOMPLISH OUR ORIGINAL GOAL.
WE CAN'T AFFORD TO LET ESEECROSS DISTRACT US RIGHT NOW.
THAT'S TRUE.
BUT I DON'T THINK COOPERATING IS REALISTIC AT THE MOMENT...
THAT'S WHY WE NEED TO TALK!
THAT'S WHY WE NEED TO FIGHT!

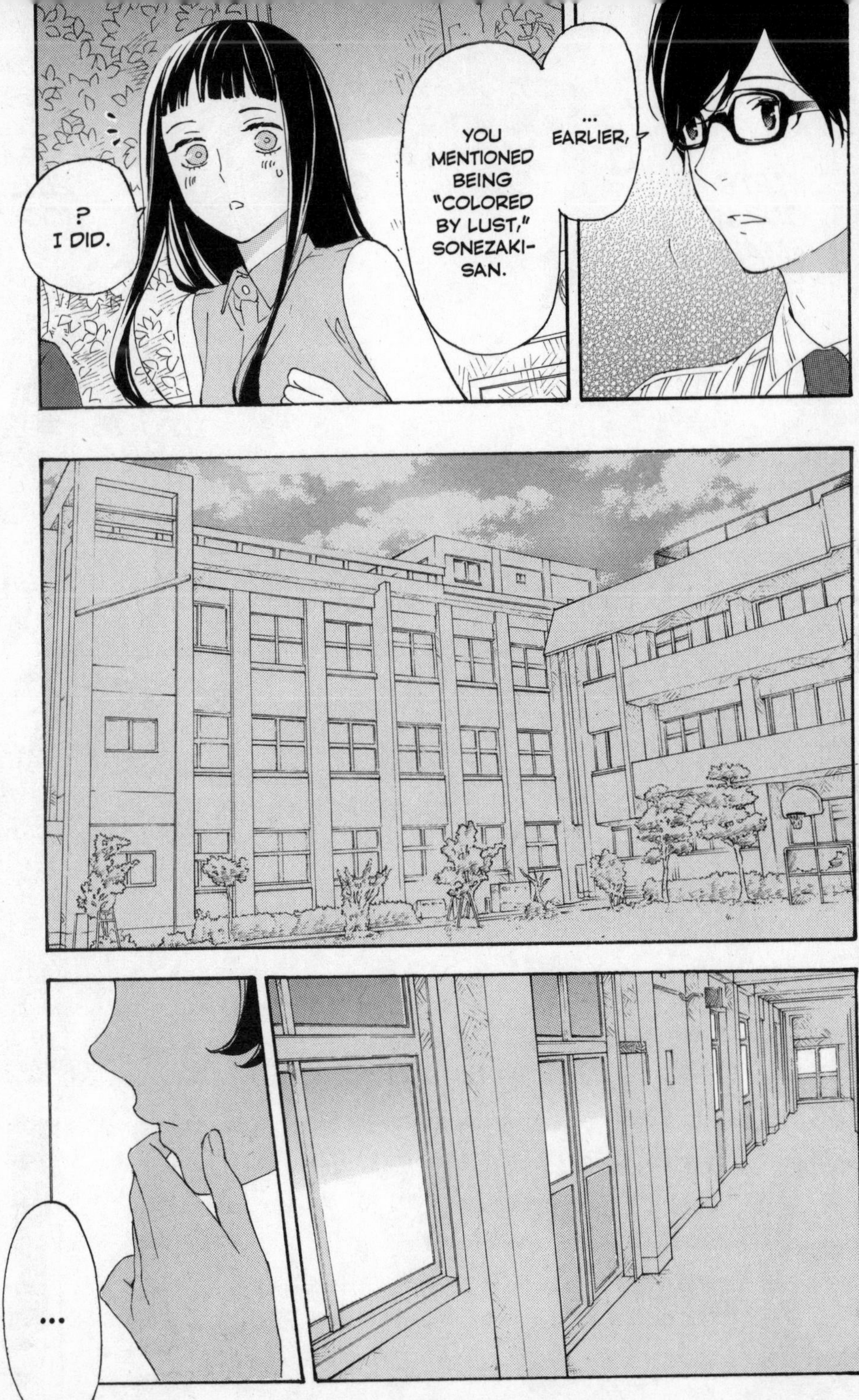
... EARLIER,
YOU MENTIONED BEING "COLORED BY LUST," SONEZAKI-SAN.
? I DID.
...

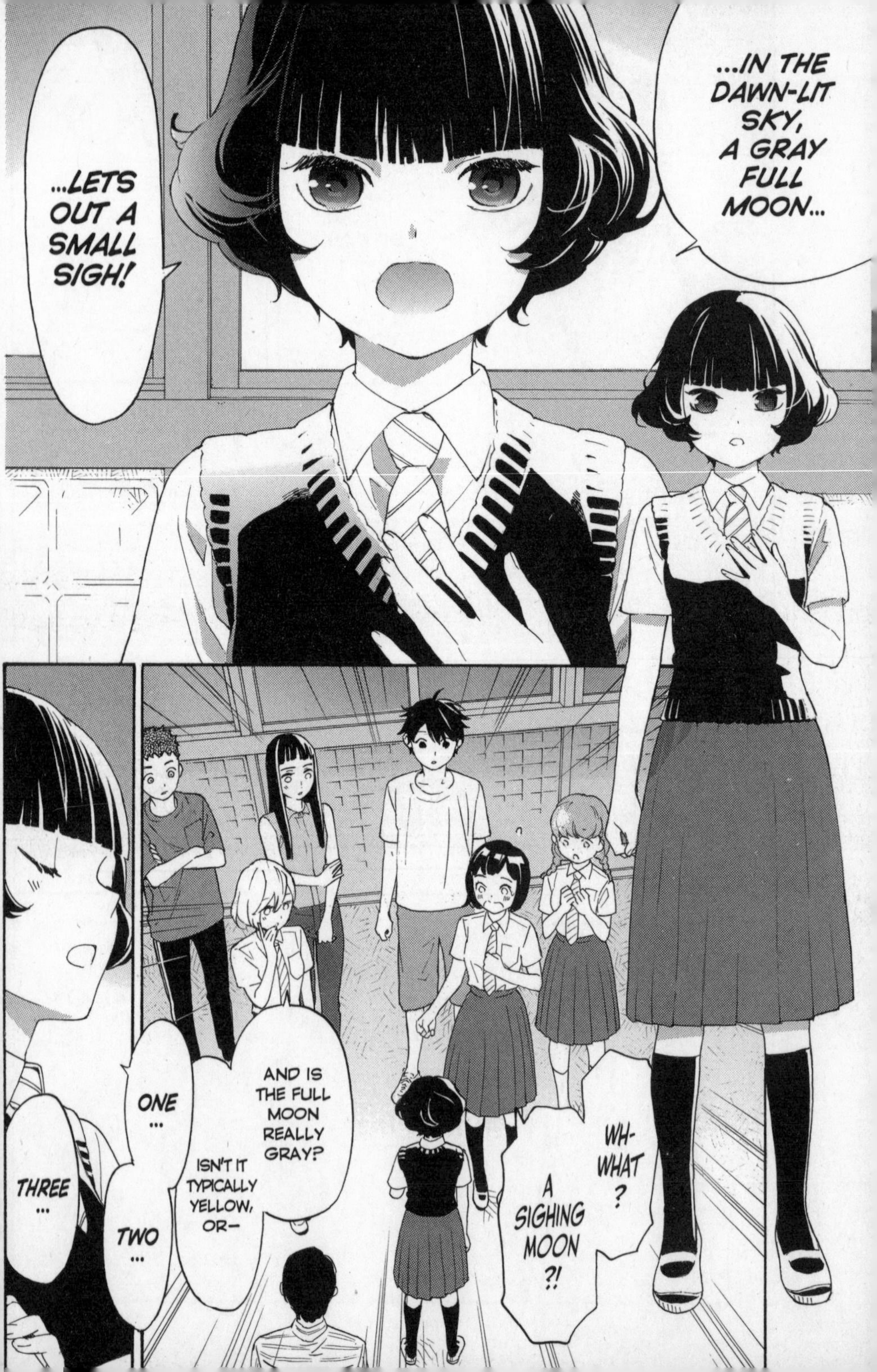
...IN THE DAWN-LIT SKY, A GRAY FULL MOON...
...LETS OUT A SMALL SIGH!
WH-WHAT?
A SIGHING MOON?!
AND IS THE FULL MOON REALLY GRAY?
ISN'T IT TYPICALLY YELLOW, OR—
ONE...
TWO...
THREE...

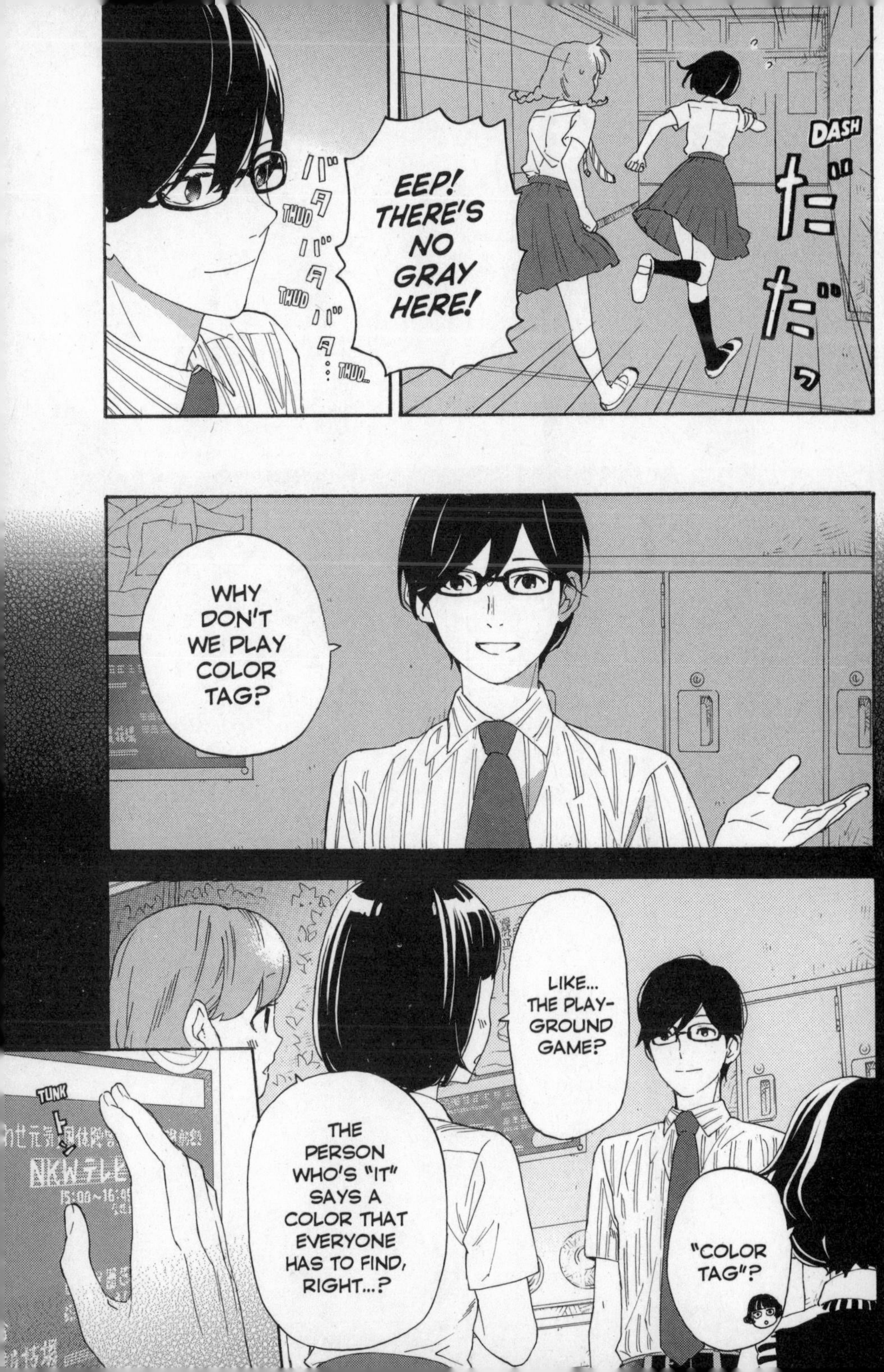
DASH
だだっ
EEP! THERE'S NO GRAY HERE!
バタ THUD
バタ THUD
バタ… THUD…
WHY DON'T WE PLAY COLOR TAG?
"COLOR TAG"?
LIKE… THE PLAY-GROUND GAME?
THE PERSON WHO'S "IT" SAYS A COLOR THAT EVERYONE HAS TO FIND, RIGHT…?
TUNK
トン
NKWテレビ

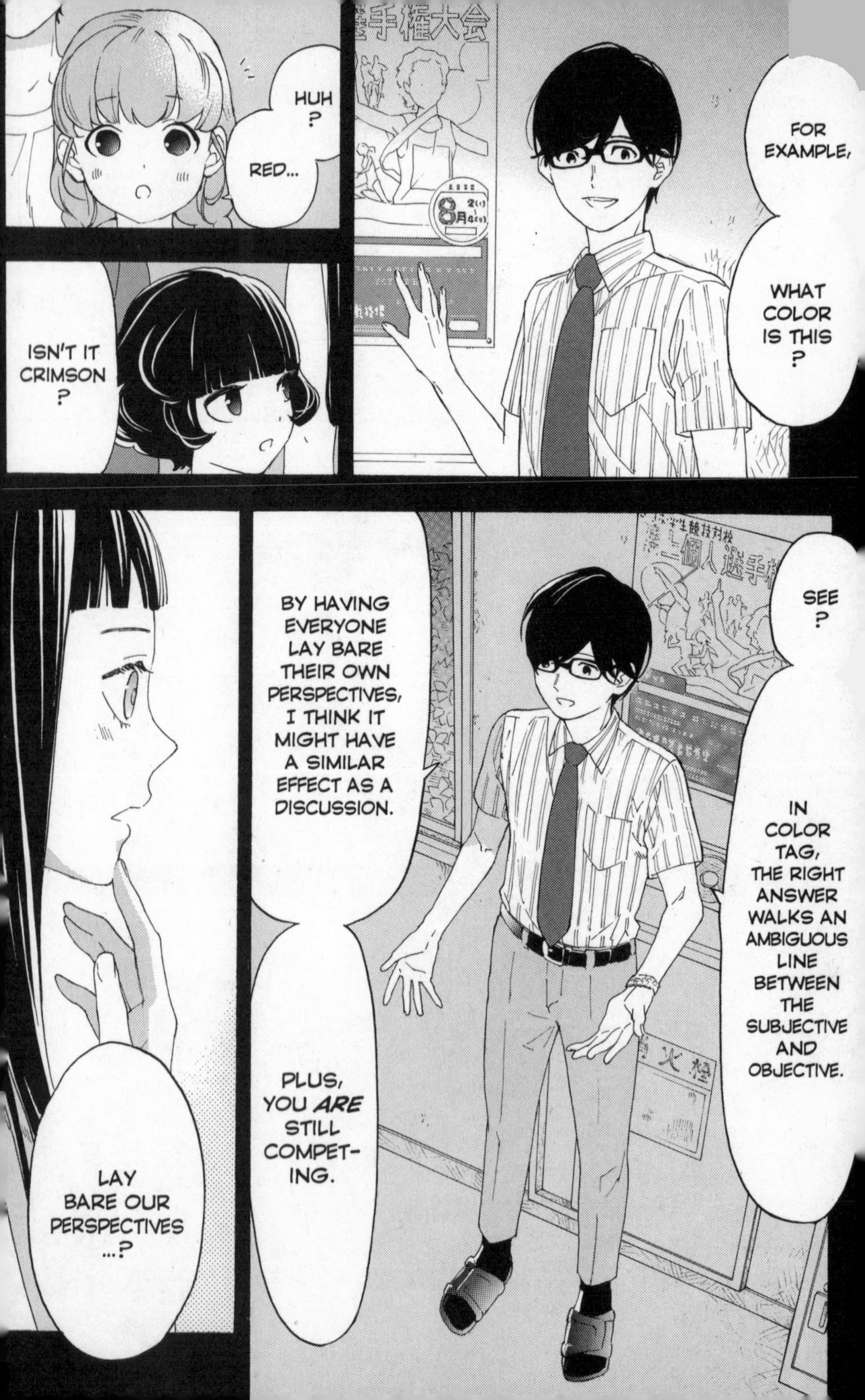
FOR EXAMPLE,
WHAT COLOR IS THIS ?
HUH ?
RED...
ISN'T IT CRIMSON ?
SEE ?
IN COLOR TAG, THE RIGHT ANSWER WALKS AN AMBIGUOUS LINE BETWEEN THE SUBJECTIVE AND OBJECTIVE.
BY HAVING EVERYONE LAY BARE THEIR OWN PERSPECTIVES, I THINK IT MIGHT HAVE A SIMILAR EFFECT AS A DISCUSSION.
PLUS, YOU *ARE* STILL COMPET-ING.
LAY BARE OUR PERSPECTIVES ...?

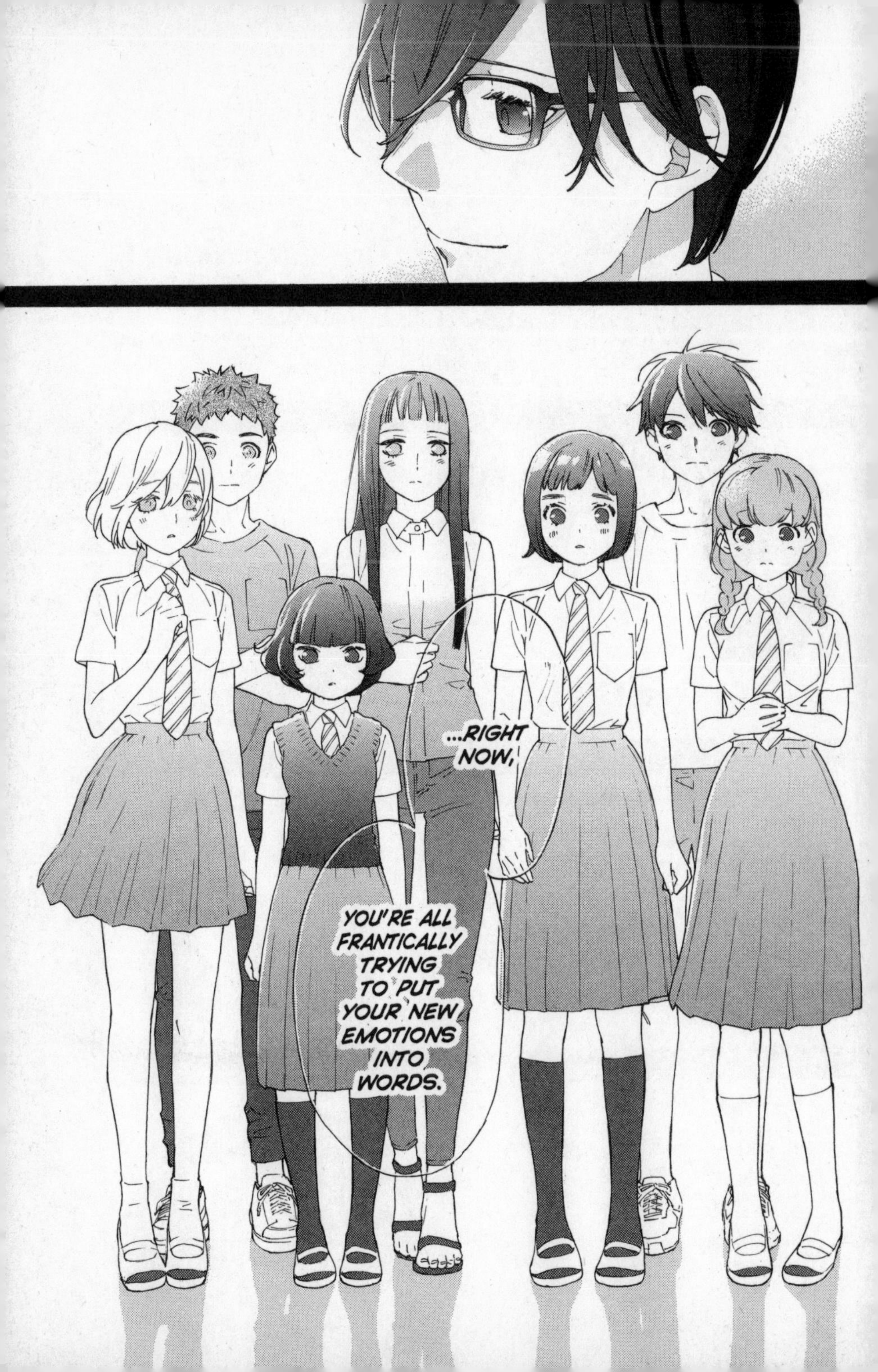
...RIGHT NOW,
YOU'RE ALL FRANTICALLY TRYING TO PUT YOUR NEW EMOTIONS INTO WORDS.

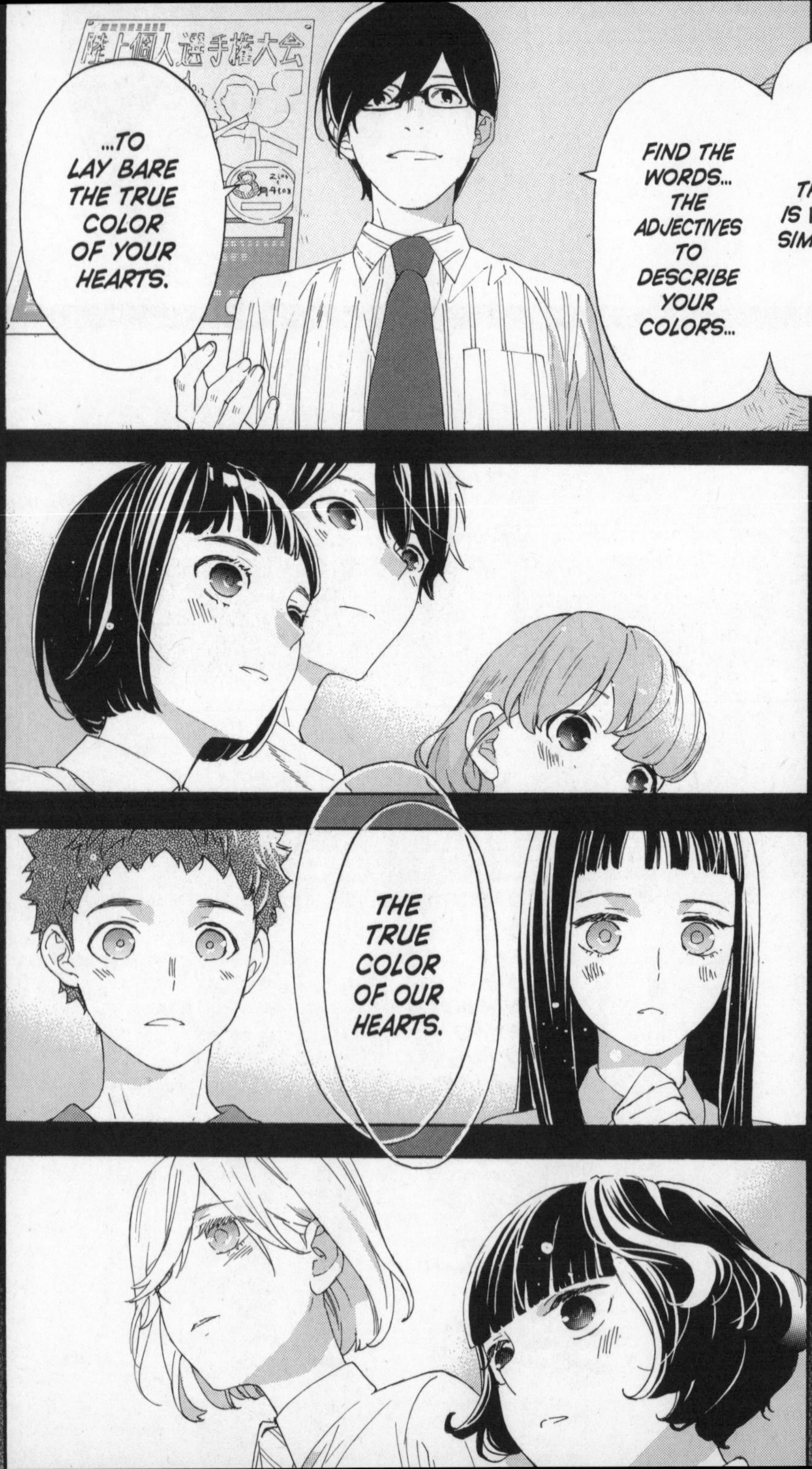
THIS IS VERY SIMILAR.
FIND THE WORDS... THE ADJECTIVES TO DESCRIBE YOUR COLORS...
陸上個人選手権大会
...TO LAY BARE THE TRUE COLOR OF YOUR HEARTS.
THE TRUE COLOR OF OUR HEARTS.

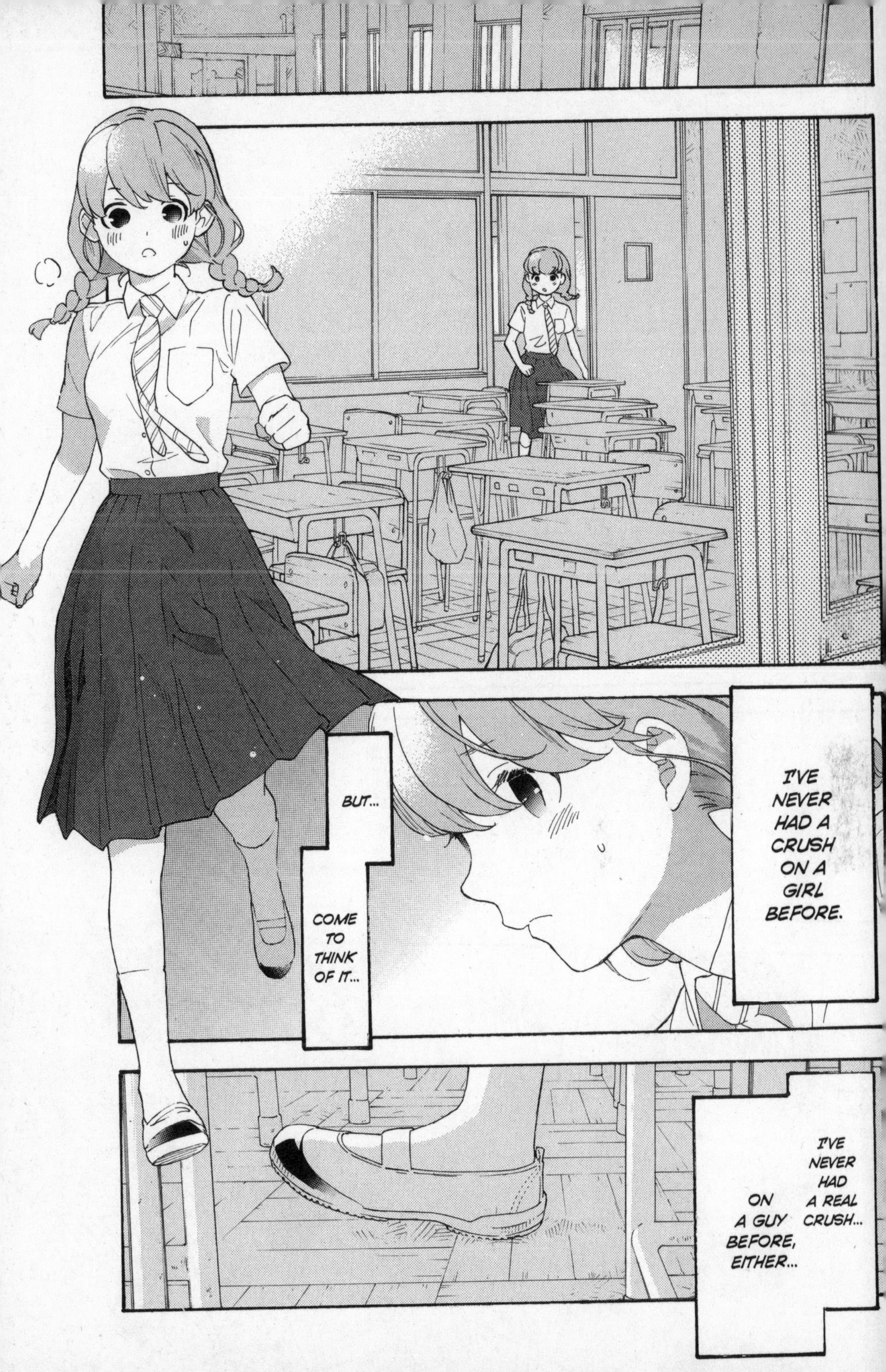
I'VE NEVER HAD A CRUSH ON A GIRL BEFORE.
BUT...
COME TO THINK OF IT...
I'VE NEVER HAD A REAL CRUSH...
ON A GUY BEFORE, EITHER...

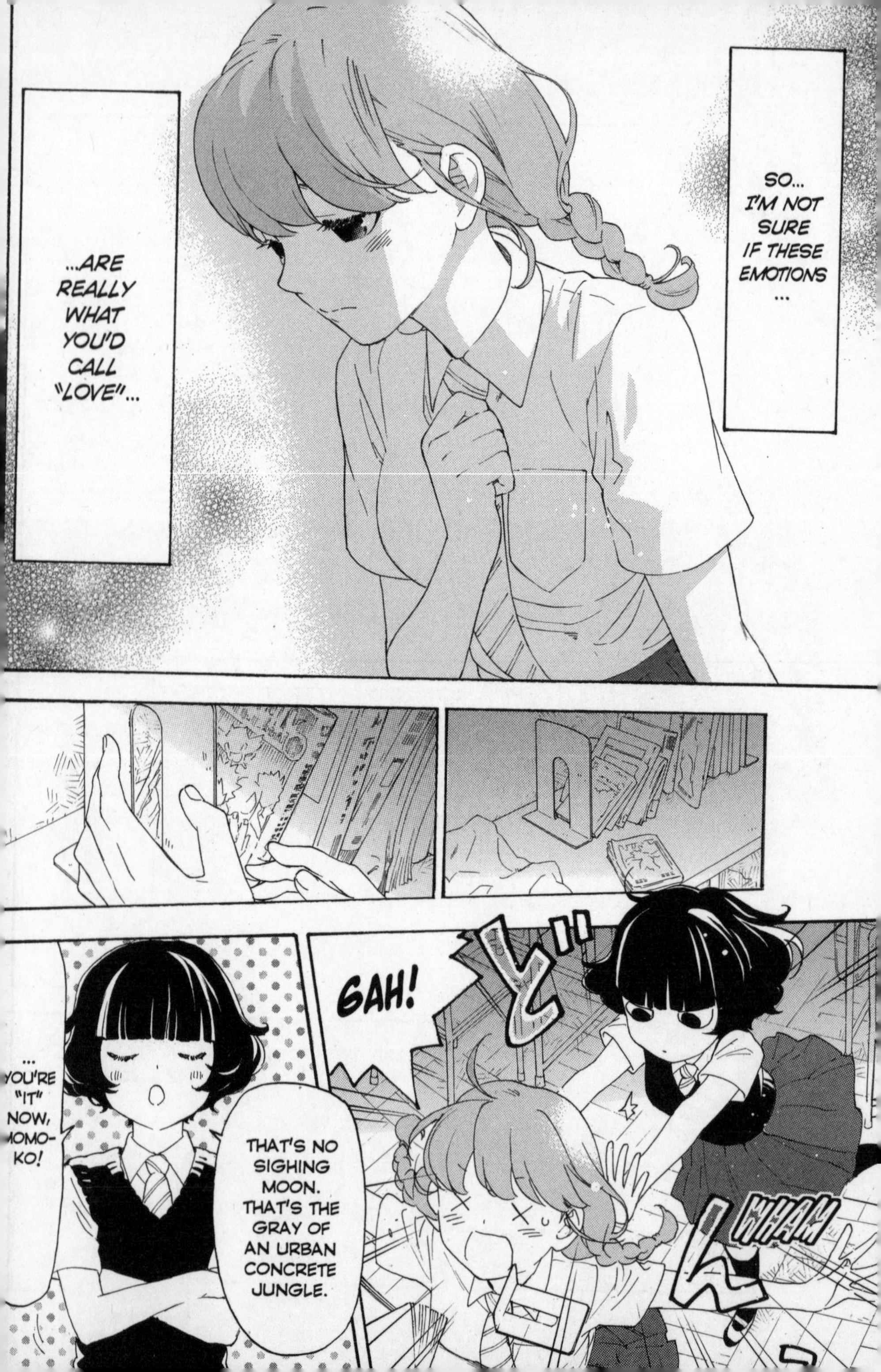
SO... I'M NOT SURE IF THESE EMOTIONS ...
...ARE REALLY WHAT YOU'D CALL "LOVE"...
GAH!
THAT'S NO SIGHING MOON. THAT'S THE GRAY OF AN URBAN CONCRETE JUNGLE.
WHAM
... YOU'RE "IT" NOW, MOMO-KO!

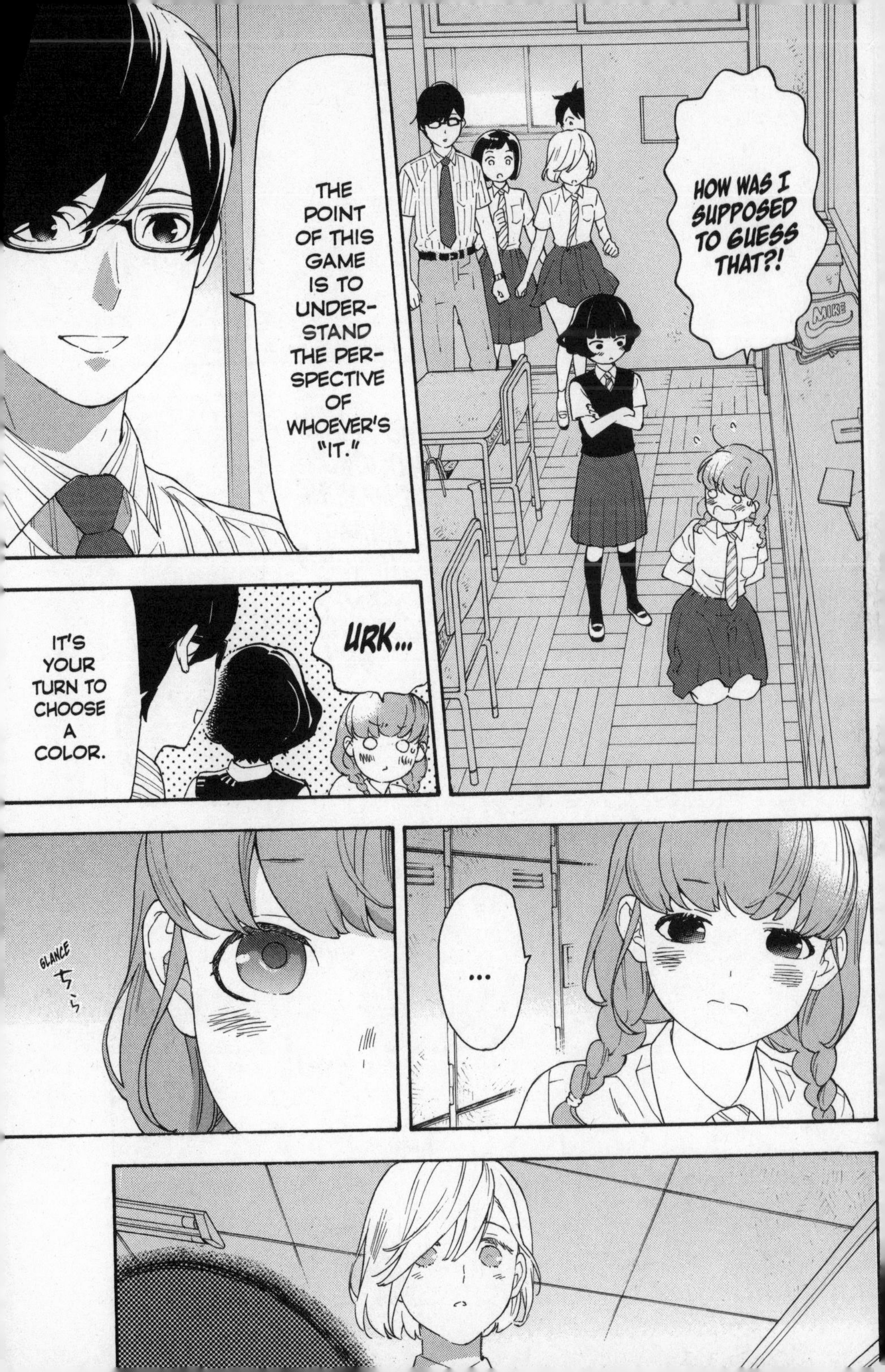
HOW WAS I SUPPOSED TO GUESS THAT?!
MIKE
THE POINT OF THIS GAME IS TO UNDER-STAND THE PER-SPECTIVE OF WHOEVER'S "IT."
URK...
IT'S YOUR TURN TO CHOOSE A COLOR.
...
GLANCE
ちら

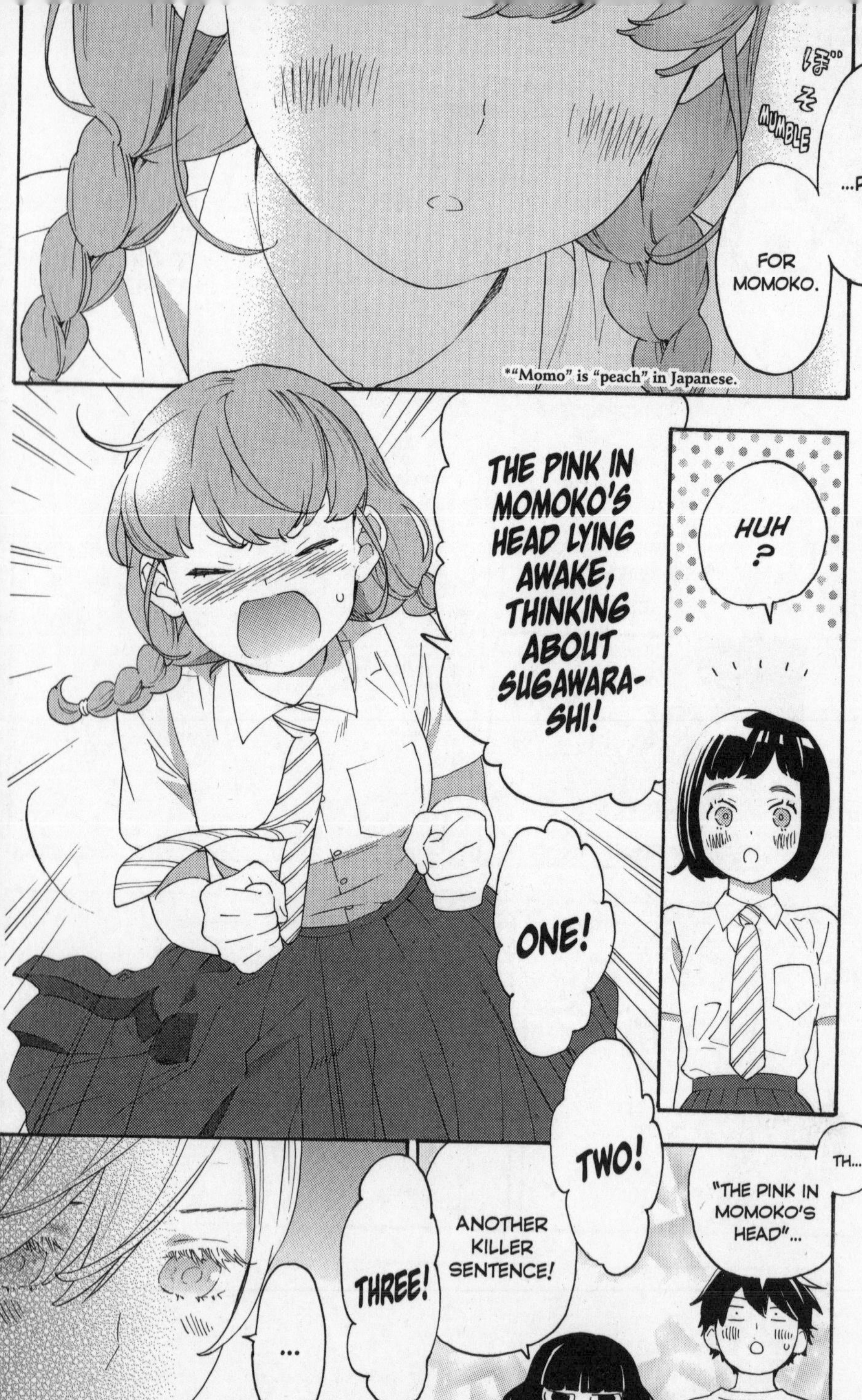
ぼそ
MUMBLE
...PINK,
FOR MOMOKO.
HUH ?
THE PINK IN MOMOKO'S HEAD LYING AWAKE, THINKING ABOUT SUGAWARA-SHI!
ONE!
TH...
"THE PINK IN MOMOKO'S HEAD"...
TWO!
ANOTHER KILLER SENTENCE!
THREE!
...
*"Momo" is "peach" in Japanese.

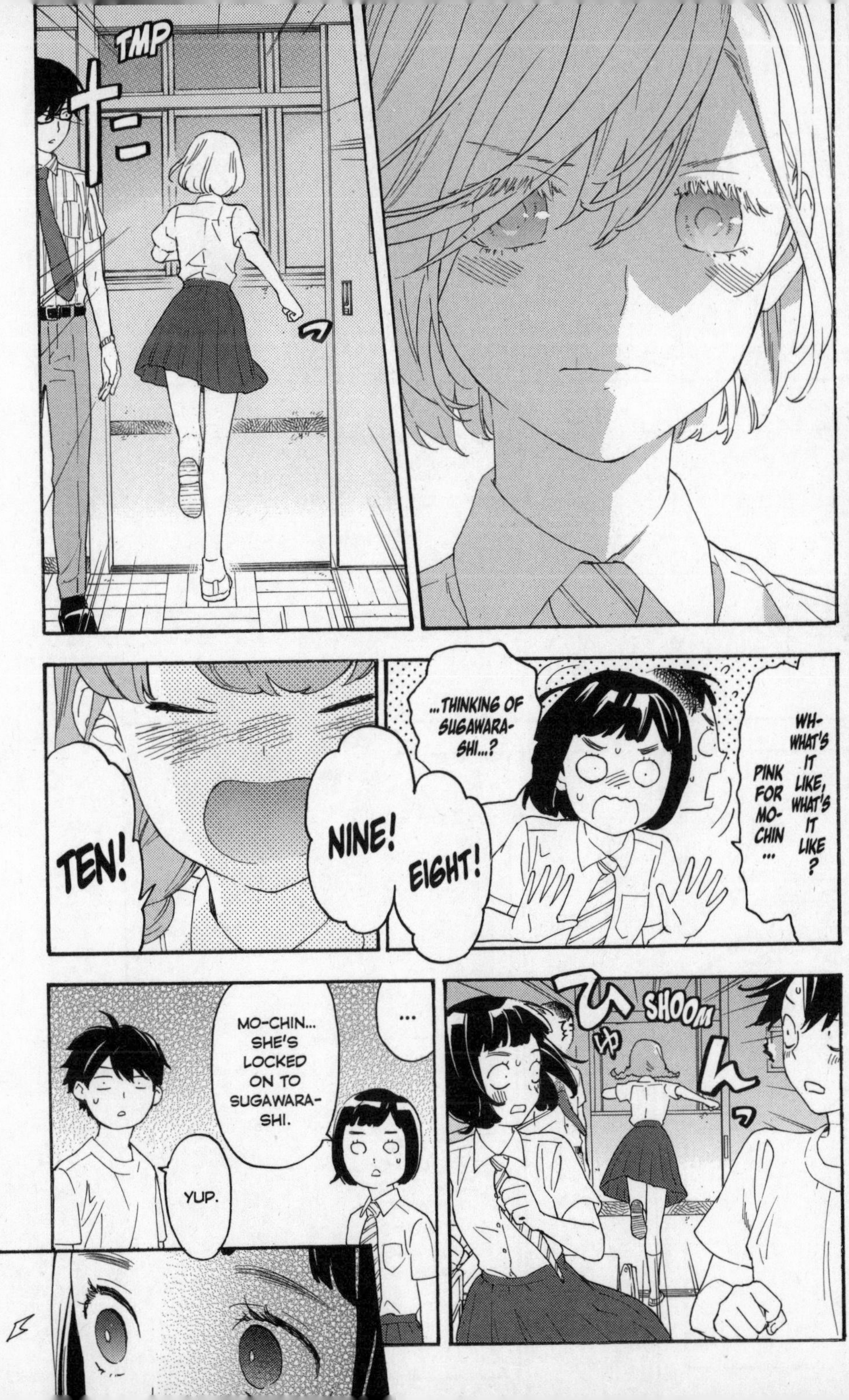
TMP
WH-WHAT'S IT LIKE, WHAT'S IT LIKE?
PINK FOR MO-CHIN...
...THINKING OF SUGAWARA-SHI...?
TEN!
NINE!
EIGHT!
SHOOM
...
MO-CHIN... SHE'S LOCKED ON TO SUGAWARA-SHI.
YUP.

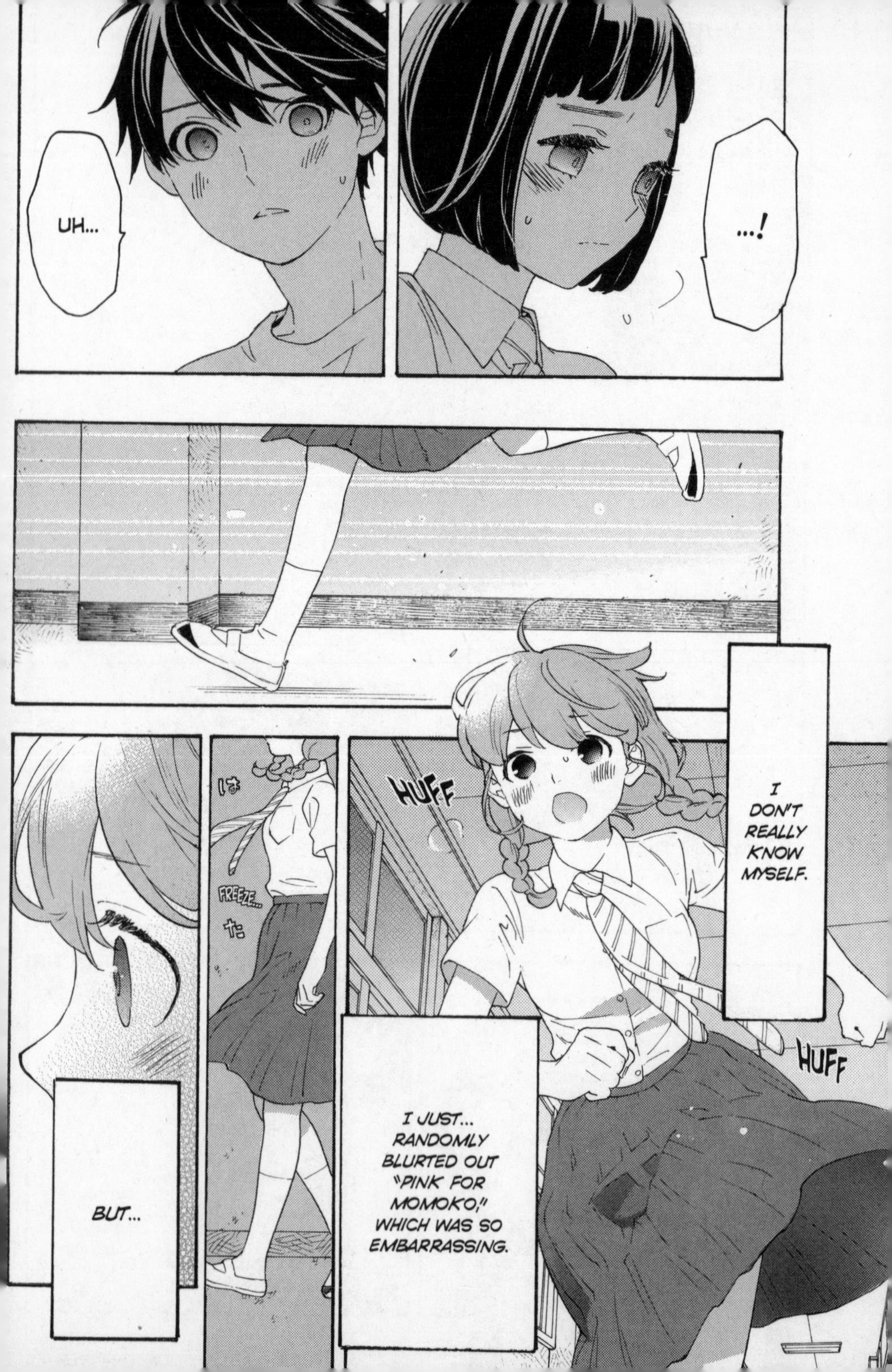
...!
UH...
I DON'T REALLY KNOW MYSELF.
HUFF
HUFF
I JUST... RANDOMLY BLURTED OUT "PINK FOR MOMOKO," WHICH WAS SO EMBARRASSING.
は
FREEZE...
た
BUT...

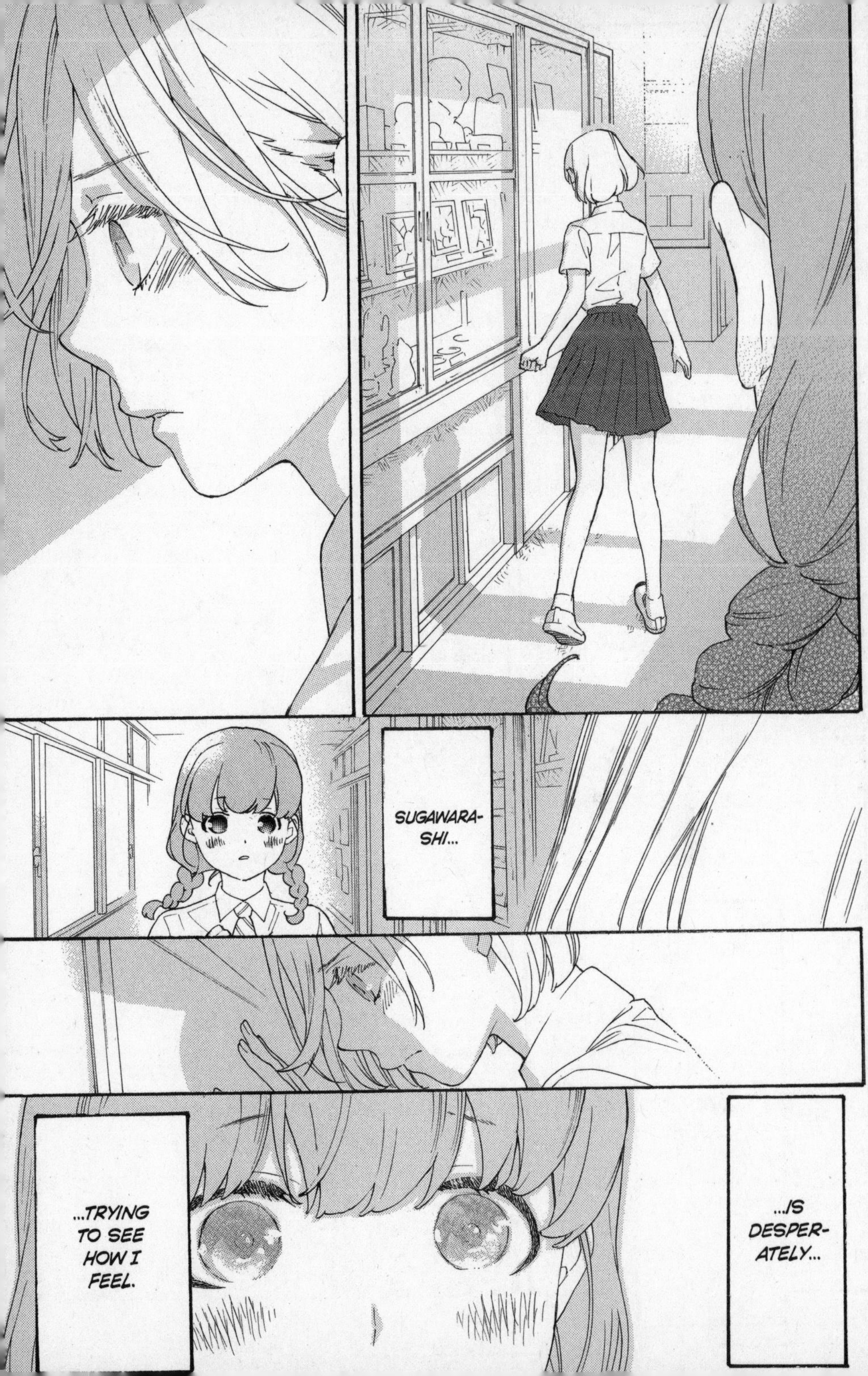
SUGAWARA-SHI...
...IS DESPER-ATELY...
...TRYING TO SEE HOW I FEEL.

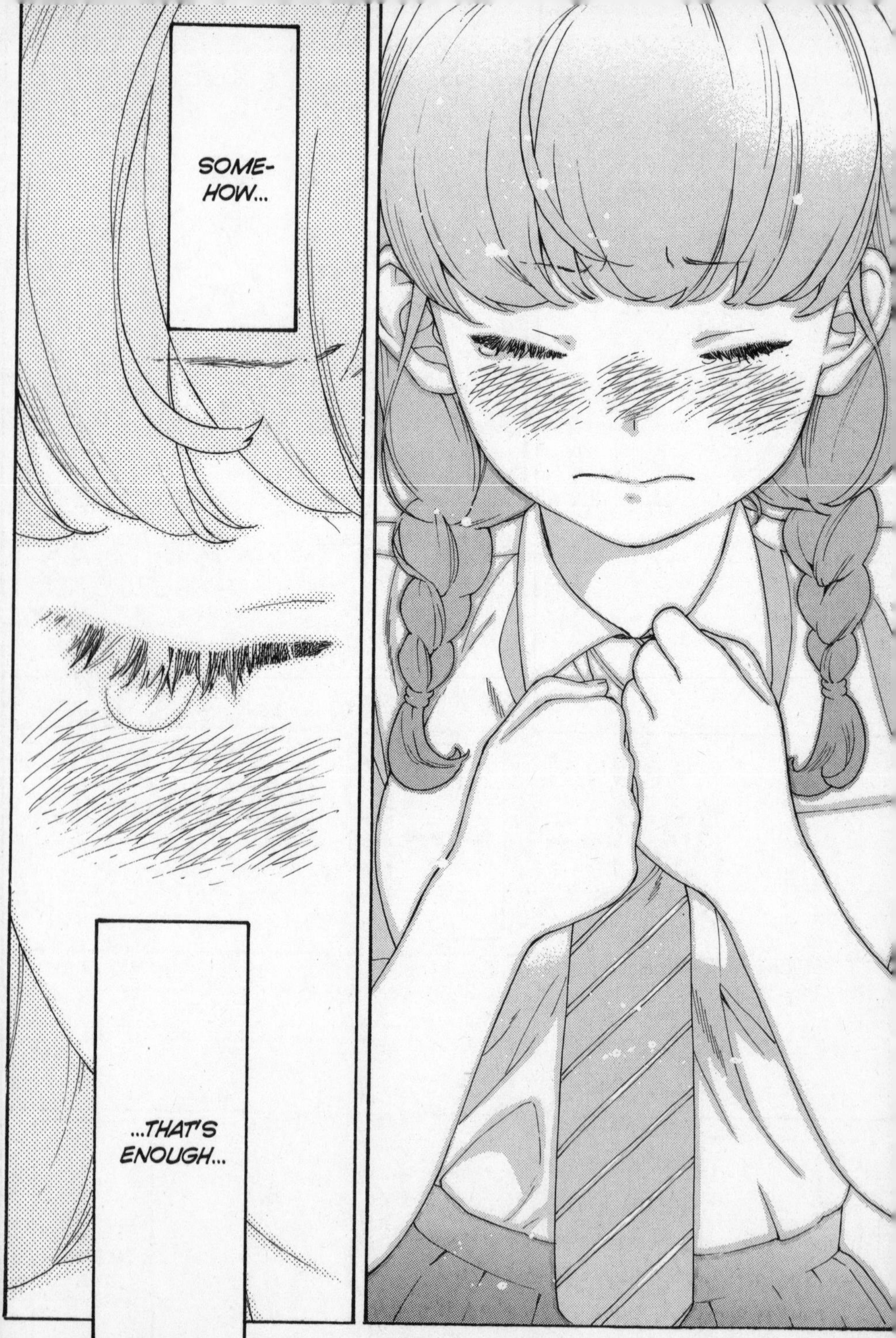
SOME-HOW...
...THAT'S ENOUGH...

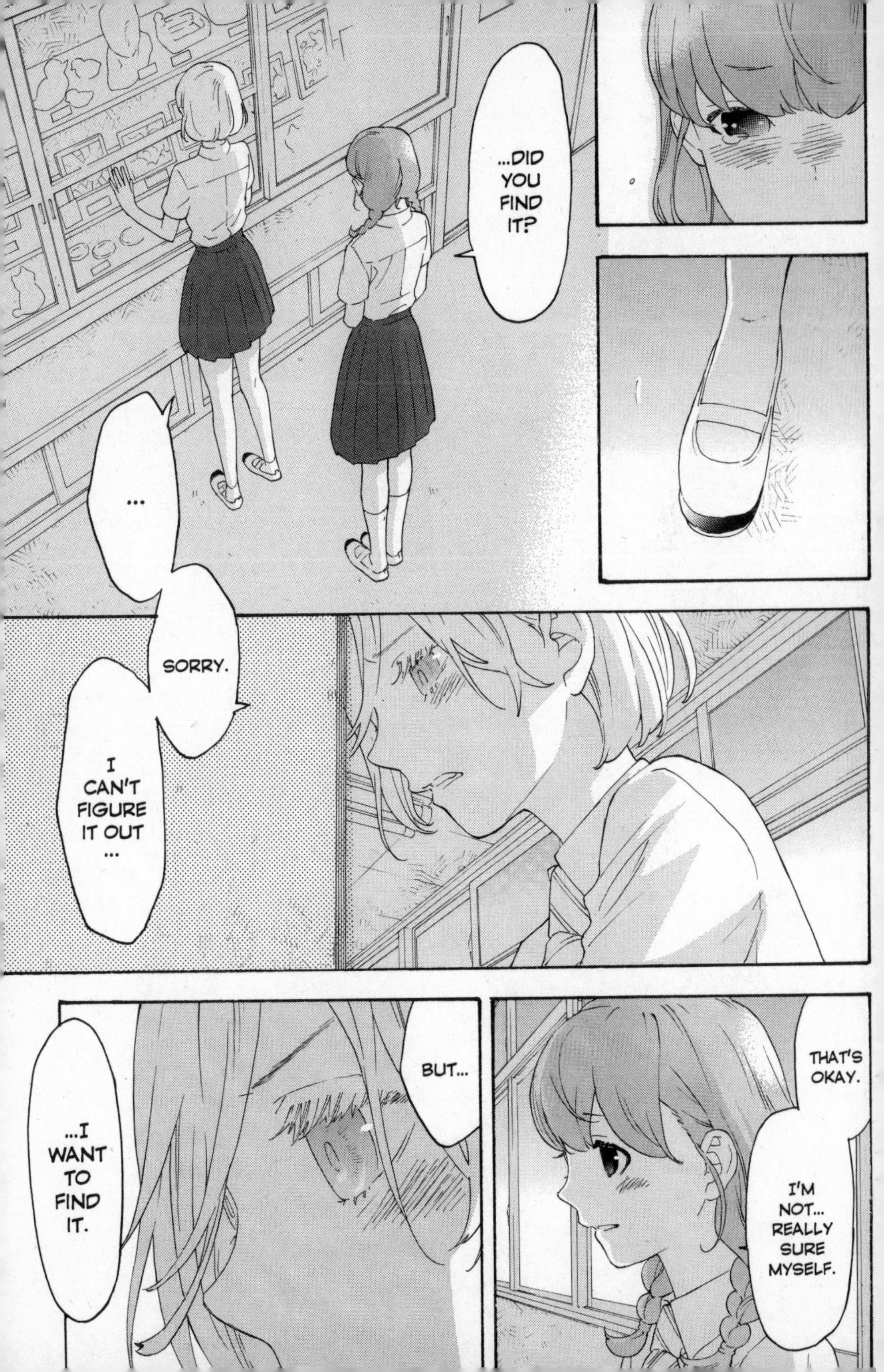
...DID YOU FIND IT?
...
SORRY.
I CAN'T FIGURE IT OUT ...
THAT'S OKAY.
I'M NOT... REALLY SURE MYSELF.
BUT...
...I WANT TO FIND IT.

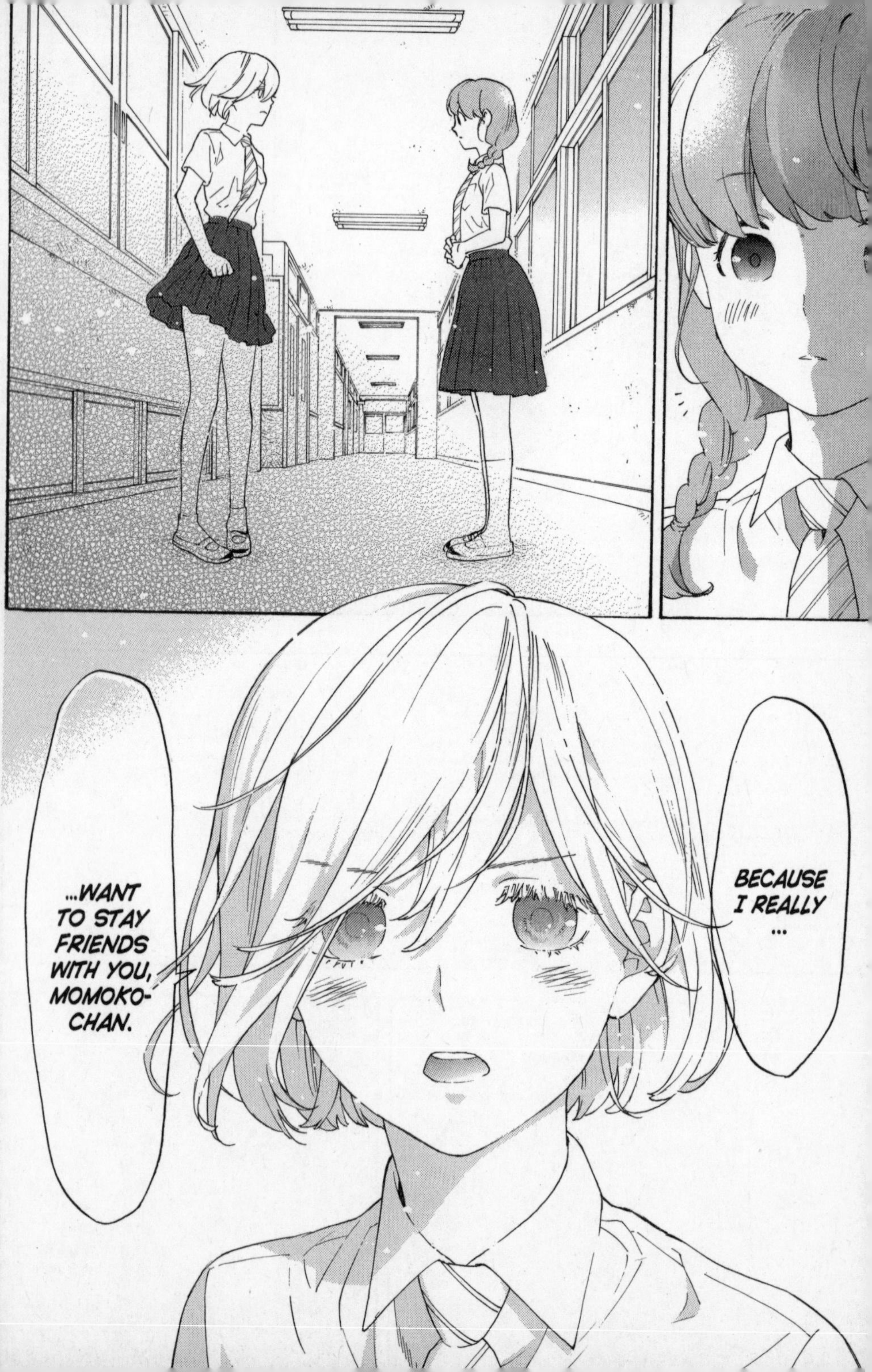
BECAUSE I REALLY ...
...WANT TO STAY FRIENDS WITH YOU, MOMOKO-CHAN.

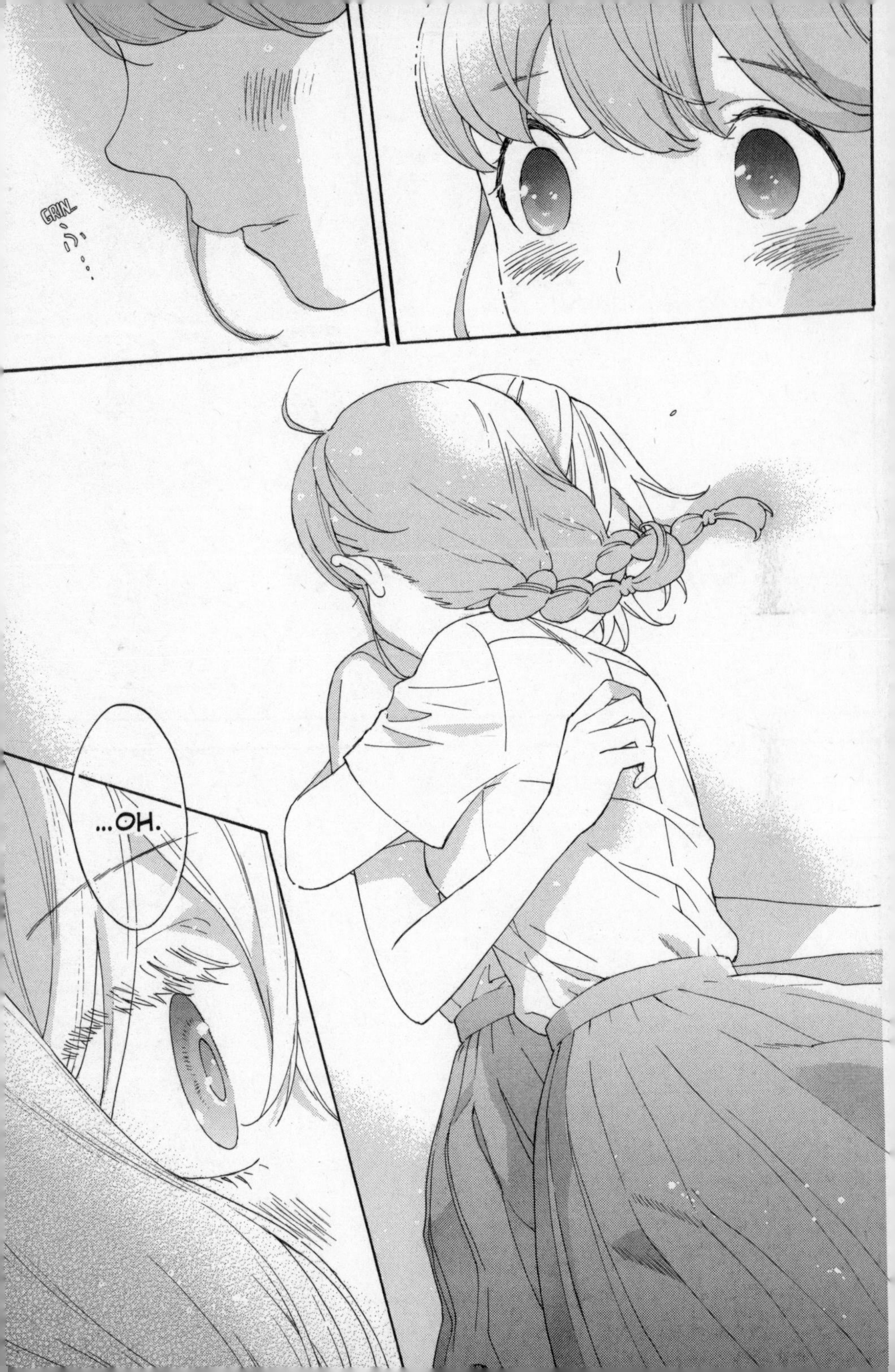
GRIN...
...OH.

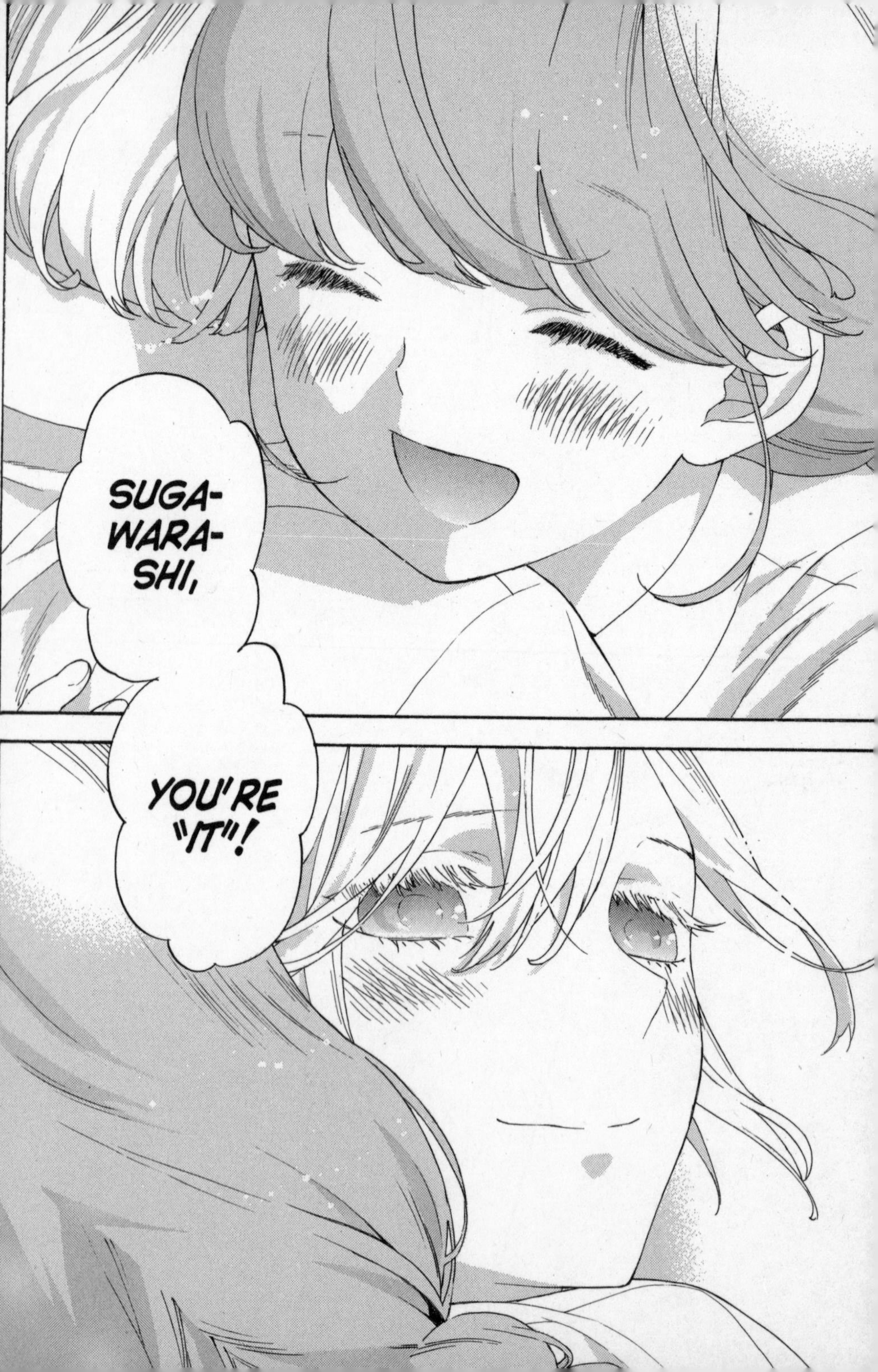
SUGA-WARA-SHI,
YOU'RE "IT"!

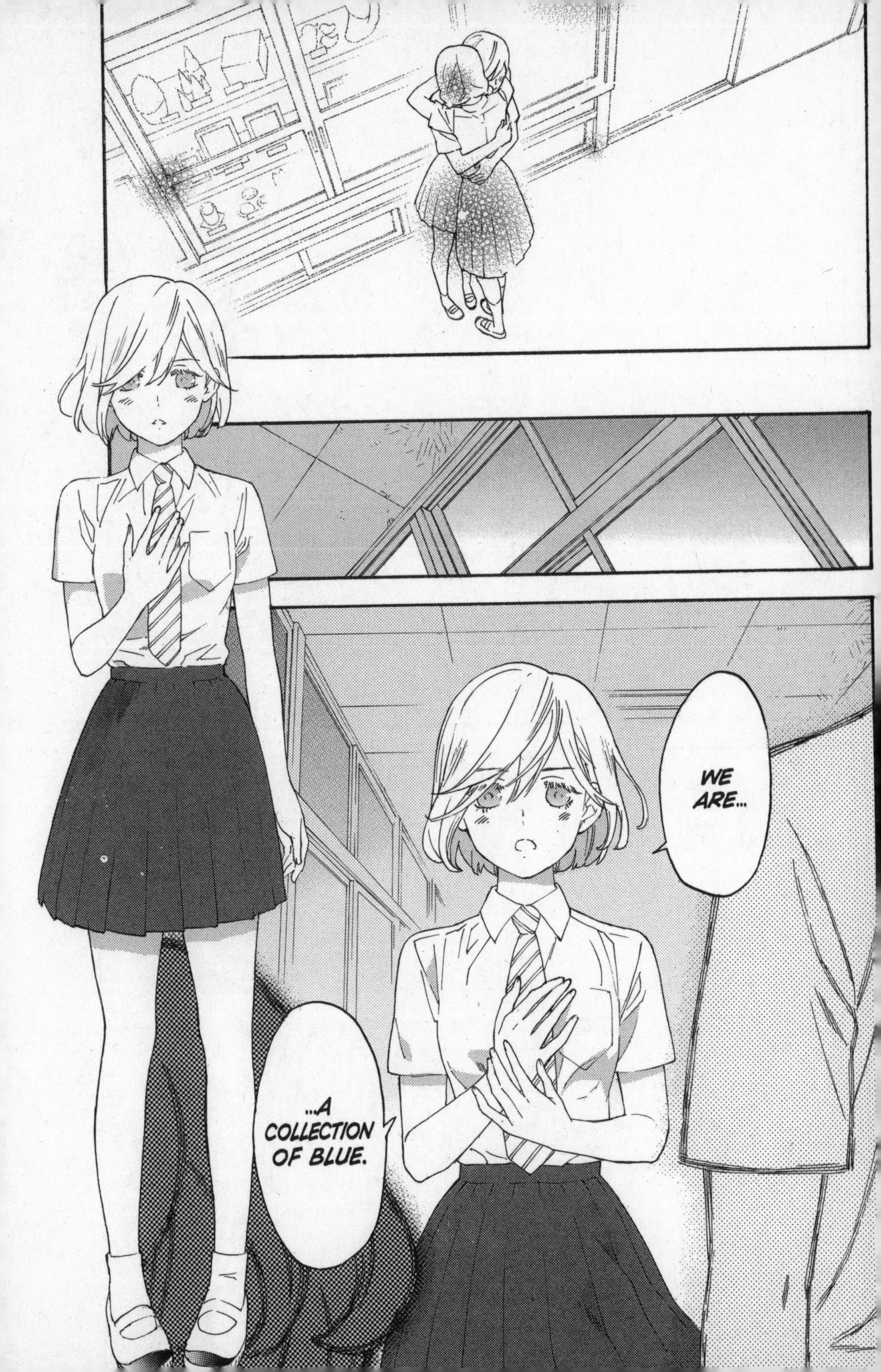
WE ARE...
...A COLLECTION OF BLUE.

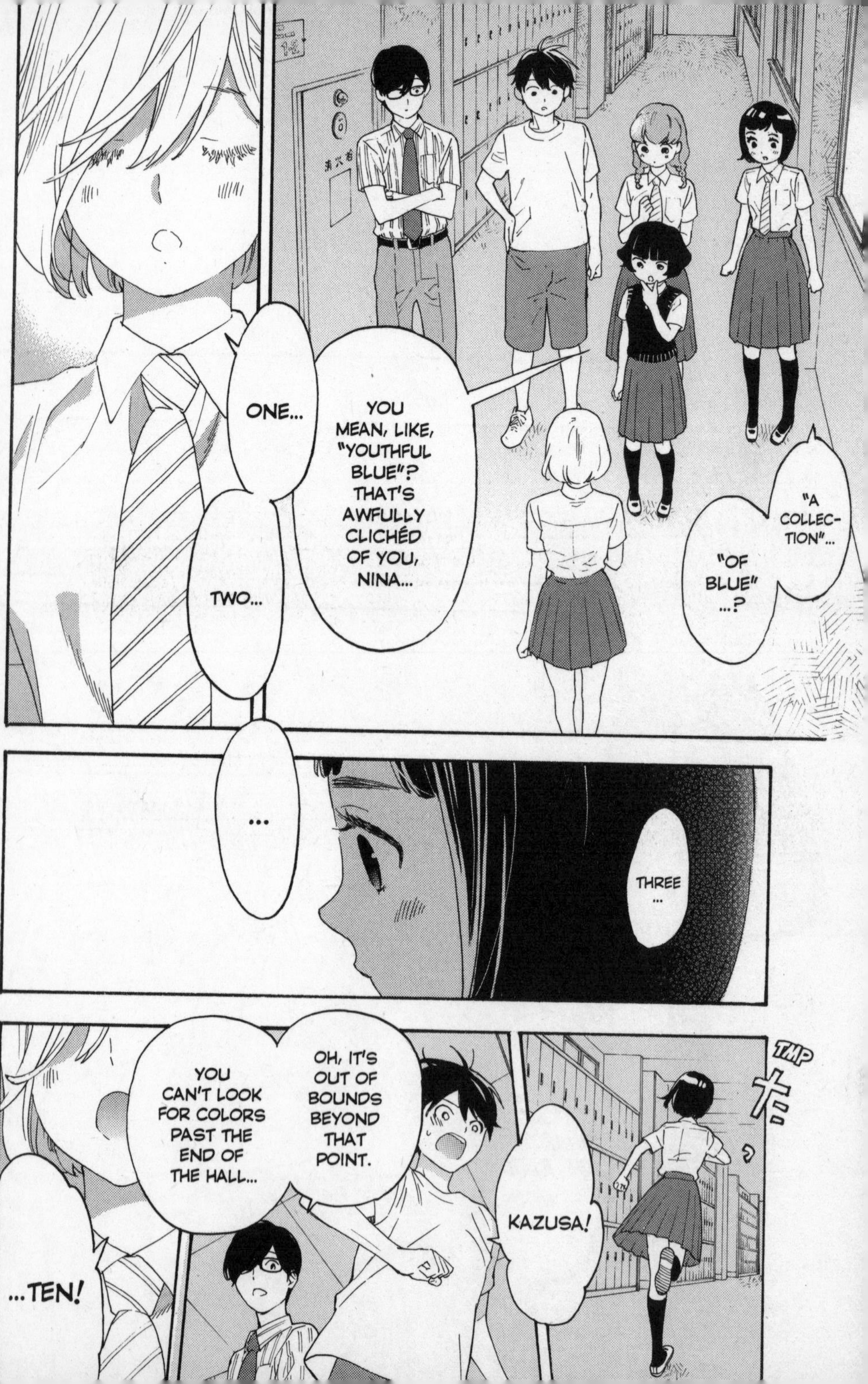
"A COLLECTION"...
"OF BLUE" ...?
YOU MEAN, LIKE, "YOUTHFUL BLUE"? THAT'S AWFULLY CLICHÉD OF YOU, NINA...
ONE...
TWO...
THREE ...
...
TMP
KAZUSA!
OH, IT'S OUT OF BOUNDS BEYOND THAT POINT.
YOU CAN'T LOOK FOR COLORS PAST THE END OF THE HALL...
...TEN!

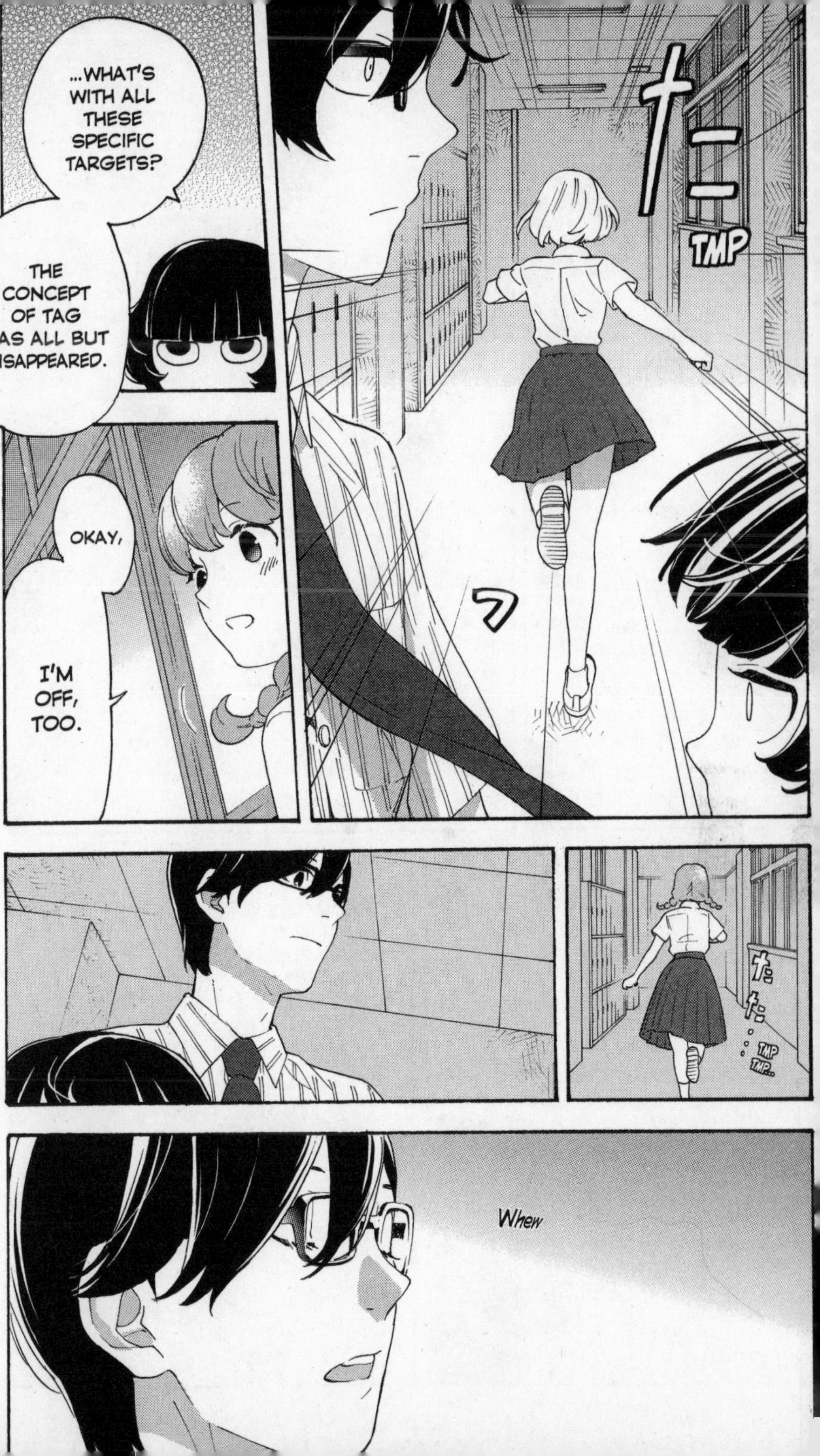
TMP
...WHAT'S WITH ALL THESE SPECIFIC TARGETS?
THE CONCEPT OF TAG HAS ALL BUT DISAPPEARED.
OKAY,
I'M OFF, TOO.
TMP TMP...
Whew

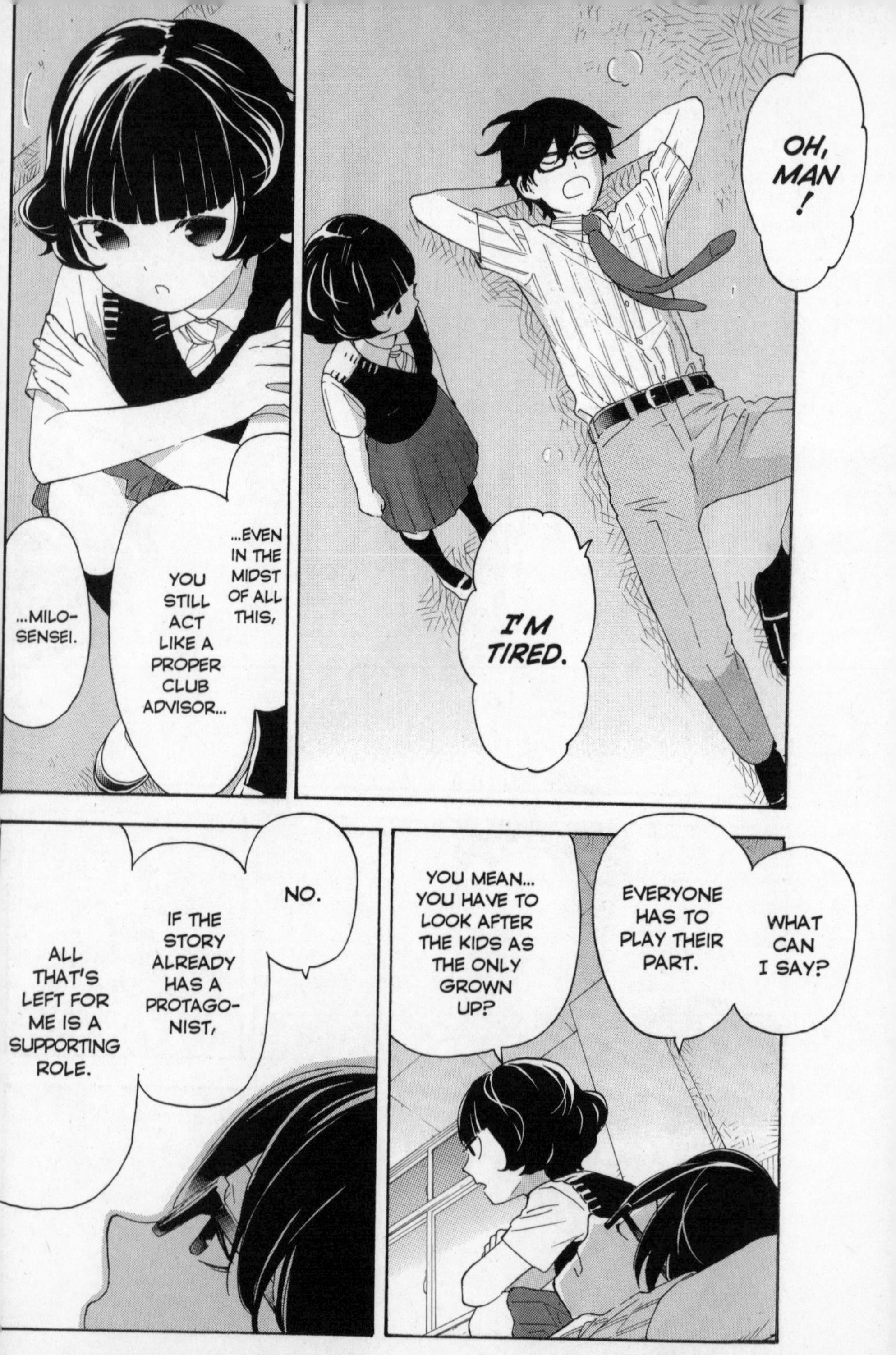
OH, MAN!
I'M TIRED.
...EVEN IN THE MIDST OF ALL THIS, YOU STILL ACT LIKE A PROPER CLUB ADVISOR...
...MILO-SENSEI.
WHAT CAN I SAY?
EVERYONE HAS TO PLAY THEIR PART.
YOU MEAN... YOU HAVE TO LOOK AFTER THE KIDS AS THE ONLY GROWN UP?
NO.
IF THE STORY ALREADY HAS A PROTAGO-NIST,
ALL THAT'S LEFT FOR ME IS A SUPPORTING ROLE.

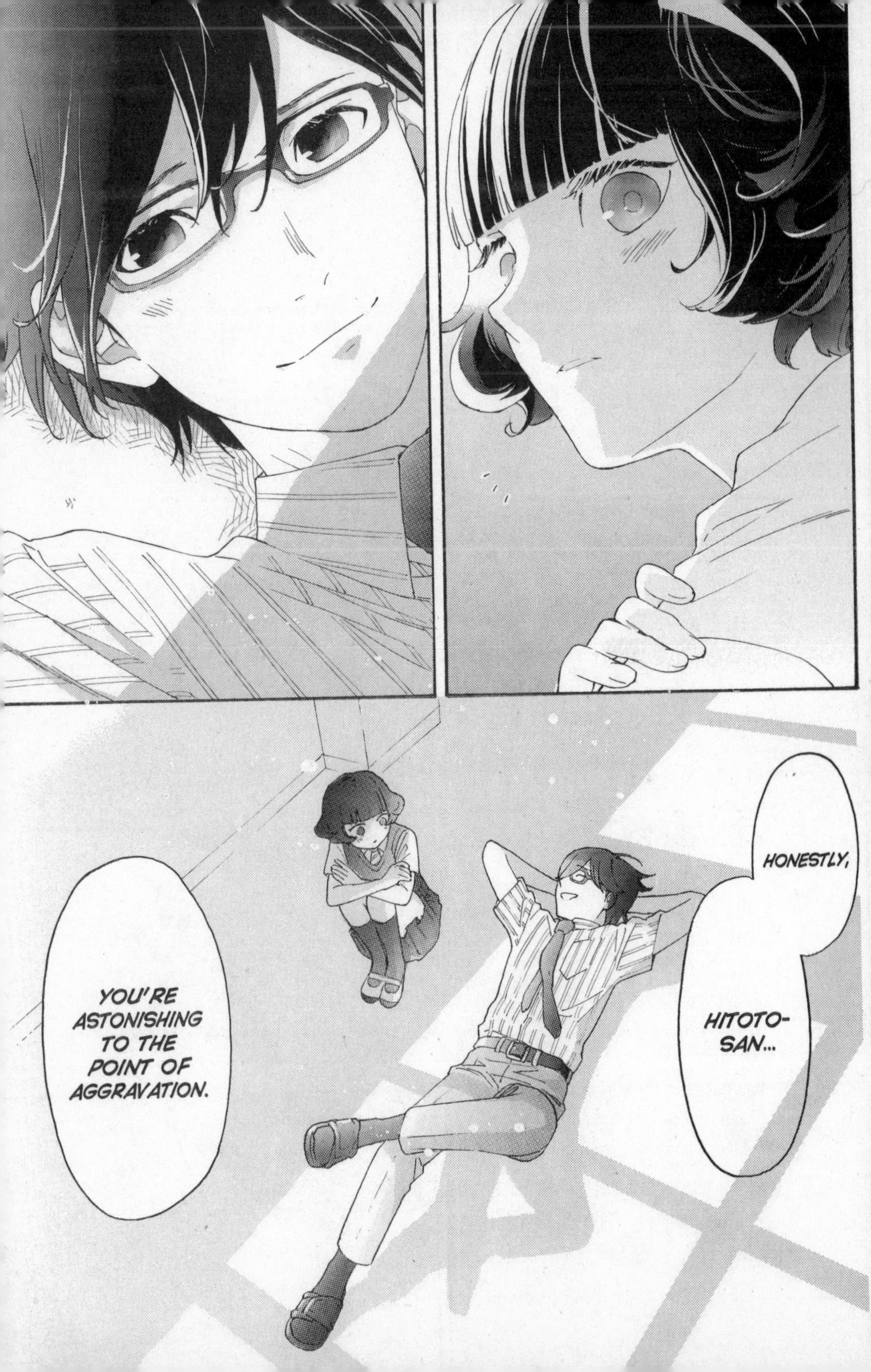
HONESTLY, HITOTO-SAN...
YOU'RE ASTONISHING TO THE POINT OF AGGRAVATION.

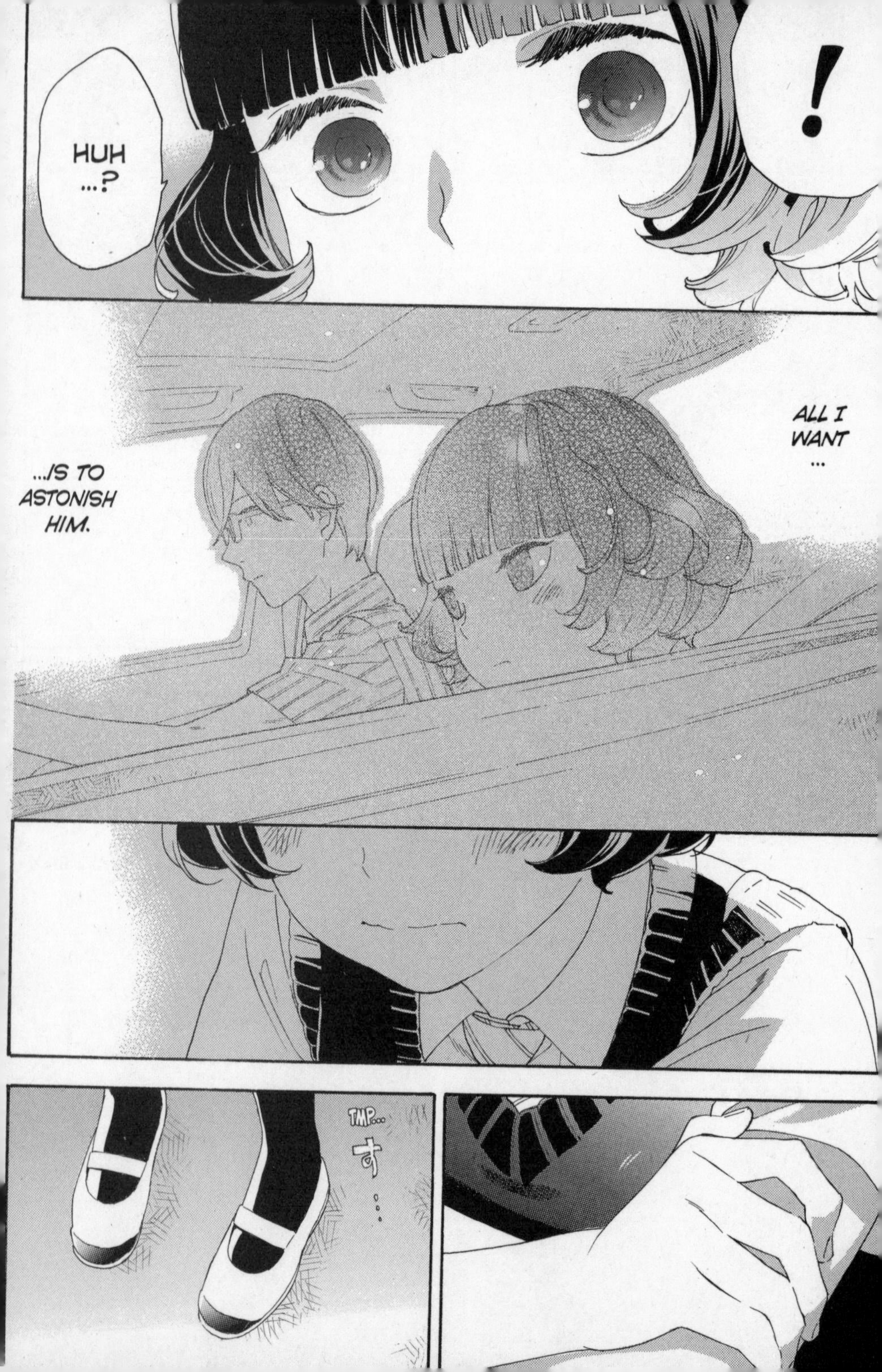
!
HUH ...?
ALL I WANT ...
...IS TO ASTONISH HIM.
TMP...
す...

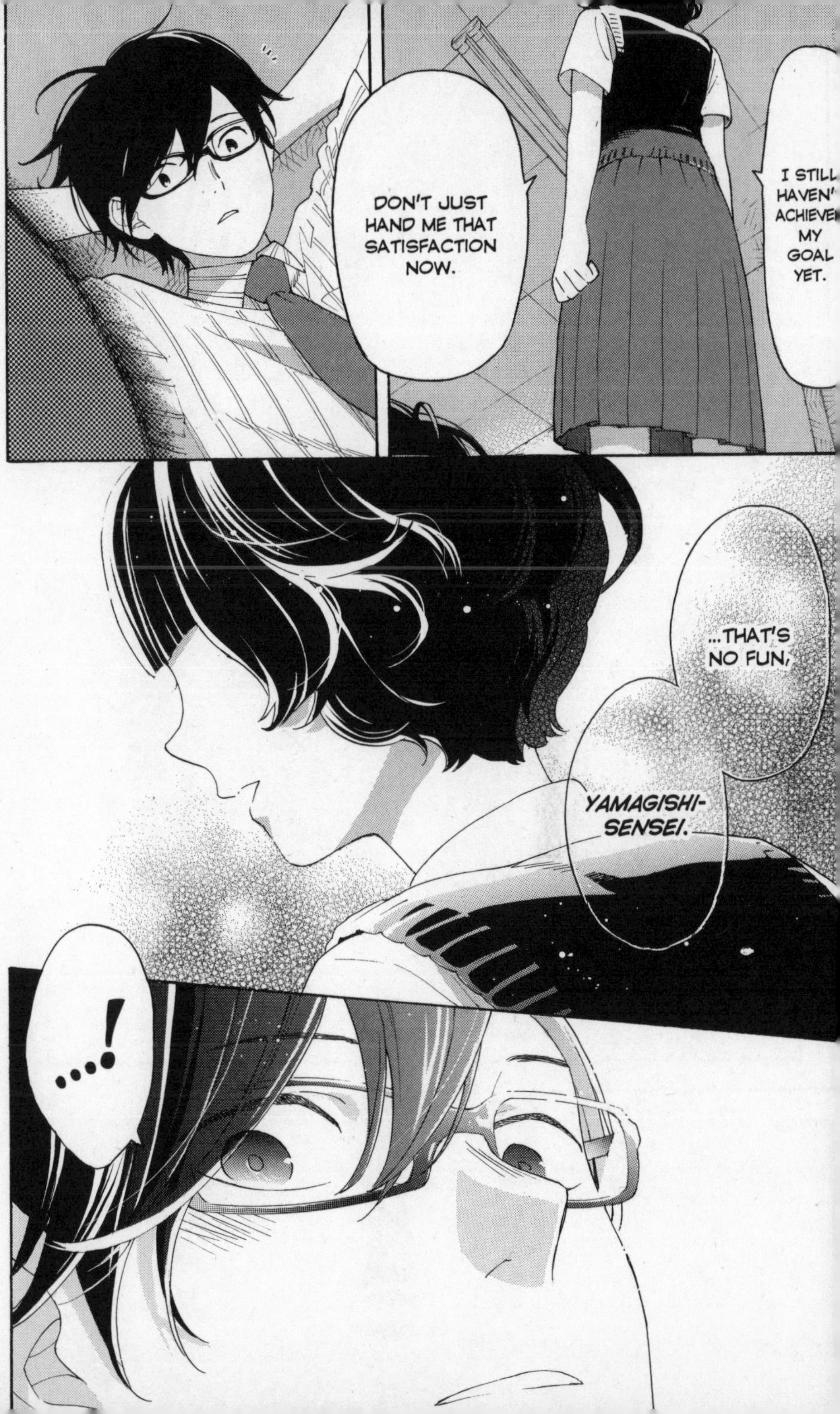
I STILL HAVEN' ACHIEVE MY GOAL YET.
DON'T JUST HAND ME THAT SATISFACTION NOW.
...THAT'S NO FUN,
YAMAGISHI-SENSEI.
...!

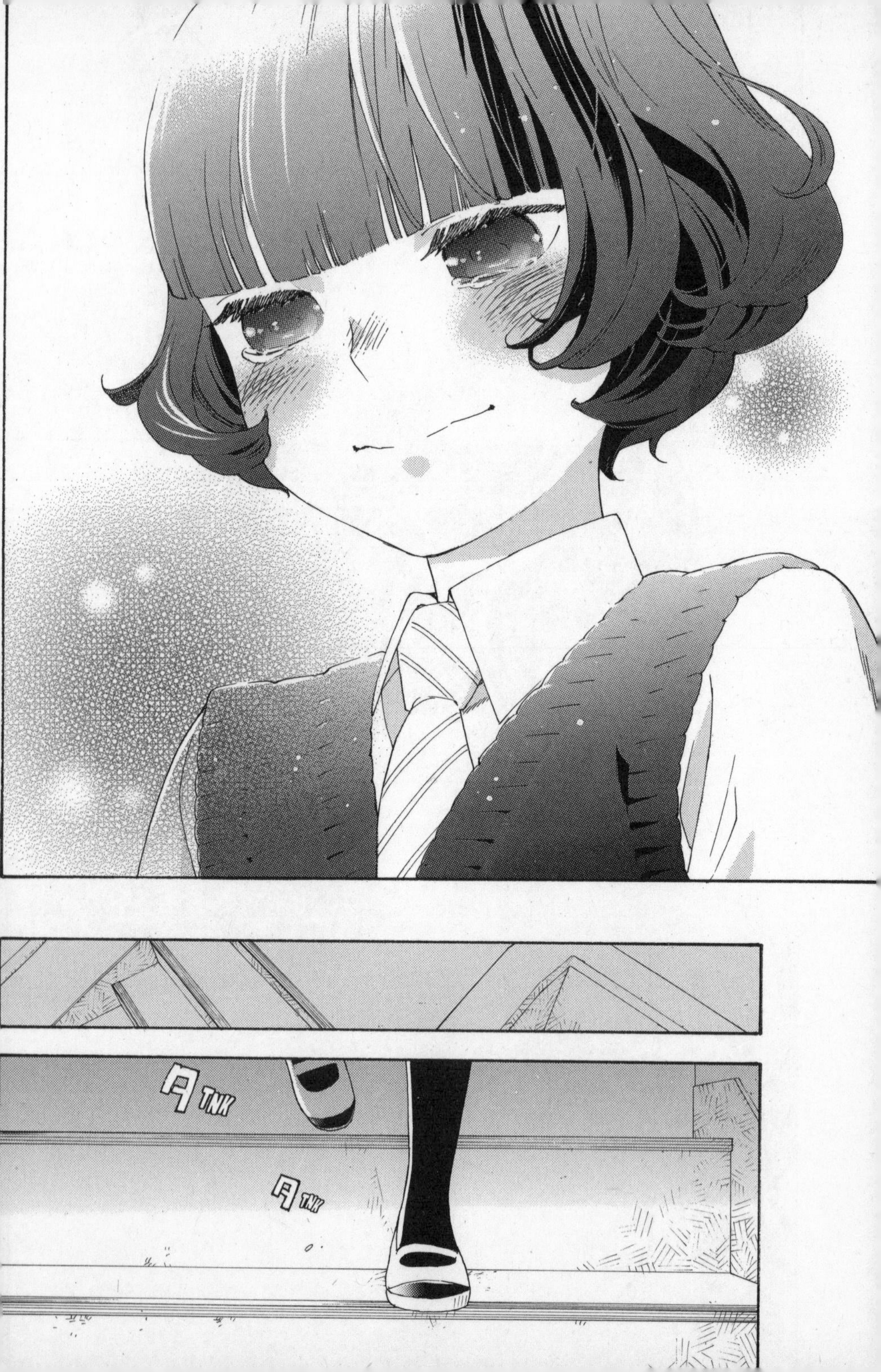
タ TNK
タ TNK

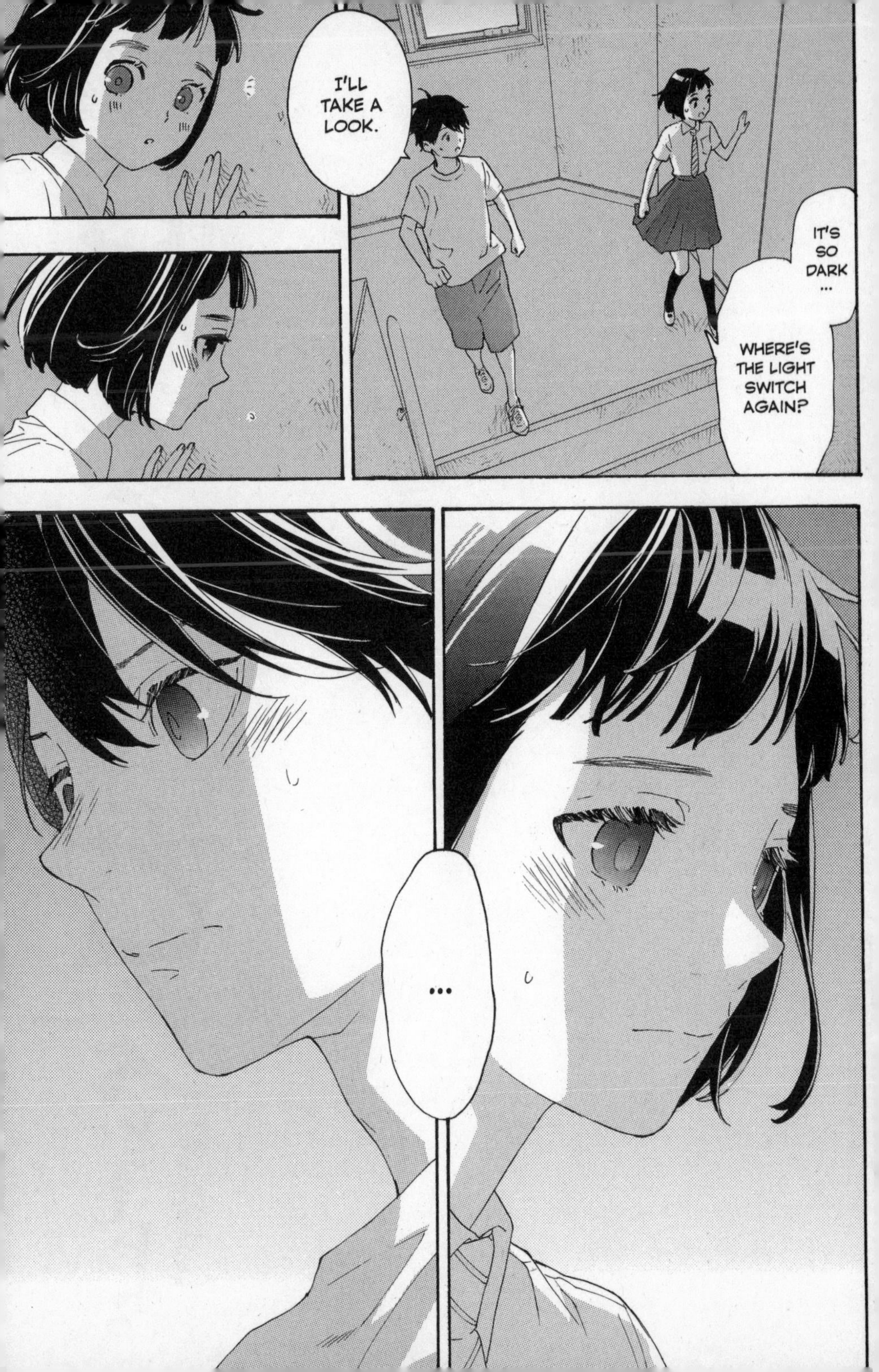
IT'S SO DARK ...
WHERE'S THE LIGHT SWITCH AGAIN?
I'LL TAKE A LOOK.
...

O Maidens in your Savage Season

荒ぶる季節の乙女どもよ。

【あらぶるきせつの
おとめどもよ】

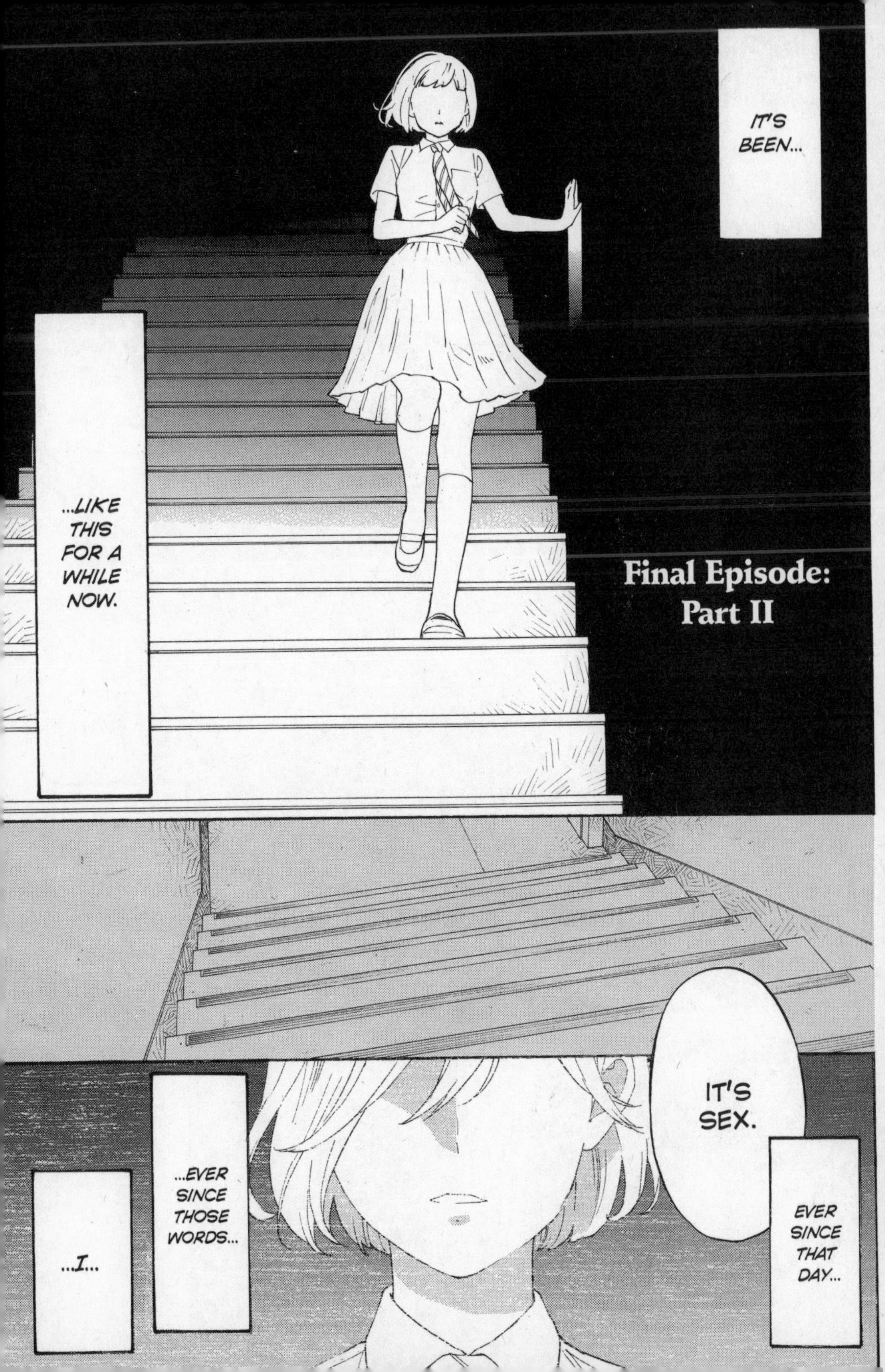
IT'S BEEN...
Final Episode: Part II
...LIKE THIS FOR A WHILE NOW.
IT'S SEX.
EVER SINCE THAT DAY...
...EVER SINCE THOSE WORDS...
...I...

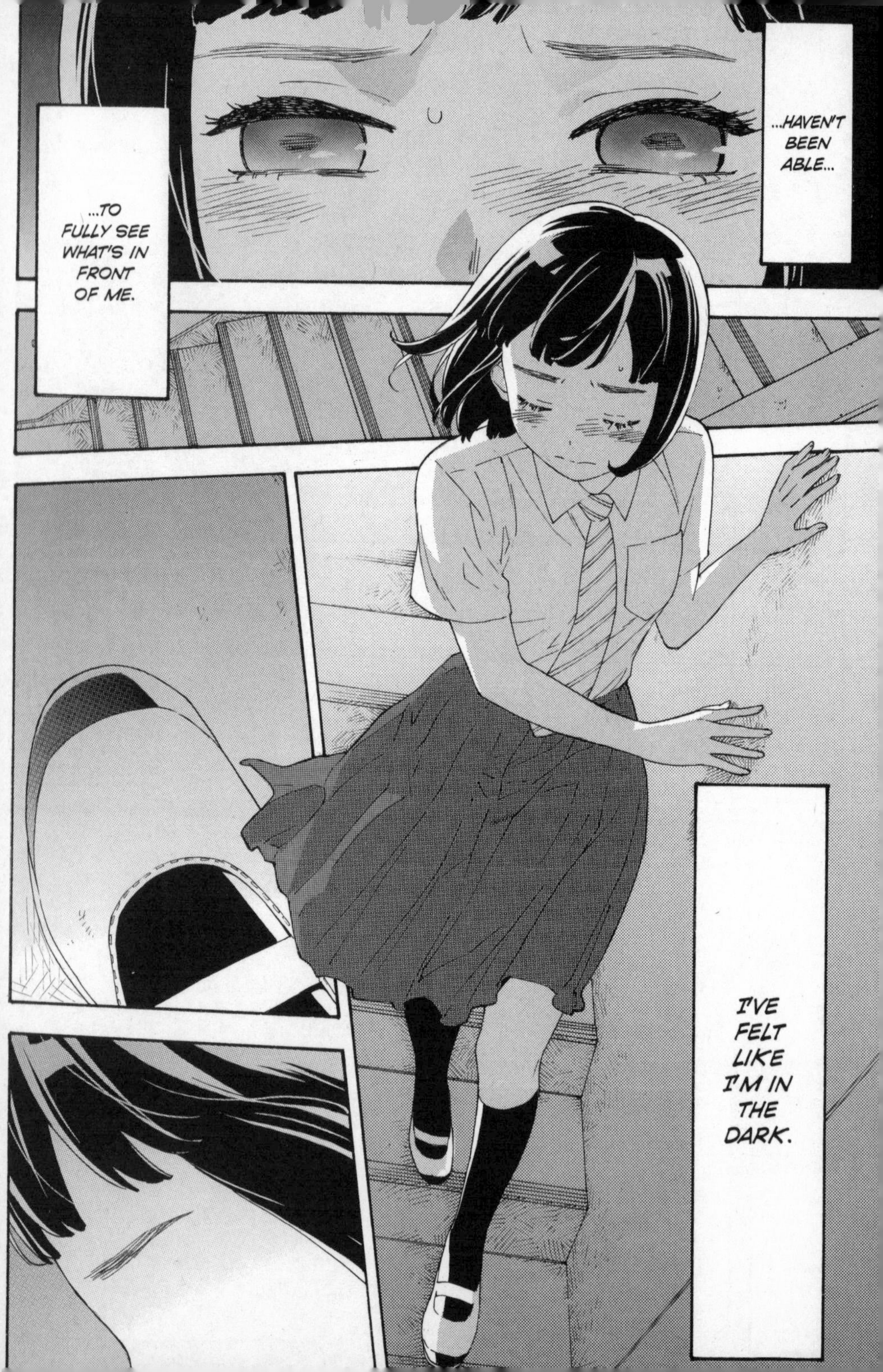
...HAVEN'T BEEN ABLE...
...TO FULLY SEE WHAT'S IN FRONT OF ME.
I'VE FELT LIKE I'M IN THE DARK.

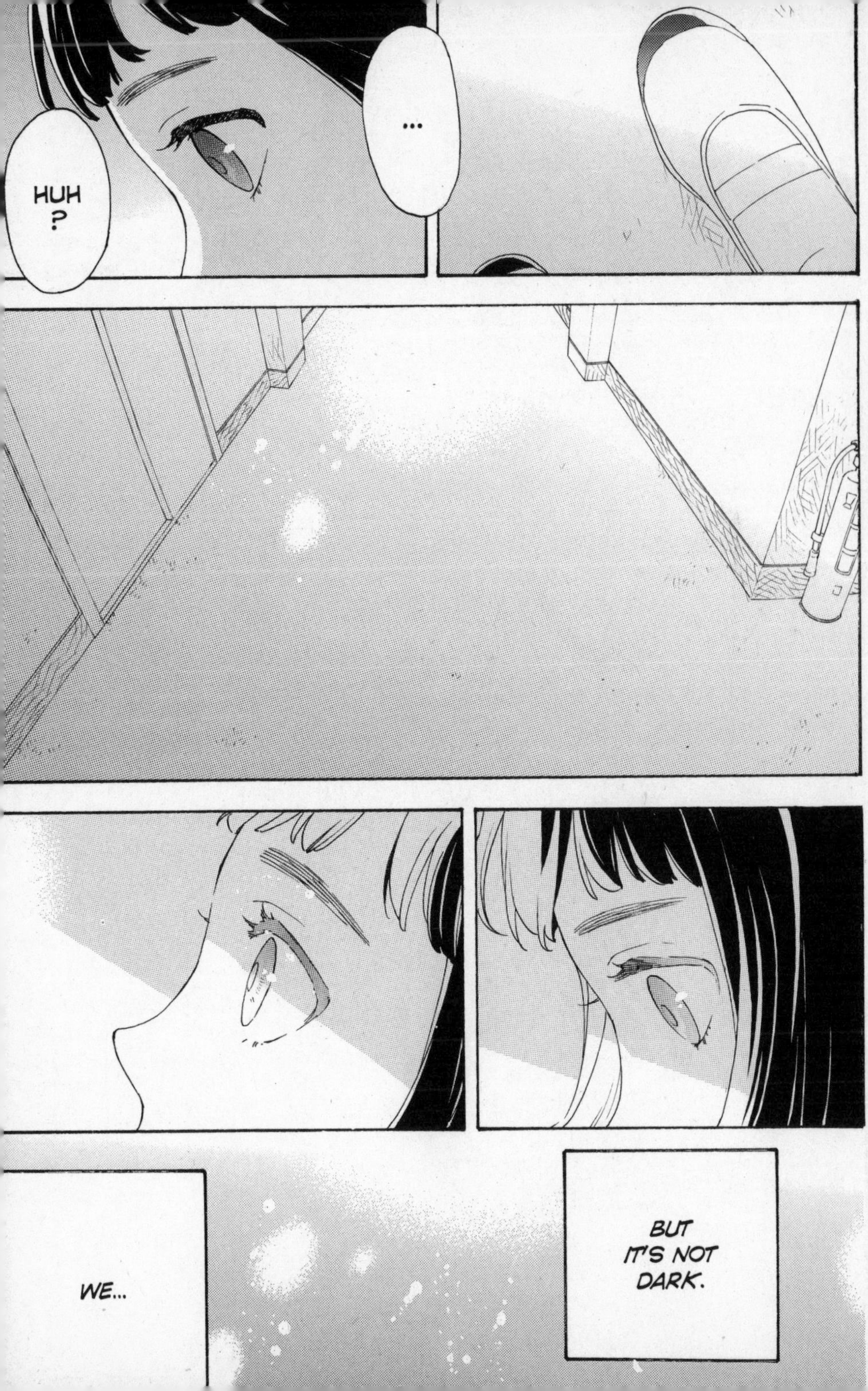
...
HUH?
BUT IT'S NOT DARK.
WE...

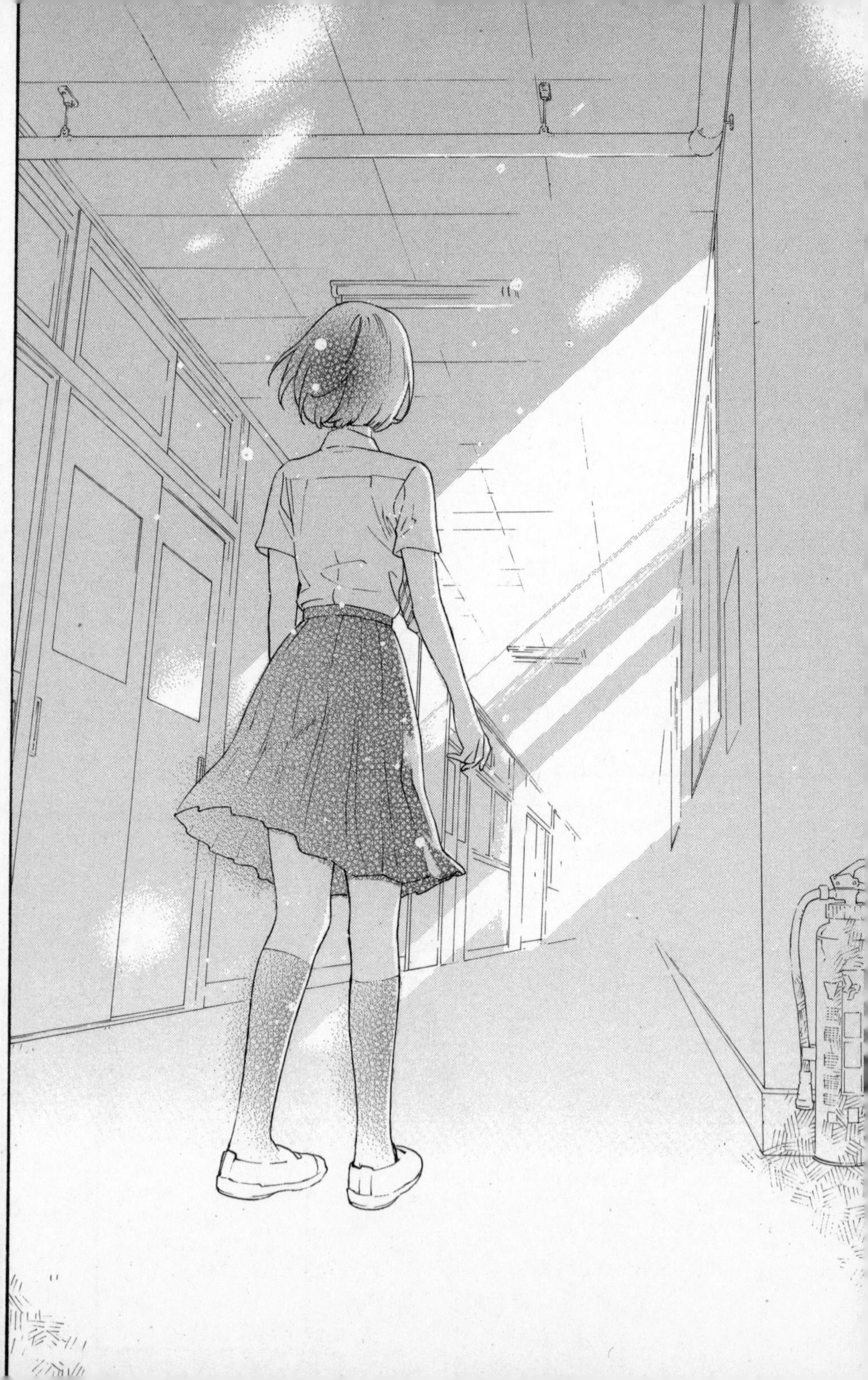

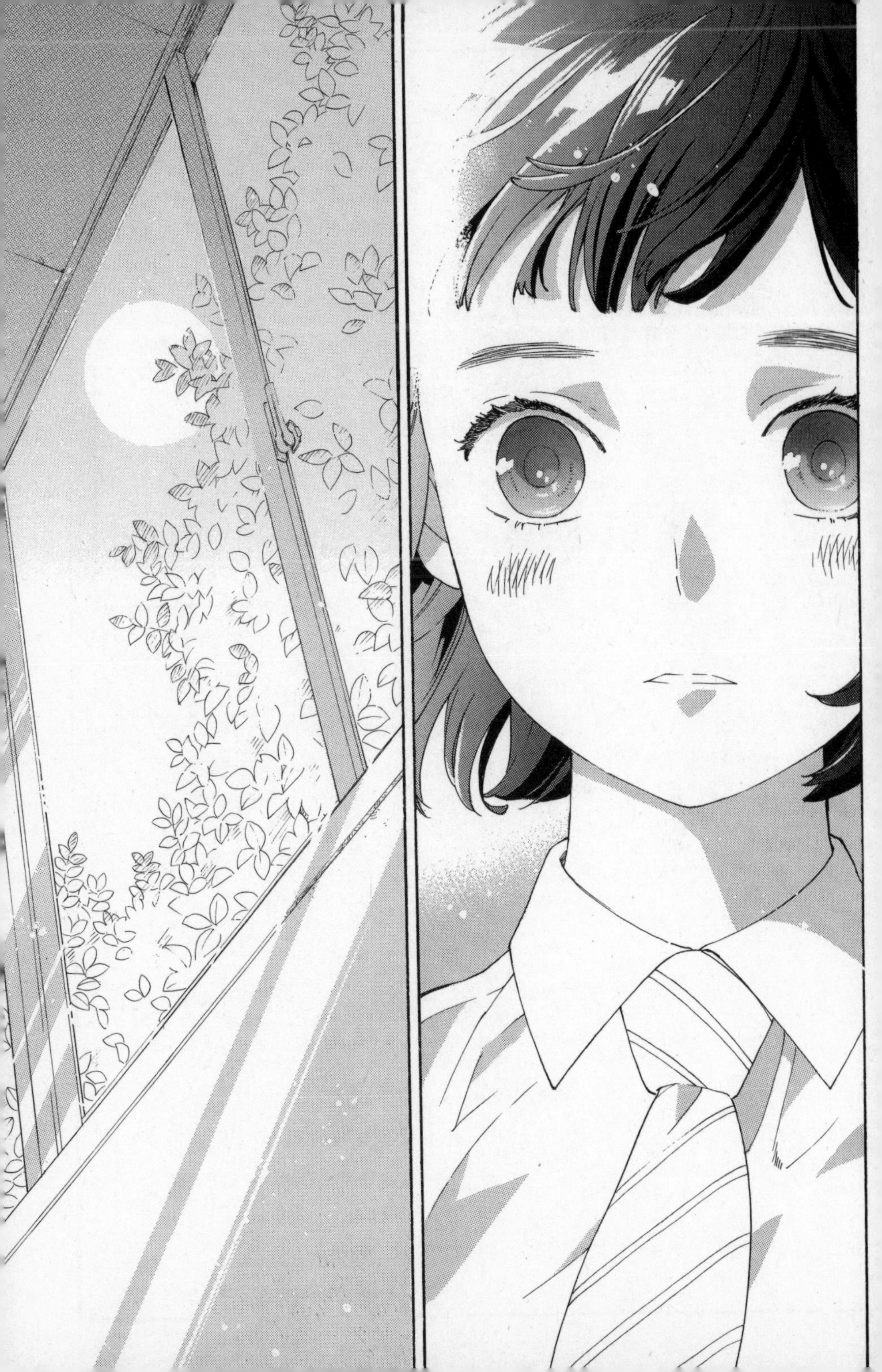

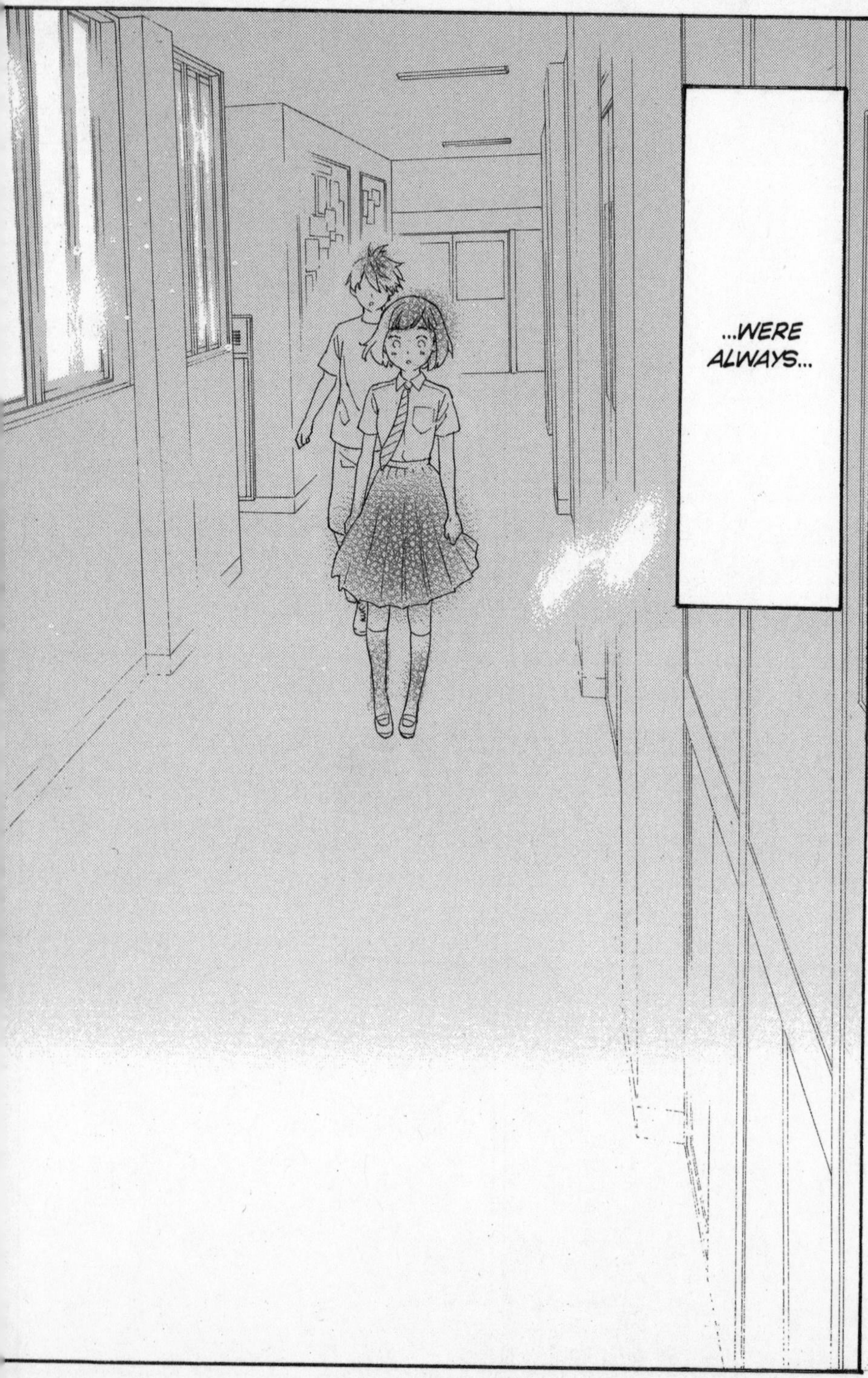
...WERE ALWAYS...

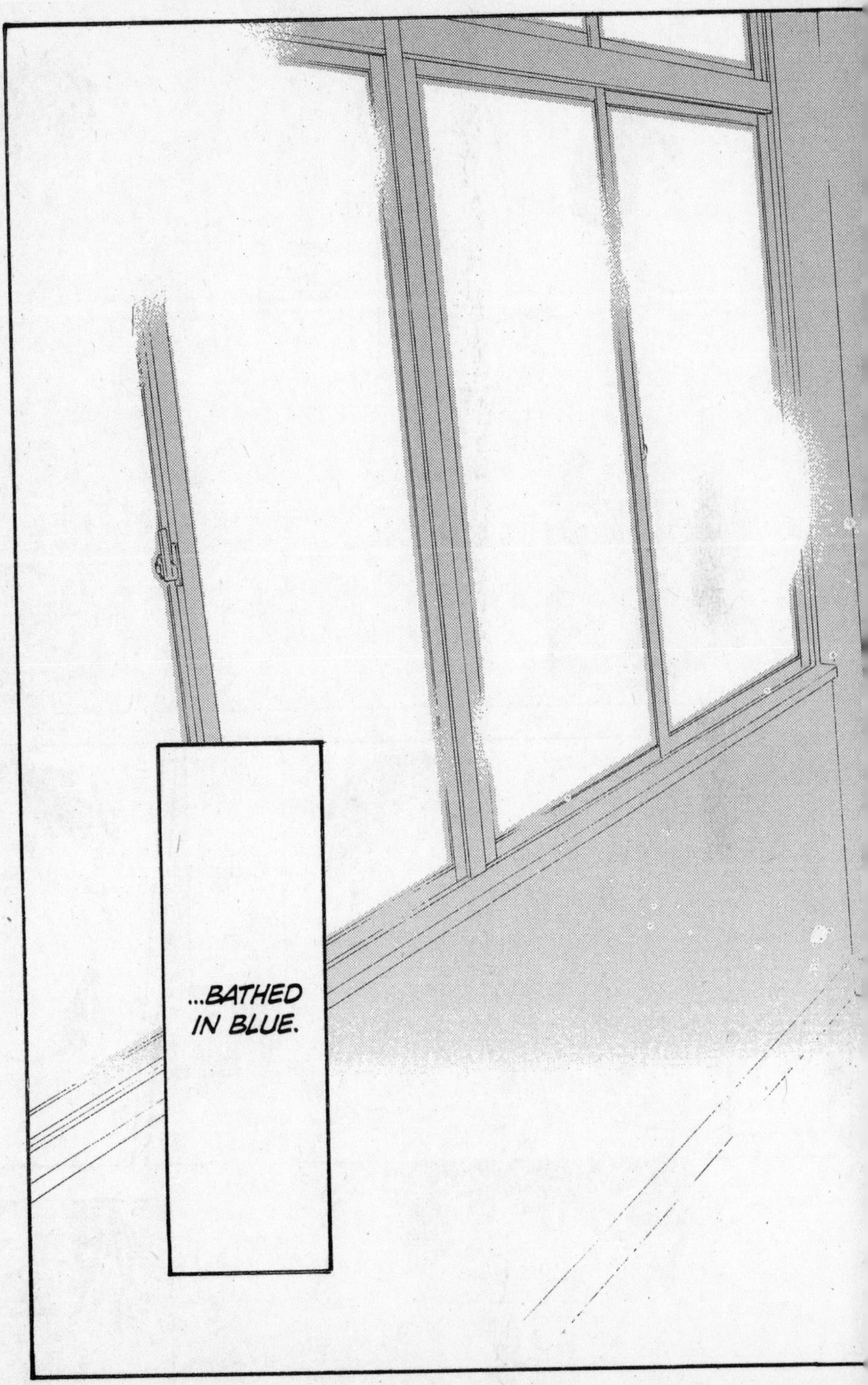
...BATHED IN BLUE.

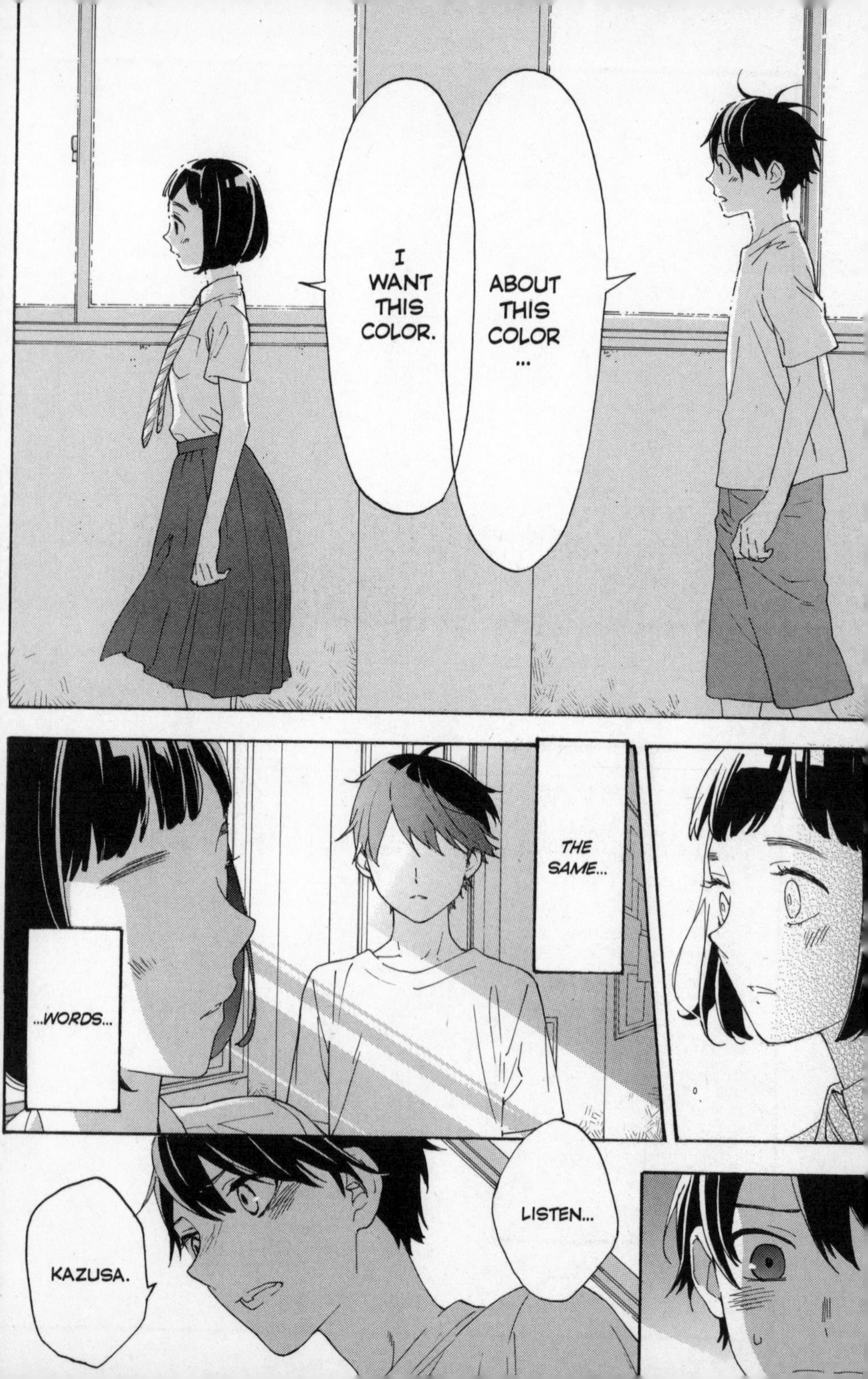
ABOUT THIS COLOR ...
I WANT THIS COLOR.
THE SAME...
...WORDS...
LISTEN...
KAZUSA.

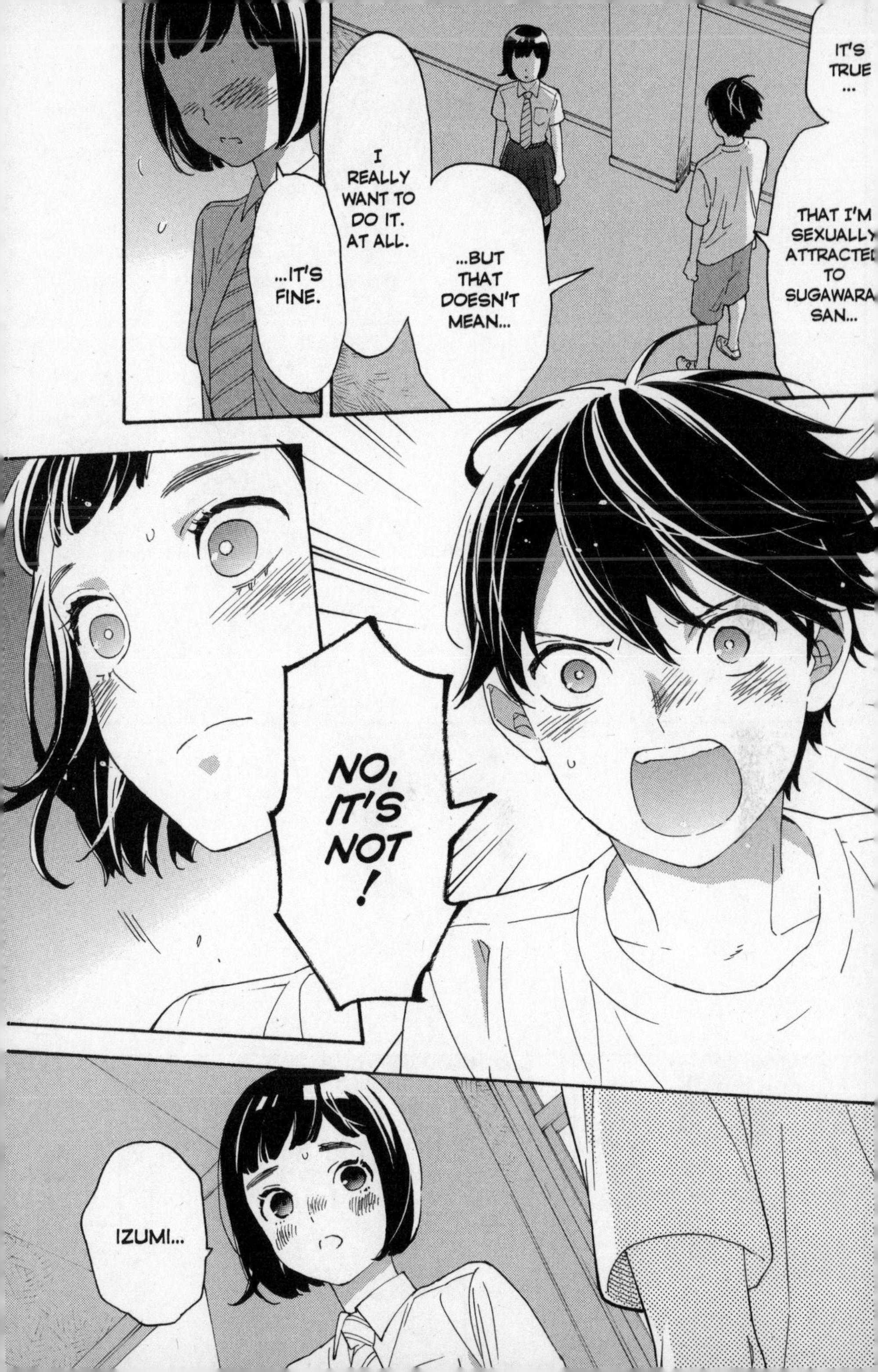
IT'S TRUE ...
THAT I'M SEXUALLY ATTRACTED TO SUGAWARA SAN...
...BUT THAT DOESN'T MEAN...
I REALLY WANT TO DO IT. AT ALL.
...IT'S FINE.
NO, IT'S NOT!
IZUMI...

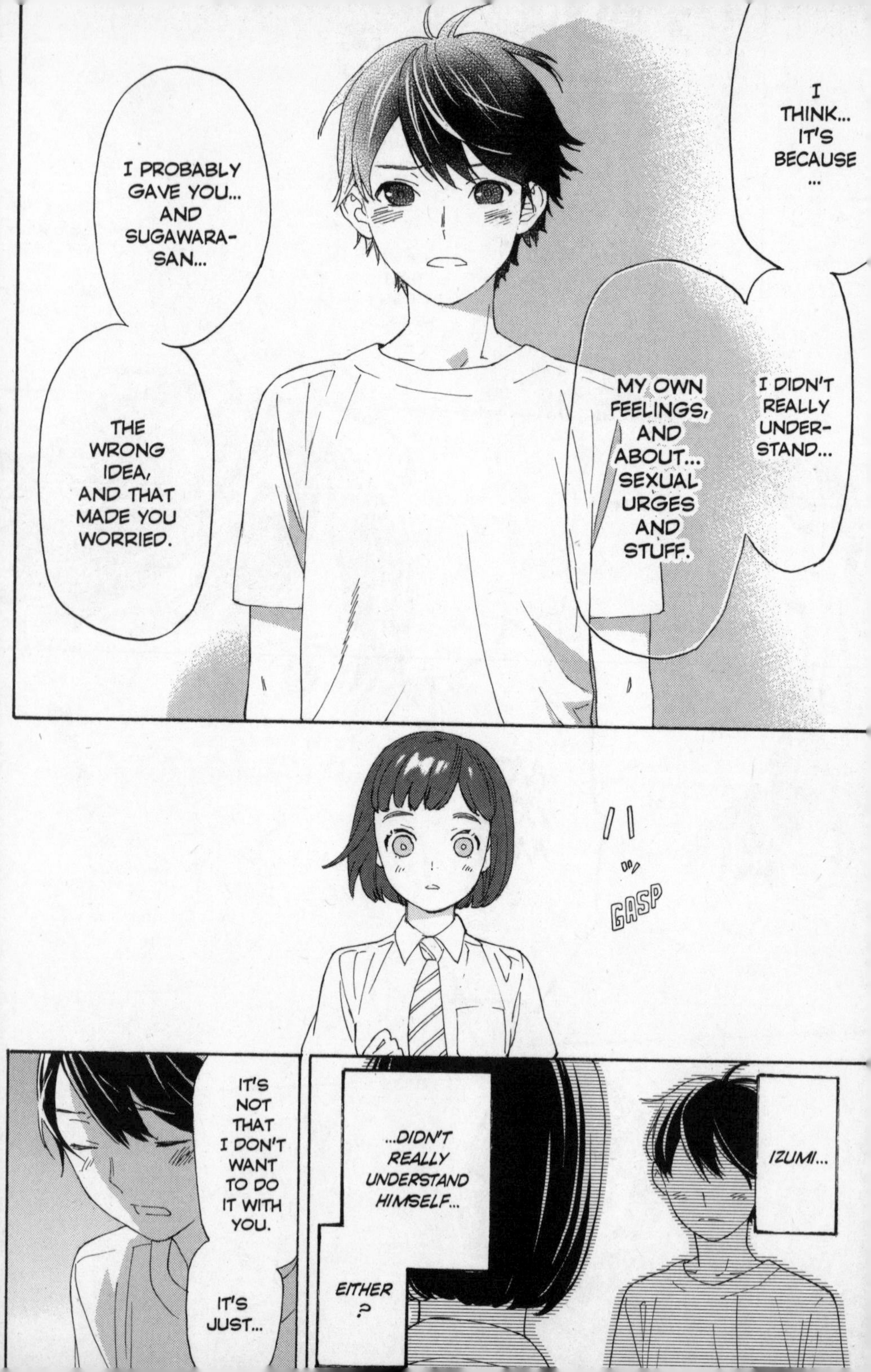
I THINK... IT'S BECAUSE ...
I DIDN'T REALLY UNDER-STAND...
MY OWN FEELINGS, AND ABOUT... SEXUAL URGES AND STUFF.
I PROBABLY GAVE YOU... AND SUGAWARA-SAN...
THE WRONG IDEA, AND THAT MADE YOU WORRIED.
GASP
IZUMI...
...DIDN'T REALLY UNDERSTAND HIMSELF...
EITHER ?
IT'S NOT THAT I DON'T WANT TO DO IT WITH YOU.
IT'S JUST...

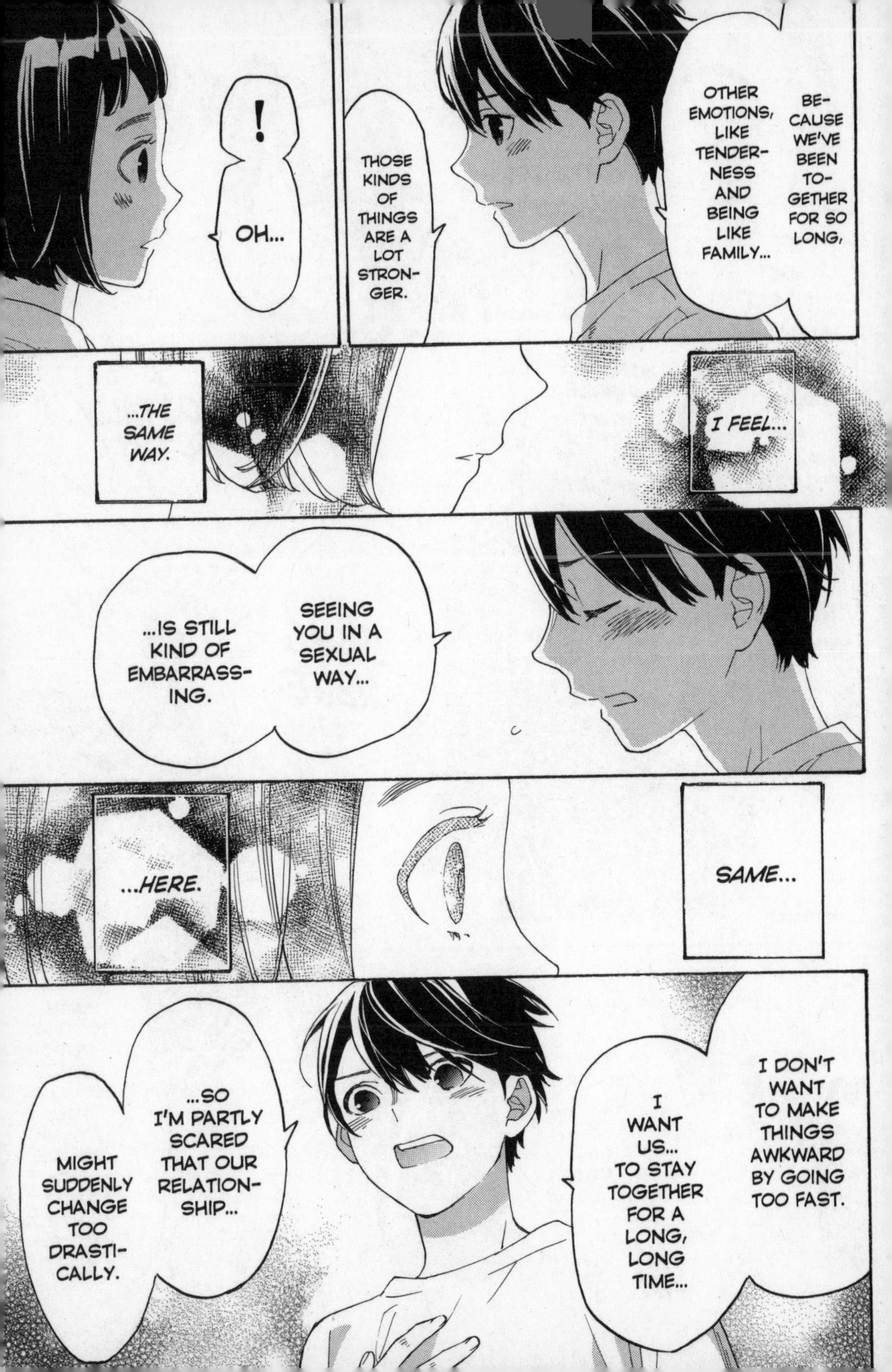
BECAUSE WE'VE BEEN TOGETHER FOR SO LONG,
OTHER EMOTIONS, LIKE TENDERNESS AND BEING LIKE FAMILY...
THOSE KINDS OF THINGS ARE A LOT STRONGER.
! OH...
I FEEL...
...THE SAME WAY.
SEEING YOU IN A SEXUAL WAY...
...IS STILL KIND OF EMBARRASSING.
SAME...
...HERE.
I DON'T WANT TO MAKE THINGS AWKWARD BY GOING TOO FAST.
I WANT US... TO STAY TOGETHER FOR A LONG, LONG TIME...
...SO I'M PARTLY SCARED THAT OUR RELATIONSHIP...
MIGHT SUDDENLY CHANGE TOO DRASTICALLY.

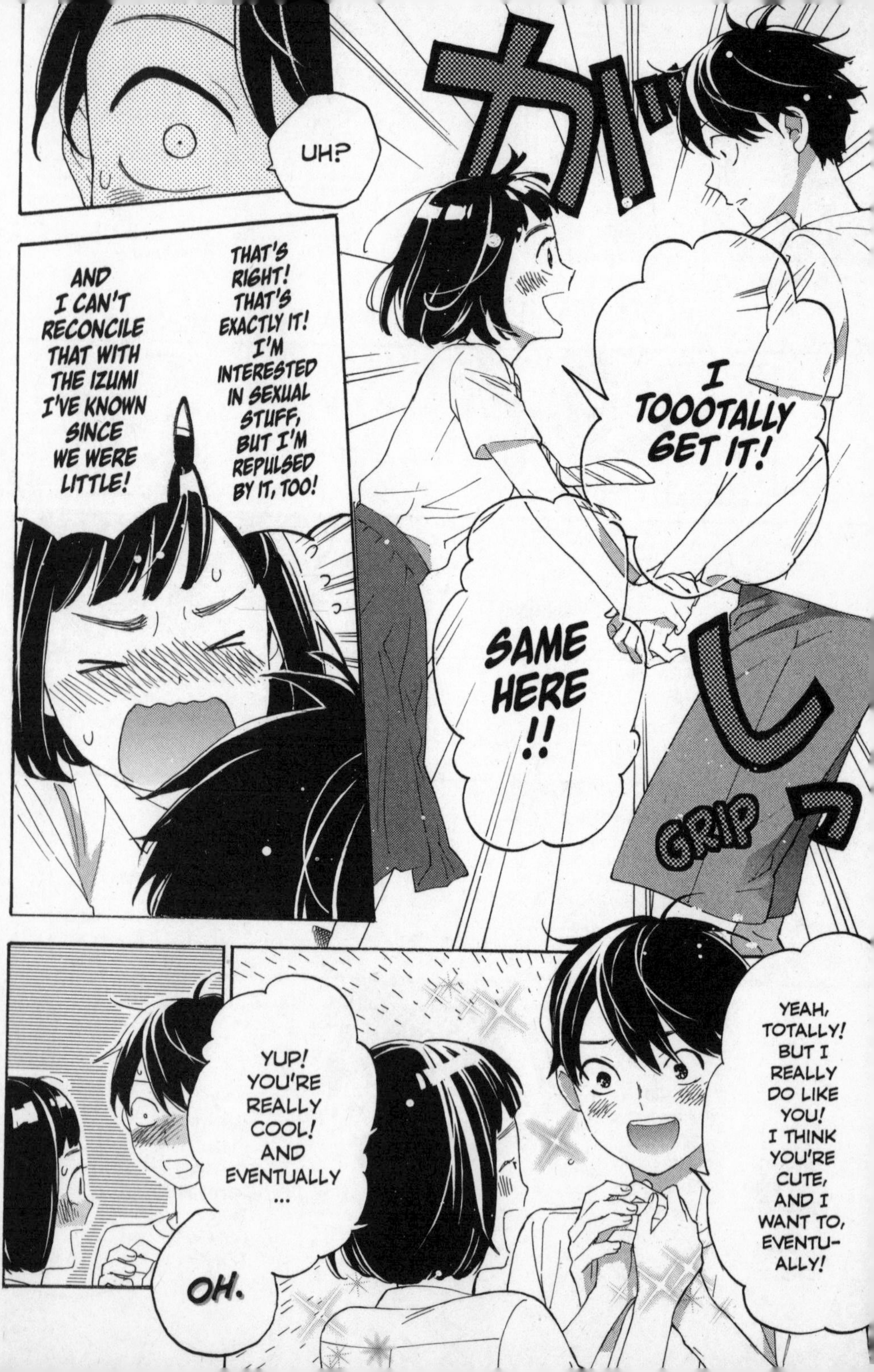
I TOOOTALLY GET IT!
SAME HERE!!
GRIP
UH?
THAT'S RIGHT! THAT'S EXACTLY IT! I'M INTERESTED IN SEXUAL STUFF, BUT I'M REPULSED BY IT, TOO!
AND I CAN'T RECONCILE THAT WITH THE IZUMI I'VE KNOWN SINCE WE WERE LITTLE!
YEAH, TOTALLY! BUT I REALLY DO LIKE YOU! I THINK YOU'RE CUTE, AND I WANT TO, EVENTU-ALLY!
YUP! YOU'RE REALLY COOL! AND EVENTUALLY ...
OH.

...I...

I'M SORRY.

NO, IT'S ME! SORRY...

I WANT TO APOLOGIZE... TO SUGAWARA-SAN, TOO.

...OH.

SUGA-WARA-SAN IS STRANGE,

BUT SHE'S A REALLY NICE PERSON.

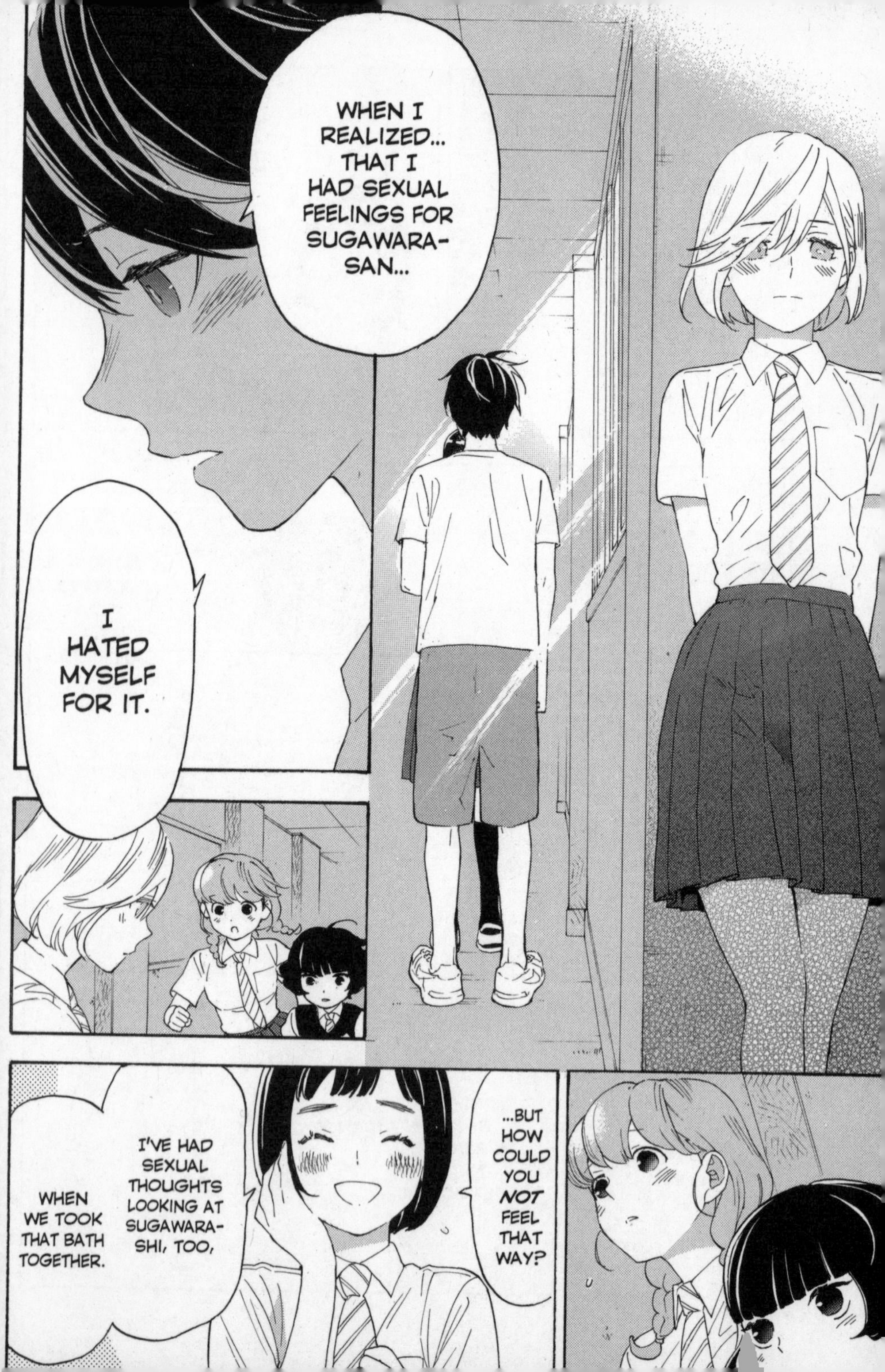
WHEN I REALIZED... THAT I HAD SEXUAL FEELINGS FOR SUGAWARA-SAN...
I HATED MYSELF FOR IT.
...BUT HOW COULD YOU *NOT* FEEL THAT WAY?
I'VE HAD SEXUAL THOUGHTS LOOKING AT SUGAWARA-SHI, TOO,
WHEN WE TOOK THAT BATH TOGETHER.

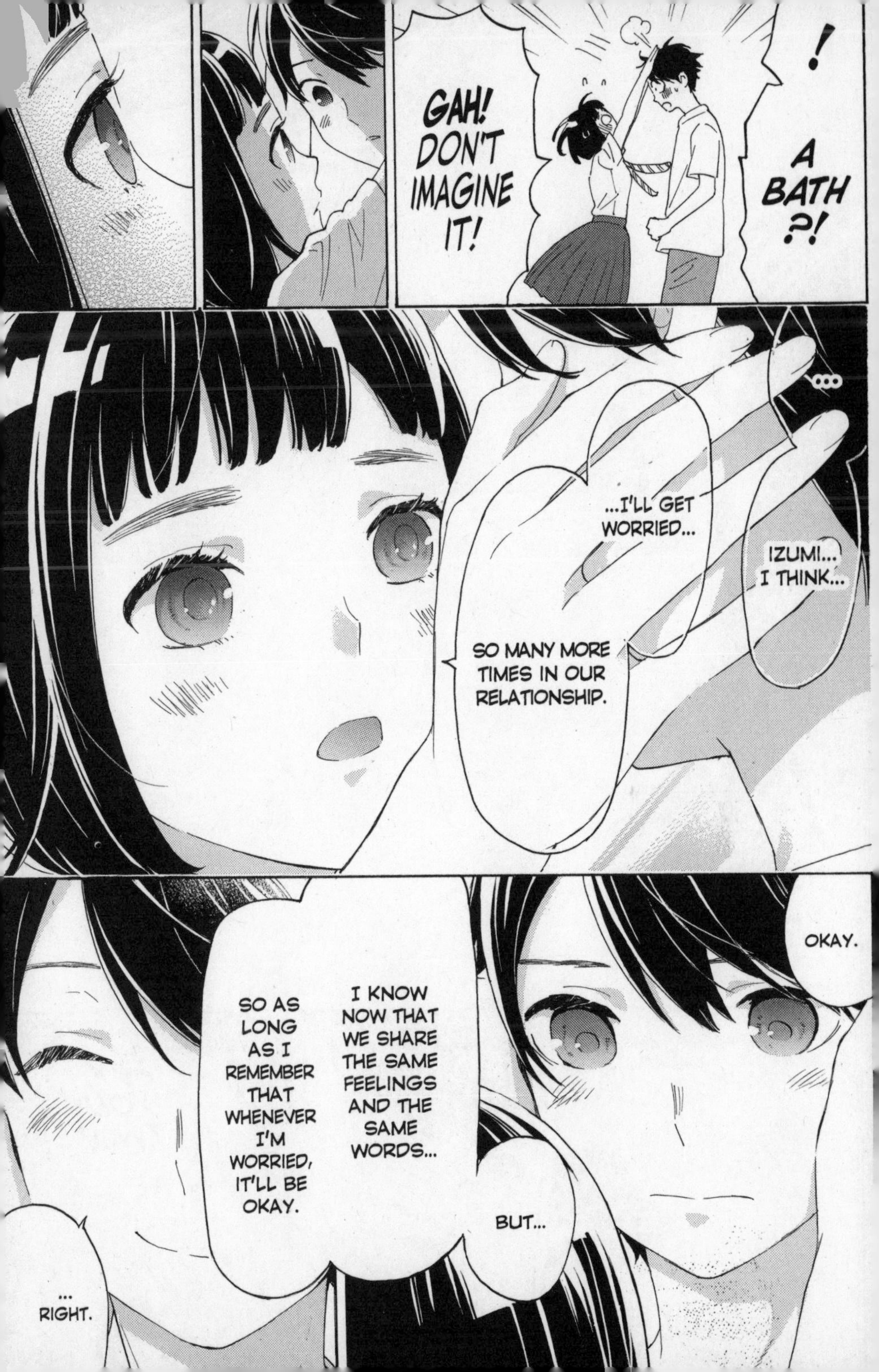
!
A BATH ?!
GAH! DON'T IMAGINE IT!
...
IZUMI... I THINK...
...I'LL GET WORRIED...
SO MANY MORE TIMES IN OUR RELATIONSHIP.
OKAY.
BUT...
I KNOW NOW THAT WE SHARE THE SAME FEELINGS AND THE SAME WORDS...
SO AS LONG AS I REMEMBER THAT WHENEVER I'M WORRIED, IT'LL BE OKAY.
...RIGHT.

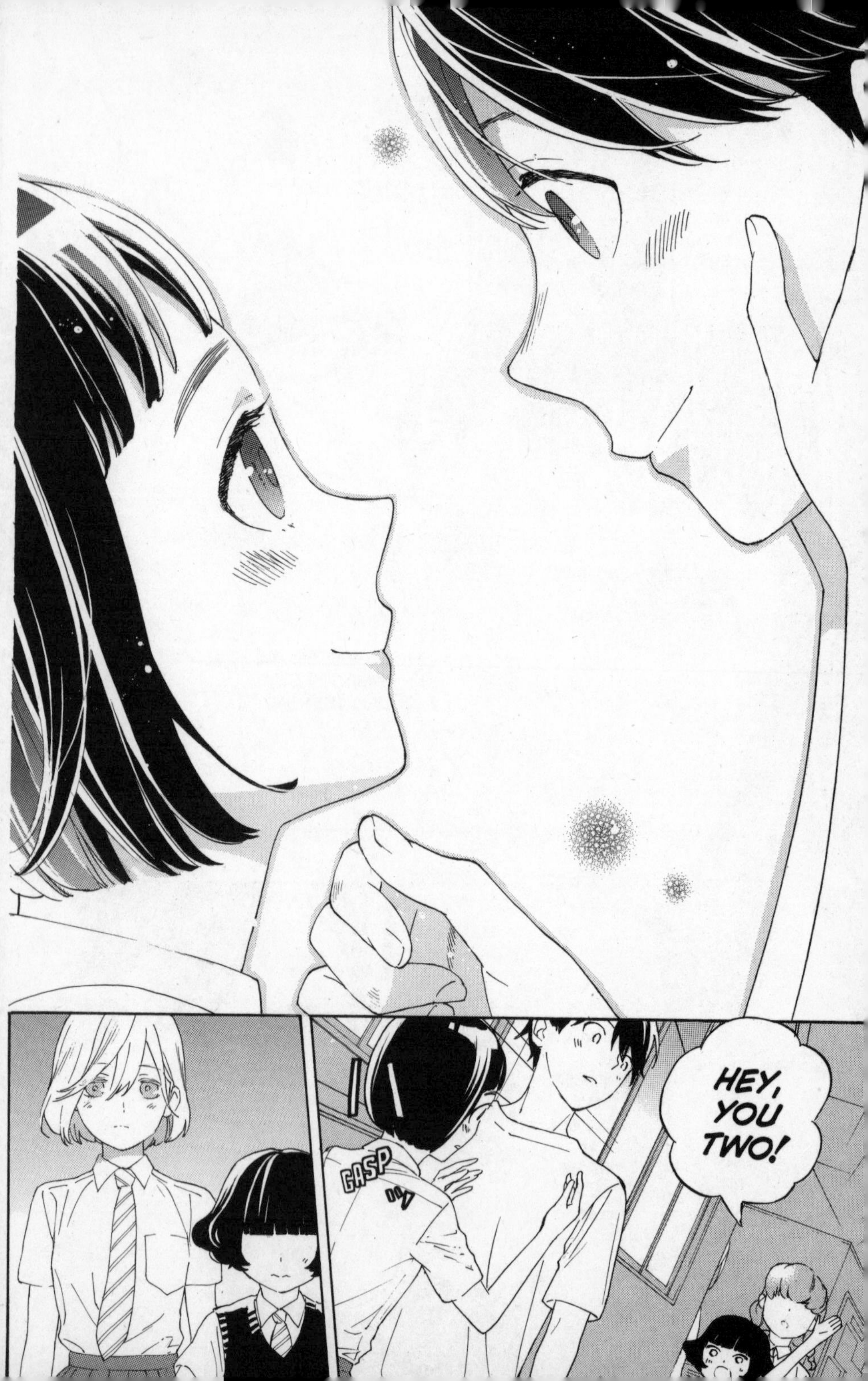
HEY, YOU TWO!
GASP

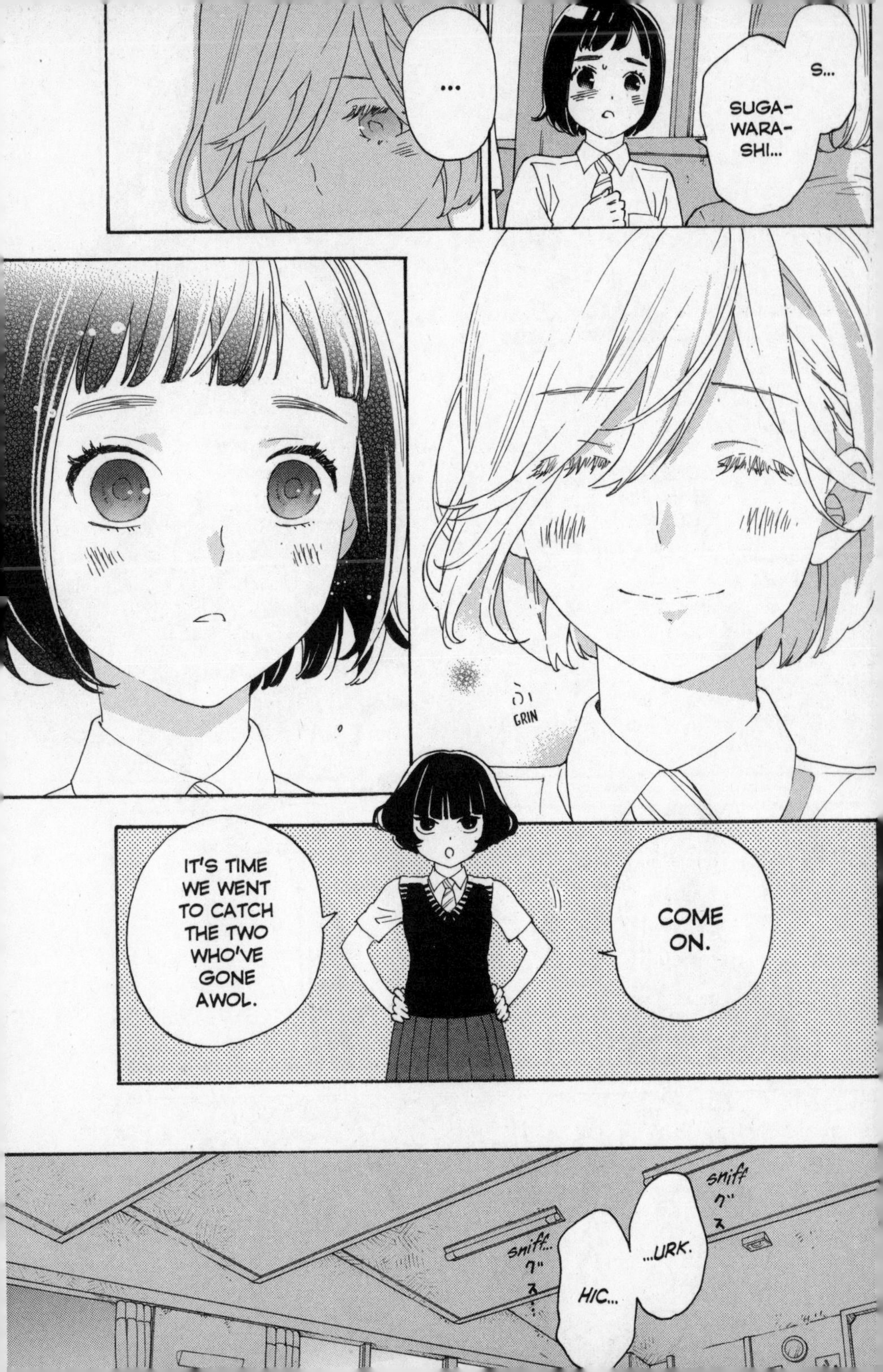

S... SUGAWARA-SHI...
...
ふ
GRIN
COME ON.
IT'S TIME WE WENT TO CATCH THE TWO WHO'VE GONE AWOL.
sniff
グス
...URK.
sniff...
グス...
HIC...

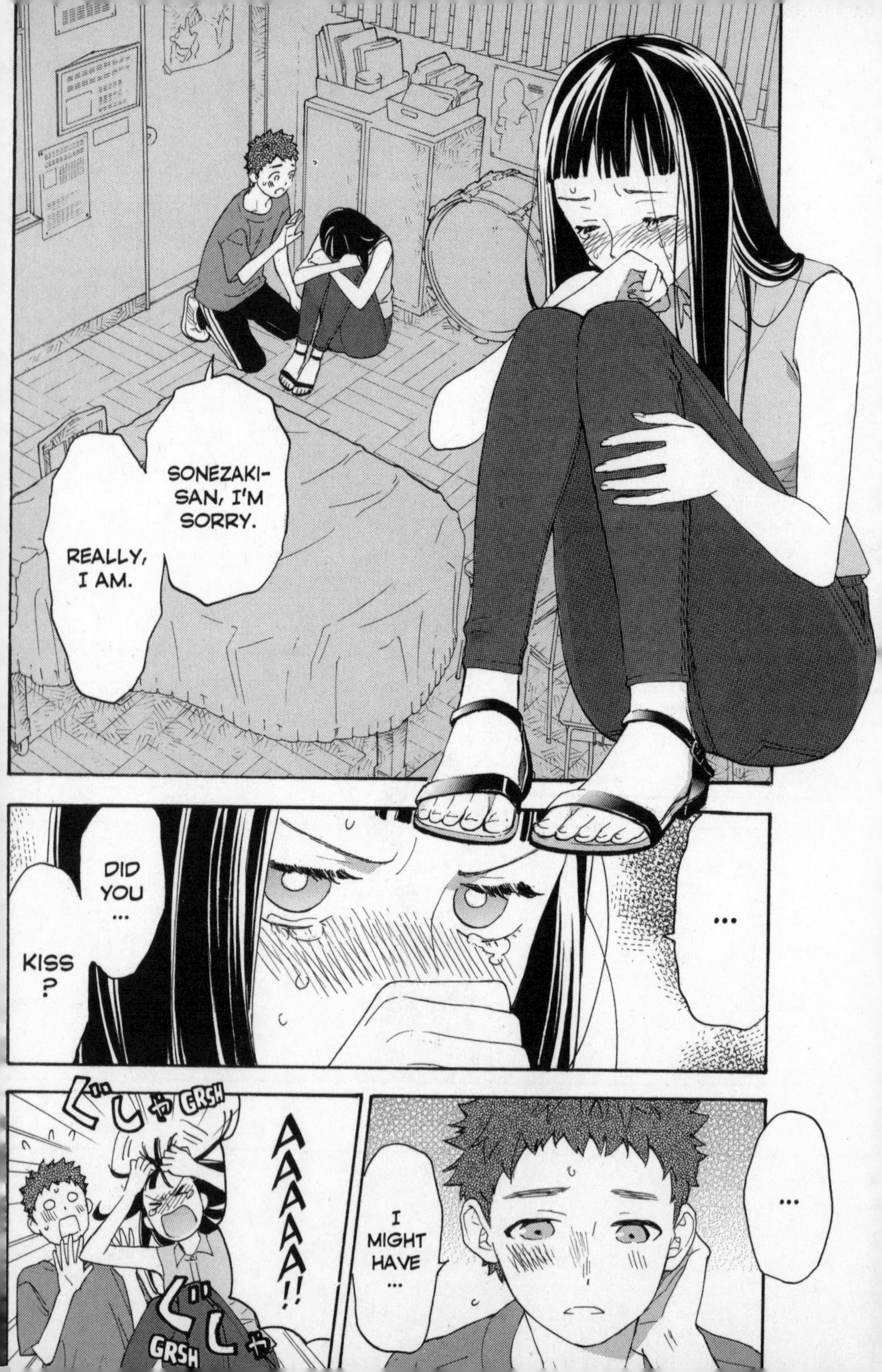
SONEZAKI-SAN, I'M SORRY.
REALLY, I AM.
DID YOU ... KISS?
...
...
I MIGHT HAVE ...
ぐしゃ GRSH
AAAAA!!
ぐしゃ GRSH

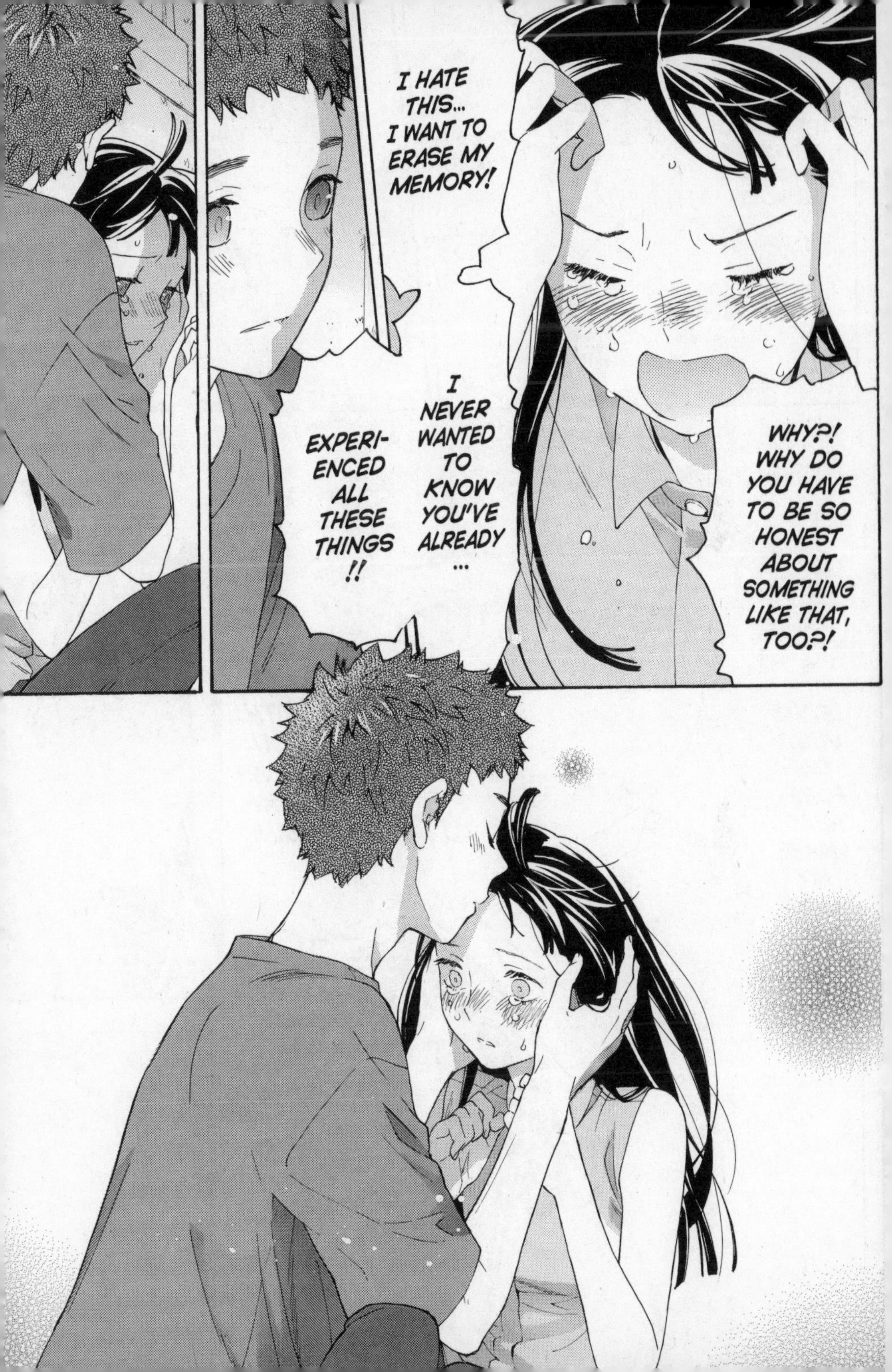
WHY?! WHY DO YOU HAVE TO BE SO HONEST ABOUT SOMETHING LIKE THAT, TOO?!
I HATE THIS... I WANT TO ERASE MY MEMORY!
I NEVER WANTED TO KNOW YOU'VE ALREADY...
EXPERI- ENCED ALL THESE THINGS!!

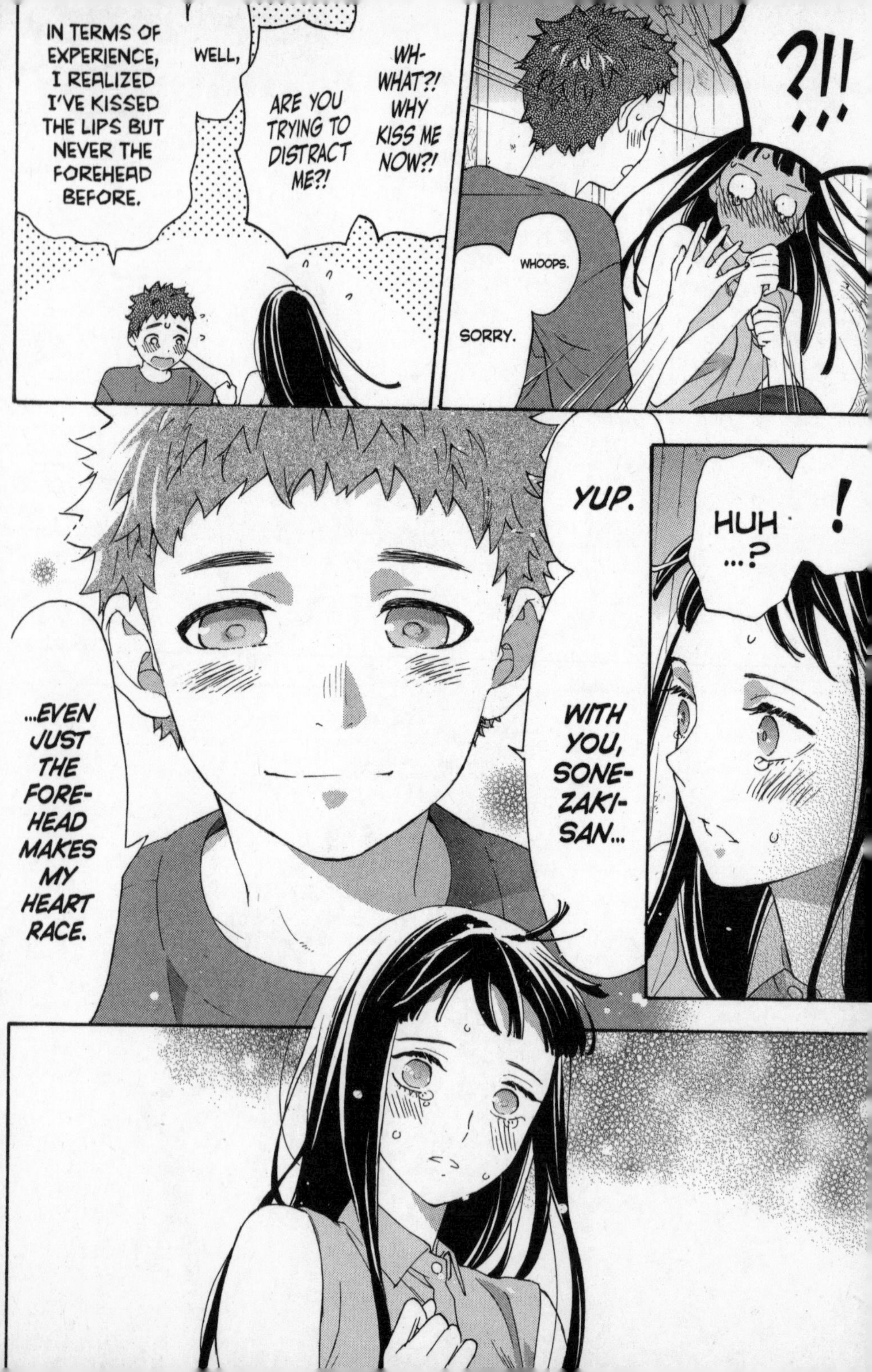
?!!
WHOOPS.
SORRY.
WH- WHAT?! WHY KISS ME NOW?!
ARE YOU TRYING TO DISTRACT ME?!
WELL,
IN TERMS OF EXPERIENCE, I REALIZED I'VE KISSED THE LIPS BUT NEVER THE FOREHEAD BEFORE.
HUH ...?
!
YUP.
WITH YOU, SONE-ZAKI-SAN...
...EVEN JUST THE FORE-HEAD MAKES MY HEART RACE.

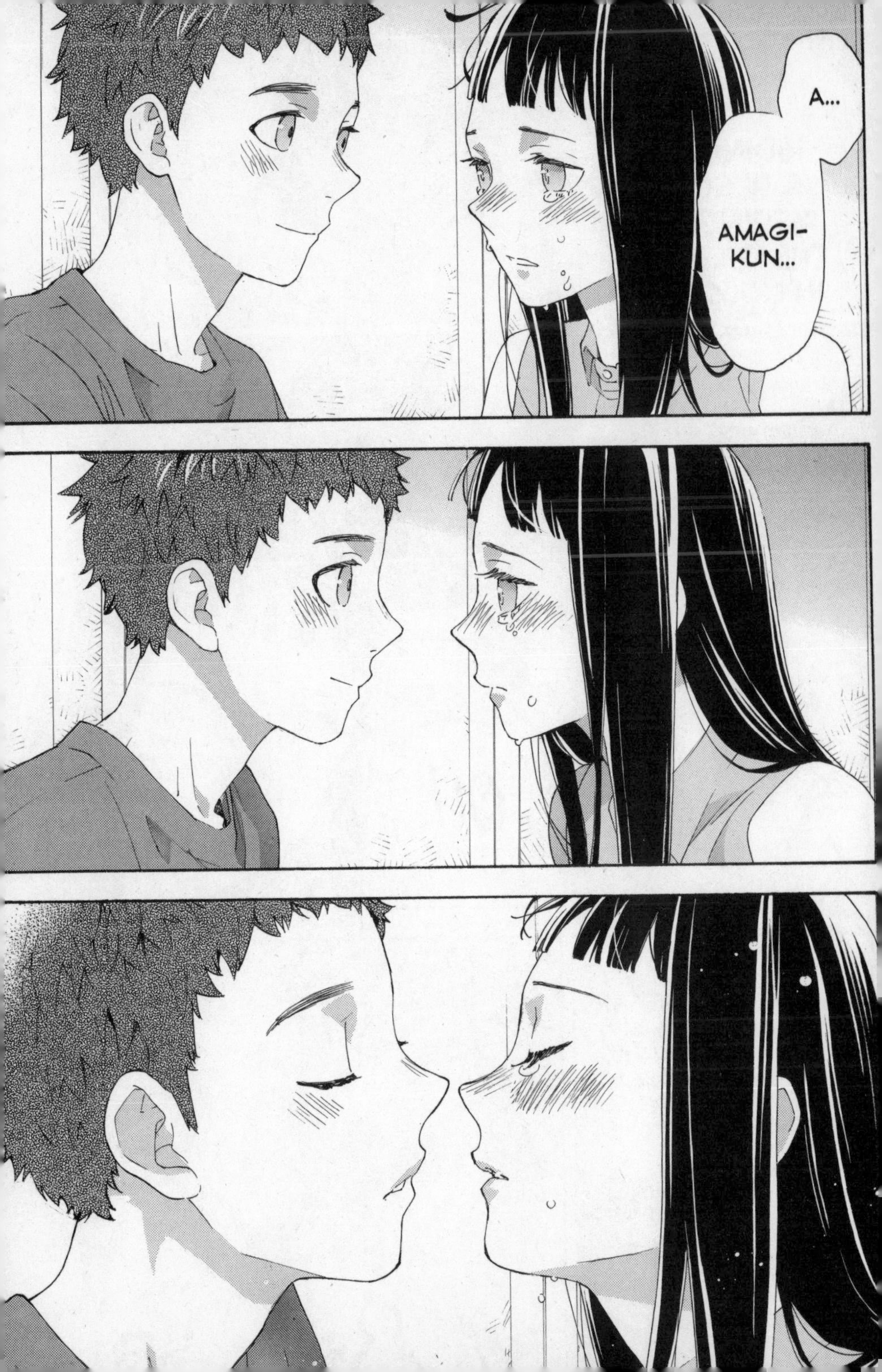
A...
AMAGI-KUN...

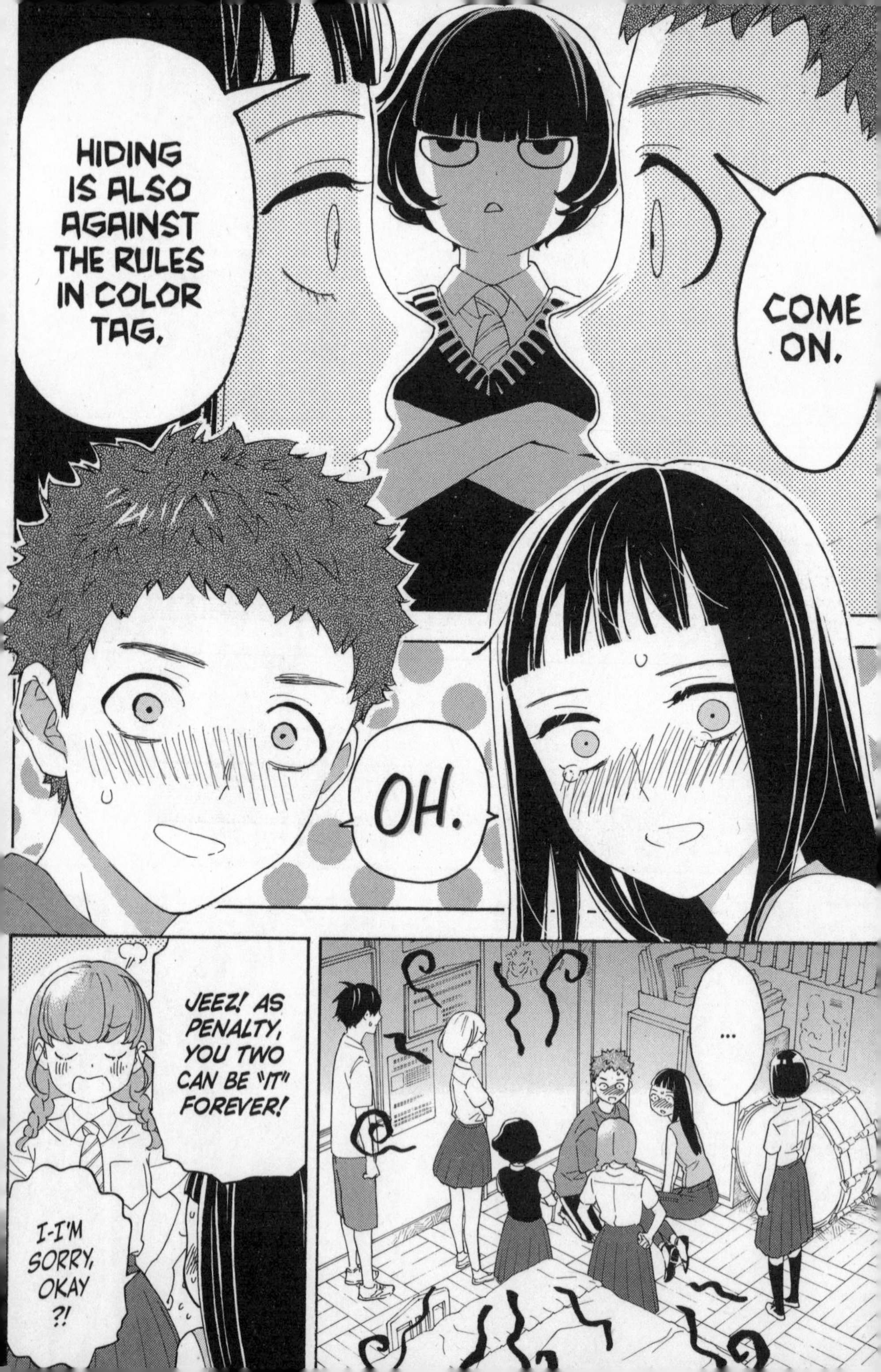
COME ON.
HIDING IS ALSO AGAINST THE RULES IN COLOR TAG.
OH.
...
JEEZ! AS PENALTY, YOU TWO CAN BE "IT" FOREVER!
I-I'M SORRY, OKAY?!

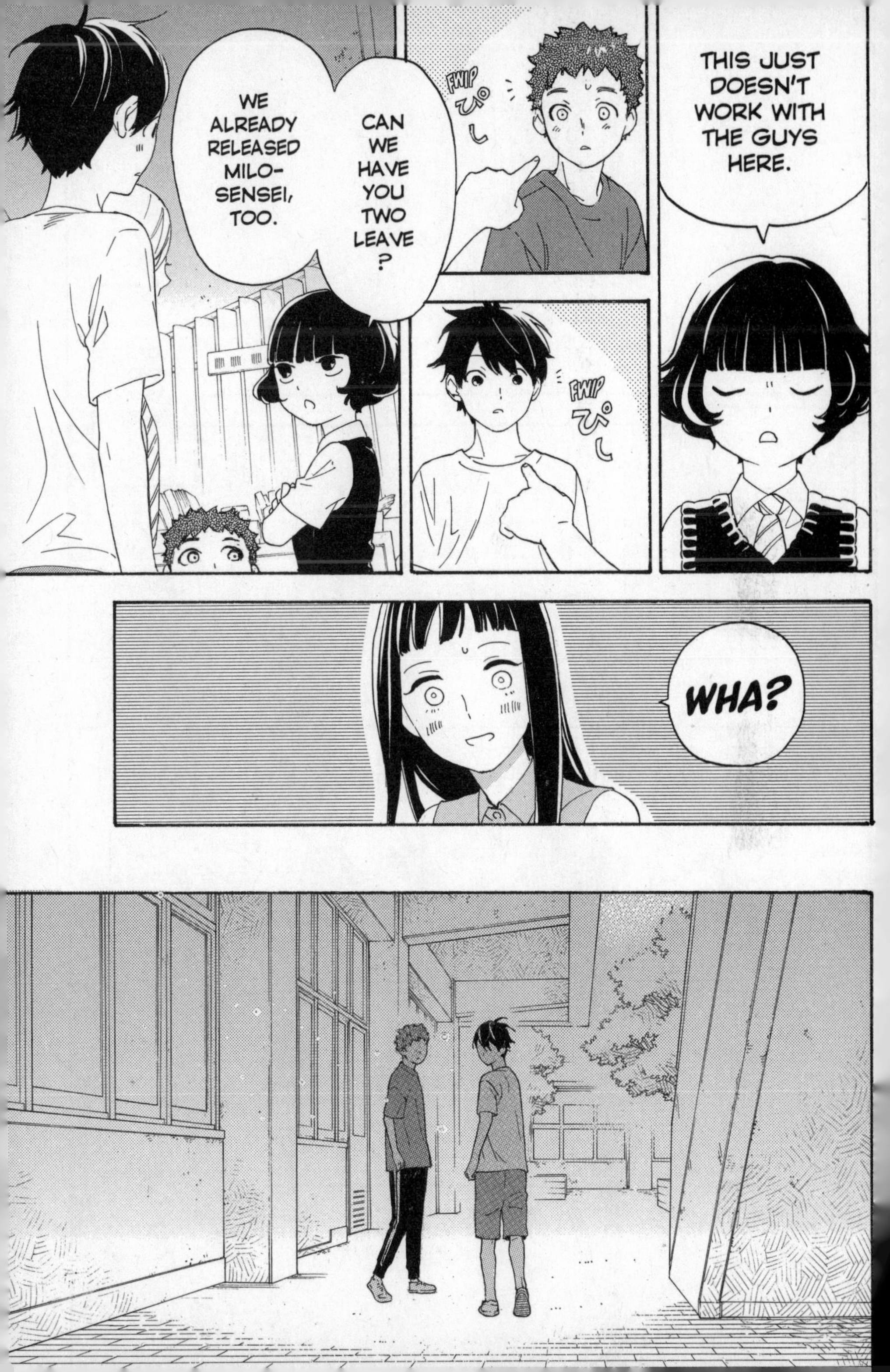
THIS JUST DOESN'T WORK WITH THE GUYS HERE.
FWIP
ぴし
FWIP
ぴし
CAN WE HAVE YOU TWO LEAVE?
WE ALREADY RELEASED MILO-SENSEI, TOO.
WHA?

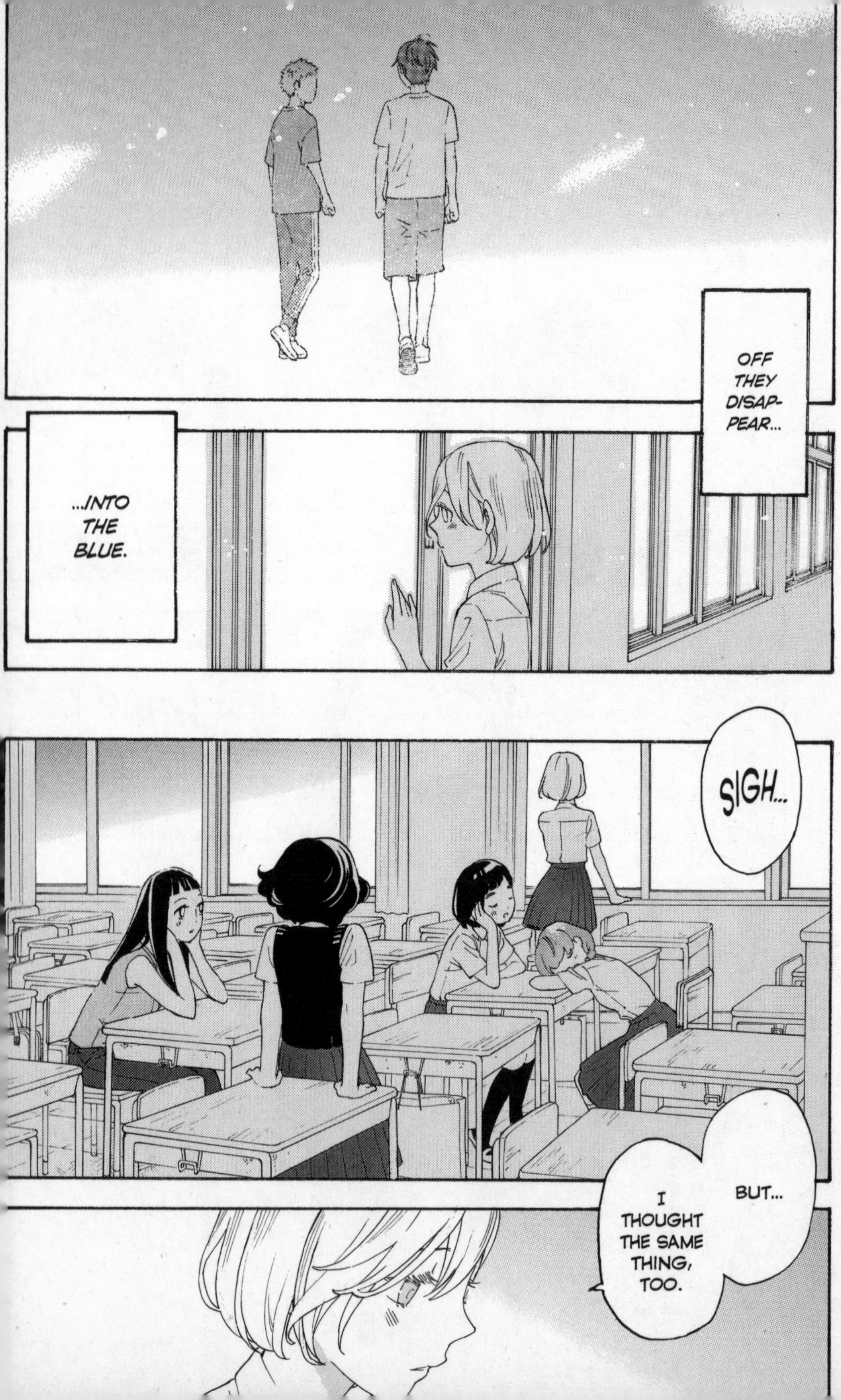
OFF THEY DISAPPEAR...
...INTO THE BLUE.
SIGH...
BUT...
I THOUGHT THE SAME THING, TOO.

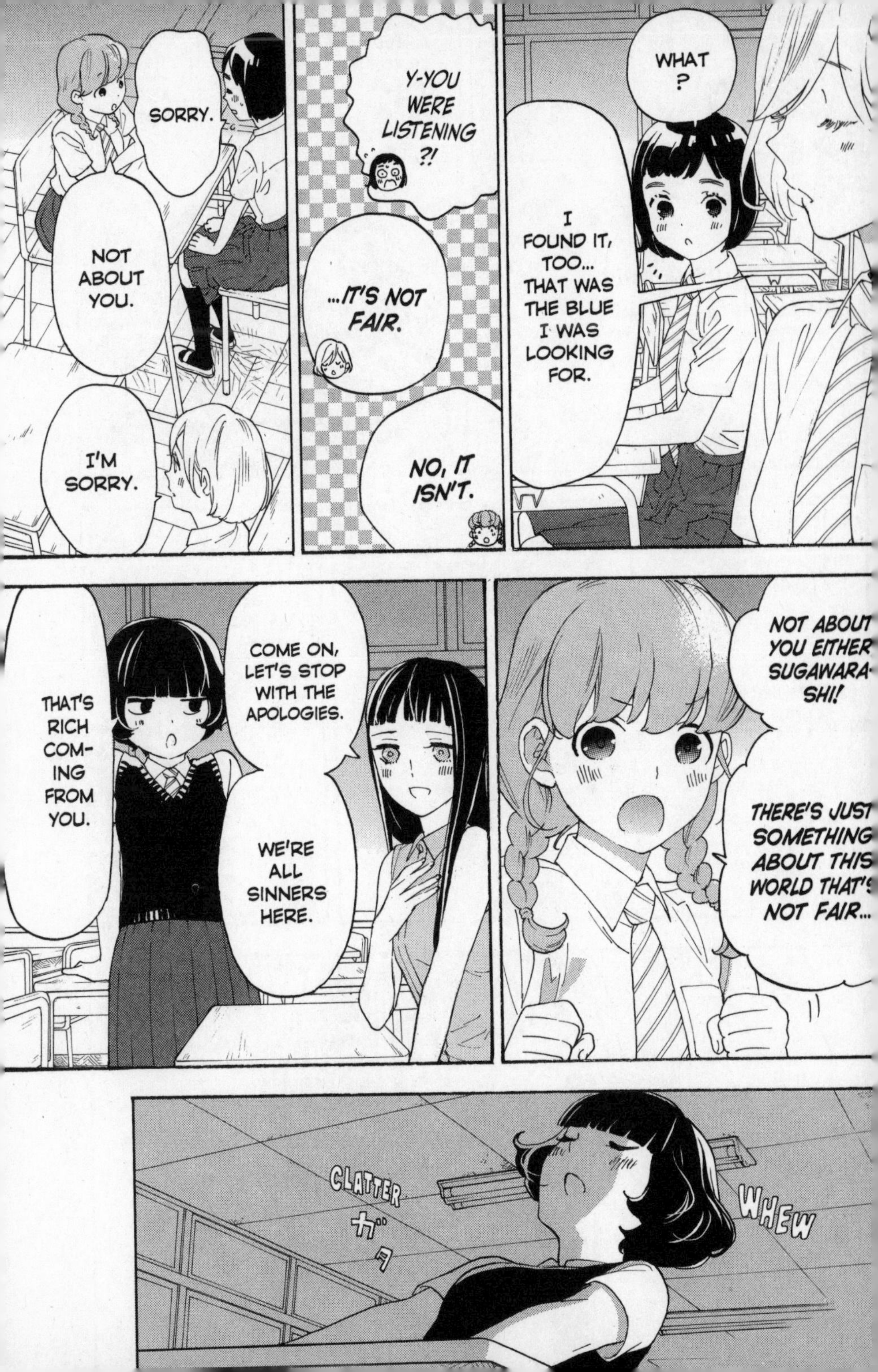
WHAT ?
I FOUND IT, TOO... THAT WAS THE BLUE I WAS LOOKING FOR.
Y-YOU WERE LISTENING ?!
...IT'S NOT FAIR.
NO, IT ISN'T.
SORRY.
NOT ABOUT YOU.
I'M SORRY.
NOT ABOUT YOU EITHER SUGAWARA-SHI!
THERE'S JUST SOMETHING ABOUT THIS WORLD THAT'S NOT FAIR...
COME ON, LET'S STOP WITH THE APOLOGIES.
WE'RE ALL SINNERS HERE.
THAT'S RICH COMING FROM YOU.
WHEW
CLATTER
ガタ

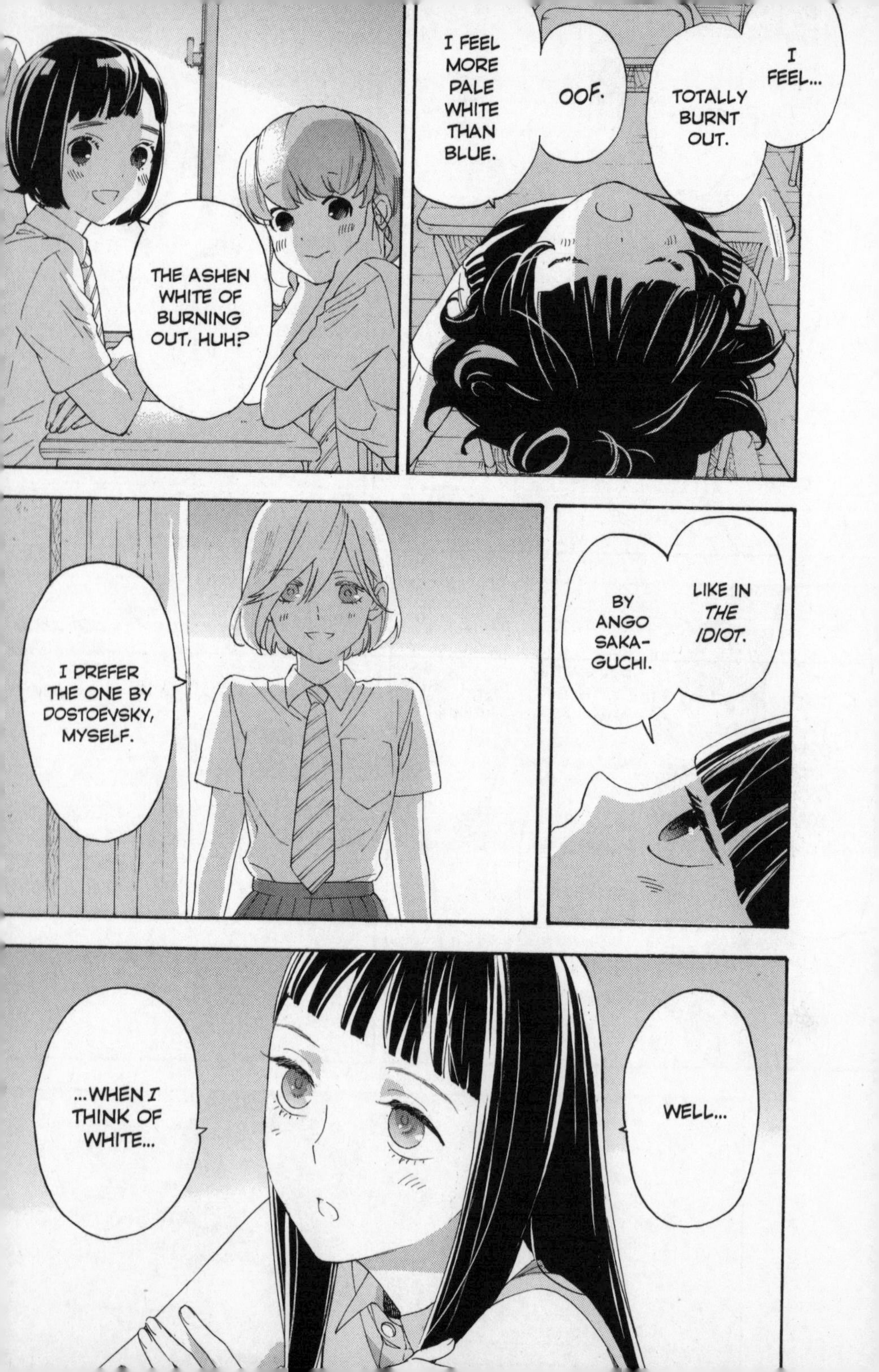
I FEEL... TOTALLY BURNT OUT.
OOF.
I FEEL MORE PALE WHITE THAN BLUE.
THE ASHEN WHITE OF BURNING OUT, HUH?
LIKE IN *THE IDIOT*.
BY ANGO SAKAGUCHI.
I PREFER THE ONE BY DOSTOEVSKY, MYSELF.
WELL...
...WHEN *I* THINK OF WHITE...

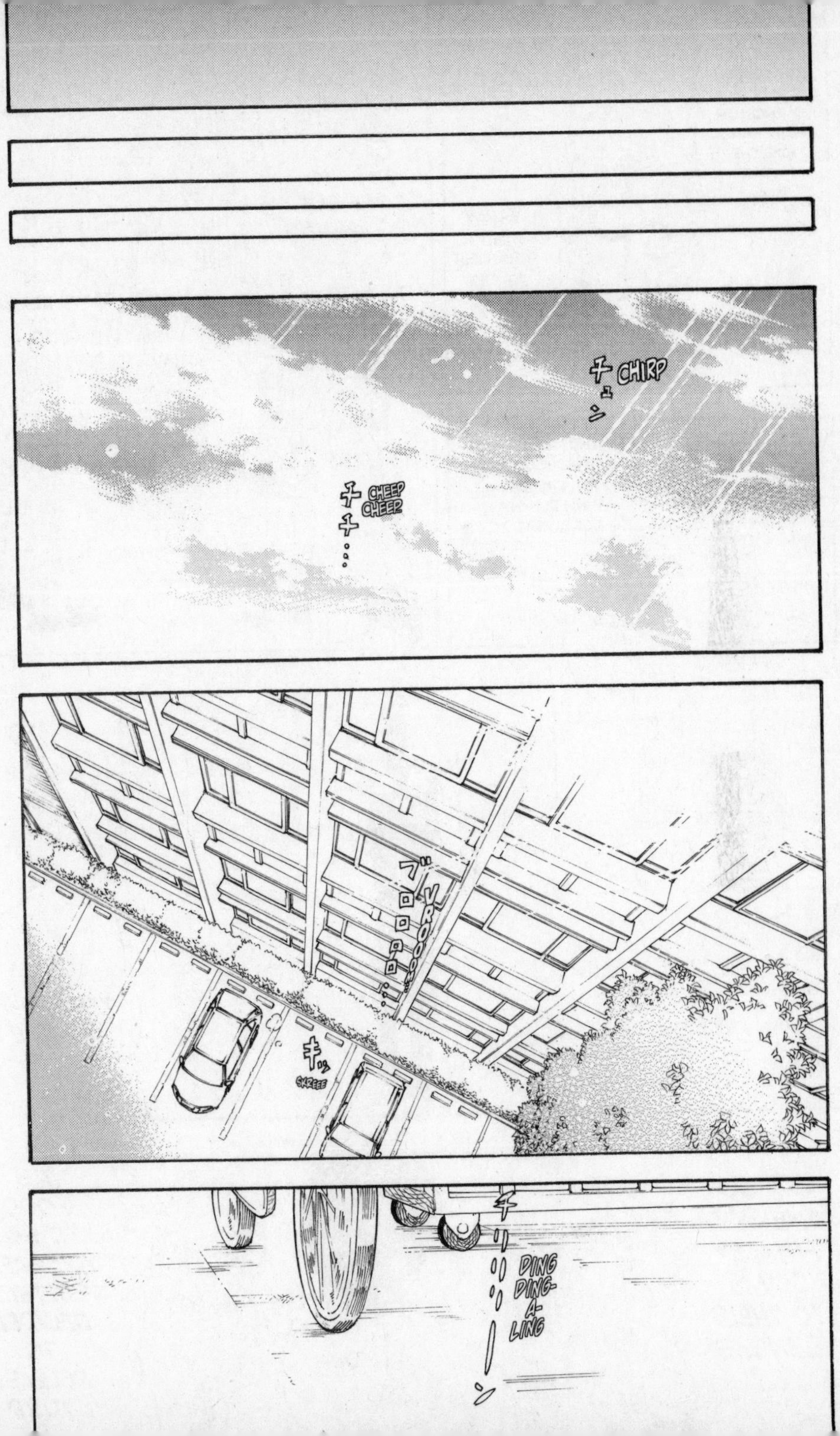

CHIRP
CHEEP CHEEP
VROOOOM...
SKREEE
DING DING-A-LING

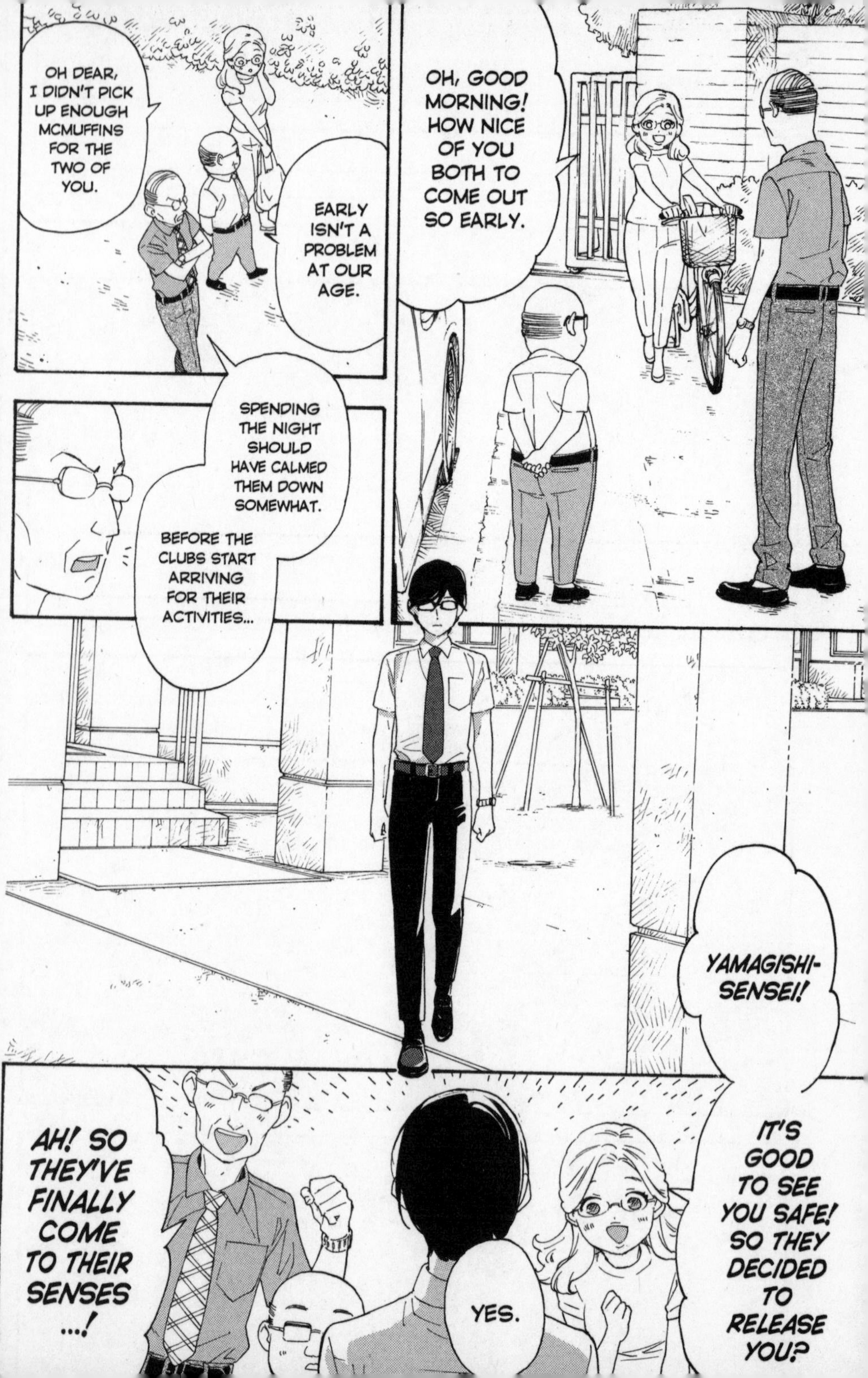
OH, GOOD MORNING! HOW NICE OF YOU BOTH TO COME OUT SO EARLY.
EARLY ISN'T A PROBLEM AT OUR AGE.
OH DEAR, I DIDN'T PICK UP ENOUGH MCMUFFINS FOR THE TWO OF YOU.
SPENDING THE NIGHT SHOULD HAVE CALMED THEM DOWN SOMEWHAT.
BEFORE THE CLUBS START ARRIVING FOR THEIR ACTIVITIES...
YAMAGISHI-SENSEI!
IT'S GOOD TO SEE YOU SAFE! SO THEY DECIDED TO RELEASE YOU?
YES.
AH! SO THEY'VE FINALLY COME TO THEIR SENSES ...!

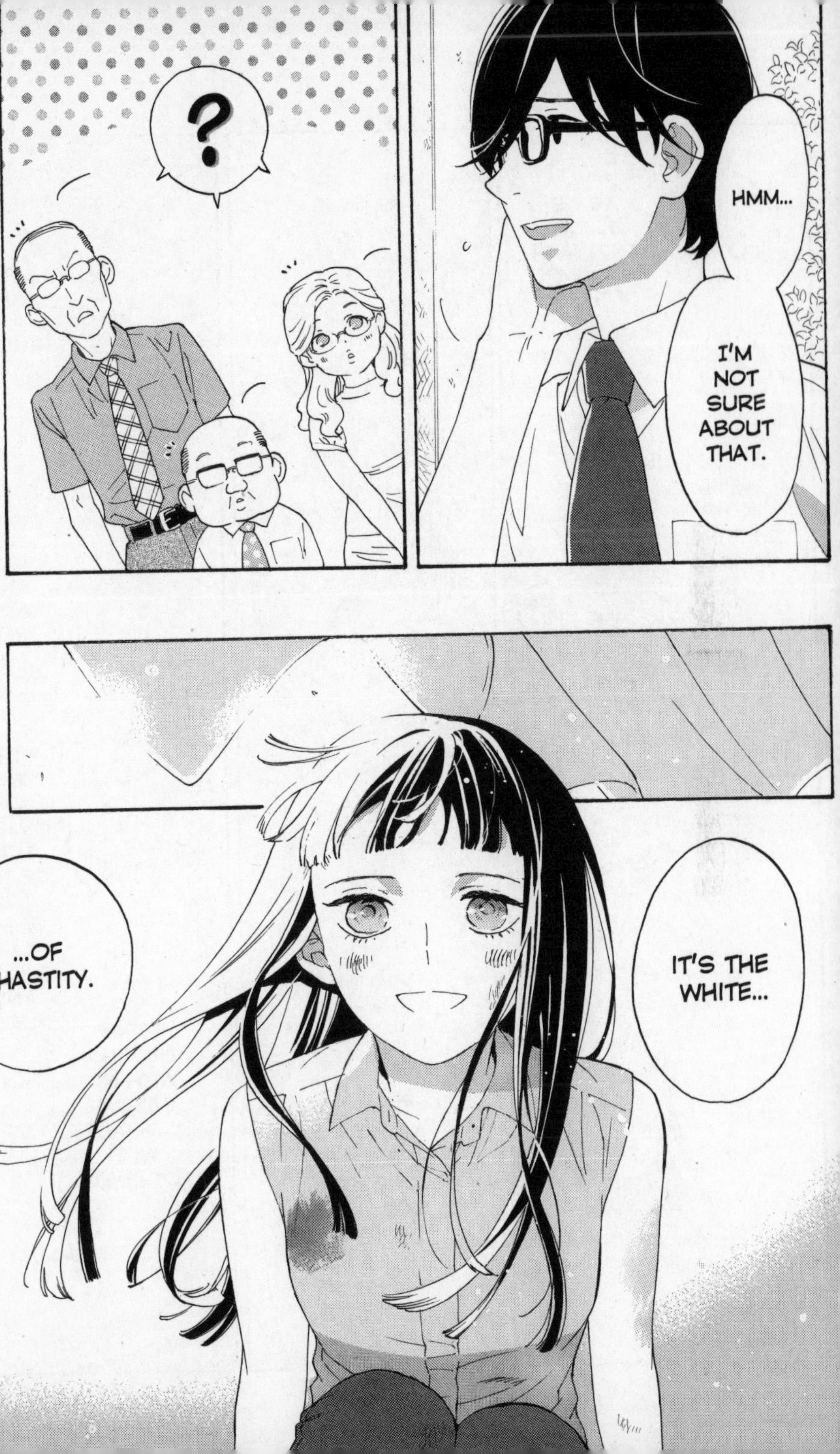
HMM...
I'M NOT SURE ABOUT THAT.
?
IT'S THE WHITE...
...OF CHASTITY.

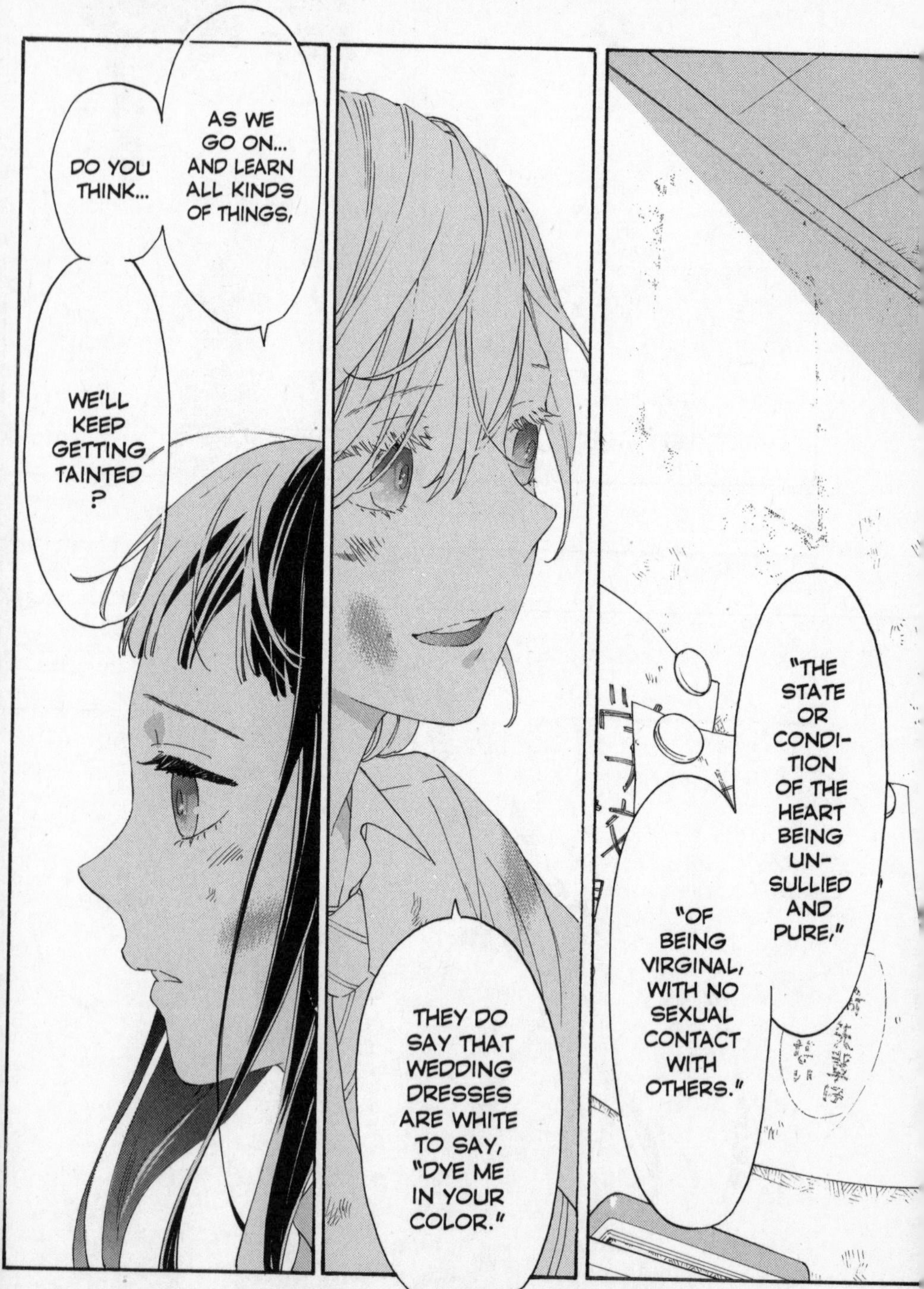
"THE STATE OR CONDITION OF THE HEART BEING UNSULLIED AND PURE,"
"OF BEING VIRGINAL, WITH NO SEXUAL CONTACT WITH OTHERS."
THEY DO SAY THAT WEDDING DRESSES ARE WHITE TO SAY, "DYE ME IN YOUR COLOR."
AS WE GO ON... AND LEARN ALL KINDS OF THINGS,
DO YOU THINK...
WE'LL KEEP GETTING TAINTED?

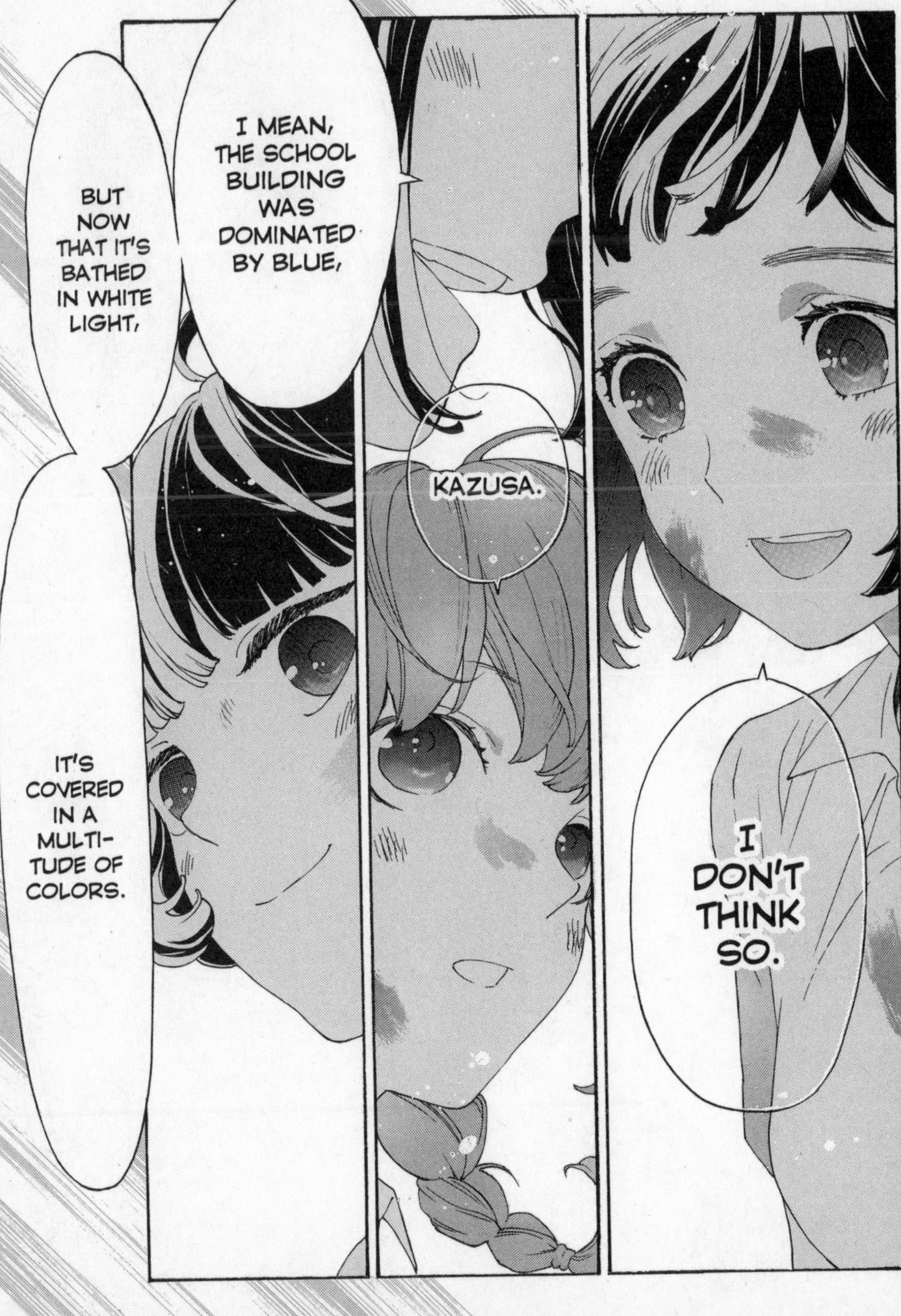
I DON'T THINK SO.
KAZUSA.
I MEAN, THE SCHOOL BUILDING WAS DOMINATED BY BLUE,
BUT NOW THAT IT'S BATHED IN WHITE LIGHT,
IT'S COVERED IN A MULTI-TUDE OF COLORS.

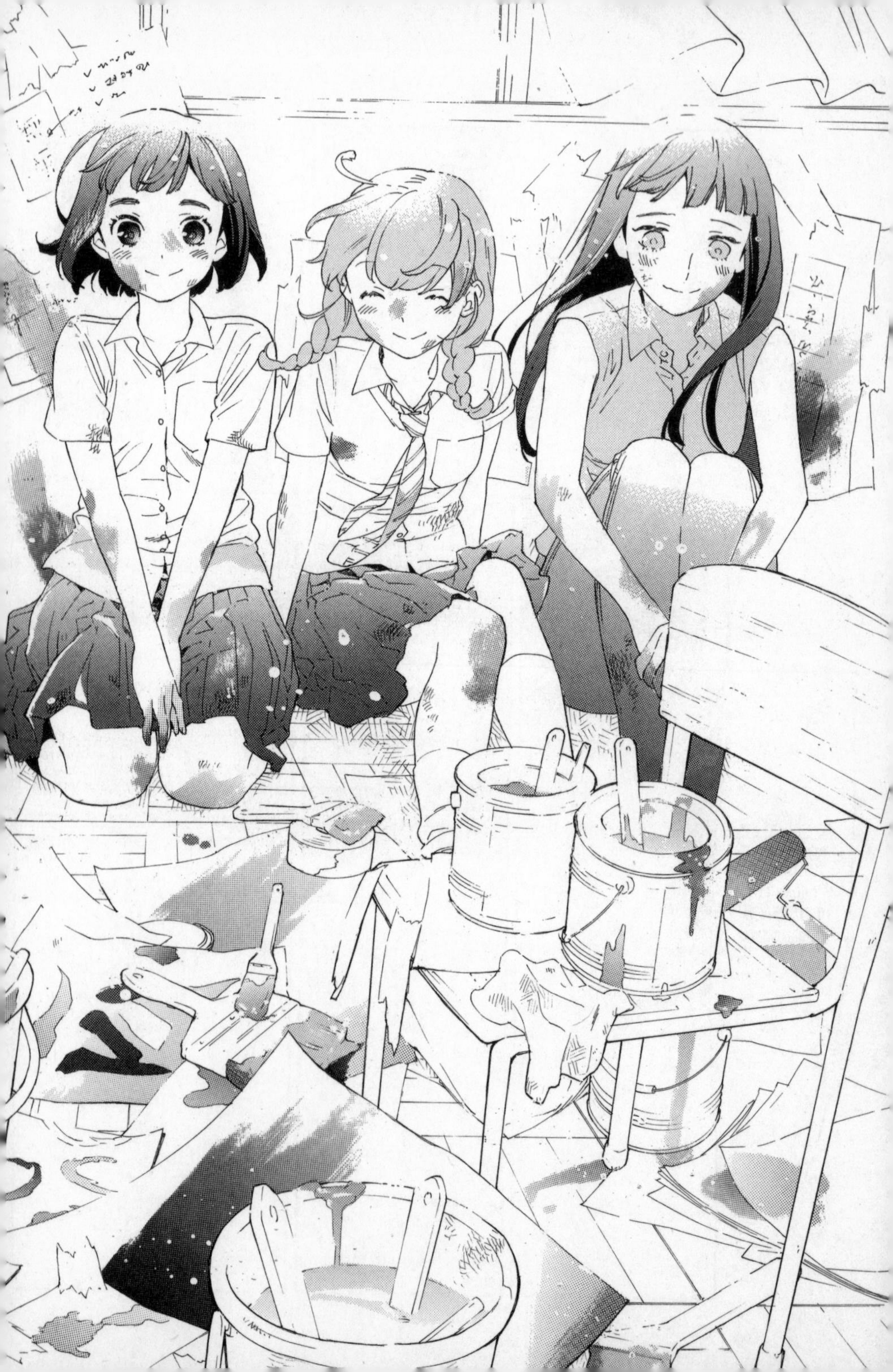

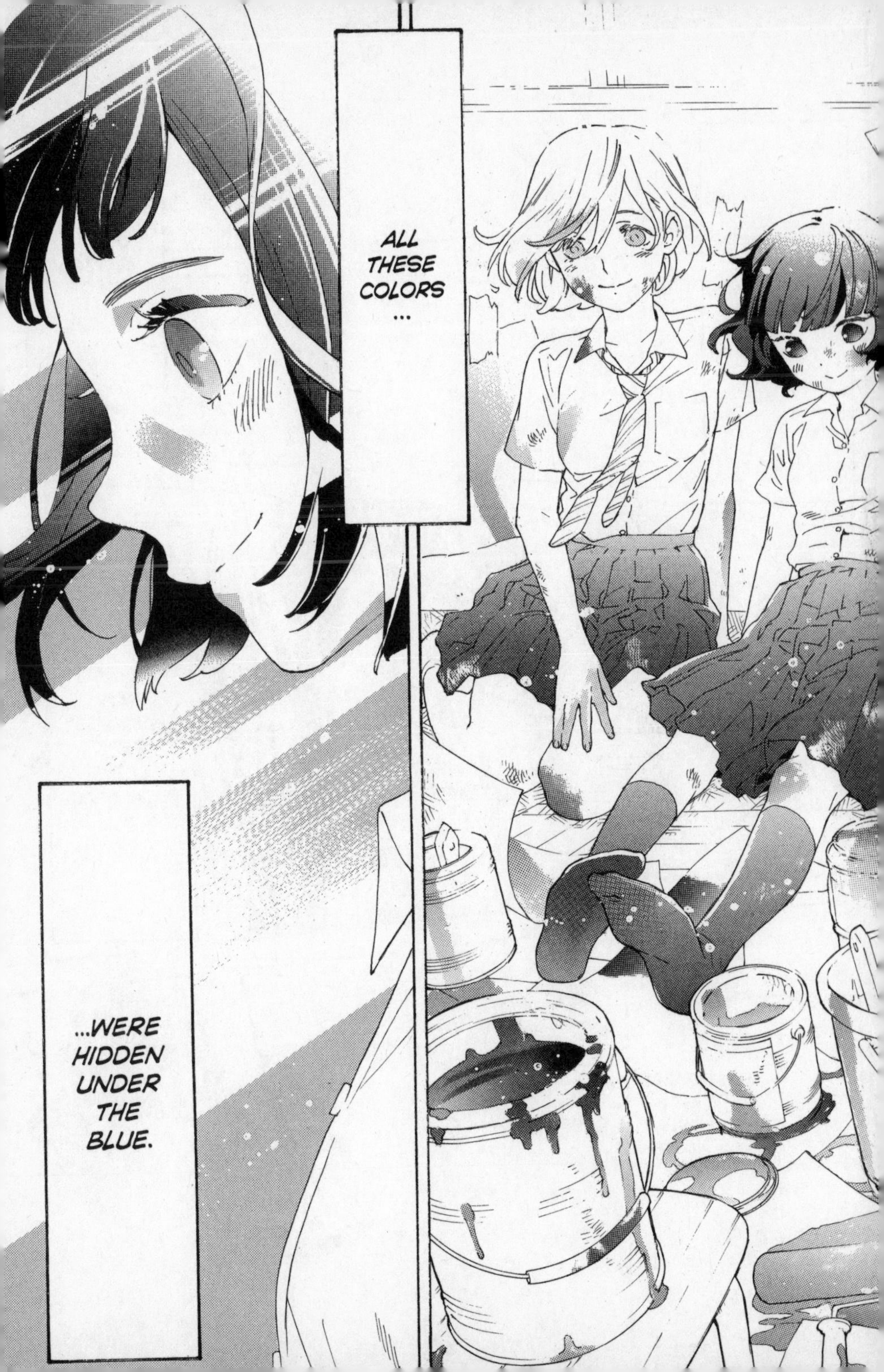
ALL THESE COLORS ...
...WERE HIDDEN UNDER THE BLUE.

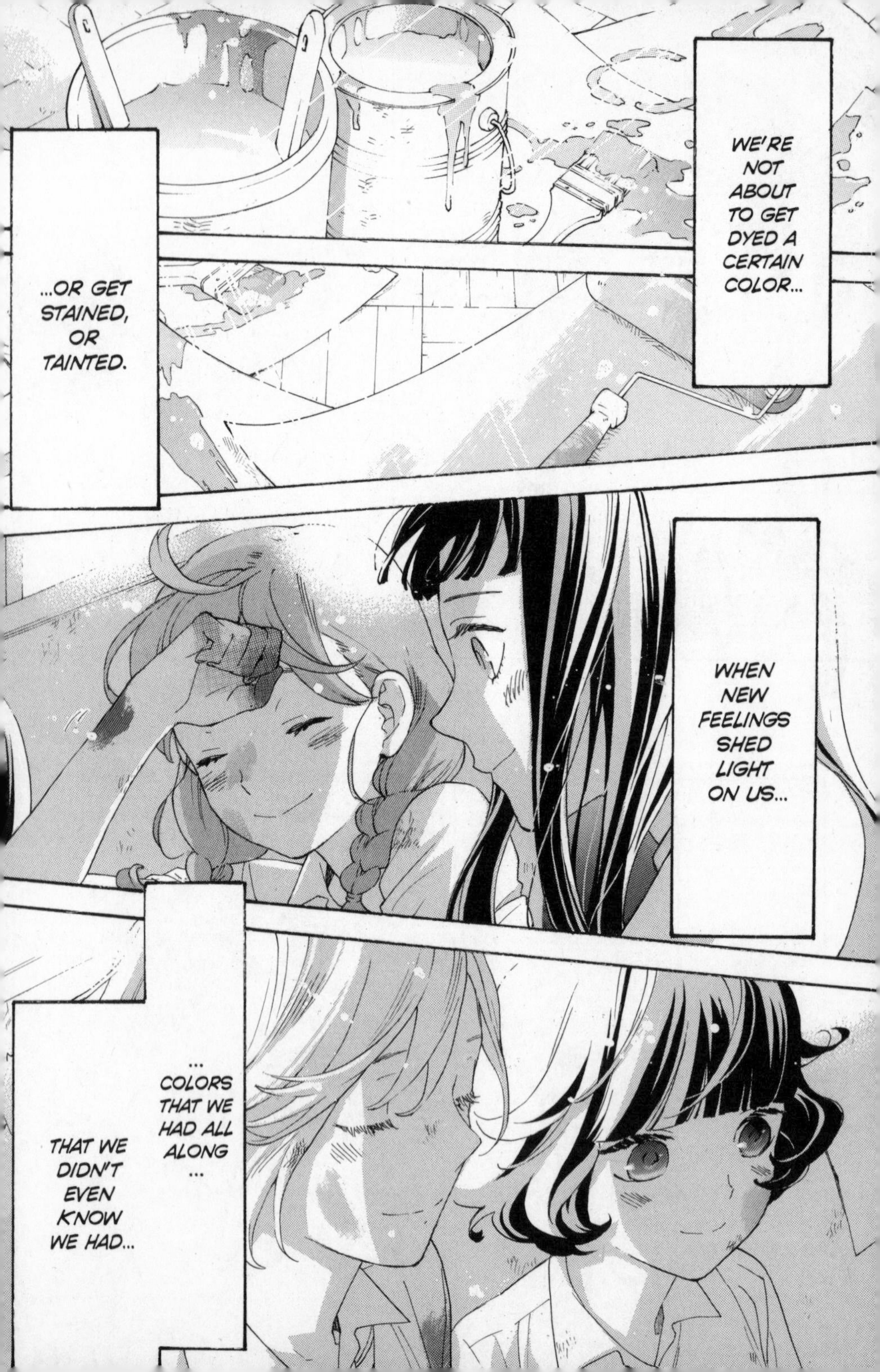
WE'RE NOT ABOUT TO GET DYED A CERTAIN COLOR...
...OR GET STAINED, OR TAINTED.
WHEN NEW FEELINGS SHED LIGHT ON US...
...COLORS THAT WE HAD ALL ALONG...
THAT WE DIDN'T EVEN KNOW WE HAD...

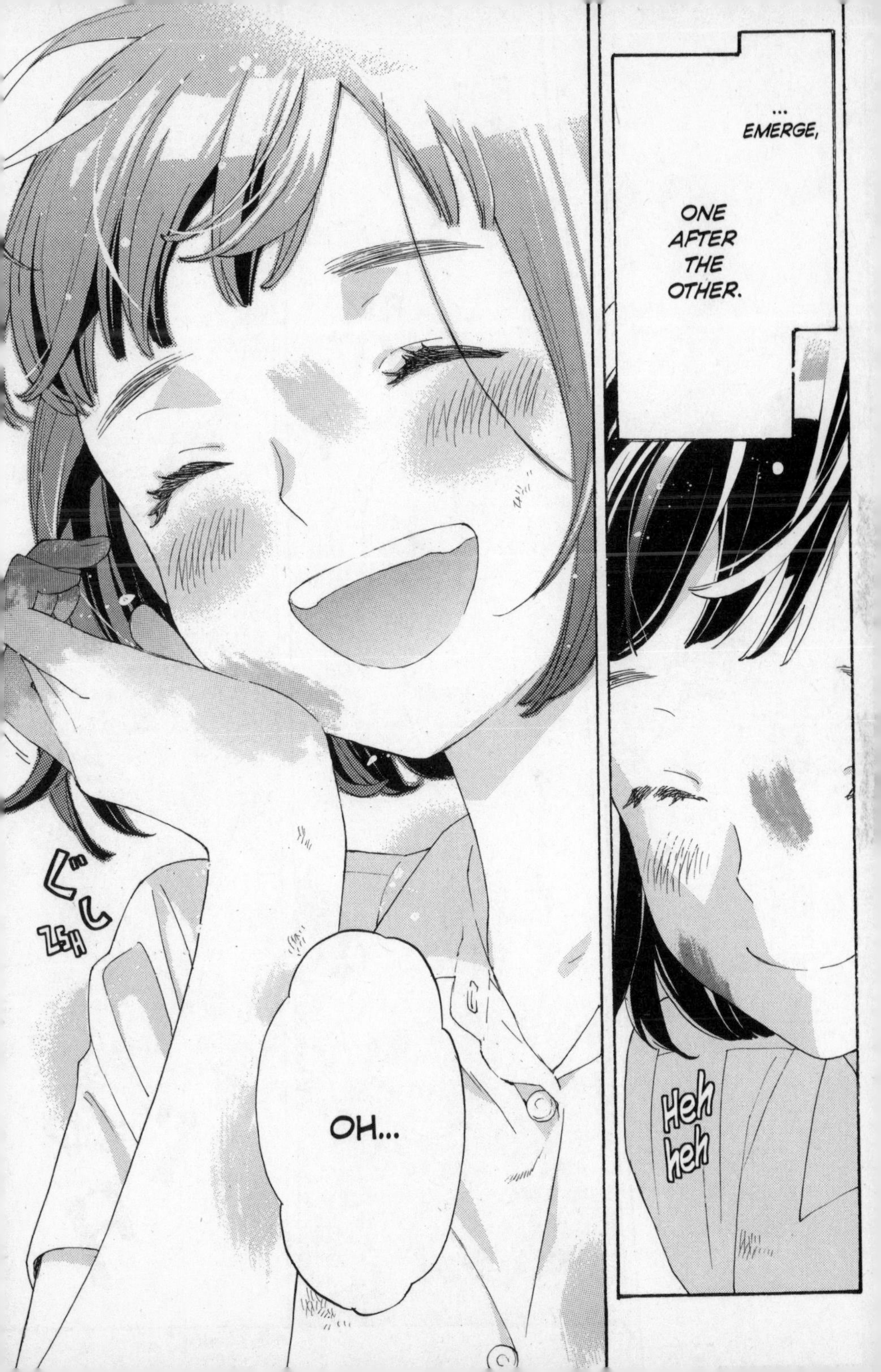
...EMERGE,
ONE AFTER THE OTHER.
Heh heh
OH...
じし
ZSH

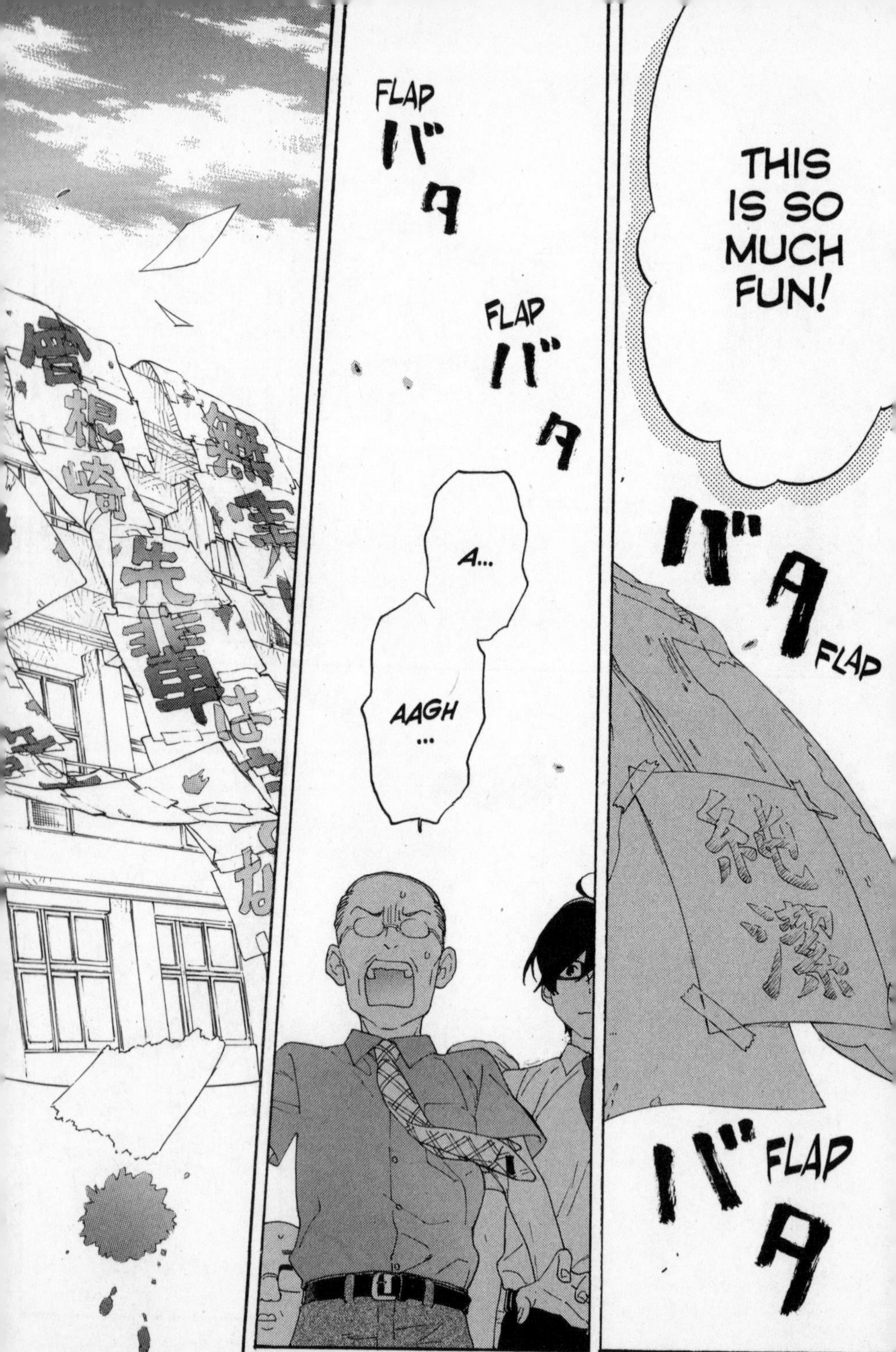
THIS IS SO MUCH FUN!
バタ FLAP
バタ FLAP
FLAP バタ
FLAP バタ
A...
AAGH ...

SIGN: Chastity

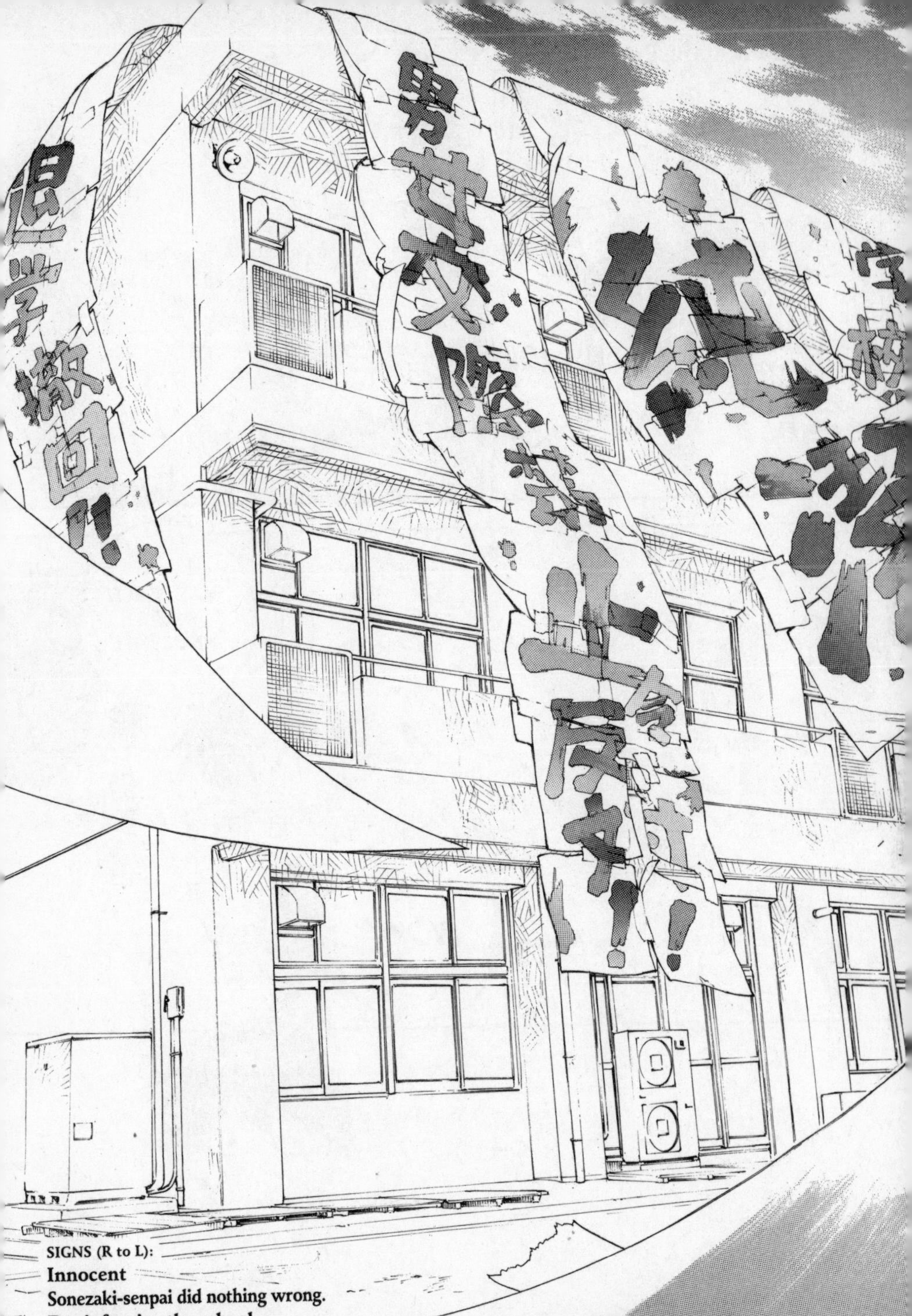

退学撤回!!
男女交際禁止反対!!

SIGNS (R to L):
Innocent
Sonezaki-senpai did nothing wrong.
Don't forgive the school…
Chastity
Say no to the Zero Dating policy!!
Retract the expulsion!!

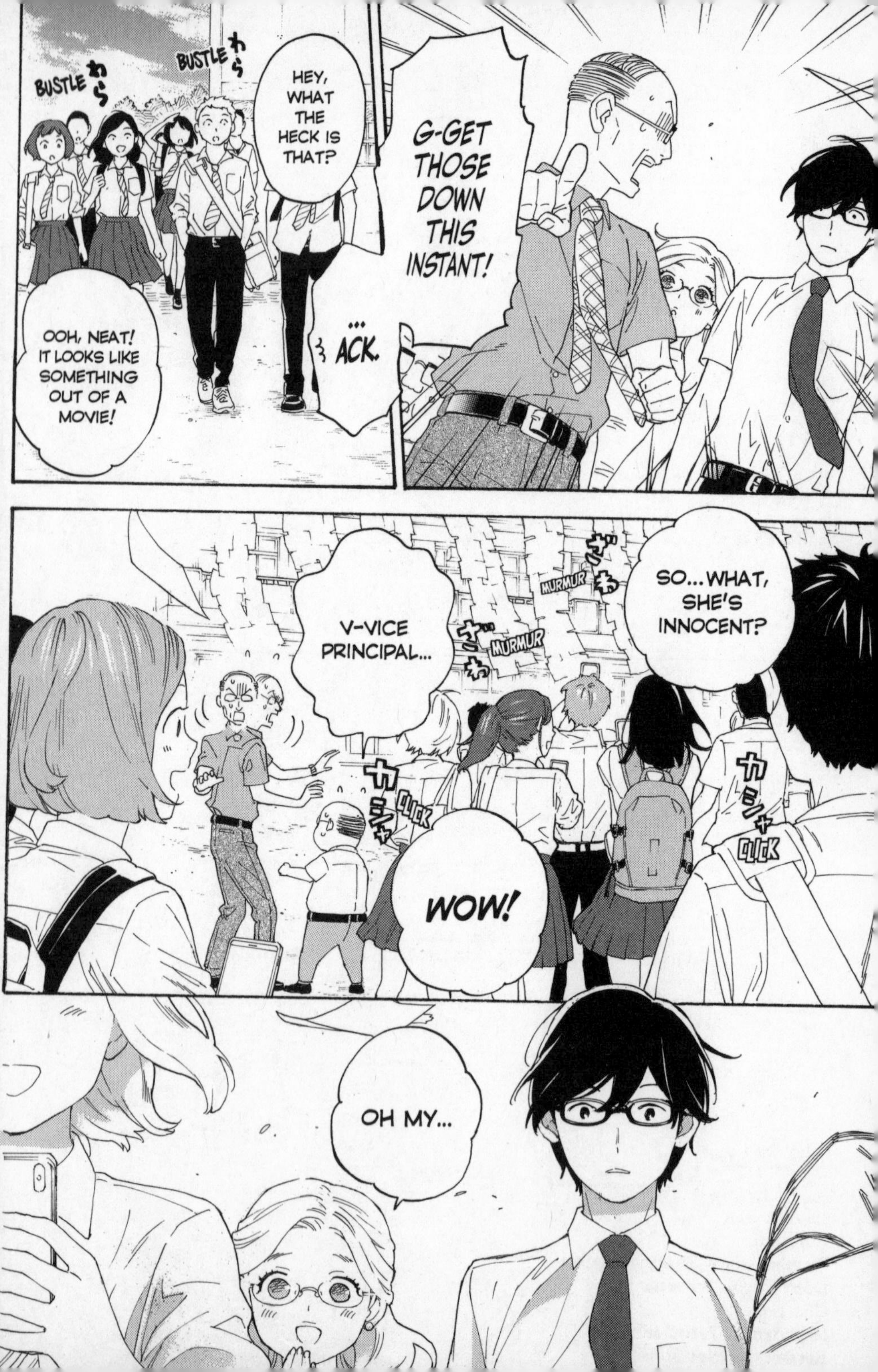
G-GET THOSE DOWN THIS INSTANT!
BUSTLE わら
BUSTLE わら
HEY, WHAT THE HECK IS THAT?
...ACK.
OOH, NEAT! IT LOOKS LIKE SOMETHING OUT OF A MOVIE!
SO...WHAT, SHE'S INNOCENT?
ざわ MURMUR
V-VICE PRINCIPAL...
ざわ MURMUR
カシャ CLICK
カシャ CLICK
WOW!
OH MY...

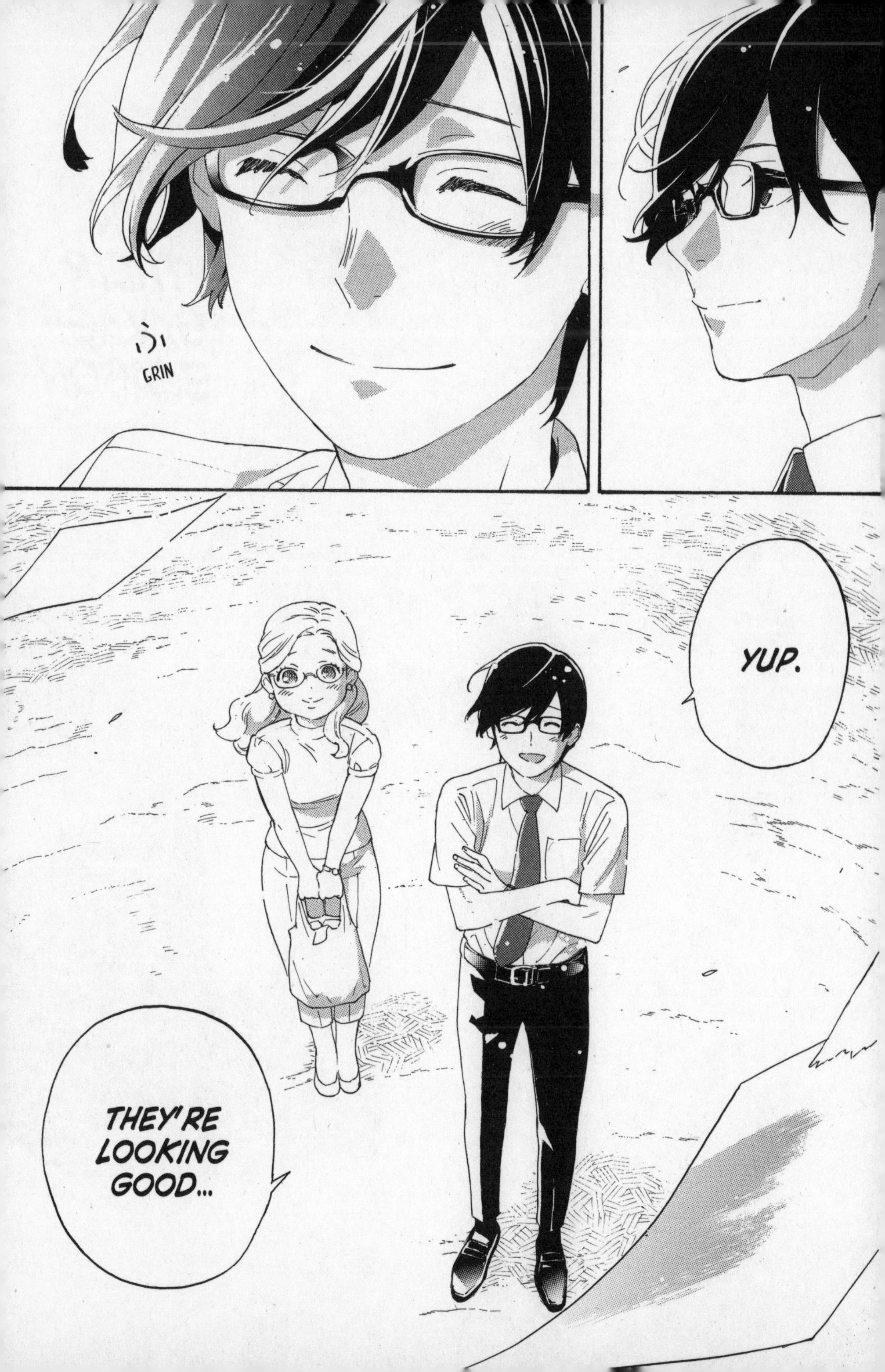
GRIN
YUP.
THEY'RE LOOKING GOOD...

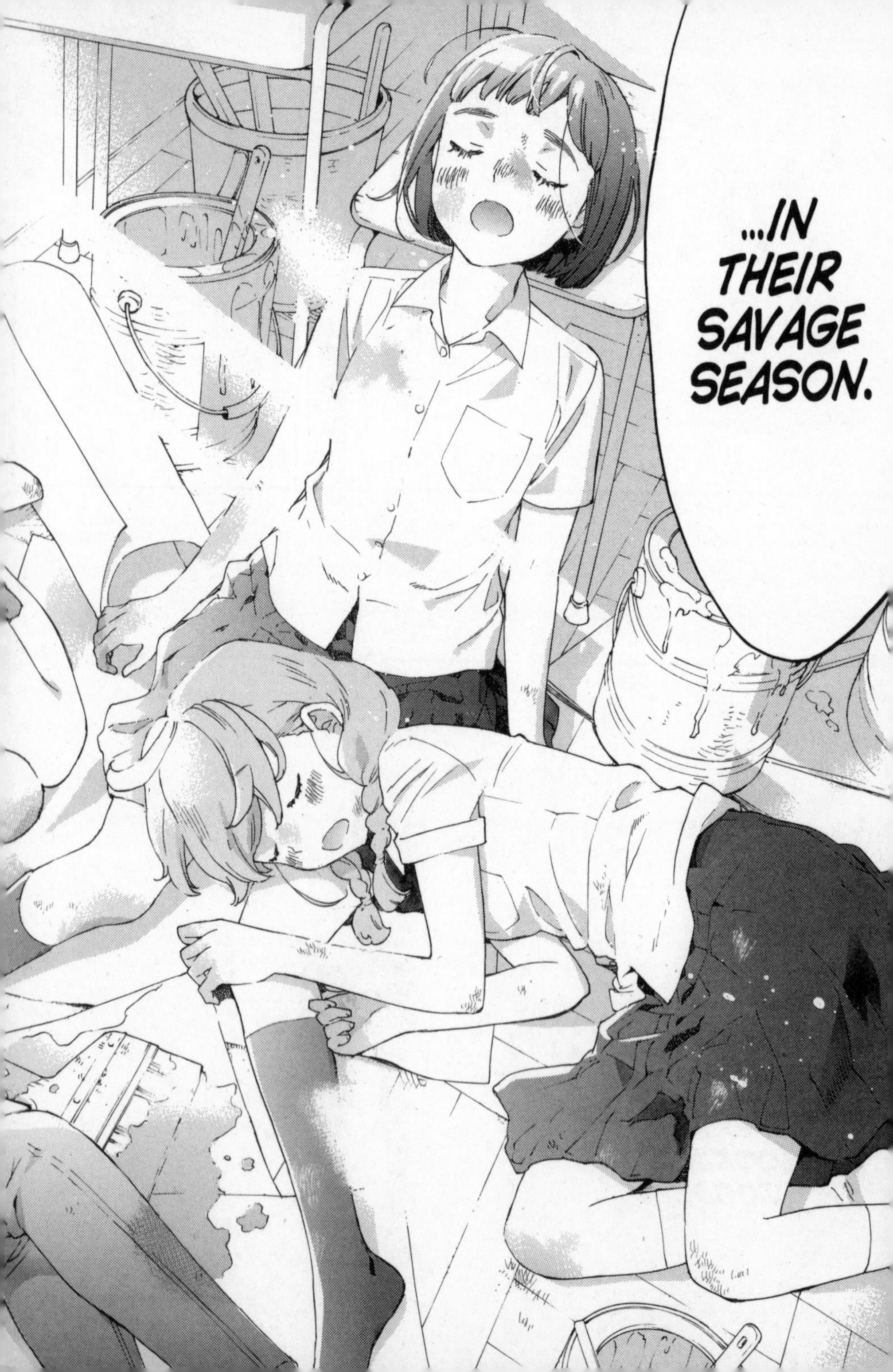
...IN THEIR SAVAGE SEASON.

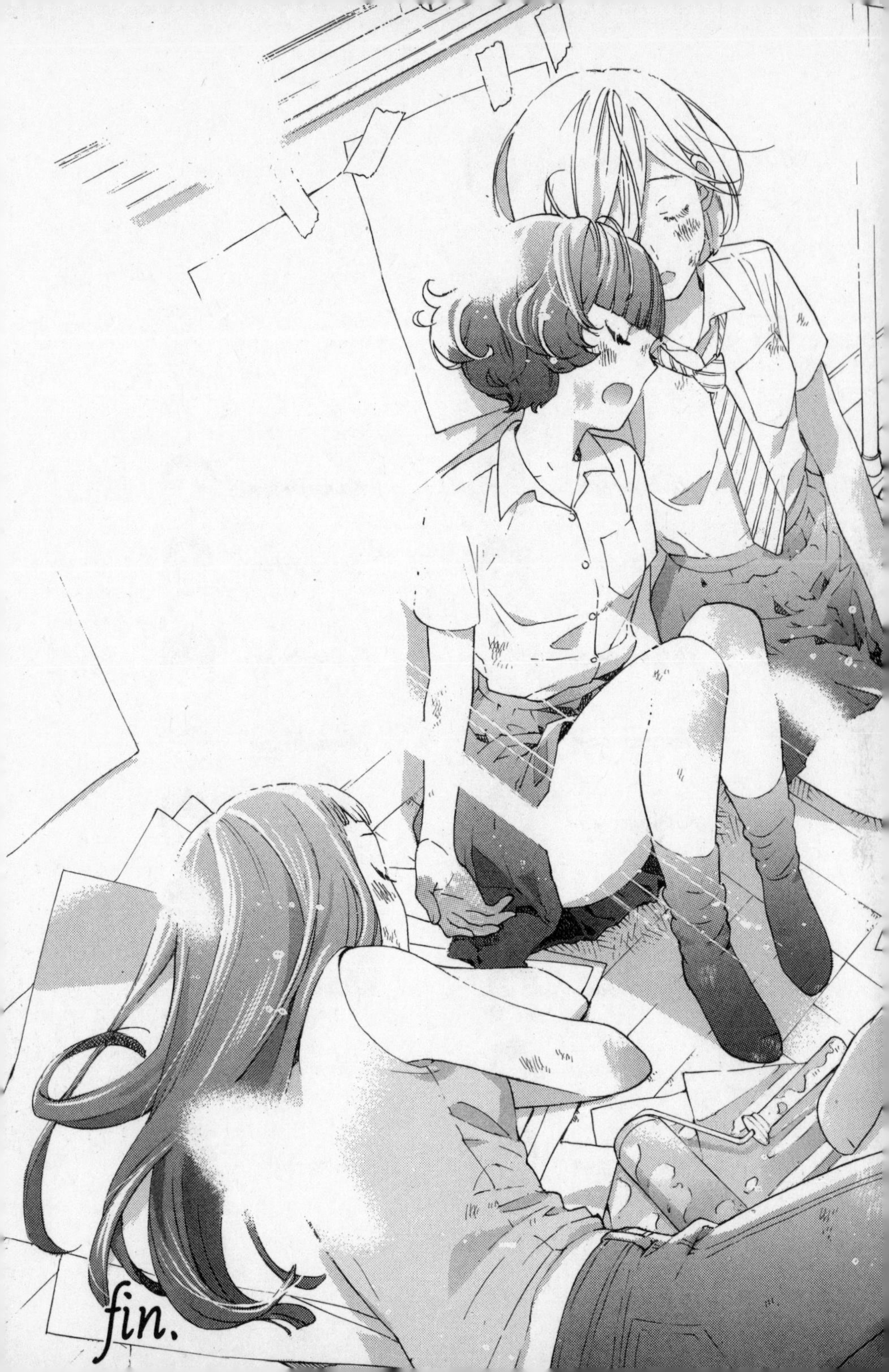
fin.

STORY　　Okada-sensei

ART　　Emoto

Kabaya-san	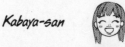	Kanzaki-san	
Endo-san		Suehiro-kun	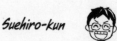
Watanabe-san	 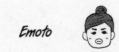	Furumoto-kun	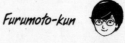
Harada-san		Maehata-kun	
Katayama-san	 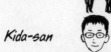	Ueda-san	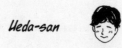
Kida-san		Matsuoka-san	
Aoyagi-san		Otake-san	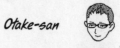
Takaniwa-san	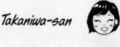	Yagi-san	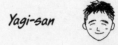
Sugiyama-san		Miura-san	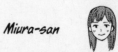

DESIGN   Kuroki-san

EDITORS   Suzuki-san

          Fujii-san 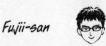   Kayama-san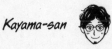

MANGA
VOLUMES   Toriumi-san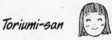

IN
COOPERATION
WITH...   Nacchan  Tsugumi-chan   Noda-san

         Funton-san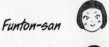

         Kodama-kun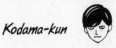

SPECIAL
THANKS   Saito-san

Thank you so much to manga artists Shuzo Oshimi-
sensei and Fujita-sensei for taking time out of their busy
schedules to draw some beautiful bonus illustrations.*

*Editor's note: Available at limited Japanese bookstores.

O Maidens
in your Savage
your Season

Epilogue

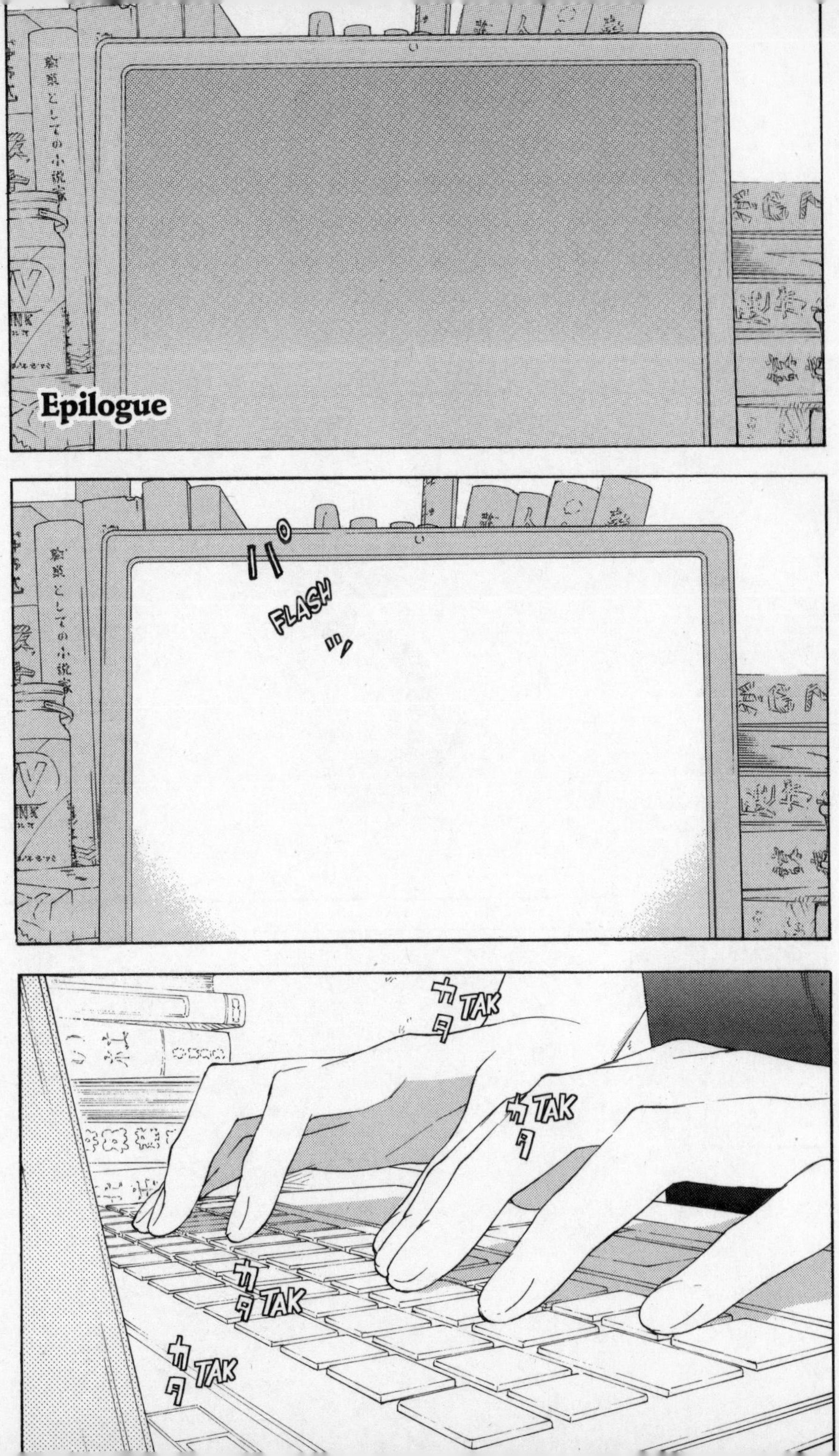
パッ
FLASH
カタ
TAK
カタ
TAK
カタ
TAK
カタ
TAK

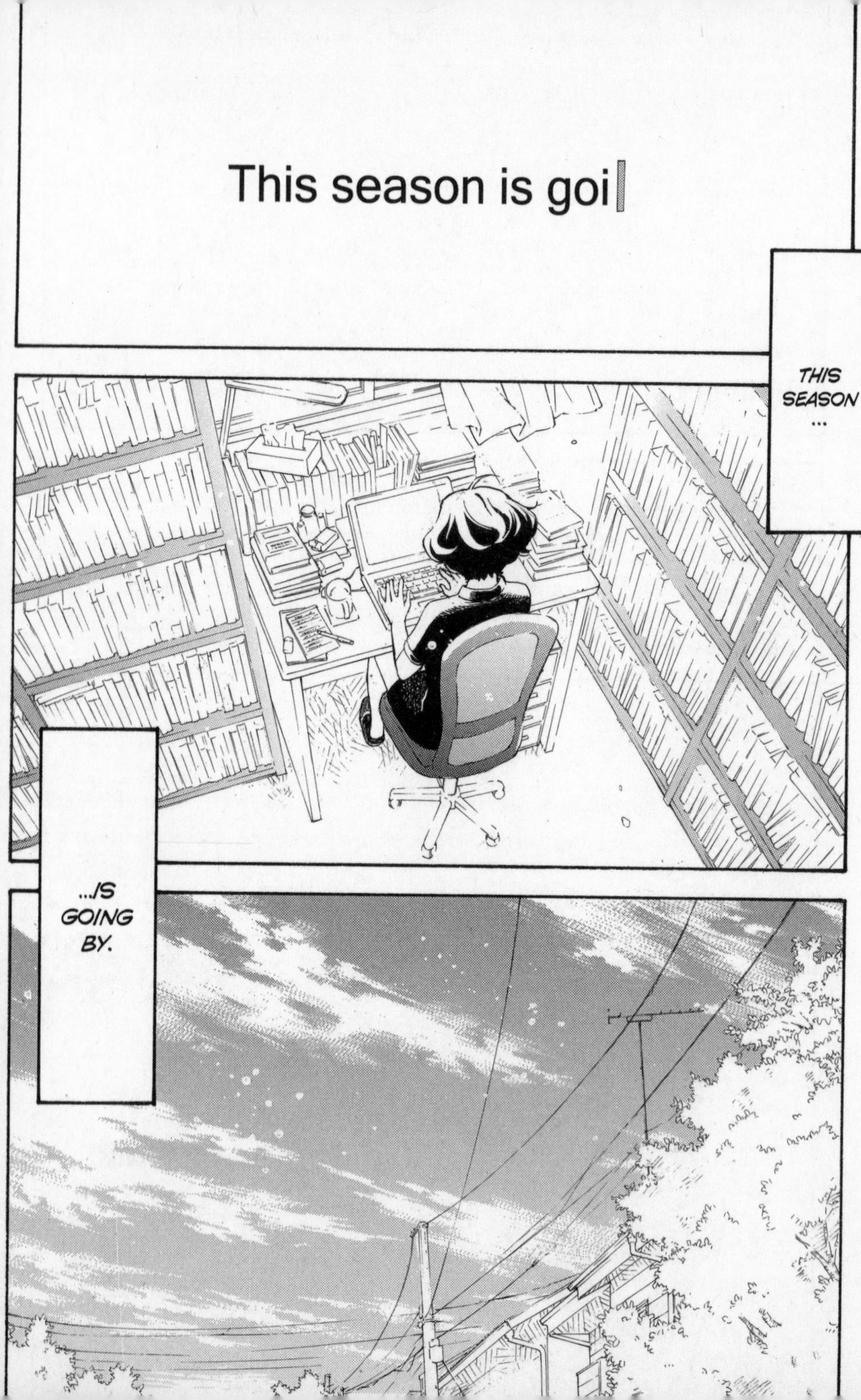
This season is goi
THIS SEASON ...
...IS GOING BY.

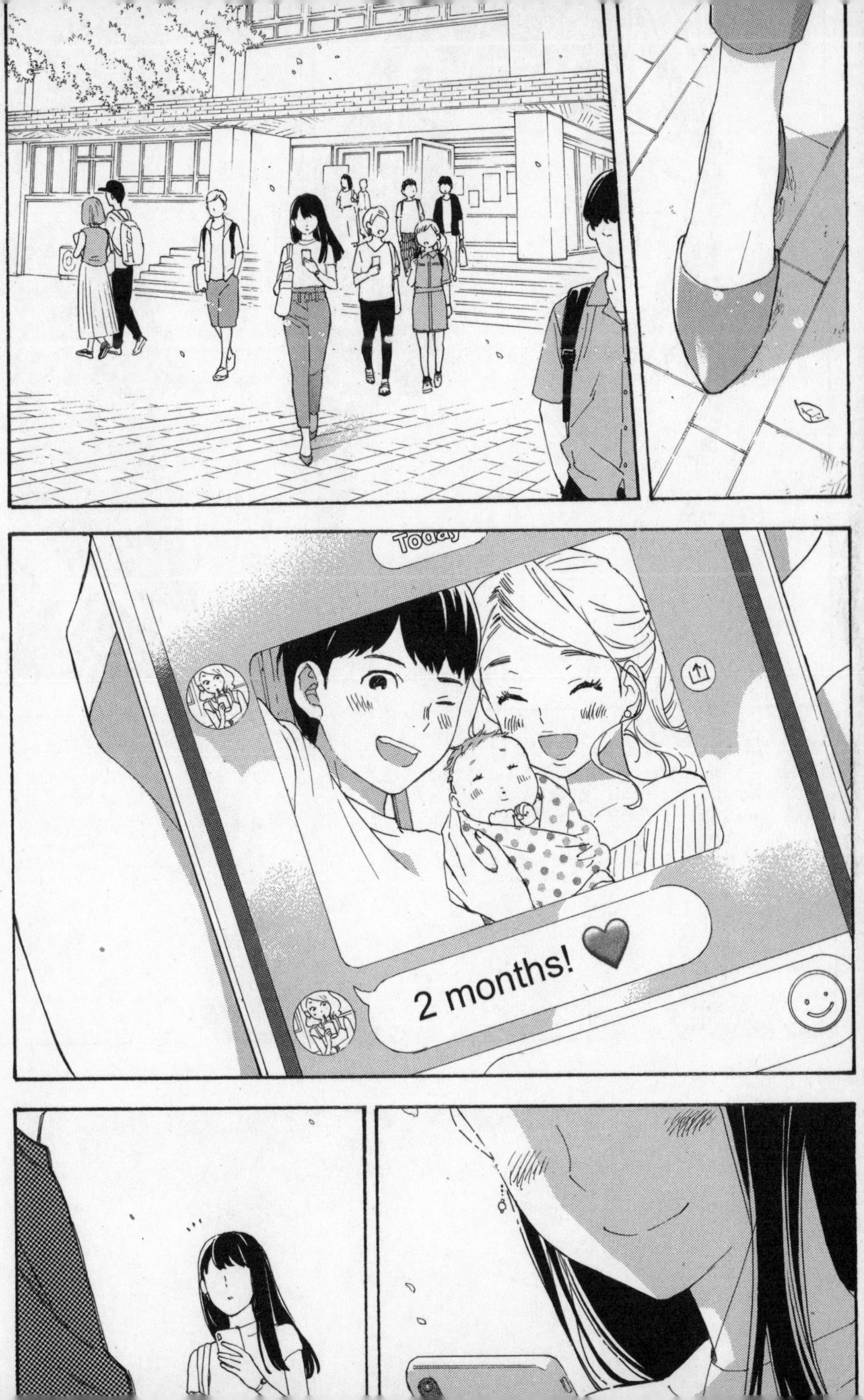
Today
2 months!

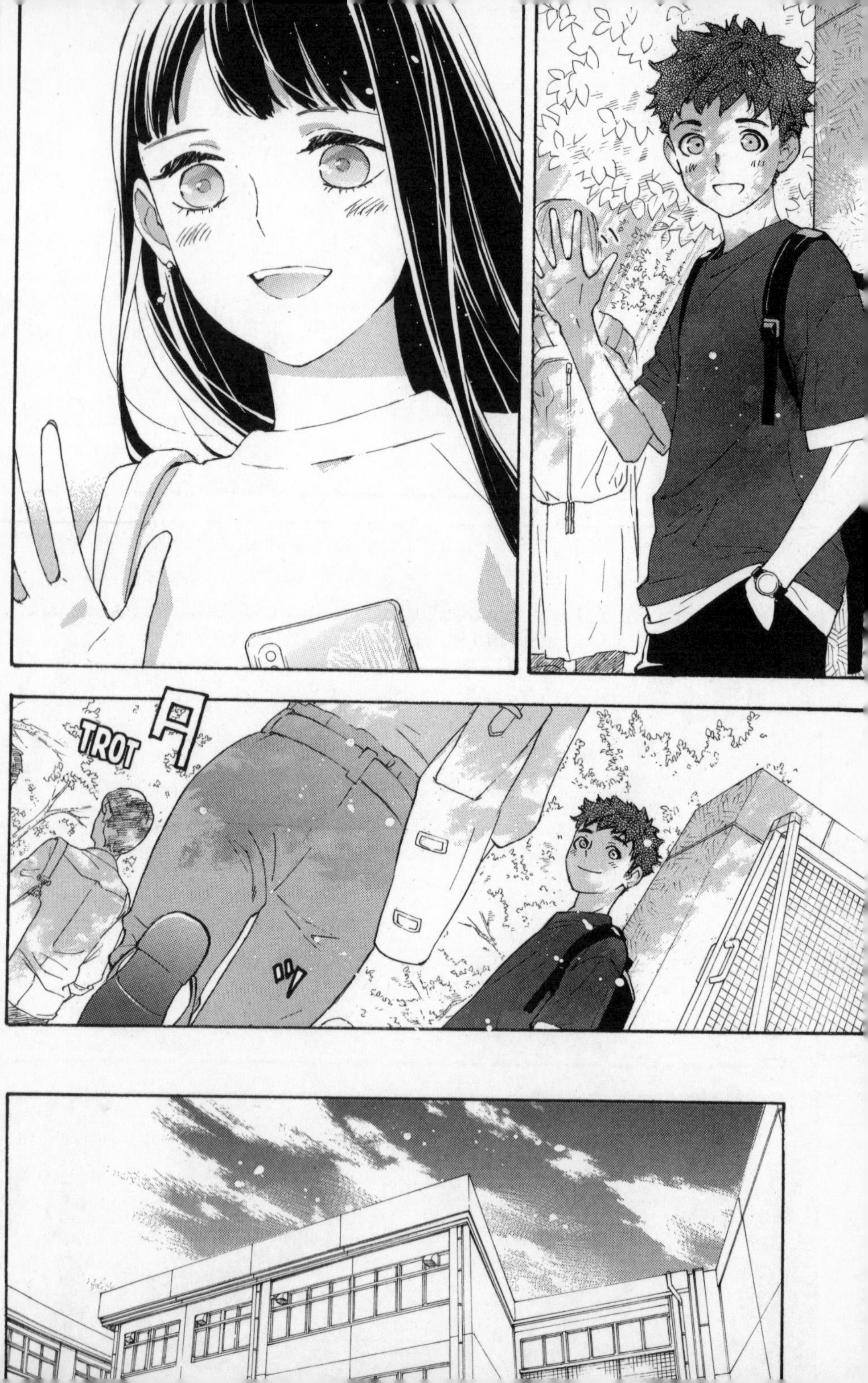
TROT

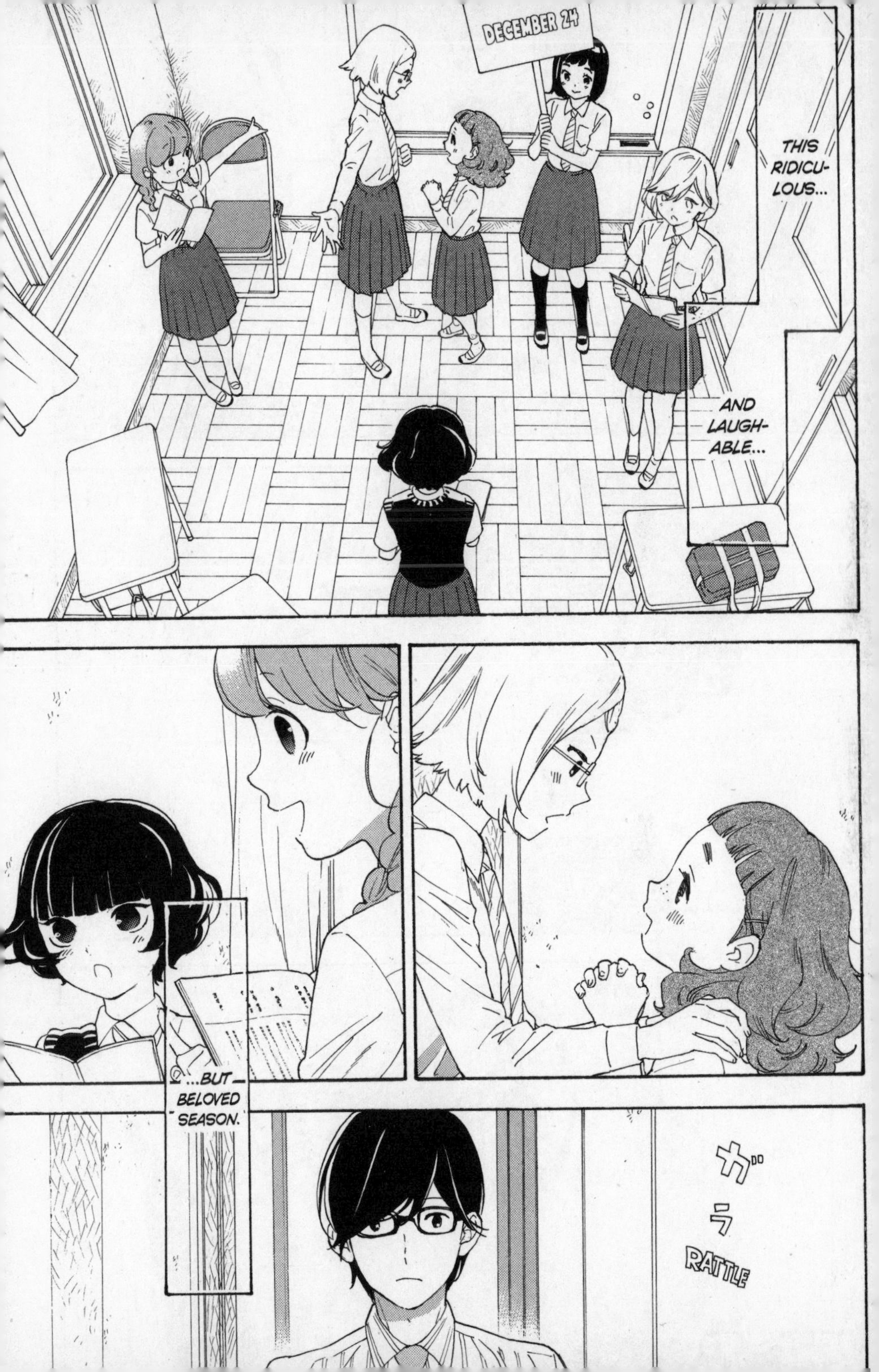
DECEMBER 24
THIS RIDICULOUS...
AND LAUGHABLE...
...BUT BELOVED SEASON.
ガラ
RATTLE

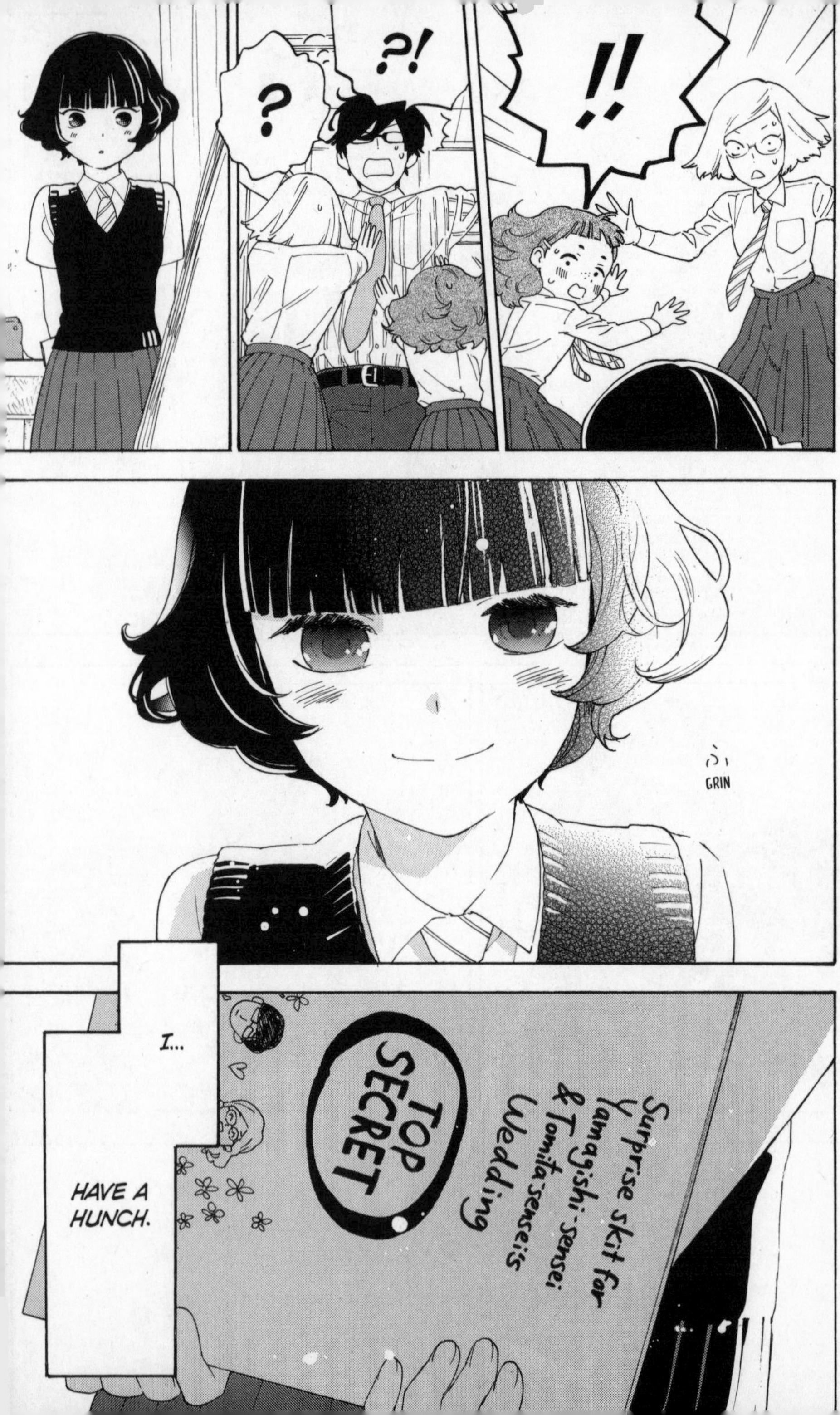
!!
?!
?
ふ
GRIN
Surprise skit for Yamagishi-sensei & Tomita-sensei's Wedding
TOP SECRET
I...
HAVE A HUNCH.

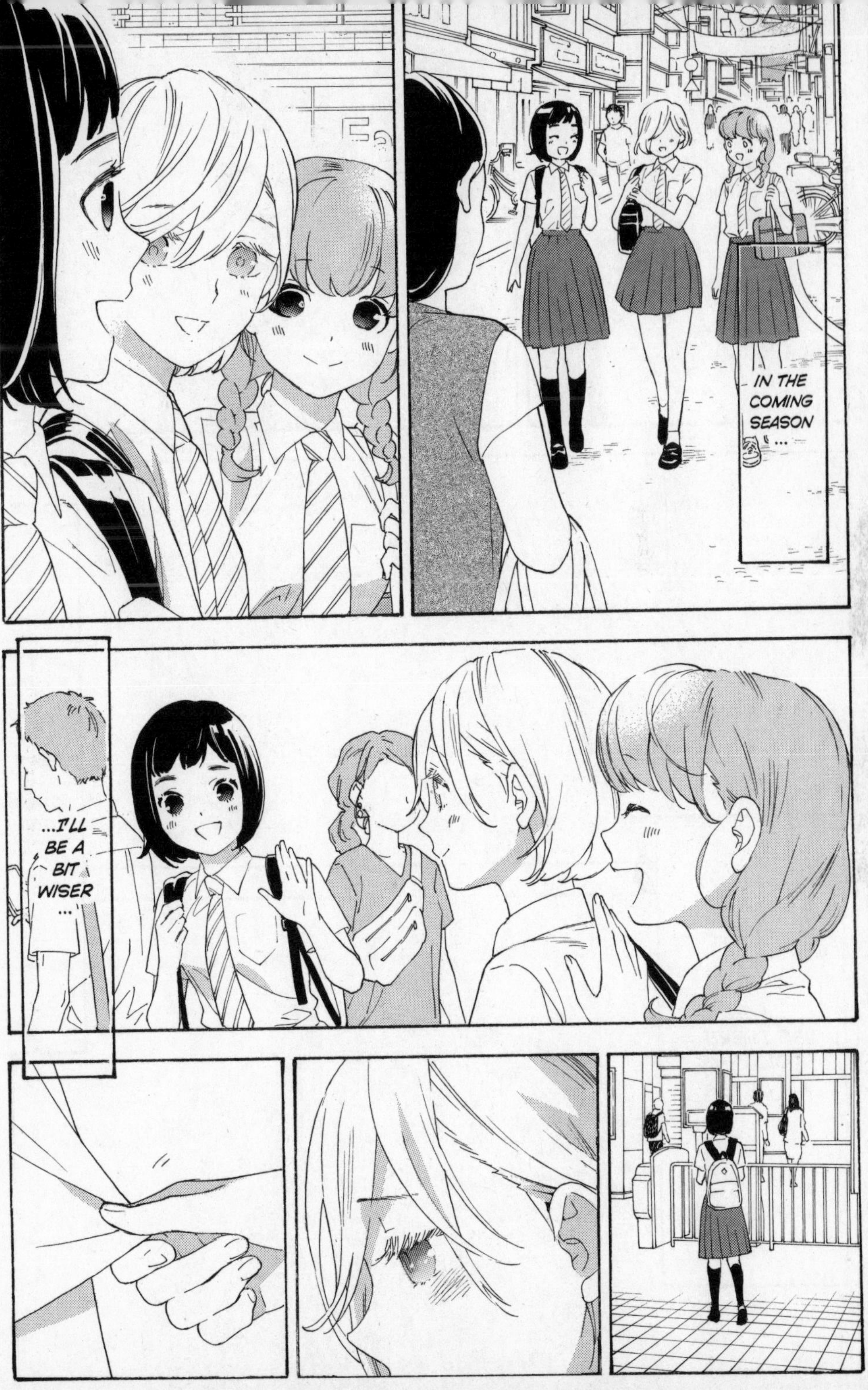
IN THE COMING SEASON ...
...I'LL BE A BIT WISER ...

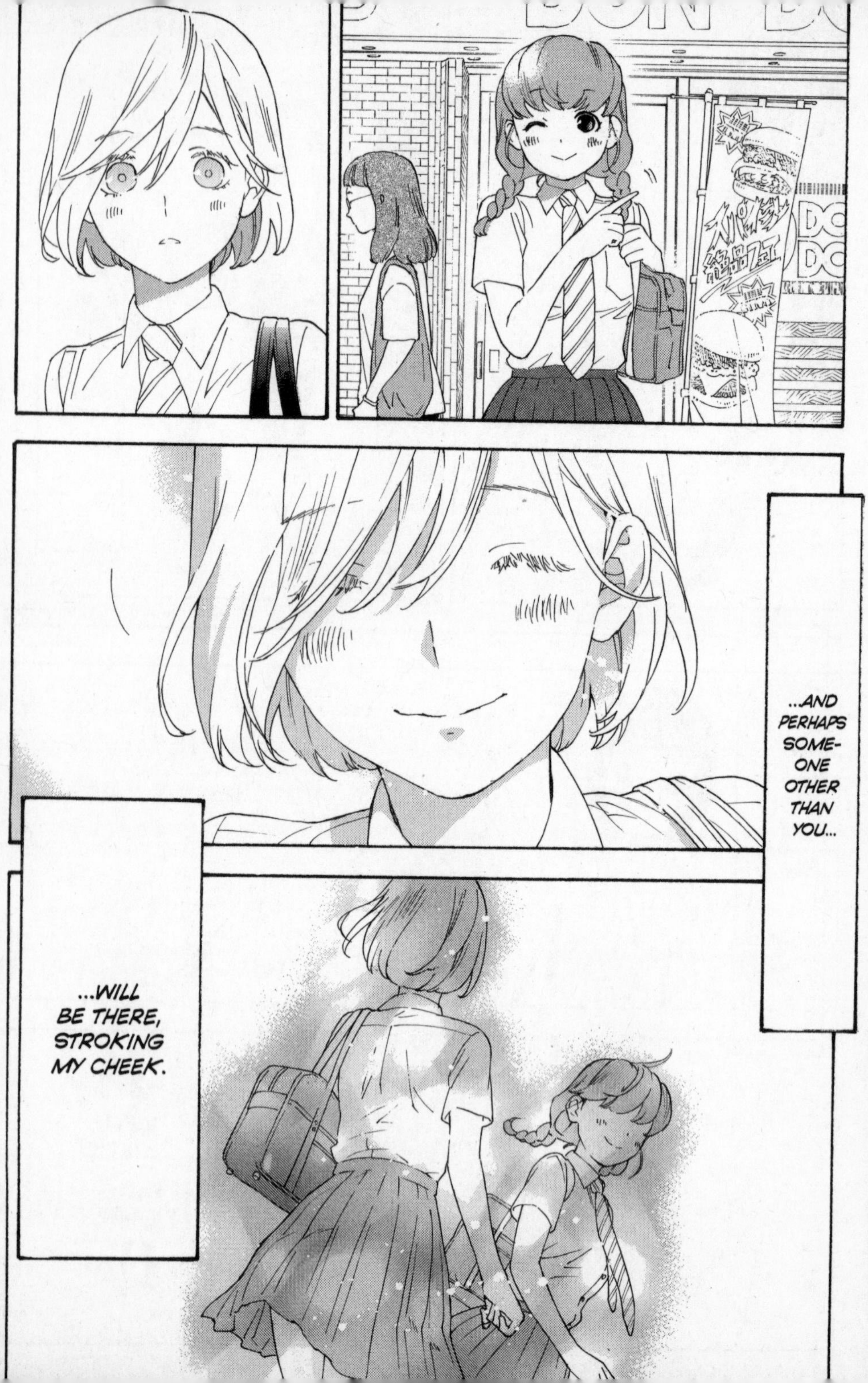
...AND PERHAPS SOME-ONE OTHER THAN YOU...
...WILL BE THERE, STROKING MY CHEEK.

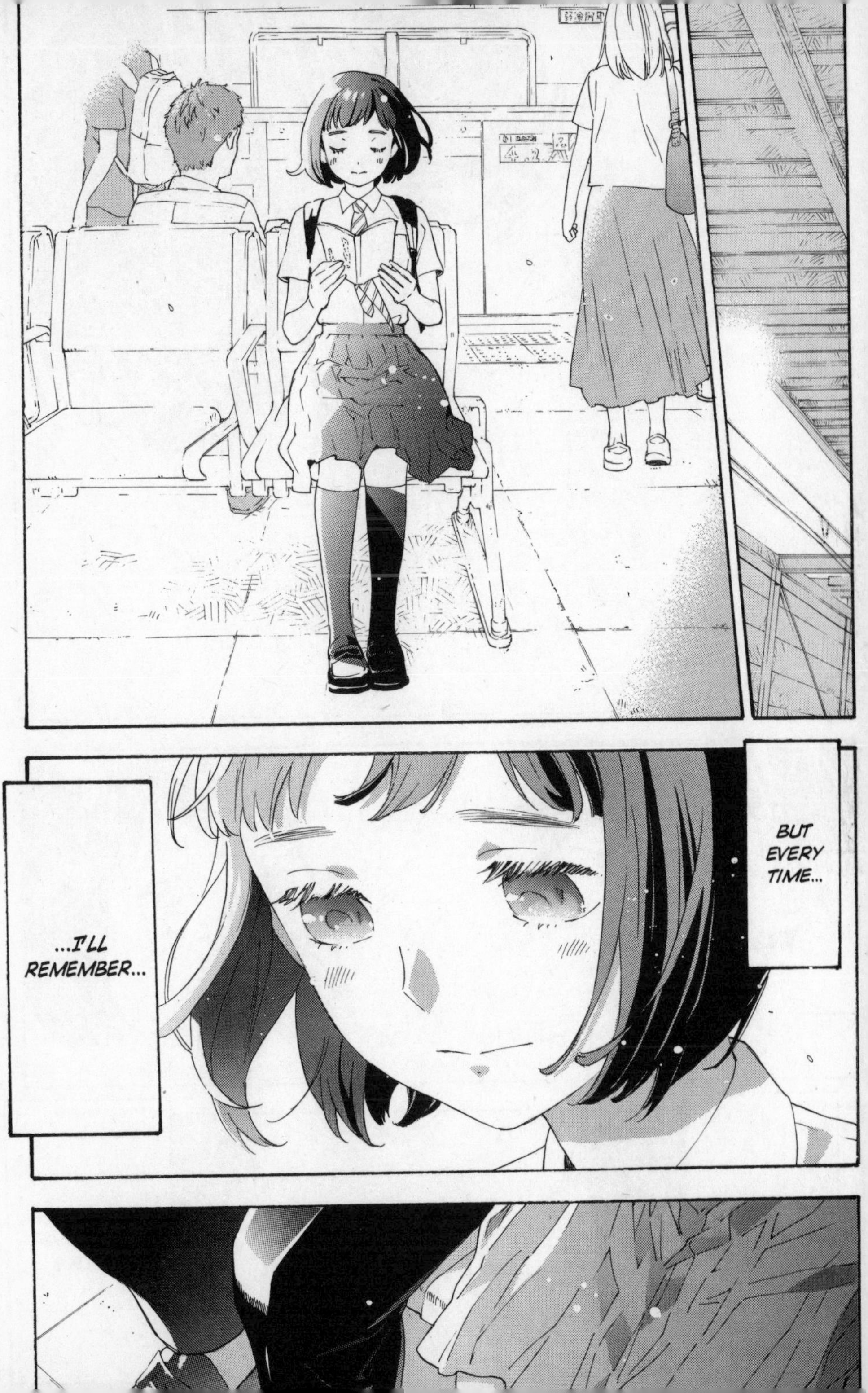
BUT EVERY TIME...
...I'LL REMEMBER...

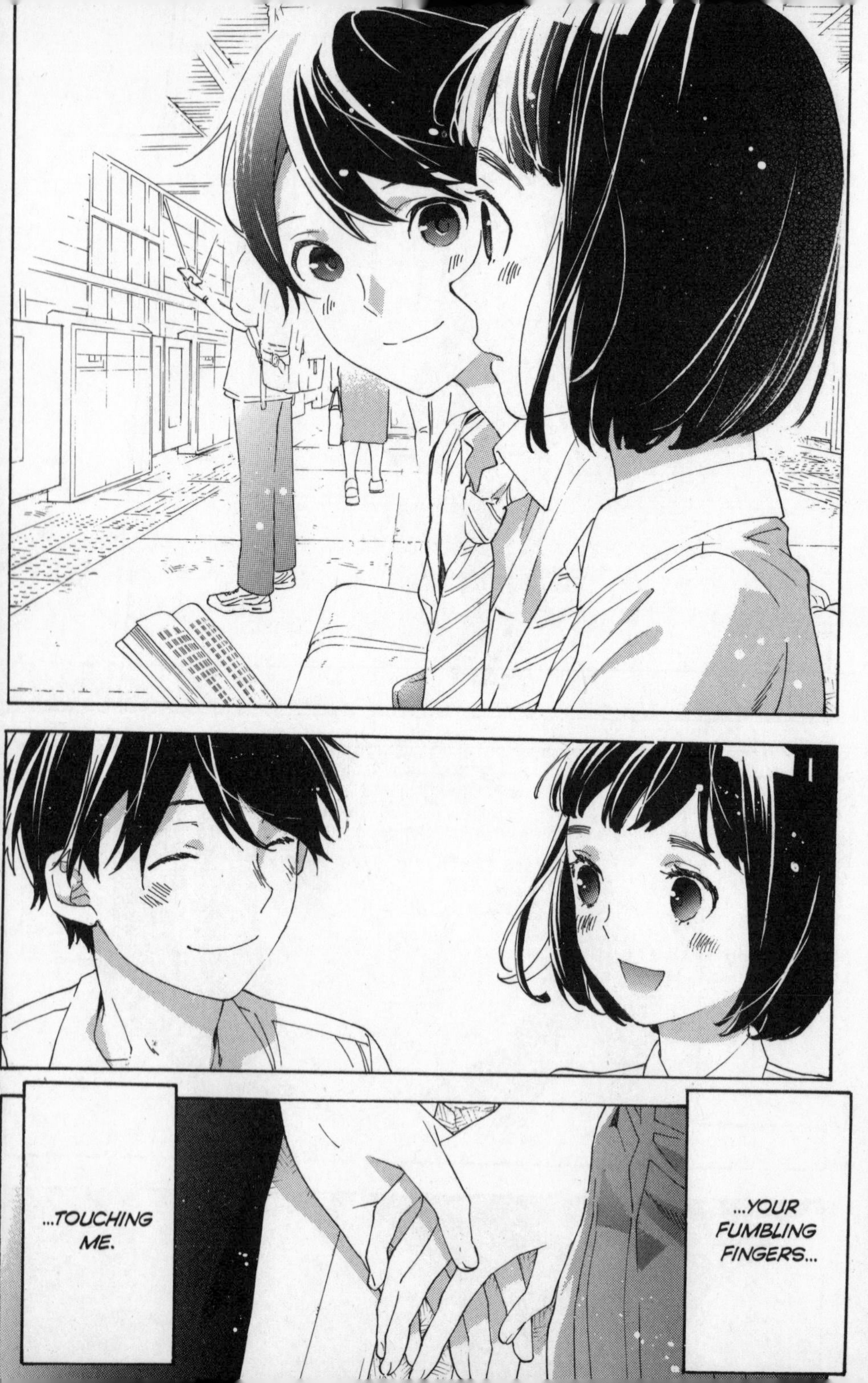
...YOUR FUMBLING FINGERS...
...TOUCHING ME.

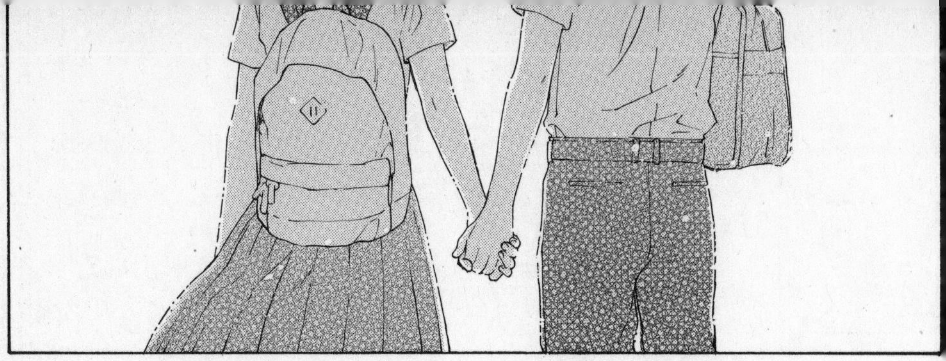

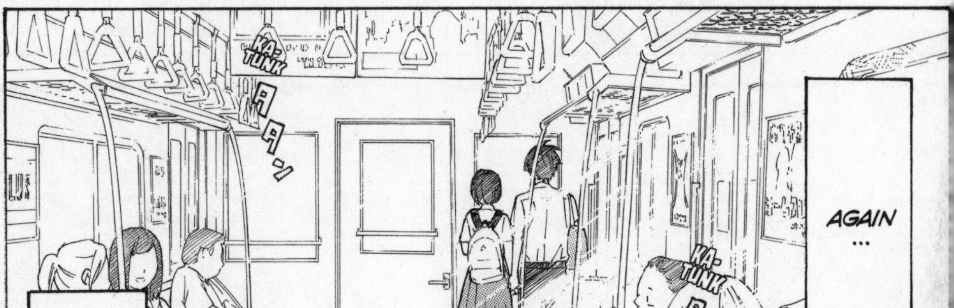
AGAIN...
AND AGAIN...
KA-TUNK
KA-TUNK
KA-TUNK
...I'LL REMEMBER.

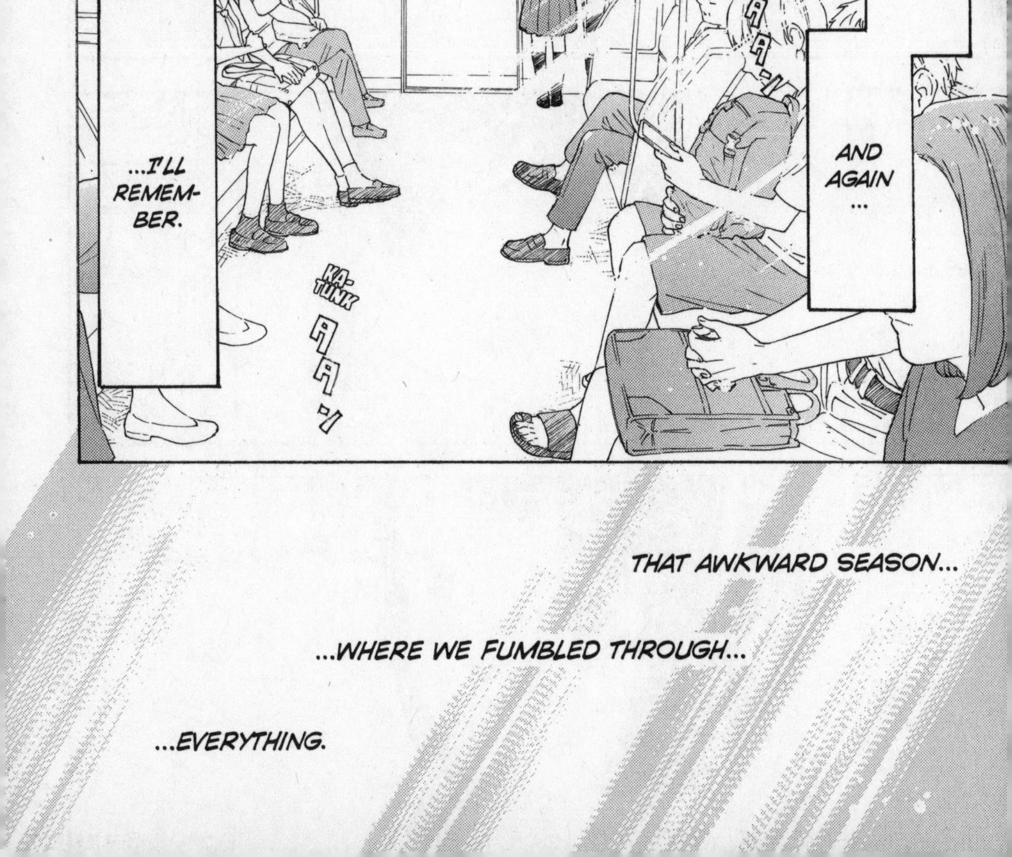
THAT AWKWARD SEASON...
...WHERE WE FUMBLED THROUGH...
...EVERYTHING.

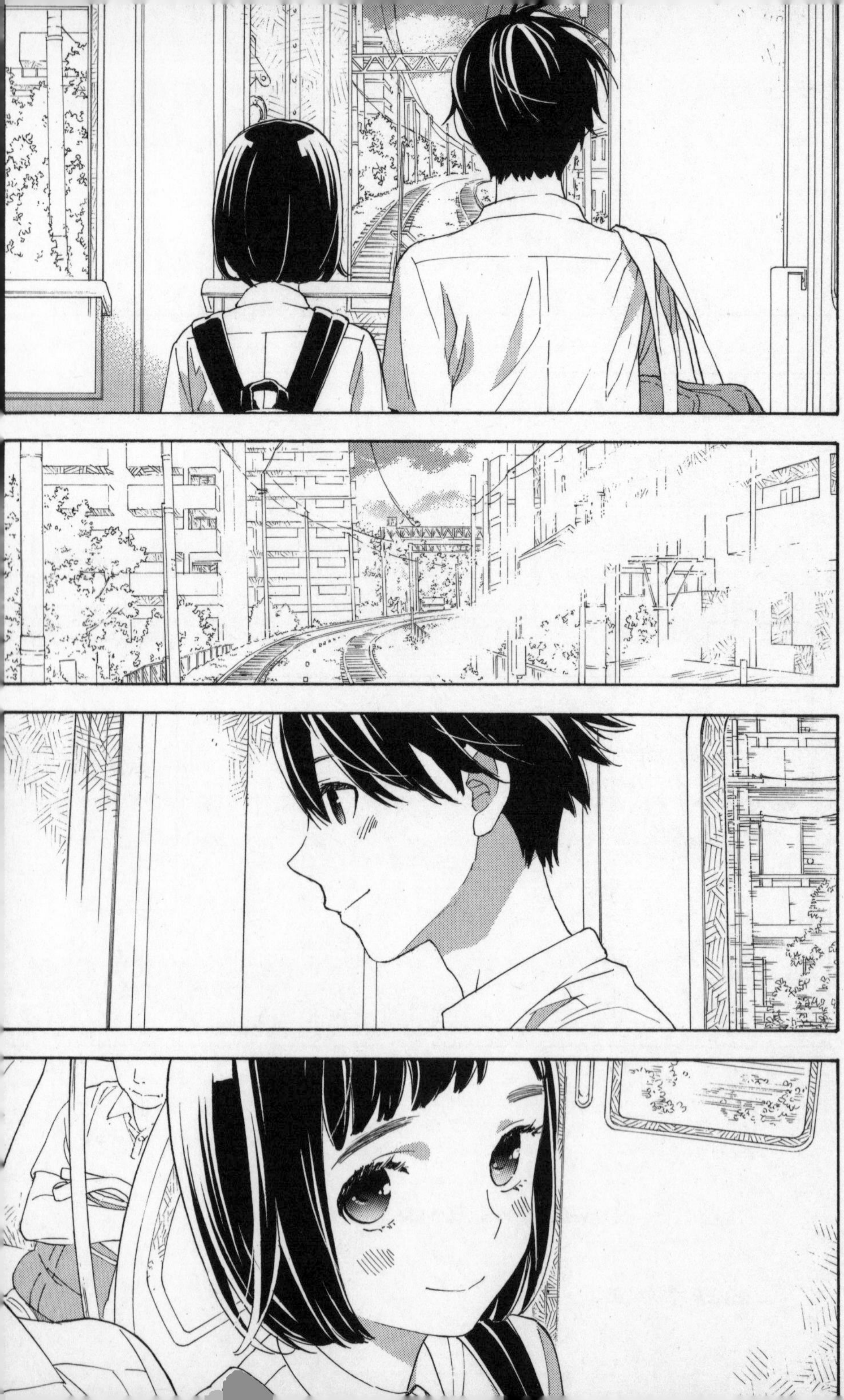

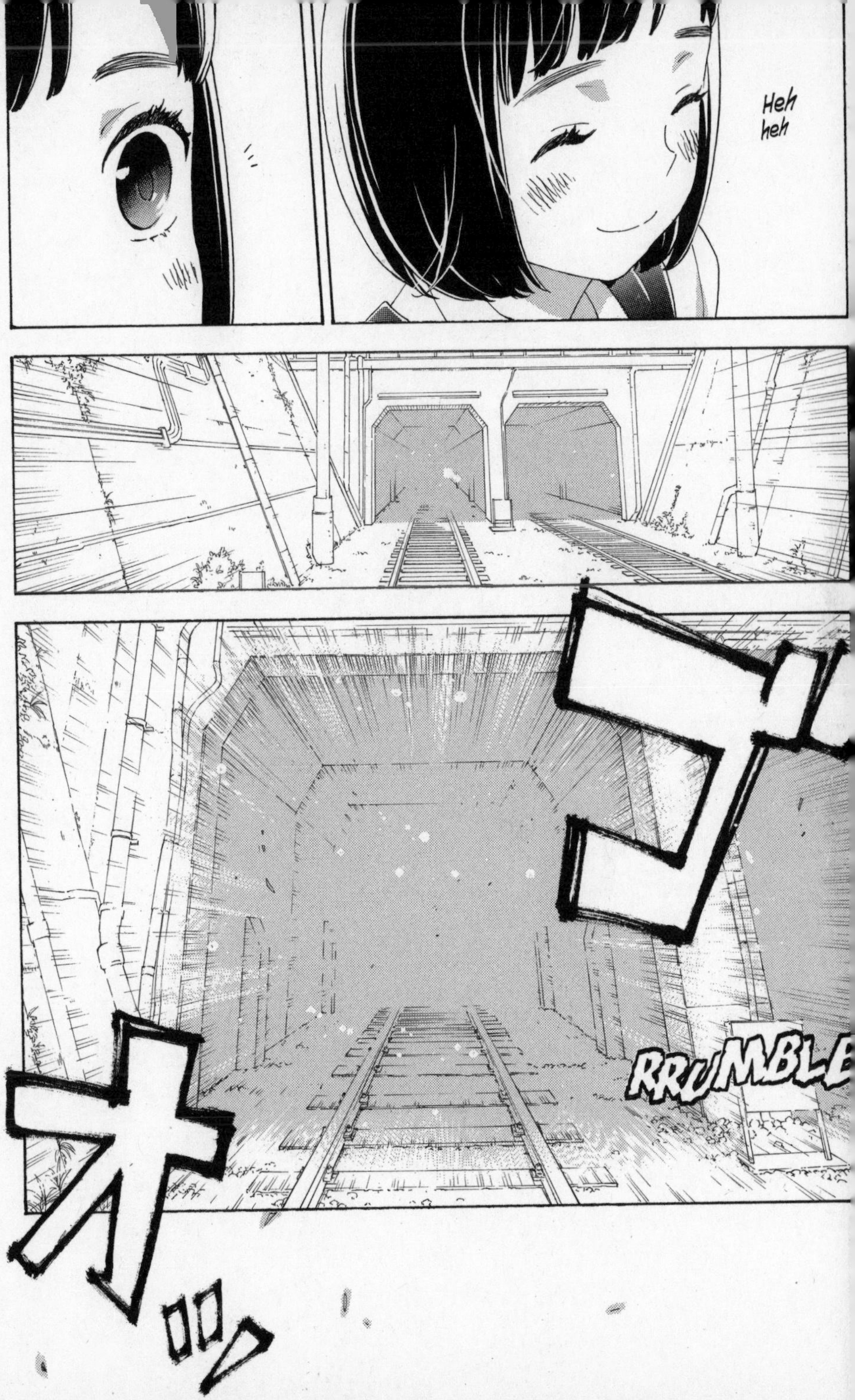
Heh heh
RRUMBLE

...IT
WENT
IN.

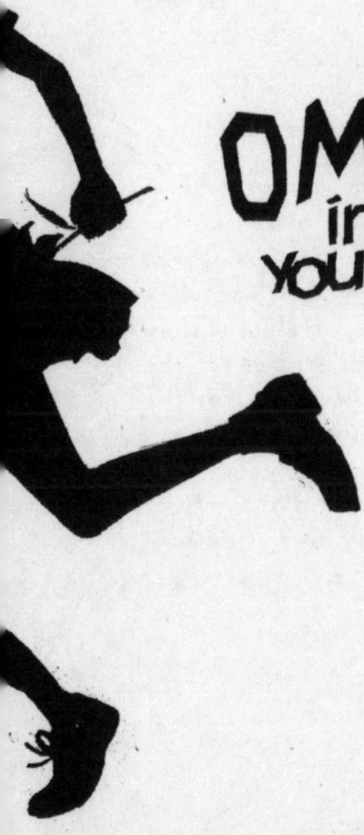

O Maidens in Your Savage Season

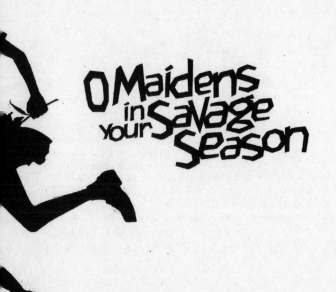

They told me I could write on any subject I wanted, so I wanted to try my hand at something that would be hard to pitch as an anime. Basically, I wanted to go wild and plunge headlong into eroticism. But once the characters started living on the page, the Literature Club members were all so pure that they didn't get into sexy mode at all, pushing eroticism further and further away. They plunged on ahead as pure as ever to the very end, so I never got to achieve my original goal...but I ended up loving all of them.

If this were an anime, I was basically only in charge of the script, but Emoto-sensei was the equivalent of director, animator, and so much more. Thanks to her outstanding style and passion, I have come to love this series so much it makes me want to scream. The editors were also always there to support us, and I'm so grateful to have been part of such a fantastic team.

Finally, to everyone who supported us: thanks to you all, I was able to go wild creating the series, just like these maidens in their savage season. Thank you so very much.

I hope to see you again somewhere soon.

Mari Okada

Because the original story was tremendously fun, creating the manga was so enjoyable that sometimes I had to stop and ask myself, "Is it really okay that I'm having this much fun this whole time?"

I got so much power every month from the girls going wild, sparkling as they laughed, cried, and worried their way through. When I read the stories for the last episode and epilogue, I felt a warmth flood through my heart, but at the same time I was sad to realize that it was almost time to say goodbye...

That's not the only reason, but I drew their sleeping faces at the end of the final episode with the sincere hope that they would truly live happily ever after.

I can't describe how honored I am to have experienced Okada-sensei's passion so directly through providing the art for this series.

Thank you, from the bottom of my heart, to Okada-sensei, everyone who helped and supported us, and all of you readers out there!

Nao Emoto

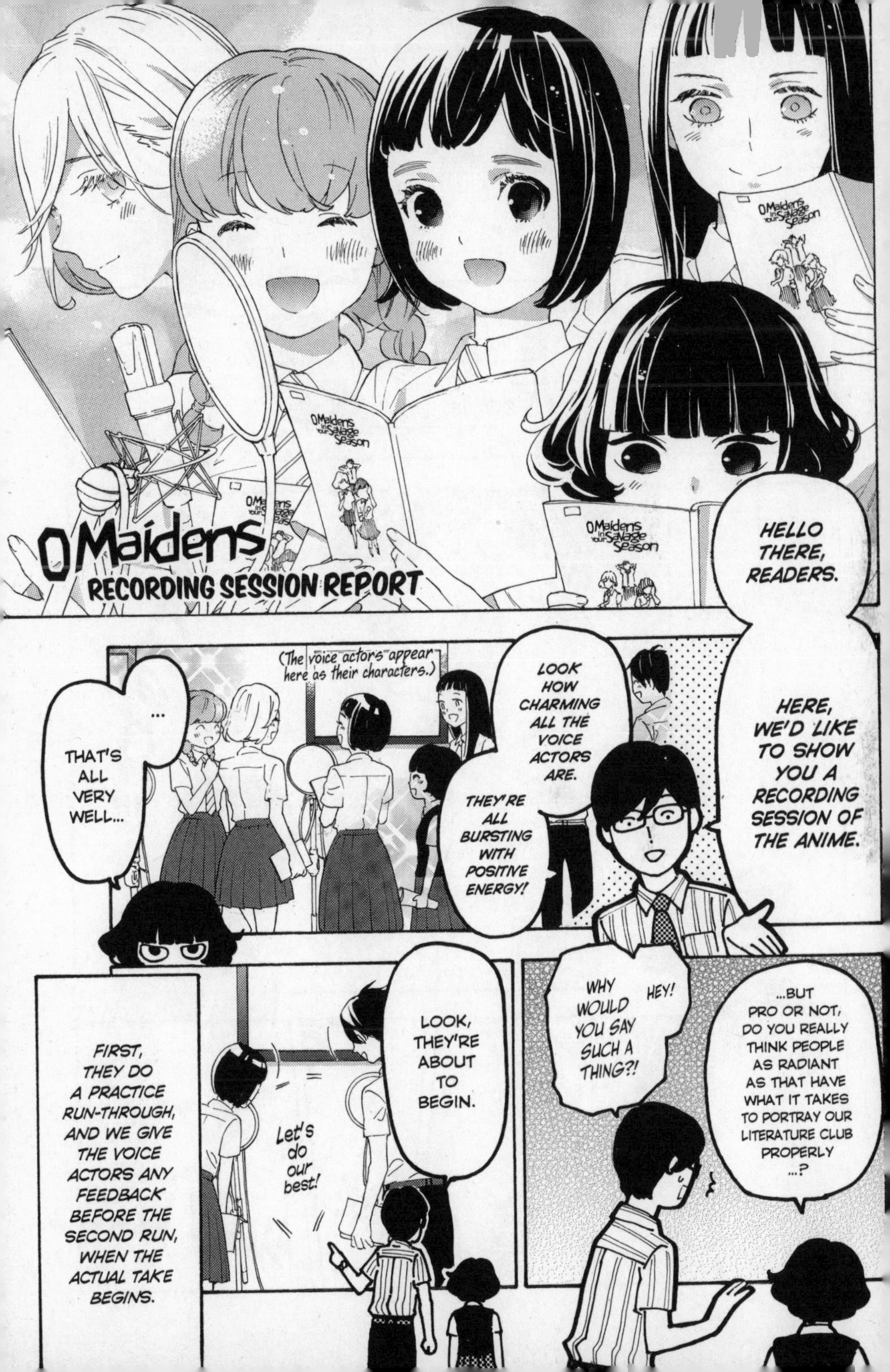
HELLO THERE, READERS.
O Maidens
RECORDING SESSION REPORT
HERE, WE'D LIKE TO SHOW YOU A RECORDING SESSION OF THE ANIME.
LOOK HOW CHARMING ALL THE VOICE ACTORS ARE.
(The voice actors appear here as their characters.)
THEY'RE ALL BURSTING WITH POSITIVE ENERGY!
...
THAT'S ALL VERY WELL...
...BUT PRO OR NOT, DO YOU REALLY THINK PEOPLE AS RADIANT AS THAT HAVE WHAT IT TAKES TO PORTRAY OUR LITERATURE CLUB PROPERLY ...?
HEY!
WHY WOULD YOU SAY SUCH A THING?!
LOOK, THEY'RE ABOUT TO BEGIN.
Let's do our best!
FIRST, THEY DO A PRACTICE RUN-THROUGH, AND WE GIVE THE VOICE ACTORS ANY FEEDBACK BEFORE THE SECOND RUN, WHEN THE ACTUAL TAKE BEGINS.

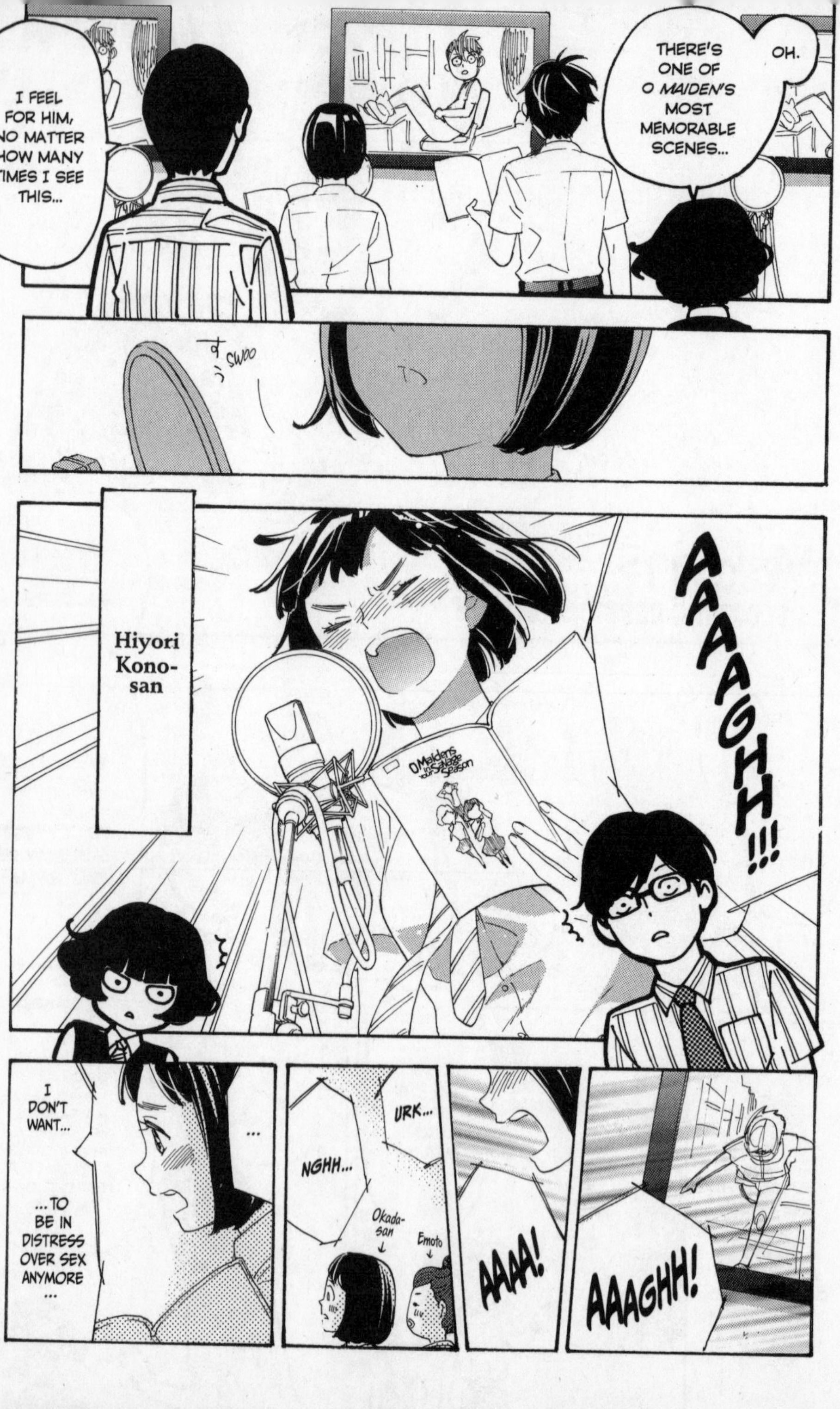
OH.
THERE'S ONE OF O MAIDEN'S MOST MEMORABLE SCENES...
I FEEL FOR HIM, NO MATTER HOW MANY TIMES I SEE THIS...
SWOO
AAAAGHH!!!
O Maidens in Your Savage Season
Hiyori Konosan
AAAGHH!
AAAA!
URK...
NGHH...
Okada-san
Emoto
...
I DON'T WANT...
...TO BE IN DISTRESS OVER SEX ANYMORE ...

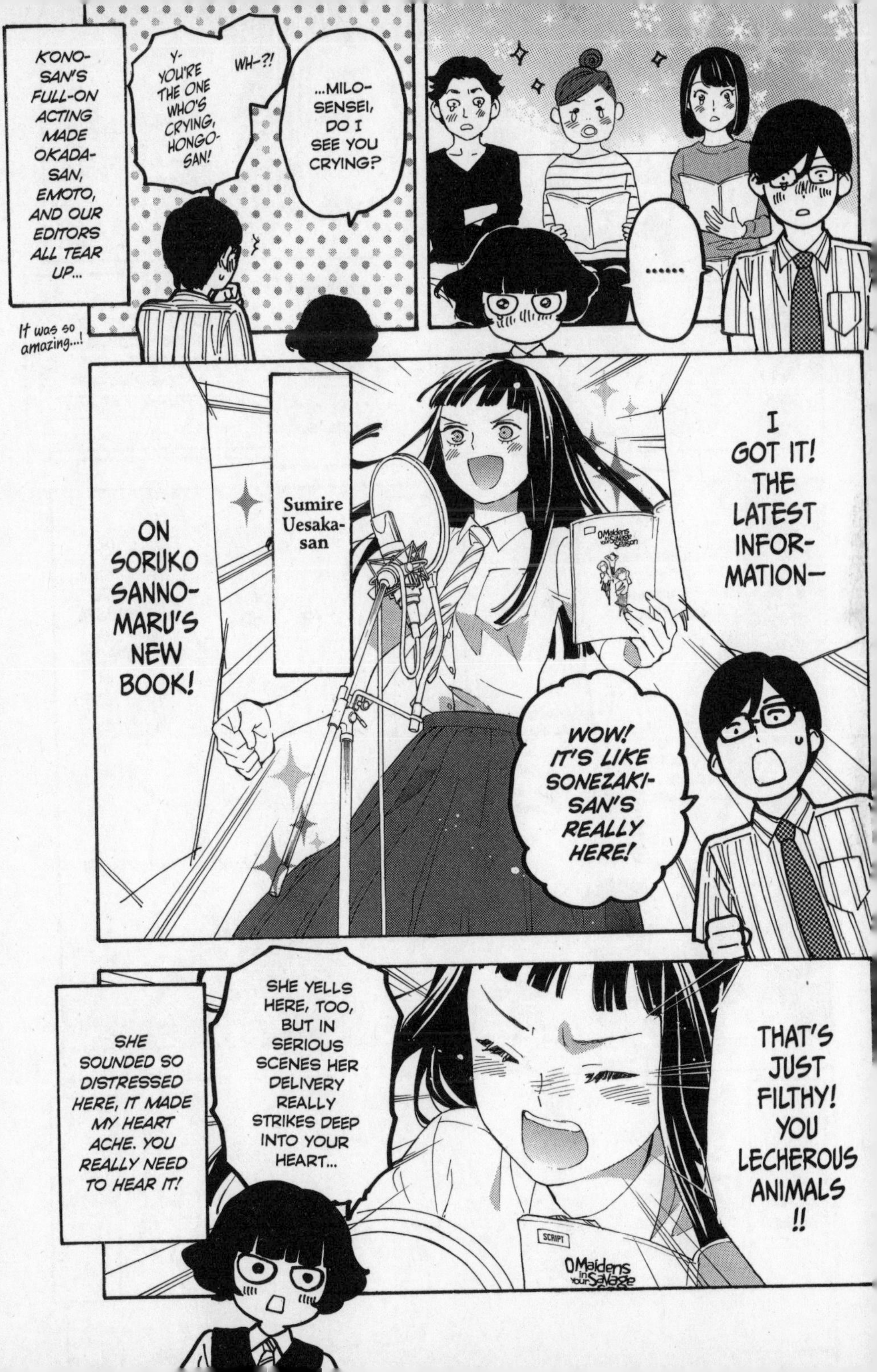
......
...MILO-SENSEI, DO I SEE YOU CRYING?
WH-?!
Y-YOU'RE THE ONE WHO'S CRYING, HONGO-SAN!
KONO-SAN'S FULL-ON ACTING MADE OKADA-SAN, EMOTO, AND OUR EDITORS ALL TEAR UP...
It was so amazing...!
I GOT IT! THE LATEST INFORMATION—
Sumire Uesaka-san
ON SORUKO SANNO-MARU'S NEW BOOK!
WOW! IT'S LIKE SONEZAKI-SAN'S REALLY HERE!
THAT'S JUST FILTHY! YOU LECHEROUS ANIMALS!!
SCRIPT
O Maidens in Your Savage Season
SHE YELLS HERE, TOO, BUT IN SERIOUS SCENES HER DELIVERY REALLY STRIKES DEEP INTO YOUR HEART...
SHE SOUNDED SO DISTRESSED HERE, IT MADE MY HEART ACHE. YOU REALLY NEED TO HEAR IT!

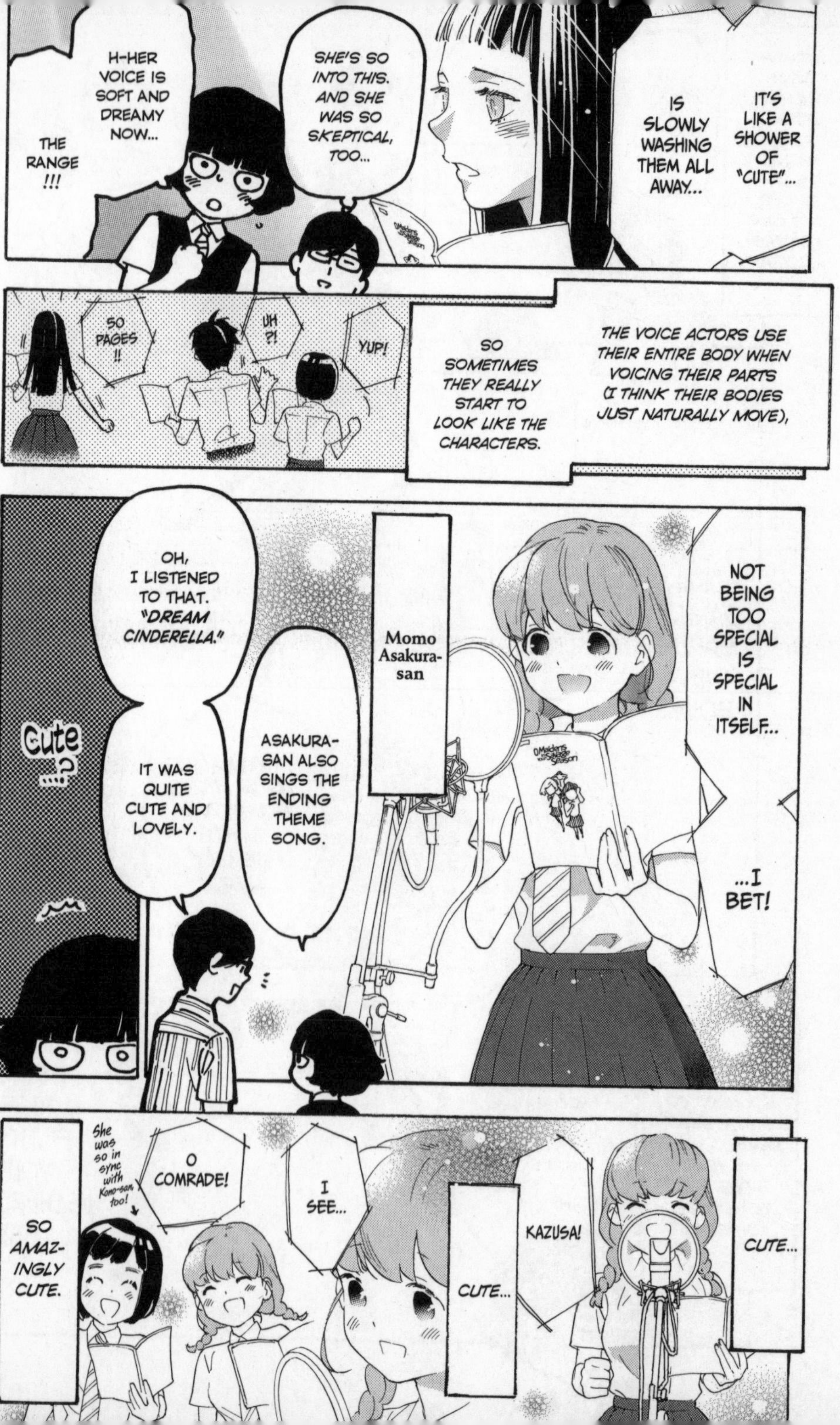
IT'S LIKE A SHOWER OF "CUTE"...
IS SLOWLY WASHING THEM ALL AWAY...
SHE'S SO INTO THIS. AND SHE WAS SO SKEPTICAL, TOO...
H-HER VOICE IS SOFT AND DREAMY NOW...
THE RANGE !!!
THE VOICE ACTORS USE THEIR ENTIRE BODY WHEN VOICING THEIR PARTS (I THINK THEIR BODIES JUST NATURALLY MOVE),
SO SOMETIMES THEY REALLY START TO LOOK LIKE THE CHARACTERS.
YUP!
UH ?!
SO PAGES !!
NOT BEING TOO SPECIAL IS SPECIAL IN ITSELF...
...I BET!
Momo Asakura-san
ASAKURA-SAN ALSO SINGS THE ENDING THEME SONG.
OH, I LISTENED TO THAT. "DREAM CINDERELLA."
IT WAS QUITE CUTE AND LOVELY.
Cute ...?
CUTE...
KAZUSA!
CUTE...
I SEE...
O COMRADE!
She was so in sync with Kono-san, too!
SO AMAZINGLY CUTE.

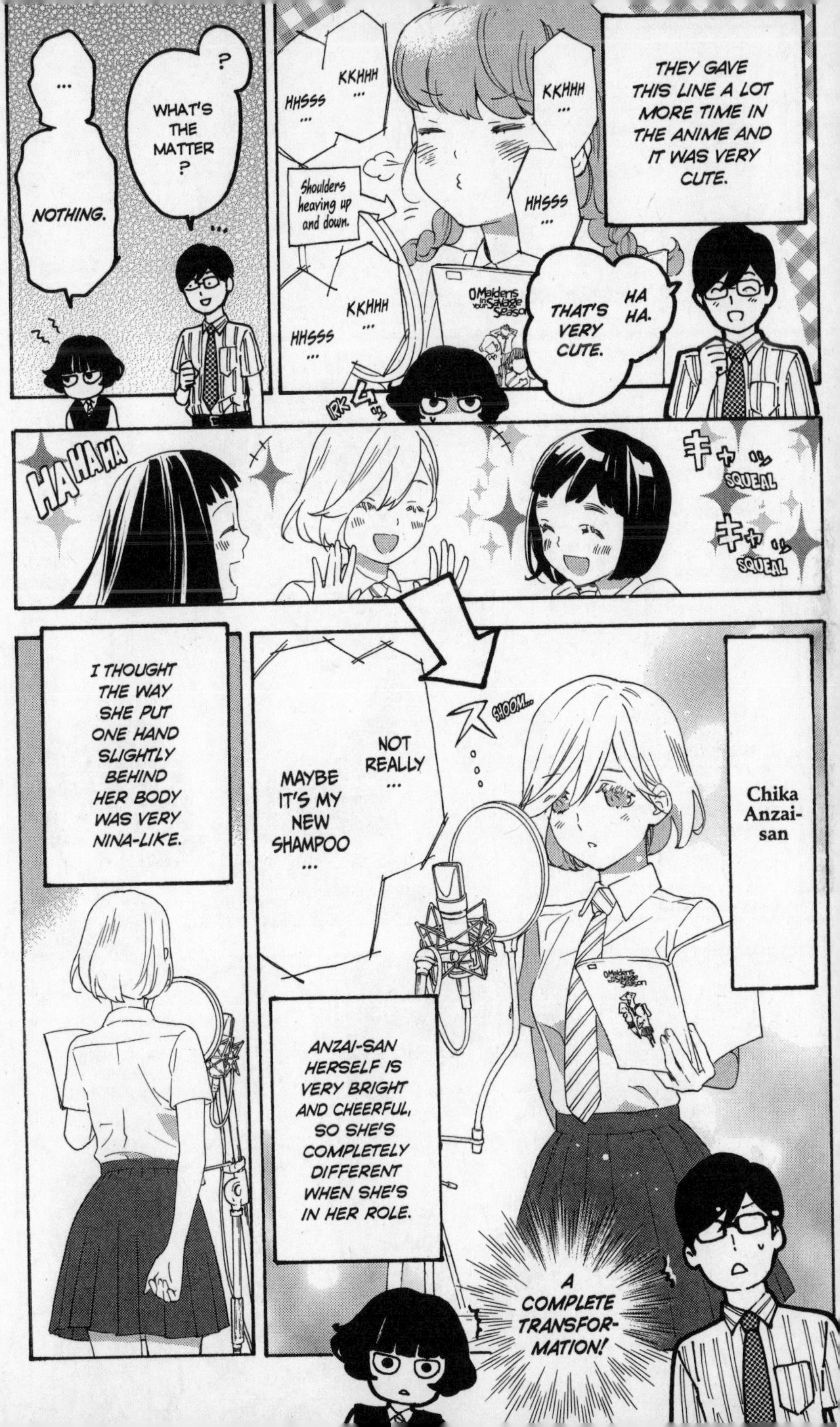
THEY GAVE THIS LINE A LOT MORE TIME IN THE ANIME AND IT WAS VERY CUTE.
HA HA.
THAT'S VERY CUTE.
KKHHH ...
HHSSS ...
KKHHH ...
HHSSS ...
Shoulders heaving up and down.
KKHHH ...
HHSSS ...
IRK
?
WHAT'S THE MATTER ?
...
...
NOTHING.
キャッ
SQUEAL
キャッ
SQUEAL
HAHAHA
Chika Anzai-san
SHOOM...
NOT REALLY ...
MAYBE IT'S MY NEW SHAMPOO ...
ANZAI-SAN HERSELF IS VERY BRIGHT AND CHEERFUL, SO SHE'S COMPLETELY DIFFERENT WHEN SHE'S IN HER ROLE.
A COMPLETE TRANSFORMATION!
I THOUGHT THE WAY SHE PUT ONE HAND SLIGHTLY BEHIND HER BODY WAS VERY NINA-LIKE.

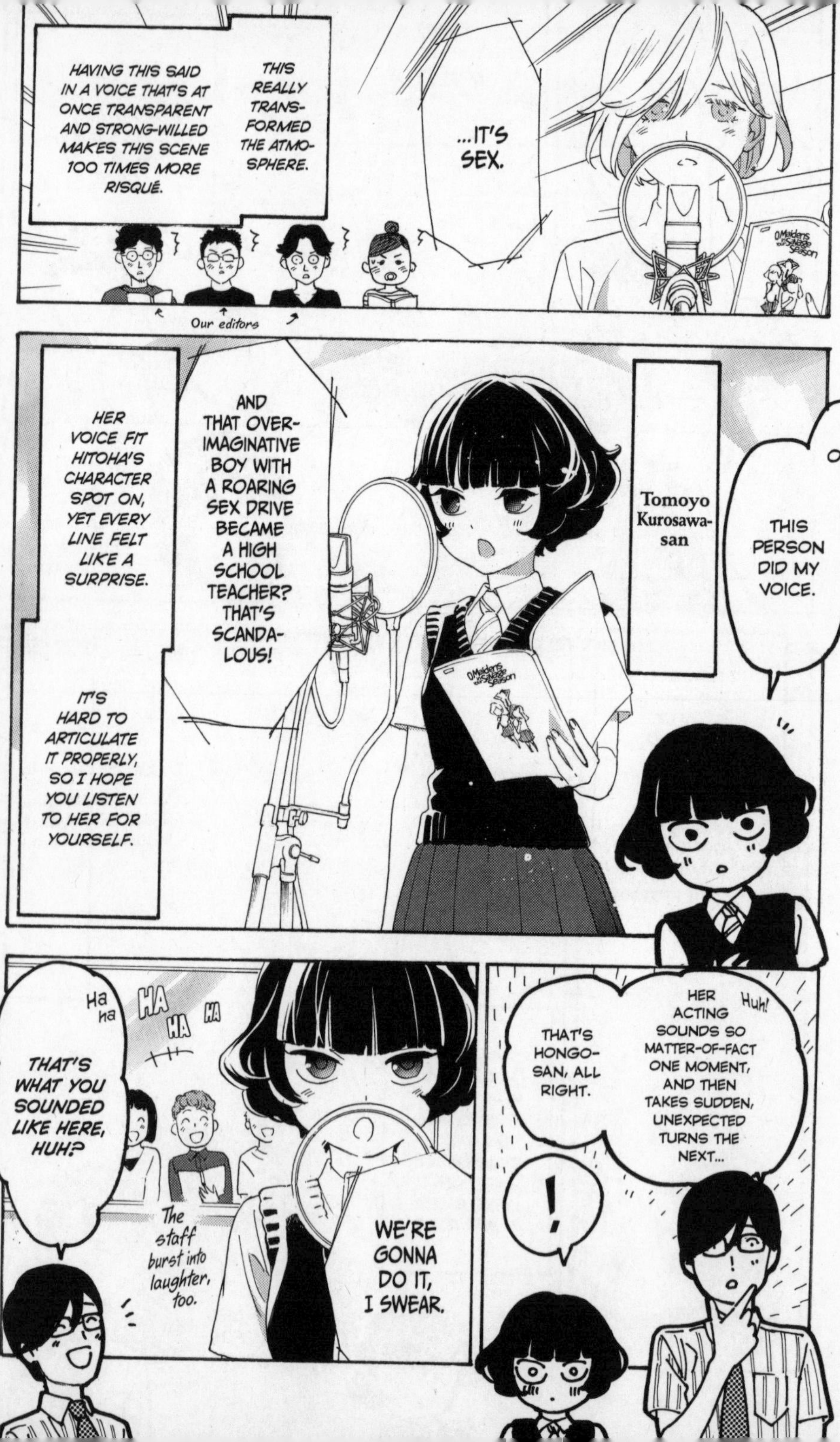
...IT'S SEX.
THIS REALLY TRANSFORMED THE ATMOSPHERE.
HAVING THIS SAID IN A VOICE THAT'S AT ONCE TRANSPARENT AND STRONG-WILLED MAKES THIS SCENE 100 TIMES MORE RISQUÉ.
Our editors
OH!
THIS PERSON DID MY VOICE.
Tomoyo Kurosawa-san
AND THAT OVER-IMAGINATIVE BOY WITH A ROARING SEX DRIVE BECAME A HIGH SCHOOL TEACHER? THAT'S SCANDALOUS!
HER VOICE FIT HITOHA'S CHARACTER SPOT ON, YET EVERY LINE FELT LIKE A SURPRISE.
IT'S HARD TO ARTICULATE IT PROPERLY, SO I HOPE YOU LISTEN TO HER FOR YOURSELF.
Huh!
HER ACTING SOUNDS SO MATTER-OF-FACT ONE MOMENT, AND THEN TAKES SUDDEN, UNEXPECTED TURNS THE NEXT...
THAT'S HONGO-SAN, ALL RIGHT.
!
WE'RE GONNA DO IT, I SWEAR.
Ha ha HA HA HA
THAT'S WHAT YOU SOUNDED LIKE HERE, HUH?
The staff burst into laughter, too.

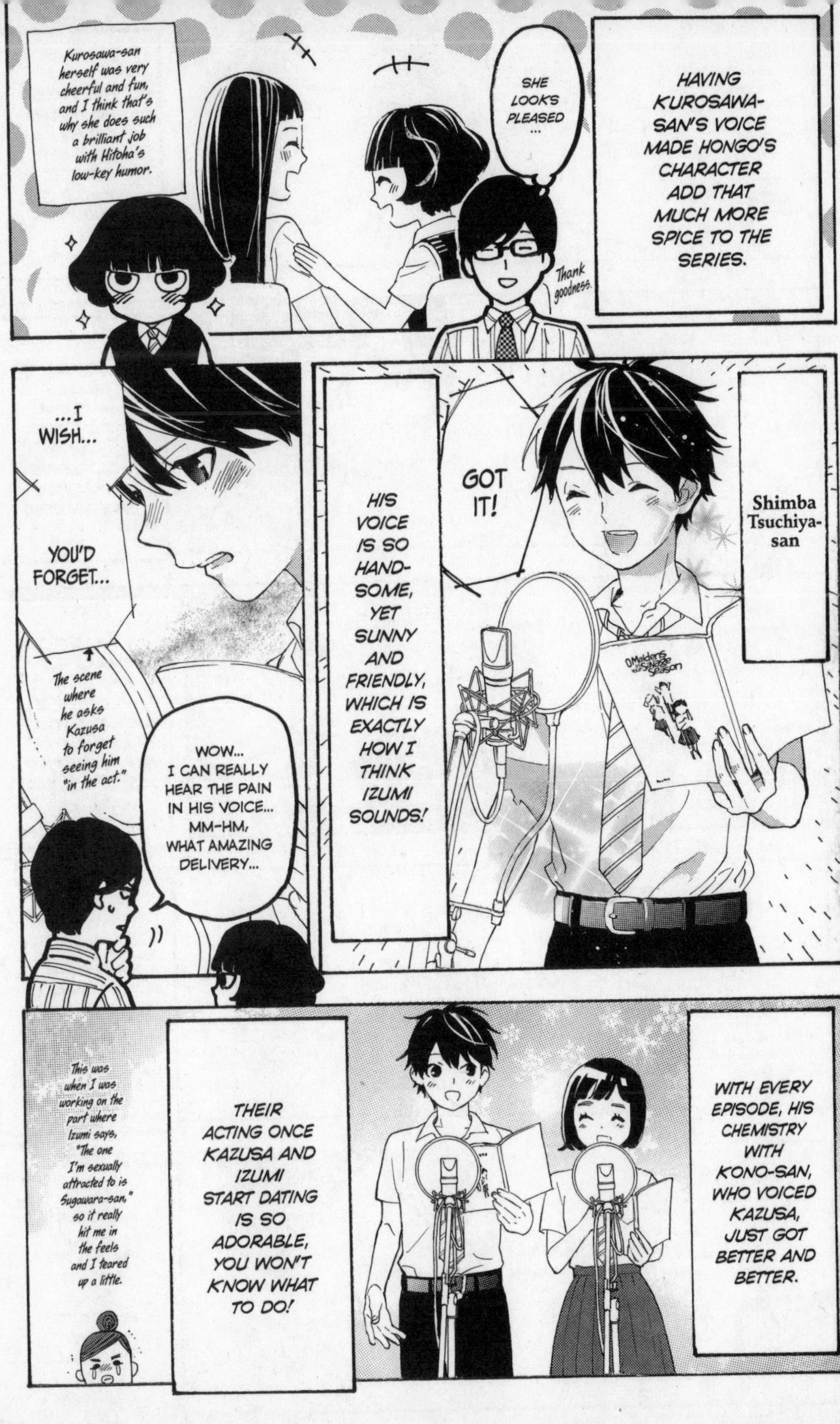
HAVING KUROSAWA-SAN'S VOICE MADE HONGO'S CHARACTER ADD THAT MUCH MORE SPICE TO THE SERIES.
SHE LOOKS PLEASED ...
Thank goodness.
Kurosawa-san herself was very cheerful and fun, and I think that's why she does such a brilliant job with Hitoha's low-key humor.
Shimba Tsuchiya-san
GOT IT!
HIS VOICE IS SO HANDSOME, YET SUNNY AND FRIENDLY, WHICH IS EXACTLY HOW I THINK IZUMI SOUNDS!
O Maidens in Your Savage Season
...I WISH...
YOU'D FORGET...
The scene where he asks Kazusa to forget seeing him "in the act."
WOW... I CAN REALLY HEAR THE PAIN IN HIS VOICE... MM-HM, WHAT AMAZING DELIVERY...
WITH EVERY EPISODE, HIS CHEMISTRY WITH KONO-SAN, WHO VOICED KAZUSA, JUST GOT BETTER AND BETTER.
THEIR ACTING ONCE KAZUSA AND IZUMI START DATING IS SO ADORABLE, YOU WON'T KNOW WHAT TO DO!
This was when I was working on the part where Izumi says, "The one I'm sexually attracted to is Sugawara-san," so it really hit me in the feels and I teared up a little.

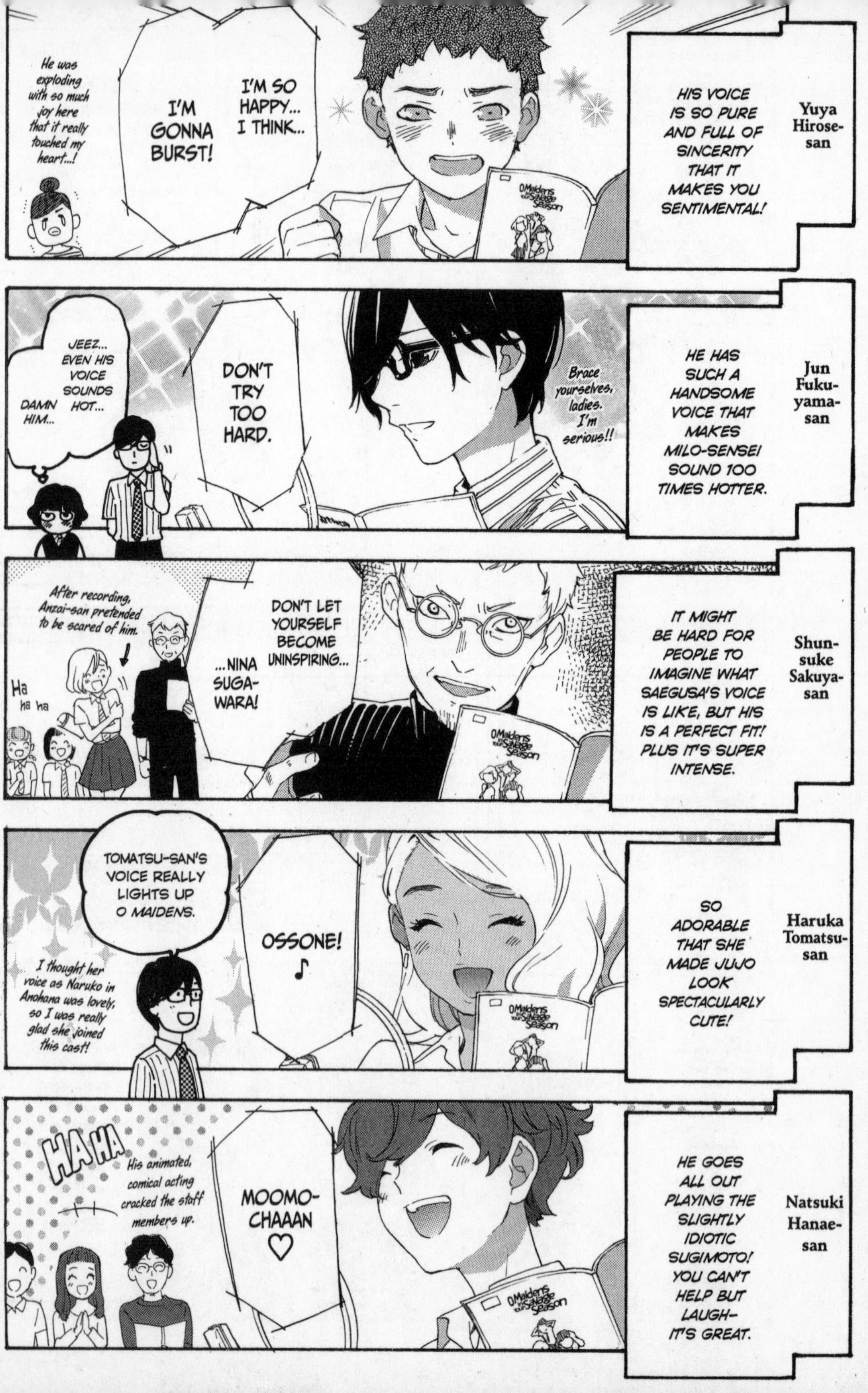
Yuya Hirose-san
HIS VOICE IS SO PURE AND FULL OF SINCERITY THAT IT MAKES YOU SENTIMENTAL!
I'M SO HAPPY... I THINK...
I'M GONNA BURST!
He was exploding with so much joy here that it really touched my heart...!
Jun Fukuyama-san
HE HAS SUCH A HANDSOME VOICE THAT MAKES MILO-SENSEI SOUND 100 TIMES HOTTER.
Brace yourselves, ladies. I'm serious!!
DON'T TRY TOO HARD.
JEEZ... EVEN HIS VOICE SOUNDS HOT... DAMN HIM...
Shunsuke Sakuya-san
IT MIGHT BE HARD FOR PEOPLE TO IMAGINE WHAT SAEGUSA'S VOICE IS LIKE, BUT HIS IS A PERFECT FIT! PLUS IT'S SUPER INTENSE.
DON'T LET YOURSELF BECOME UNINSPIRING...
...NINA SUGAWARA!
After recording, Anzai-san pretended to be scared of him.
Ha ha ha
Haruka Tomatsu-san
SO ADORABLE THAT SHE MADE JUJO LOOK SPECTACULARLY CUTE!
OSSONE! ♪
TOMATSU-SAN'S VOICE REALLY LIGHTS UP O MAIDENS.
I thought her voice as Naruko in Anohana was lovely, so I was really glad she joined this cast!
Natsuki Hanae-san
HE GOES ALL OUT PLAYING THE SLIGHTLY IDIOTIC SUGIMOTO! YOU CAN'T HELP BUT LAUGH—IT'S GREAT.
MOOMO-CHAAAN ♡
HAHA
His animated, comical acting cracked the staff members up.

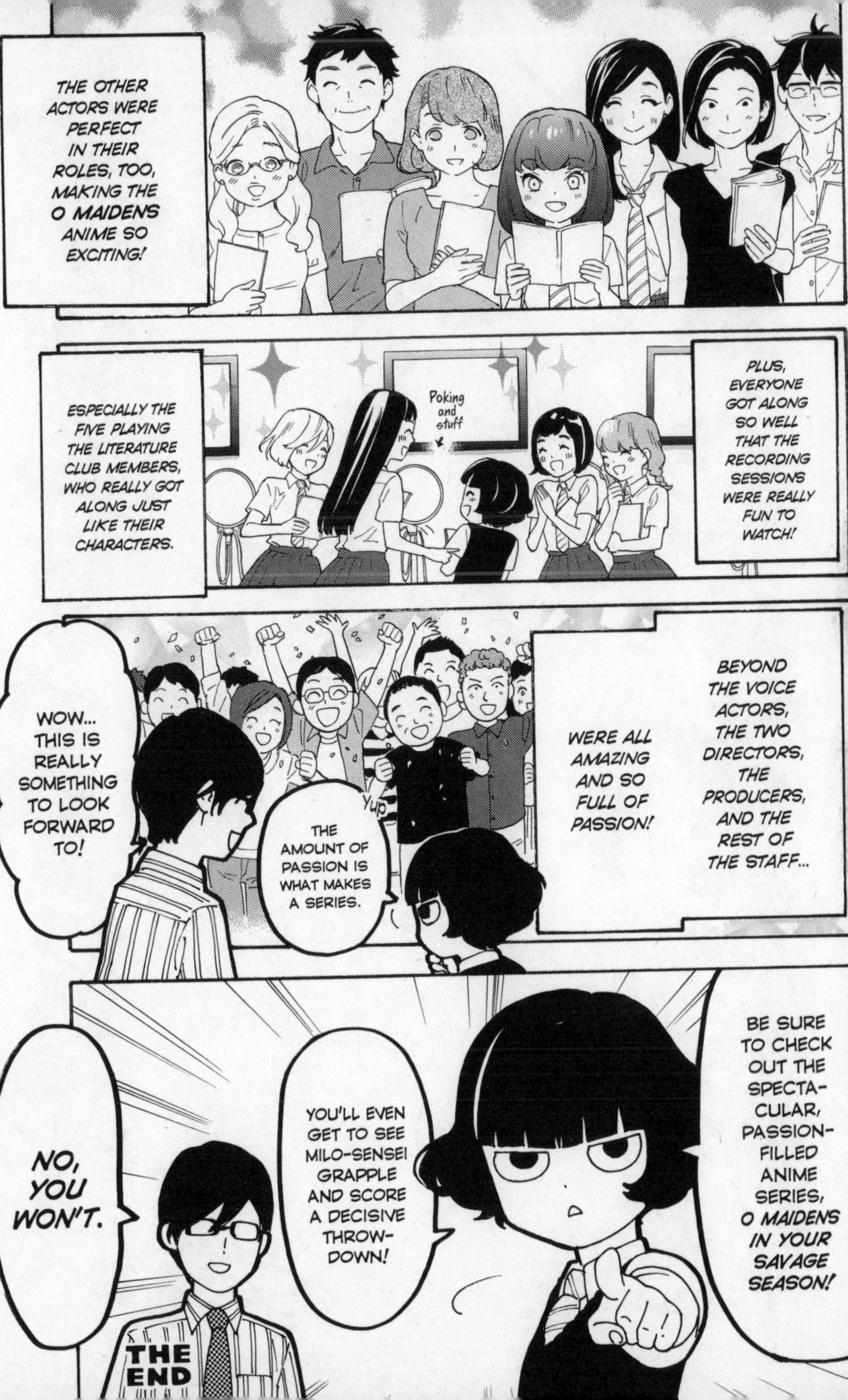
THE OTHER ACTORS WERE PERFECT IN THEIR ROLES, TOO, MAKING THE *O MAIDENS* ANIME SO EXCITING!
PLUS, EVERYONE GOT ALONG SO WELL THAT THE RECORDING SESSIONS WERE REALLY FUN TO WATCH!
Poking and stuff
ESPECIALLY THE FIVE PLAYING THE LITERATURE CLUB MEMBERS, WHO REALLY GOT ALONG JUST LIKE THEIR CHARACTERS.
BEYOND THE VOICE ACTORS, THE TWO DIRECTORS, THE PRODUCERS, AND THE REST OF THE STAFF...
WERE ALL AMAZING AND SO FULL OF PASSION!
WOW... THIS IS REALLY SOMETHING TO LOOK FORWARD TO!
Yup
THE AMOUNT OF PASSION IS WHAT MAKES A SERIES.
BE SURE TO CHECK OUT THE SPECTACULAR, PASSION-FILLED ANIME SERIES, *O MAIDENS IN YOUR SAVAGE SEASON!*
YOU'LL EVEN GET TO SEE MILO-SENSEI GRAPPLE AND SCORE A DECISIVE THROW-DOWN!
NO, YOU WON'T.
THE END

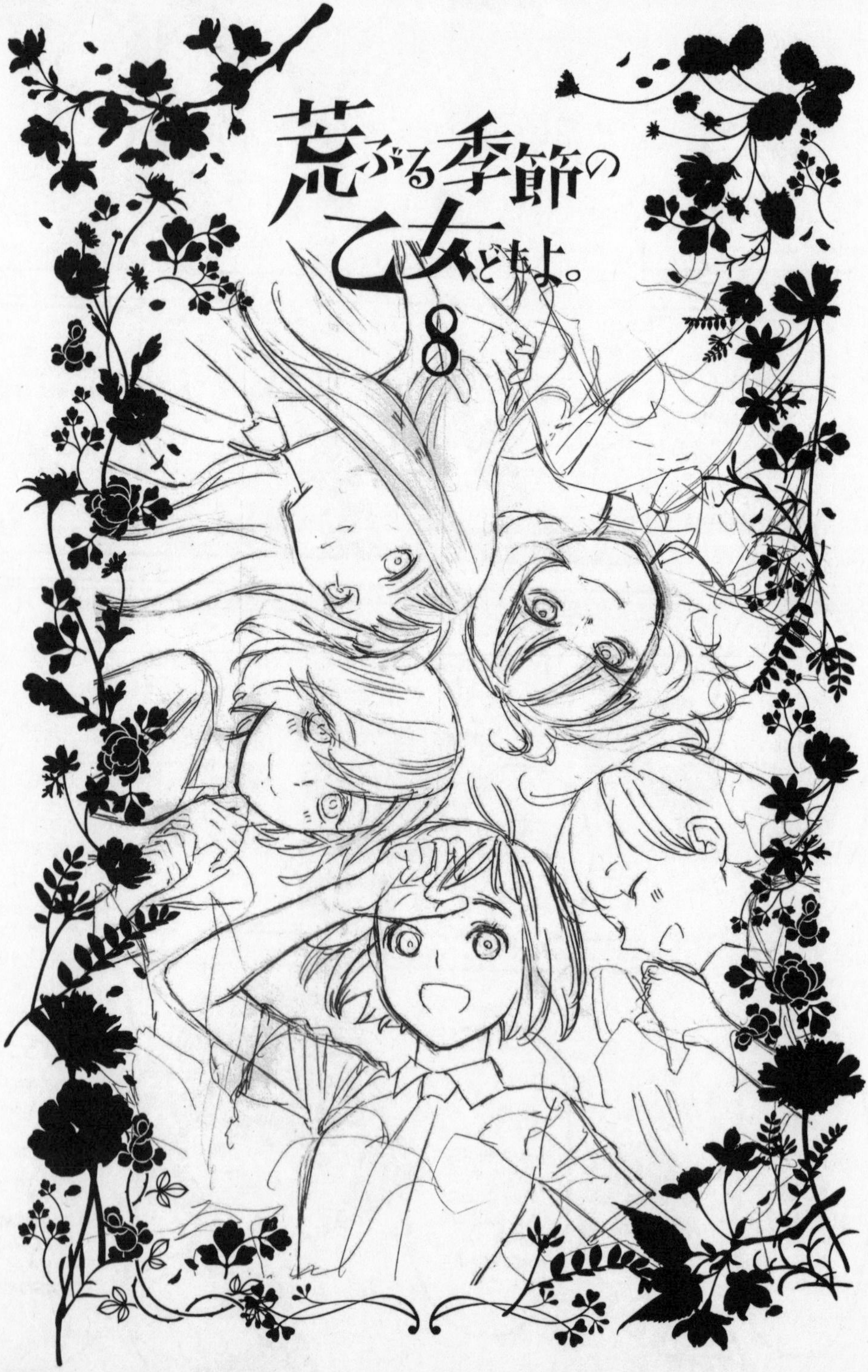
荒ぶる季節の乙女どもよ。
8

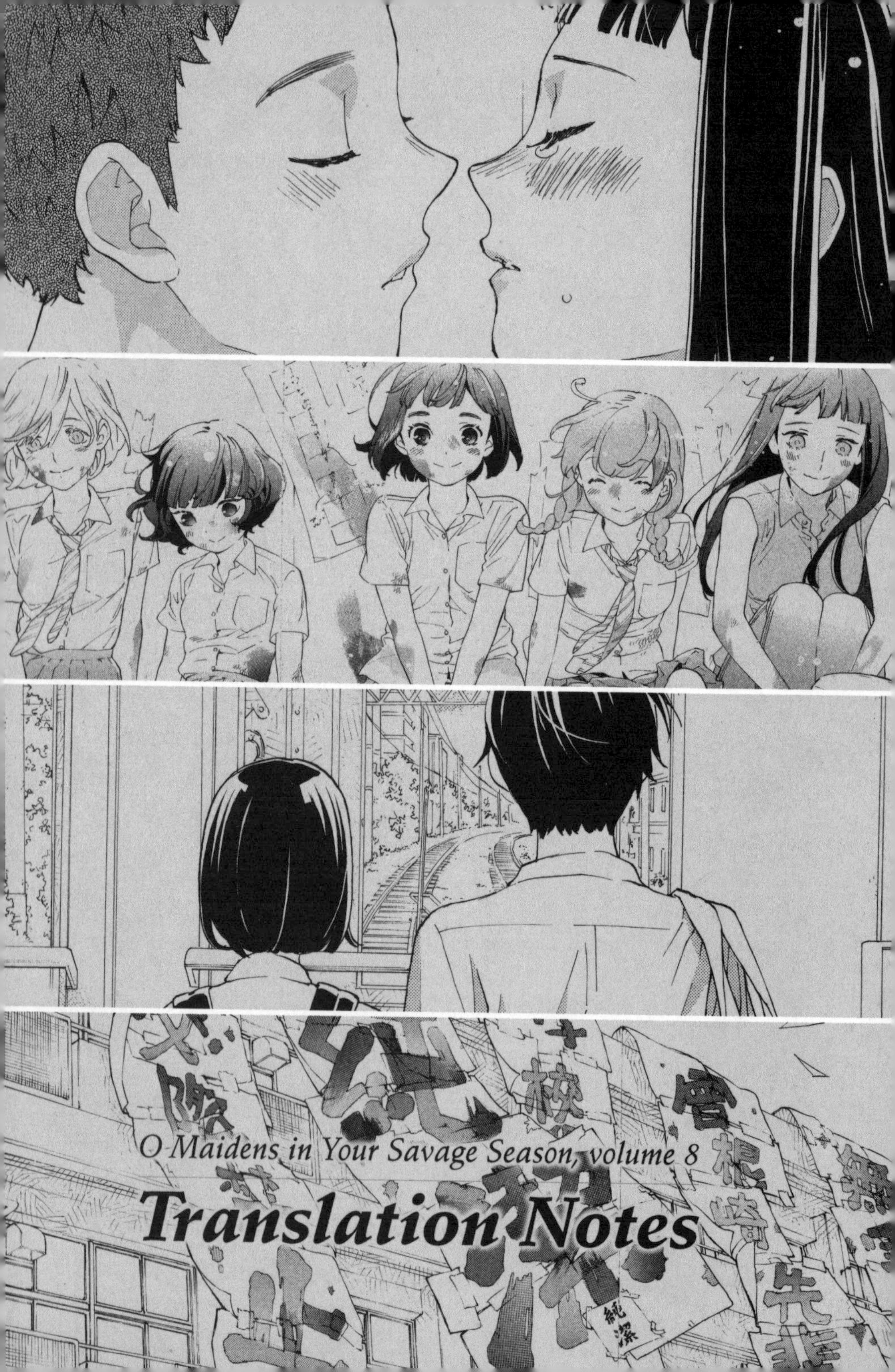

O Maidens in Your Savage Season, volume 8

Translation Notes

page 82

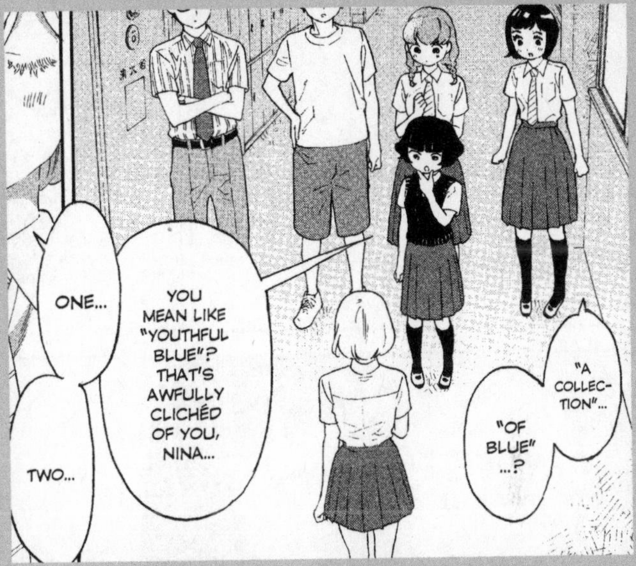
"A COLLECTION"...
"OF BLUE" ...?
YOU MEAN LIKE "YOUTHFUL BLUE"? THAT'S AWFULLY CLICHÉD OF YOU, NINA...
ONE...
TWO...

Youthful blue

The Japanese word *seishun,* which uses the *kanji* characters for "blue spring," refers to the lush and exciting period of adolescence.

page 116

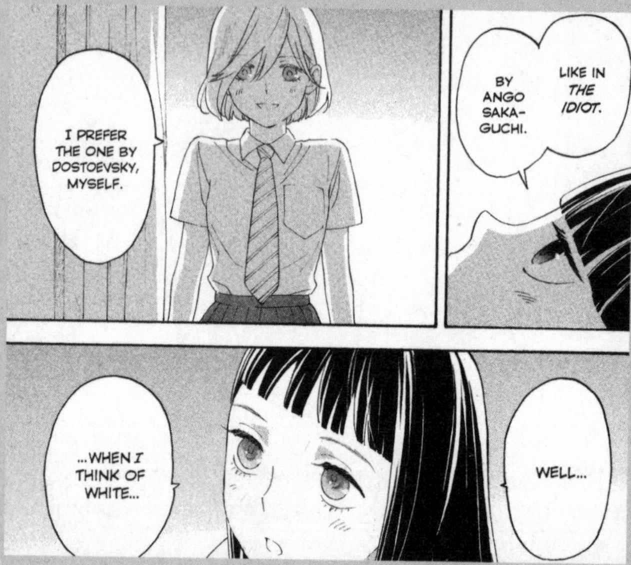
LIKE IN *THE IDIOT*.
BY ANGO SAKAGUCHI.
I PREFER THE ONE BY DOSTOEVSKY, MYSELF.
WELL...
...WHEN I THINK OF WHITE...

The Idiot

A short story by 20th century author Ango Sakaguchi about a man's twisted relationship with an intellectually disabled woman just before Japan's surrender during World War II. The Japanese title, *Hakuchi,* is an obsolete term for developmentally disabled people, now considered derogatory. The "*haku*" means white, which is why Hitoha references it here. Dostoevsky also wrote a novel entitled *The Idiot* (known also as *Hakuchi* in Japanese), but the two are unrelated.

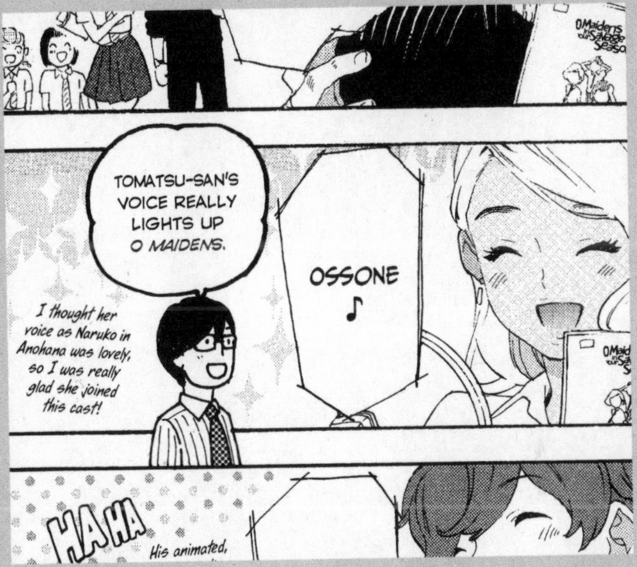
OSSONE ♪
TOMATSU-SAN'S VOICE REALLY LIGHTS UP O MAIDENS.
I thought her voice as Naruko in Anohana was lovely, so I was really glad she joined this cast!
HAHA
His animated,

Anohana

Also written by Mari Okada, *Anohana: The Flower We Saw That Day* is a 2011 anime series about a group of friends coming to terms with the death of a mutual childhood friend. Naruko Anjo is one of the leading characters.

A picture-perfect shojo series from Yoko Nogiri, creator of the hit *That Wolf-Boy is Mine!*

Mako's always had a passion for photography. When she loses someone dear to her, she clings onto her art as a relic of the close relationship she once had... Luckily, her childhood best friend Kei encourages her to come to his high school and join their prestigious photo club. With nothing to lose, Mako grabs her camera and moves into the dorm where Kei and his classmates live. Soon, a fresh take on life, along with a mysterious new muse, begin to come into focus!

LOVE IN FOCUS

Love in Focus © Yoko Nogiri/Kodansha Ltd.

KC KODANSHA COMICS

A SMART, NEW ROMANTIC COMEDY FOR FANS OF *SHORTCAKE CAKE* AND *TERRACE HOUSE!*

A romance manga starring high school girl Meeko, who learns to live on her own in a boarding house whose living room is home to the odd (but handsome) Matsunaga-san. She begins to adjust to her new life away from her parents, but Meeko soon learns that no matter how far away from home she is, she's still a young girl at heart — especially when she finds herself falling for Matsunaga-san.

PERFECT WORLD

Rie Aruga

A TOUCHING
NEW SERIES
ABOUT LOVE AND
COPING WITH
DISABILITY

An office party reunites Tsugumi with her high school crush Itsuki. He's realized his dream of becoming an architect, but along the way, he experienced a spinal injury that put him in a wheelchair. Now Tsugumi's rekindled feelings will butt up against prejudices she never considered — and Itsuki will have to decide if he's ready to let someone into his heart...

"Depicts with great delicacy and courage the difficulties some with disabilities experience getting involved in romantic relationships... Rie Aruga refuses to romanticize, pushing her heroine to face the reality of disability. She invites her readers to the same tasks of empathy, knowledge and recognition."
—Slate.fr

"An important entry [in manga romance]... The emotional core of both plot and characters indicates thoughtfulness... [Aruga's] research is readily apparent in the text and artwork, making this feel like a real story."
—Anime News Network

KC
KODANSHA
COMICS

THE SWEET SCENT OF LOVE IS IN THE AIR! FOR FANS OF OFFBEAT ROMANCES LIKE *WOTAKOI*

Sweat and Soap © Kintetsu Yamada / Kodansha Ltd.

In an office romance, there's a fine line between sexy and awkward... and that line is where Asako — a woman who sweats copiously — meets Koutarou — a perfume developer who can't get enough of Asako's, er, scent. Don't miss a romcom manga like no other!

KC
KODANSHA
COMICS

KC KODANSHA COMICS

In love, there are no save points.

NOW AN ANIME!

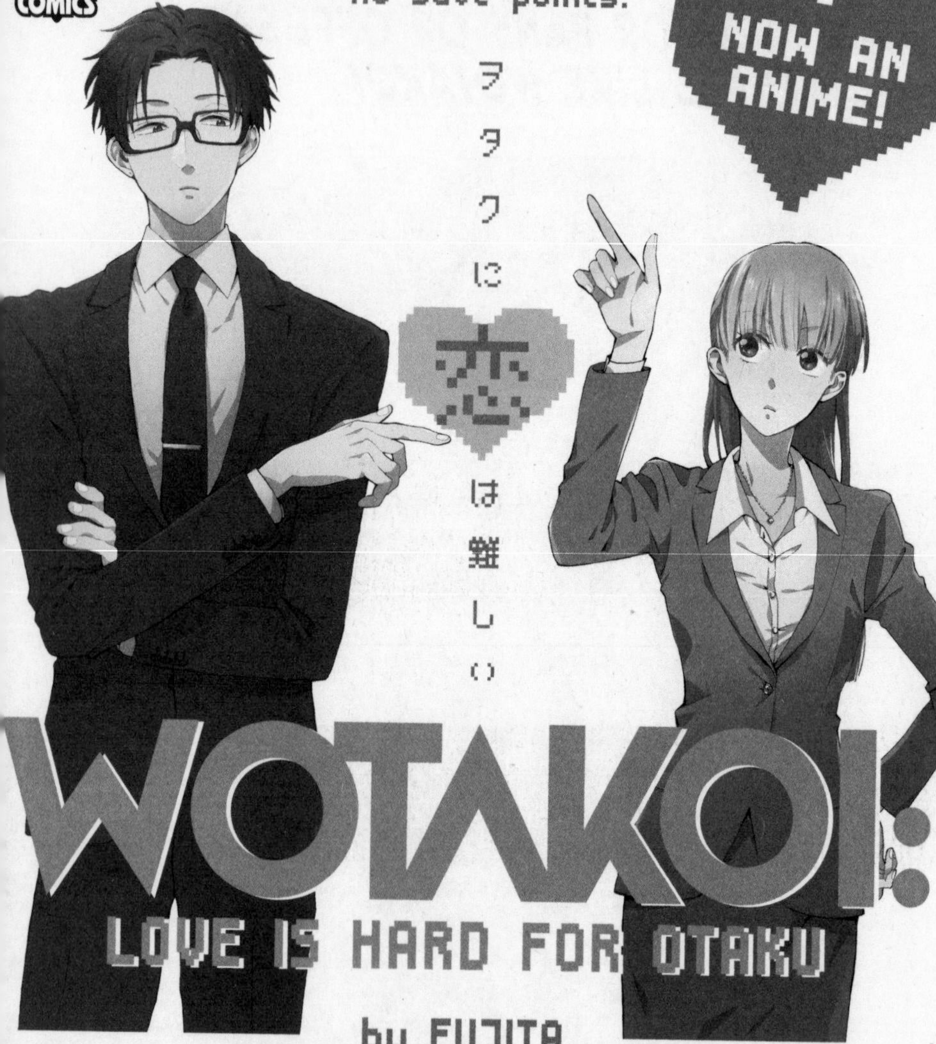
ヲタクに恋は難しい

WOTAKOI:
LOVE IS HARD FOR OTAKU

by FUJITA

Narumi has had it rough: Every boyfriend she's had dumped her once they found out she was an otaku, so she's gone to great lengths to hide it. At her new job, she bumps into Hirotaka, her childhood friend and fellow otaku. When Hirotaka almost gets her secret outed at work, she comes up with a plan to keep him quiet. But he comes up with a counter-proposal: Why doesn't she just date him instead?

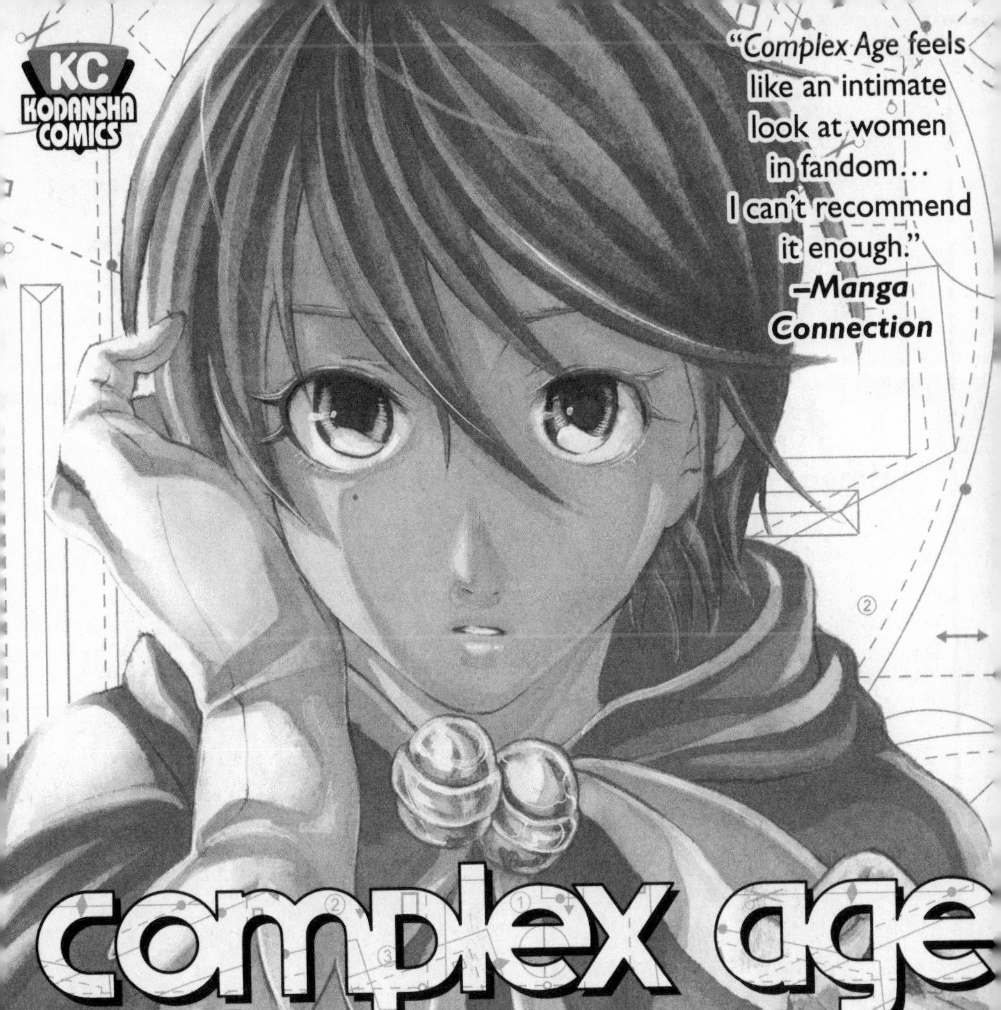
KC
KODANSHA COMICS
"Complex Age feels like an intimate look at women in fandom… I can't recommend it enough."
–Manga Connection
complex age
yui sakuma

26-year-old Nagisa Kataura has a secret. Transforming into her favorite anime and manga characters is her passion in life, and she's earned great respect amongst her fellow cospayers. But to the rest of society, her hobby is a silly fantasy. As demands from both her office job and cosplaying begin to increase, she may one day have to make a tough choice—what's more important to her, cosplay or being "normal"?

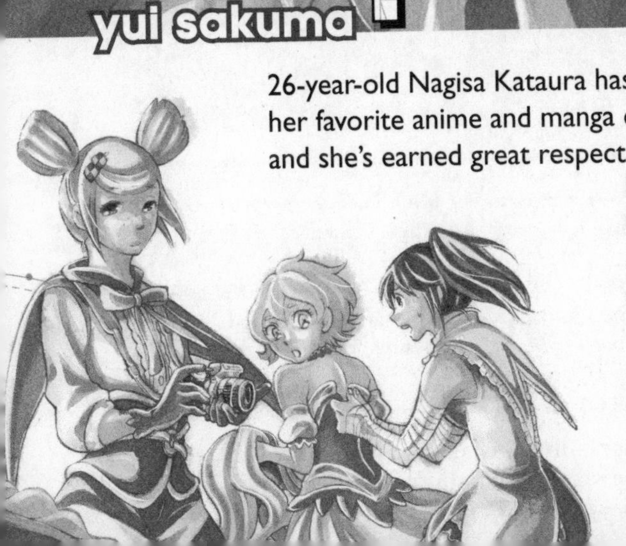

Yuri Is My Job!

miman

JOIN US FOR AFTERNOON TEA WITH EQUAL PARTS YURI, ROM-COM, AND DRAMA!

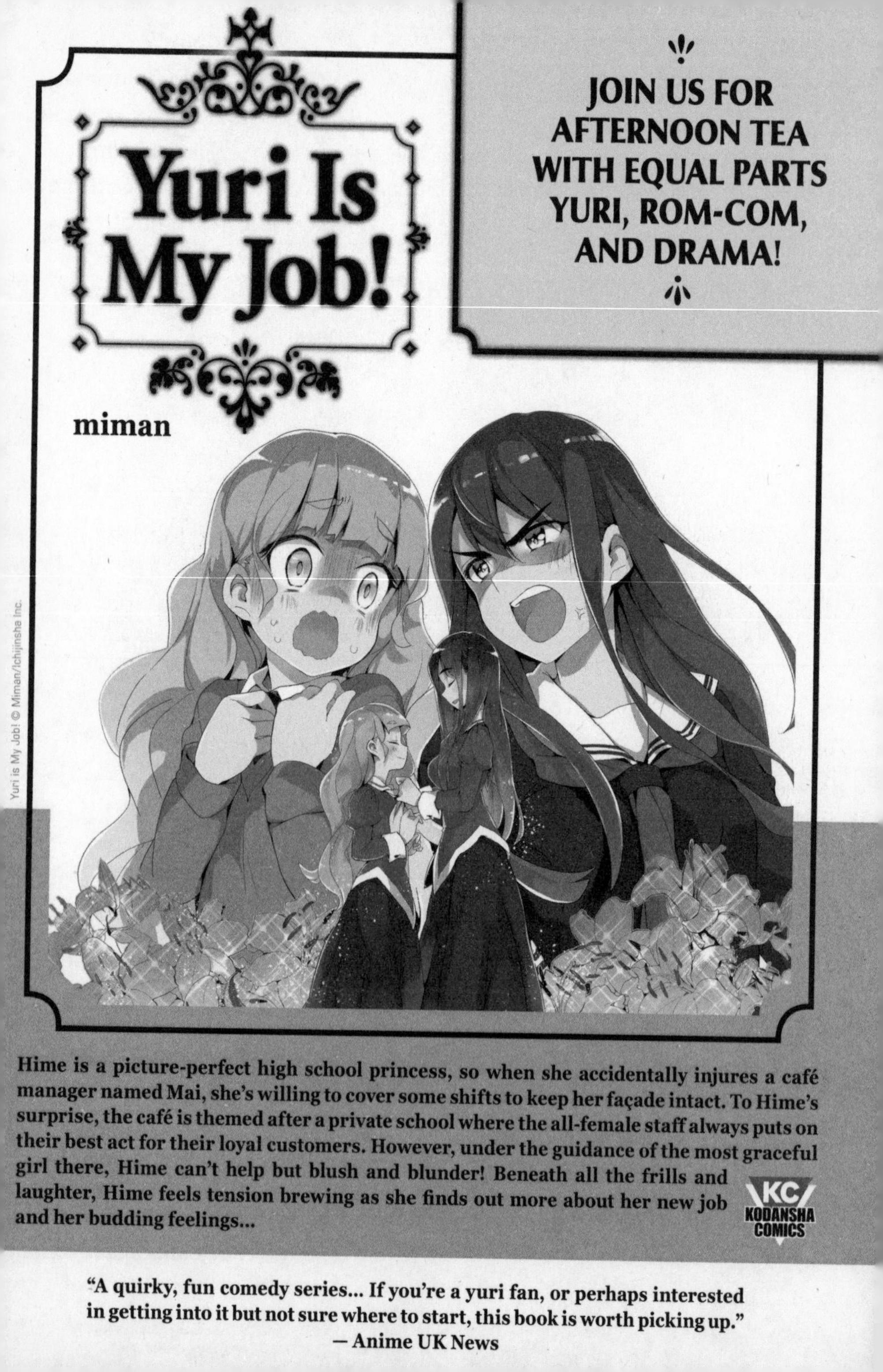

Hime is a picture-perfect high school princess, so when she accidentally injures a café manager named Mai, she's willing to cover some shifts to keep her façade intact. To Hime's surprise, the café is themed after a private school where the all-female staff always puts on their best act for their loyal customers. However, under the guidance of the most graceful girl there, Hime can't help but blush and blunder! Beneath all the frills and laughter, Hime feels tension brewing as she finds out more about her new job and her budding feelings...

"A quirky, fun comedy series... If you're a yuri fan, or perhaps interested in getting into it but not sure where to start, this book is worth picking up."
— Anime UK News

Having lost his wife, high school teacher Kōhei Inuzuka is doing his best to raise his young daughter Tsumugi as a single father. He's pretty bad at cooking and doesn't have a huge appetite to begin with, but chance brings his little family together with one of his students, the lonely Kotori. The three of them are anything but comfortable in the kitchen, but the healing power of home cooking might just work on their grieving hearts.

"This season's number-one feel-good anime!" —Anime News Network

"A beautifully-drawn story about comfort food and family and grief. Recommended." —Otaku USA Magazine

sweetness & lightning

By Gido Amagakure

A Kodansha Comics Trade Paperback Original
O Maidens in Your Savage Season 8 copyright © 2019 Mari Okada/Nao Emoto
English translation copyright © 2020 Mari Okada/Nao Emoto

All rights reserved.

Published in the United States by Kodansha Comics, an imprint of
Kodansha USA Publishing, LLC, New York.

Publication rights for this English edition arranged through
Kodansha Ltd., Tokyo.

First published in Japan in 2019 by Kodansha Ltd., Tokyo
as *Araburu Kisetsu no Otomedomoyo*, volume 8.

ISBN 978-1-63236-992-5

Printed in the United States of America.

www.kodanshacomics.com

9 8 7 6 5 4 3 2 1
Translation: Sawa Matsueda Savage
Lettering: Evan Hayden
Editing: Haruko Hashimoto
Kodansha Comics edition cover design by Phil Balsman

Publisher: Kiichiro Sugawara

Director of publishing services: Ben Applegate
Associate director of operations: Stephen Pakula
Publishing services managing editor: Noelle Webster
Assistant production manager: Emi Lotto, Angela Zurlo